SEEING RED

INDIAN LAND FOR S[ALE]

GET A HOME

OF

YOUR OWN

❈

EASY PAYMENTS

PERFE[CT]

POSS[ESSION]

WI[TH]

THIRT[Y]

FINE LANDS IN THE W[EST]

IRRIGATED
IRRIGABLE

GRAZING

AGRICULTU[RAL]
DRY FARM[ING]

IN 1910 THE DEPARTMENT OF THE INTERIOR SOLD UNDER SEALED BIDS ALLOTTED INDIAN L[AND]

Location.	Acres.	Average Price per Acre.	Location.	Acres
Colorado	5,211.21	$7.27	Oklahoma	34,66[ ]
Idaho	17,013.00	24.85	Oregon	1,02[ ]
Kansas	1,684.50	33.45	South Dakota	120,44[ ]
Montana	11,034.00	9.86	Washington	4,87[ ]
Nebraska	5,641.00	36.65	Wisconsin	1,06[ ]
North Dakota	22,610.70	9.93	Wyoming	86[ ]

FOR THE YEAR 1911 IT IS ESTIMATED THAT 350,000 ACRES WILL BE OFF[ERED]

For information as to the character of the land write for booklet, "INDIAN LANDS F[OR SALE]
Superintendent U. S. Indian School at any one of the following places:

CALIFORNIA:
Hoopa.
COLORADO:
Ignacio.
IDAHO:
Lapwai.
KANSAS:
Horton.
Nadeau.

MINNESOTA:
Onigum.
MONTANA:
Crow Agency.
NEBRASKA:
Macy.
Santee.
Winnebago.

NORTH DAKOTA:
Fort Totten.
Fort Yates.
OKLAHOMA:
Anadarko.
Cantonment.
Colony.
Darlington.
Muskogee, SUPT. OF UNION AGENCY.
Pawnee.

OKLAHOMA—Con.
Sac and Fox Agency.
Shawnee.
Wyandotte.
OREGON:
Klamath Agency.
Pendleton.
Roseburg.
Siletz.

SOUTH DAKOTA:
Cheyenne Agency.
Crow Creek.
Greenwood.
Lower Brule.
Pine Ridge.
Rosebud.
Sisseton.

WALTER L. FISHER,
Secretary of the Interior.

ROBERT G. VALE[NTINE,]
Commiss[ioner]

Seeing Red

INDIGENOUS LAND, AMERICAN EXPANSION,

AND THE POLITICAL ECONOMY OF PLUNDER

IN NORTH AMERICA

Michael John Witgen

Published by the
OMOHUNDRO INSTITUTE OF
EARLY AMERICAN HISTORY AND CULTURE,
Williamsburg, Virginia,
and the
UNIVERSITY OF NORTH CAROLINA PRESS,
Chapel Hill

*The Omohundro Institute of Early American History & Culture (OI) is
an independent research organization sponsored by William & Mary.
On November 15, 1996, the OI adopted the present name in honor of a
bequest from Malvern H. Omohundro, Jr., and Elizabeth Omohundro.*

Cover illustration: Detail of *Indian Land for Sale. . . .* Broadside,
[1911]. U.S. Department of the Interior, signed by Walter L. Fisher,
Secretary of the Interior, and Robert G. Valentine, Commissioner
of Indian Affairs. Printed Ephemera Collection, Library of
Congress, Washington, D.C.

Library of Congress Cataloging-in-Publication Data
Names: Witgen, Michael J., author. | Omohundro Institute of
Early American History & Culture, issuing body.
Title: Seeing red : Indigenous land, American expansion, and the
political economy of plunder in North America / Michael John Witgen.
Description: Williamsburg, Virginia : Omohundro Institute of Early American History
and Culture ; Chapel Hill : University of North Carolina Press, [2022] | ". . . I [author
Michael John Witgen] use the term Anishinaabeg for the Great Lakes people also known
as the Odawaag, Ojibweg, and Boodewaadamiig even though these same people most
often are presented in historical sources as Ottawas, Chippewas, and Potawatomi and
are written about generically as Algonquian"—Author's Note on terminology. |
Includes bibliographical references and index.
Identifiers: LCCN 2021038335 | ISBN 9781469664842 (cloth ; alk. paper) |
ISBN 9781469677774 (pbk. ; alk. paper) | ISBN 9781469664859 (ebook)
Subjects: LCSH: Algonquian Indians—Northwest, Old—Government relations. |
Algonquian Indians—Treaties—History—19th century. | Ojibwa Indians—Northwest,
Old. | Ottawa Indians—Northwest, Old. | Potawatomi Indians—Northwest, Old. | Settler
colonialism—Economic aspects—Northwest, Old. | Racially mixed people—Northwest,
Old—Politics and government. | Northwest, Old—History—1775–1865. | United States—
Territorial expansion. | United States—Race relations—History—19th century. |
BISAC: SOCIAL SCIENCE / Ethnic Studies / American / Native American Studies |
HISTORY / United States / General
Classification: LCC E99.A35 W57 2022 | DDC 305.800973—dc23
LC record available at https://lccn.loc.gov/2021038335

For Kelly and Kieran

ACKNOWLEDGMENTS

My family, at least part of it, has lived in the Great Lakes region of North America for millennia. This book is in part a love letter to the Anishinaabe peoples and to our Great Lakes homeland. The Boodewaadamii, Odawa, and Ojibwe peoples fought to preserve this homeland, Anishinaabewaki, and did preserve it as a Native space even as much of Native North America suffered through dispossession, genocide, and ethnic cleansing. It is a triumph that so many Anishinaabe people fought off removal to the federal Indian Territory, a policy mandated by the government of the United States. It is a testimony to survivance that we managed to preserve some remnant of our homelands east of the Mississippi River and learned to reassert and insist upon our sovereignty in the wake of the devastation that the nineteenth-century Republic wrought on Native peoples. This book is also a lament. It is impossible to live in the twenty-first-century Midwest, amid the decaying exoskeleton of the industrial United States, the Rust Belt, and not feel a sense of sadness and loss at how the Republic used up and squandered the bounty of Anishinaabewaki. This lament is tempered by a sense of wonder at how much the people, land, resources, and wealth of Anishinaabewaki contributed to the emergence of an economically successful and politically viable post-Revolutionary United States. It is astonishing to acknowledge this fact and understand that it is widely unknown. Indeed, this absence represents a profound failure to properly account for the Indigenous history of North America. That most people acquainted with U.S. history remain unaware of this contribution means that they are also unaware of the true history of this continent. I hope this book can begin to correct this gap in our knowledge about the place of the Anishinaabeg in the historical development of North America. Any failure to advance this historical truth is entirely my own.

Any success in this endeavor, however, would not be possible without the help and support of so many people and institutions. I am deeply grateful to the College of Literature, Science, and the Arts (LSA) at the University of Michigan for awarding me a Humanities Fellowship. This fellowship and additional funding from the Associate Professor Support Fund allowed me to take two semesters to complete the research and write the manuscript for this book. Being able to take this leave while also having access to the William L. Clements Library and its stellar staff allowed me to research and write simultaneously. Having this time and space was a luxury, and I am well aware of how fortunate I was to have it. I especially want to thank the Clement Library's Mary Pedley, Jayne Ptolemy, and Cheney Schopieray. I was similarly fortunate to have ready access to the Bentley Historical Library at the University of Michigan, where Nancy Bartlett provided invaluable assistance in chasing down Michigan-specific sources.

After the initial research and writing, this project really found a home at the Omohundro Institute of Early American History and Culture (OI). Karin Wulf has been enormously supportive of my work and was enthusiastic about this book project and helped to make sure that I would be happy and well supported. The arrival of Catherine Kelly as Editor of Books at the OI sealed the deal, for me at least, in seeking a publisher for this project. I had the opportunity to work with Cathy on the publication of an article at the *Journal of the Early Republic* and realized how truly brilliant she was as an editor. Cathy helped to refine and develop this project, working with me at the conceptual as well as at the editorial level. She has been instrumental in bringing this project to fruition, and I am sincerely grateful for the work she was willing to put into this book. Similarly, Virginia Chew has offered indefatigable editorial assistance.

One of the qualities that makes an excellent editor is the ability to find insightful and generous readers for an author. Accordingly, this project has benefited tremendously in early stages from close and careful readings by Anne Hyde and Lucy Eldersveld Murphy. Also, during the formative stages of this project, I received discerning and insightful readings by Tiya Miles and Gregory Evans Dowd. I am greatly indebted to Christina Snyder, who read the entire manuscript and offered brilliant and illuminating comments. She, along with the anonymous readers for the OI, provided an invaluable critique of the work. At the beginning stages of this project, I also received crucial support and inspiration from L'École des hautes études en sciences sociales (EHESS). Jean Hébrard brought me to Paris, France, for the colloquium "Circulation des catégories juridiques et des catégories raciales dans l'espace atlantique," along with Rebecca Scott and Martha Jones. This proved to be a formative opportunity to share work and think collaboratively about race and citizenship in the early Atlantic. All of these scholars improved my work, and their willingness to read, think through, and critique the project is a humbling reminder that at its best scholarly production is a collective endeavor. While all faults and failures are squarely mine, any success is shared with those who labored along with me to make this a better book.

I also benefited greatly from presenting my work at a number of institutions, including the Department of History at the University of Washington, New York University, Columbia University, Harvard University, Washington University in St. Louis, and Stanford University as well as the Indigenous Peoples' Rights Program at Columbia University. I sincerely appreciate the feedback I received from faculty and students on these occasions. The chairs of my departments at the University of Michigan, Jay Cook in History and Alex Stern and Greg Dowd in American Culture, supported my scholarship and my teaching. Native American Studies provided a true intellectual home for my work and teaching at Michigan, and I was nurtured and supported by this community. I offer a heartfelt *miigwech* to Greg Dowd, Bethany Hughes, Barbara Meek, Cherry Meyer, Alphonse Pitawanakwat, Amy Stillman, David Temin, Arland Thornton, and Gustavo Verdisio. Adam Kosto, serving as chair of the Department of History at Columbia University, and my colleague and friend Karl Jacoby were enormously helpful in guiding my transition to Columbia—and in the midst of a global pandemic. In these same trying circumstances, I am also grateful for Zoe Waldman and Alana Venable, who worked as research assistants during the conclusion of this project.

As always, my work is deeply informed by my family, my wife and partner Kelly Cunningham and my son Kieran Witgen. Like it or not, they heard a spoken version of this book, for years on end, before and during the process of getting the thing into print. Both were excellent companions as we struggled to figure out how to live and work from home during a global pandemic. Like me, they are believers in the power of storytelling and in the importance of history. I am so grateful to you both.

CONTENTS

ILLUSTRATIONS

NOTE ON TERMINOLOGY

How we talk about and think about Native people in North America, within academia and in popular culture, has changed a great deal during my lifetime. For much of the twentieth century in the United States, it was common to refer to Native people as American Indians, which, for many good reasons, is no longer the case. For the most part, as a scholar, when referring to the Indigenous peoples of North America, I use the terms Native and Indigenous. Whenever possible, however, I try to use the specific names and signifiers of identity that Indigenous people use for themselves. For example, I use the term Anishinaabeg for the Great Lakes people also known as the Odawaag, Ojibweg, and Boodewaadamiig even though these same people most often are presented in historical sources as Ottawas, Chippewas, and Potawatomi and are written about generically as Algonquians. These Anglicized versions of Anishinaabe names are given only when quoting sources directly.

At times, I do use the term Indian and American Indian, most often when quoting sources directly but also occasionally as a descriptor in historical context. The term Indian worked as a racialized category of social identity during the early Republic, signifying a savage or uncivilized person who was considered to be socially and politically excluded from the civil society of the Republic, or any other civilized polity. I also use the term "half-breed" most often when quoting a source. For both Native and non-Native people in nineteenth-century North America, the term "half-breed" indicated an Indigenous person of mixed racial descent. Similarly, sources use the terms "mulatto" and "quarteroon" ("quadroon") to mean African American or Black persons of mixed racial descent. These racialized terms are almost always used in quotations and always in historical context.

SEEING RED

The Indian Liberating Army

Re-imagining Native Identity in Colonial North America

Late at night on August 23, 1836, the steamboat *General Gratiot* forced a black schooner sailing without colors to allow the Saint Clair sheriff to board the ship as it entered the Saint Clair River en route to Lake Huron. The crew aboard the schooner, twenty-three men, were heavily armed and wearing what appeared to be some combination of British and American military uniforms. The sheriff charged the men with piracy, accusing them of stealing and butchering three head of cattle from a local farmer. The uniformed men sailed without official identification papers, and they refused to provide the sheriff with their names. The sheriff detained the crew and vessel for two days until an American military officer acquainted with the man in command of the schooner brokered a deal enabling the detainees to pay a fine in return for their release. The *Vermont Phoenix*, reporting the event, concluded: "Whatever may have been the occupation or design of these men, it is certain that their appearance and that of their vessel, was such as to create mistrust in the minds of those who met them." This might well have been the case, for these men had set out to filibuster California from the newly independent nation-state of Mexico with the intent of founding an American Indian empire. Their mission, if not their appearance, certainly ought to have aroused the suspicion and mistrust of Americans living in the Northwest Territory during the era of Indian removal.[1]

The man in charge of the crew aboard the schooner called himself General James Dickson, although he also represented himself as Montezuma II, general and leader of the Indian Liberating Army. For approximately a year before his arrest in 1836, he made appearances in Montreal, New York, and Washington, D.C., talking up his expedition to the West and recruiting soldiers for his filibustering army. According to George

---

1. "Piracy on the Lakes," *Vermont Phoenix* (Brattleboro), Sept. 9, 1836, [2].

Simpson, governor of the Northern Department of the Hudson's Bay Company, Dickson made quite an impression everywhere he went. Simpson described Dickson as "an Englishman by birth of bold and desperate character" and noted that he cut quite a figure, "being dressed in handsome uniform" and sporting a large mustache and a face "seamed with Sabre wounds."[2]

Dickson declared California to be the ultimate objective of his Indian Liberating Army. He claimed to have traveled extensively in Mexico and seemed familiar with the Anglo-American leadership fighting for an independent Texas. Dickson planned to add to Mexico's distraction by leading his army against Santa Fe. With Mexican forces on the defensive and concentrated east of the Rocky Mountains, the Indian Liberating Army would proceed to California, "where they purpose remaining till joined by the Cherokees etc." This at least, is what Dickson told the Hudson's Bay Company trader William Nourse at Sault Sainte Marie, who reported further "that with their aid, they mean to endeavour obtaining possession of that Country for the Indian Tribes, and locate them there under a Military Government." This newly formed Indigenous government would prevent "all except those of Indian blood, from possessing an acre of land." The general spoke of his plans freely with American and Canadian officials as he made his way west. He talked at length with the missionary Edmund Ely at the American Fur Company post at Fond du Lac, on the western shore of Lake Superior. "He keeps nothing back," Ely wrote in his journal; "His plan is to form a government in California of the scattered Indian tribes of the west, Cherokee, Creeks and all others who may be disposed to join them." What impression did Dickson, the Indian Liberating Army, and their quixotic quest make on Catherine Ely, Edmund's mixed-race Native wife? Could she have imagined an Indian empire as a plausible future for herself and her mixed-race Native children?[3]

Dickson's journey west began in Buffalo, New York, with an army of approximately sixty men. By the time he reached Detroit, he was down

2. George Simpson to J. H. Pelly, Oct. 31, 1836, in Grace Lee Nute, "Documents Relating to James Dickson's Expedition," *Mississippi Valley Historical Review*, X (1923), 174.

3. William Nourse to John Siveright, Sept. 15, 1836, Series G, Governor General's papers, 78, no. 124, Library and Archives Canada, cited in Grace Lee Nute, "James Dickson: A Filibuster in Minnesota in 1836," *Mississippi Valley Historical Review*, X (1923), 128; Theresa M. Schenck, ed., *The Ojibwe Journals of Edmund F. Ely, 1833–1849* (Lincoln, Nebr., 2012), Oct. 23, 1836, 234.

to twenty-three, and when he reached Sault Sainte Marie, he had only a dozen. The diminishing Indian Liberating Army spent a month sailing across Lake Erie and up to the Sault, swamping the boat on two occasions, crashing into reefs, getting arrested and detained for two days, and losing many more days tacking outside Detroit in search of favorable winds. Their bumbling progress, and the need to fortify their provisions with stolen cattle so early in their expedition, foreshadowed the fate of their adventure. That their route west brought the Indian Liberating Army north into the country of Anishinaabeg, rather than into Mexican territory in the Southwest, also signaled the quixotic nature of the expedition. Yet, even with such a beleaguered start, Martin McLeod, commissioned as a major by General Dickson, wrote in his diary, "If I may judge from so short an acquaintance, he is somewhat visionary in his views."[4]

Dickson's route into the West reveals a great deal about the kind of people who found the general to be a visionary leader. Rather than heading immediately southwest toward Santa Fe, the remaining members of the Indian Liberating Army planned to travel along the southern shore of Lake Superior, exiting at Fond du Lac and journeying overland up the Mississippi River valley, and continuing north to the Red River colony established by the Hudson's Bay Company in Rupert's Land in present-day Manitoba. At Red River, according to Nourse, they "hoped to obtain from one to two hundred Recruits, mounted and armed."[5]

This curious route makes sense given the Indian Liberating Army's officer corps. In addition to Martin McLeod, his cousin Alexander McLeod, John McLoughlin, and Charles McBean served as junior officers. Hudson's Bay Company governor John H. Pelly informed the Colonial Office about the expedition and described the officers as "well educated young men." He also noted that McLoughlin, the McLeods, and McBean were "half breed, or the sons by native or Indian women of gentlemen now or lately connected with the fur trade." Simpson described these "half breed" "sons" less charitably as "wild thoughtless young men." It would be easy to imagine mere adventure as a motive for joining the Indian Liberating Army, particularly for the non-Native rank and file, mostly Americans, all of whom deserted by the time the party reached Sault Sainte Marie.

4. Grace Lee Nute, ed., "The Diary of Martin McLeod," *Minnesota History Bulletin*, IV (1922), 359.

5. Nourse to Siveright, Sept. 15, 1836, in *Mississippi Valley Historical Review*, X (1923), 128.

"Americans," McLeod wrote in his diary, "d——d impertinent and use-less fellows."[6]

For the "half breed" "sons" of Hudson's Bay Company traders, however, Dickson's expedition clearly represented an attempt to control their future in a world where race increasingly limited their possibilities. None of the officers who joined Dickson's army had been offered a position in the fur trade. In fact, at this moment the Hudson's Bay Company was at best ambivalent about employing the mixed-race children of their white traders. For years the company had relied on mixed-race voyageurs to conduct the mundane labor-intensive aspects of their business—collecting and hauling pelts and trade goods. A few mixed-race men who had been taught to read and write by their fathers or in missionary schools in the West worked as clerks. But the company did not trust so-called half-breeds with posts of their own. The officers of the Indian Liberating Army did not fit neatly into the world created by the fur trade. They had been educated at universities in the East, where Dickson recruited them. But their eastern education, combined with the facts of their parentage, left these young men in an awkward place both within the culture of the Hudson's Bay Company and within the society of British Canada. Judging by their decision to join Dickson's army, their social and political status in the Canadian settlements must have seemed as uncertain as their place in the trade. In his journal, Martin McLeod expressed disdain for the capital of Upper Canada. "Remained one day at Toronto," he wrote, "do not like the place." He described the people as "some what pompous" and then wrote: "What have they to bost of. Their town or city . . . is a muddy hole." McLeod also complained that "they are up to their ears in politics, (damn politics)."[7]

Imagining the Future of
Native Peoples in Canada West

In 1836, Toronto was in the midst of considerable political turmoil in large part because of the rapid expansion of Upper Canada. A reform movement pushing for parliamentary democracy, and even colonial indepen-

6. J. H. Pelly to Lord Palmerston, Nov. 25, 1836, Colonial Office Files Relating to James Dickson's Filibustering Expedition, 482, Minnesota Historical Society, Saint Paul; Simpson to Pelly, Oct. 31, 1836, in Nute, "Documents Relating to James Dickson's Expedition," *Mississippi Valley Historical Review*, X (1923), 174; Nute, ed., "Diary of Martin McLeod," *Minnesota History Bulletin*, IV (1922), 372.

7. M. Elizabeth Arthur, "General Dickson and the Indian Liberating Army in the North," *Ontario History*, LXII (1970), 151–162; Nute, ed., "Diary of Martin McLeod," *Minnesota History Bulletin*, IV (1922), 356.

dence, had resulted in the appointment in 1835 of Sir Francis Bond Head as lieutenant governor of Upper Canada. McLeod noted the recent arrival of Head in his journal and linked his presence to the "damn politics" troubling the capital of Canada West. In August 1836, Head, in a letter to the colonial secretary, Charles Grant, Lord Glenelg, proposed consolidating the Native population of Upper Canada by removing them to Manitoulin Island in Lake Huron: "We could persuade those Indians, who are now impeding the Progress of Civilization in Upper Canada, to resort to a Place possessing the double Advantage of being admirably adapted to *them* . . . and yet in no Way adapted to the White Population."[8]

Although the officials of British Canada failed to implement Head's removal policy, as part of the reform process Britain's Colonial Office raised the idea of getting rid of the Indian Department in both an effort to save money and an attempt to change the nature of the relationship between British Canada and its Native allies. Specifically, Glenelg recommended that the governors of British Canada stop giving gifts annually to its Native allies. In effect, he proposed that Native peoples be treated as colonial subjects rather than as political and military allies. In November 1836, Head pushed back, "This Expense will shortly be defrayed altogether by the Sale of Lands they have this Year liberally surrendered to me." In addition, "Enjoying as we do Possession of this noble Province, it is our bounden Duty to consider as Heirlooms the Wreck of that simple-minded, ill-fated Race." The fate of Native Canada "is daily and yearly fading before the Progress of Civilization." Moreover, "the regular Delivery of the Presents," Head argued, "proves and corroborates the Testimony of the Wampums." Head was referencing the ceremonial belts made from quahog shells that colonial officials had exchanged with Native peoples as a signifier of alliance from the establishment of Canada through the War of 1812. The annual giving of gifts reaffirmed this political relationship, and

8. Nute, ed., "Diary of Martin McLeod," *Minnesota History Bulletin*, IV (1922), 356; Sir Francis Bond Head to Lord Glenelg, Aug. 20, 1836, in Great Britain, House of Commons, *Copies or Extracts of Correspondence since April 1st 1835 between the Secretary of State for the Colonies and the Governors of the British North American Provinces respecting the Indians in Those Provinces* (London, 1839), 122. For the ideology behind the removal policy in British Canada, see Elizabeth Jane Errington, *Emigrant Worlds and Transatlantic Communities: Migration to Upper Canada in the First Half of the Nineteenth Century* (Montreal and Kingston, 2007); and Theodore Binnema and Kevin Hutchings, "The Emigrant and the Noble Savage: Sir Francis Bond Head's Romantic Approach to Aboriginal Policy in Upper Canada, 1836–1838," *Journal of Canadian Studies*, XXXIX, no. 1 (Winter 2005), 115–138.

Head signaled the continued importance of this diplomatic practice. As a concession, however, he agreed to stop giving gifts to the Anishinaabeg who lived on the U.S. side of the border. In another letter to the secretary in April of the following year, Head emphasized that the Native nations aligned with Canada continued to identify themselves as the "Children" of the governor, "'their Father.'" Changing this status would prevent British Canada from "parentally governing these People according to their simple Habits." The alliance, imagined as a form of kinship, in essence allowed Head to secure both the political allegiance of and peaceful land concessions from the Native peoples of Canada West.[9]

The Western Expansion of Colonial Powers in North America

In many respects, the expansion of British Canada resembled the western expansion of the U.S. Republic. But there were crucial political and cultural differences. Organized originally as the French colony New France, Canada became part of the British Empire when the French lost the Seven Years' War. Following this transfer of power, the inhabitants or settlers of what would become British Canada understood themselves to be the colonial subjects of the king of Great Britain. The United States, in contrast, defined itself as a republic that had cut its ties with Great Britain, the colonial power that had established thirteen colonies along the Eastern Seaboard now organized as a union of thirteen independent states. Both the United States and British Canada recognized their shared origin as colonial settlements created and organized politically according to the natural law ideology used by European empires to claim possession of territory in North America. Both imagined that the continent had been an unsettled wilderness inhabited by Indigenous peoples who had failed

9. Head to Glenelg, Nov. 20, 1836, in Great Britain, House of Commons, *Copies or Extracts of Correspondence,* 128 ("Wampums"), 129 ("Expense"); Head to Glenelg, Apr. 4, 1837, ibid., 137 ("Children"). For the significance of wampum, see J. N. B. H[ewitt], "Wampum," in Frederick Webb Hodge, ed., *Handbook of the American Indians North of Mexico,* Smithsonian Institution, Bureau of American Ethnology, Bulletin 30, part 2 (Washington, D.C., 1910), 904–909; Frank G. Speck, "Wampum in Indian Tradition and Currency," *Proceedings of the Numismatic and Antiquarian Society of Philadelphia, for the Years 1913, 1914, 1915,* XXVII (Philadelphia, 1916), 121–131; Margaret M. Bruchac, "Broken Chains of Custody: Possessing, Dispossessing, and Repossessing Lost Wampum Belts, *Proceedings of the American Philosophical Society,* CLXII, (2018), 56–105.

to create, from their perspective, a legitimate form of government or recognizable property regime. By creating colonies in North America, the
French and British Empires believed that they had established dominion, or sovereignty, over an unsettled territory that they claimed by right
of discovery. Within this New World political imaginary, Great Britain
maintained an ongoing relationship with its colonial subjects in Canada,
which included settlers (both immigrants and those born in Canada) and
Indigenous peoples organized as subordinate but allied Native nations.
The United States, in contrast, had been established with a settler colonial ideology that envisioned citizens of the Republic eliminating the
Indigenous population, replacing or supplanting the Natives with its own
settlers. Accordingly, even though it existed in the same New World political imaginary as British Canada, the Republic refused to see itself as
a colonial power and instead saw itself as a postcolonial state, a political
entity that refashioned the meaning of "native" through the elimination
of the Indigenous.[10]

Whereas British Canada could imagine a future for Native peoples, or
Indians, as colonial subjects, the United States could only conceive of its
republic without Natives / Indians.[11] In the first decades after the Revolution, a few political figures, most prominently Thomas Jefferson, advocated "amalgamation," or the assimilation of Native peoples into American
society as they became "civilized." This process would, of course, require
Native peoples to assimilate as individuals, meaning that over time Indian nations would dissolve, vanishing from history. By 1836, however,
this dream of a gradual amalgamation had given way to the idea of Indian removal, a call for the immediate elimination of Native peoples. Native nations would be forcibly removed onto territory west of the Mississippi River, outside the boundaries of the Republic. Removal policy was

10. For settler colonialism and the "logic of elimination," see Patrick Wolfe, "Settler
Colonialism and the Elimination of the Native," *Journal of Genocide Research*, VIII
(2006), 387–409; Frederick E. Hoxie, "Retrieving the Red Continent: Settler Colonialism and the History of American Indians," *Ethnic and Racial Studies*, XXXI (2008),
1153–1167; Lorenzo Veracini, *Settler Colonialism: A Theoretical Overview* (London,
2010); David Armitage, *The Ideological Origins of the British Empire* (Cambridge,
2000), 96–99.

11. For the most part, when writing generally about Native peoples, I use the term
"Indigenous" or "Native." However, I occasionally use the term "Indian" as it was employed by U.S. and Canadian settlers and officials, a signifier of identity for the Indigenous non-settler population of North America.

predicated on two interconnected ideas. Some policymakers and religious missionaries believed that Native peoples needed to be isolated from white society until they became civilized. Others believed that Indigenous people were simply not capable of becoming civilized and needed to be removed beyond the boundaries of the Republic for their own protection.[12]

In truth, both approaches reflected a self-serving political justification for dispossessing Native peoples of their lands east of the Mississippi. The leading advocate of removal in the United States was Lewis Cass, governor of the Michigan Territory from 1812 until 1831 and the secretary of war under Andrew Jackson, who implemented the forced removal of people such as the Creeks and Cherokees west of the Mississippi to the "Indian Territory." These were the Native peoples that James Dickson hoped to coax into joining him in California to form a new Indigenous empire. Cass believed Native people were incapable of accepting the rigors of a civilized life and accordingly insisted that they needed to yield their territory to settlers who were willing to bring progress and civilization to the North American wilderness. Articulating this vision of the future in the *North American Review,* a nationwide publication, Cass argued "that a removal from their present position and from the vicinity of our settlements, to the regions beyond the Mississippi, can alone preserve from final extinction the remnant of our aboriginal population." Dickson and his followers believed that Native peoples might escape extinction by removing to the West and creating their own empire.[13]

12. For Jefferson and the idea of amalgamation, see Thomas Jefferson to Benjamin Hawkins, Feb. 18, 1803, in Thomas Jefferson, *Writings,* ed. Merrill Peterson (New York, 1984), 1115; Nicholas Guyatt, *Bind Us Apart: How Enlightened Americans Invented Racial Segregation* (New York, 2016), 87–114. For the policy of Indian removal, see An Act to Provide for an Exchange of Lands with the Indians Residing in Any of the States or Territories, and for Their Removal West of the River Mississippi, May 28, 1830, in Richard Peters, ed., *The Public Statutes at Large of the United States of America, from the Organization of the Government in 1799, to March 3, 1845, Arranged in Chronological Order . . .*, IV (Boston, 1850), Twenty-first Congress, Sess. 1, Chap. 148, 411–412; Tiya Miles, *Ties That Bind: The Story of an Afro-Cherokee Family in Slavery and Freedom* (Berkeley, Calif., 2005), 150–157; John P. Bowes, *Land Too Good for Indians: Northern Indian Removal* (Norman, Okla., 2016), 6–11, 63–64; Jeffery Ostler, *Surviving Genocide: Native Nations and the United States from the American Revolution to Bleeding Kansas* (New Haven, Conn., 2019), 201–206; Claudio Saunt, *Unworthy Republic: The Dispossession of Native Americans and the Road to Indian Territory* (New York, 2020), 53–84.

13. Review of [Lewis Casss], *Documents and Proceedings Relating to the Formation and Progress of a Board in the City of New York, for the Emigration, Preservation,*

Extinction or Liberation:
Alternate Visions of the Indigenous Future

Governor Head also hinted at the extinction or vanishing of Native peoples, and the expansion of Canadian settlers into the West certainly resembled American settler colonialism. It would be more accurate, however, to think of cities like Toronto as settler enclaves that existed within a larger British colonial regime. As noted previously, unlike American settler colonialism, the colonial relationship between Great Britain and its Canadian provinces did not imagine the elimination of the Native. Head might have wanted to isolate independent Native nations within Upper Canada. Like his American counterparts, he seemed to think Native peoples were fading away or diminishing in numbers. But he and the Colonial Office were not calling for their displacement, destruction, or cultural and political assimilation. The Colonial Office wanted to change the nature of the political relationship between the empire and its Native nations in British Canada, treating Native peoples as colonial subjects rather than as allies. The colonial governors of British Canada, however, recognized the value of having Native nations as military allies along their exposed border with the United States.[14]

Governors of British Canada, like Head, wanted to preserve their alliance with Native peoples in the Great Lakes, where the U.S.-Canadian boundary was ill-defined, because the United States possessed a rapacious appetite for Indigenous land. The expansion of the Republic was predicated on the idea of transforming Native homelands, imagined as unsettled wilderness, into American homesteads that could be incorporated into new states that would be added to the union of the original thirteen. In the Old Southwest, in places like Alabama and Georgia where cotton was king and the soil of the Black Belt represented an ideal growing environment, the settler colonial ambitions of the U.S. Republic met with great success. In the cold climate of the Old Northwest, particularly north of the Ohio River in the Michigan Territory, the Republic found it far more difficult to eliminate the Native population, which was needed to hunt and process animal peltry. In the Southwest, commercial farming formed the basis of the regional economy, and with the widespread adaptation of slavery, Indian labor was not required to facilitate the expansion

and Improvement of the Aborigines of America, North American Review, XXX, no. 66 (January 1830), 104.

14. For the distinction between colonialism and settler colonialism, see Lorenzo Veracini, "Introducing Settler Colonial Studies," _Settler Colonial Studies,_ I (2011), 1–12.

of the Republic. Only their land was needed. In the Michigan Territory, the northern tier of the Old Northwest, the fur trade dominated economic life, and the fur trade required Indians to continue living and working as Indians.[15]

Economic conditions in the Michigan Territory provided little incentive for Native peoples to assimilate to an American frontier existence of commercial or subsistence farming. Similarly, the region and its economy failed to entice non-Native settlers in large numbers for exactly the same reason. When the remaining members of the Indian Liberating Army finally arrived at Sault Sainte Marie in the early fall of 1836, Martin McLeod described a small and rather dilapidated settlement consisting of twenty houses and a small military garrison on the U.S. side of the river. In his journal, he wrote: "There is here a Cantonment of two Companies of very awkward American *Soldados* commanded by a Major Cobb a singular veteran who prefers any thing to a clean shirt and any duty but a military one. His 18 feet picket fort is his world and I verily believe his ideas never extend beyond the old saw mill above the fort."[16]

McLeod also noted the presence of a correspondingly large number of Anishinaabeg: "There are here at present quite a number of Chippewas with their Wigwams on their return from the island of Mackinaw where they have been to receive their annuities for lands sold in this vicinity and along lake Superior." He described the territory west of the Sault as "an immense tract but of little value for Agricultural purposes," and he noted that although the region had significant copper deposits, "there appears to be some doubt whether even that can ever be made available." In other words, in the Northwest Territory, at least on the U.S. side of the border, Native peoples were not, as Governor Head claimed, "daily and yearly fading" before the progress of an advancing settler state. They remained on their land living as Indigenous people even as they signed treaties forfeiting large swaths of their territory.[17]

In fact, it was the presence and political dominance of this large Native population that caused officials of the Hudson's Bay Company and British Canada to express alarm at the idea of the Indian Liberating Army. They were not worried about the creation of an Indian empire in California.

15. On the Old Southwest, see, for example, Claudio Saunt, "Financing Dispossession: Stocks, Bonds, and the Deportation of Native Peoples in the Antebellum United States," *Journal of American History*, CVI (2019), 315–337.

16. Nute, ed., "Diary of Martin McLeod," *Minnesota History Bulletin*, IV (1922), 369.

17. Ibid., 370.

Rather, they worried about a Native uprising in Rupert's Land, Canada's Northwest. Simpson of the Northern Department reported to Pelly, the governor of the Hudson's Bay Company, the de facto colonial government in the vast northwestern interior of British Canada, "I learnt that their views were, to proceed by Lakes Huron and Superior towards the Missippi [sic], thence up the River St.Peters, and through the Scieux Country to the Red River Settlement." Once there they would "excite dissatisfaction in the minds of the different Indian Tribes and half breeds under the plea of encroachments on their territory by the British and United States Governments." The end goal, according to Simpson, was "forming themselves into a great and independent Nation." Simpson reported that his "intimate knowledge of the Indian Character" caused him to worry that "such representations from such sources might lead to much excitement among the different tribes thro' whom the party would pass."[18]

Simpson believed the threat posed by the Indian Liberating Army to be credible. Before writing his report to the Hudson's Bay Company governor, he received a letter from James McKay, a Montreal-based trader. McKay informed Simpson of the arrival of John George McKenzie, the mixed-blood son of a fur trader with a long history in the Northwest who resented the monopoly of the Hudson's Bay Company. McKenzie had been part of the expedition but was forced to return home because of illness. McKay reported, "They claim the whole of the Company's Territory on their inheritance by birth-right."[19]

This claim suggests that at least some members of the expedition might have aspired to the liberation of Native and mixed-race peoples in the Red River region from British colonial rule. They also claimed an unextinguished Native title to this territory. This was precisely the danger that the Indian Liberating Army represented from the perspective of British Canadian officials: Native peoples with national aspirations of their own who possessed the design to create an independent Indigenous homeland in the West that excluded white settlers. The members of the Indian Liberating Army imagined just such a future for Indigenous people in North America.

The fear that the Indian Liberating Army might actually pull off such a thing proved grossly exaggerated. Perhaps it was that the men Dickson recruited possessed a university education, as opposed to the skills of

18. Simpson to Pelly, Oct. 31, 1836, in Nute, "Documents Relating to James Dickson's Expedition," *Mississippi Valley Historical Review*, X (1923), 175.

19. James McKay to Simpson, Oct. 7, 1836, ibid., 179.

voyageurs, that made the dream impossible. Once they left Lake Superior, the men of the Indian Liberating Army needed Native guides in order to find their way west and north, traveling overland up the Mississippi River valley and onto northern plains in canoes and on foot. With the season so advanced, their guides deserted them after they departed the American Fur Company post at Red Lake. The Indian Liberating Army, reduced to twelve men, struggled as it advanced into the North. The men became lost. Their inadequate provisions reduced them to a ration of a single biscuit a day until they found two Canadian voyageurs willing to escort them by cart to Red River. At this point, the Indian Liberating Army dissolved, and James Dickson vanished from the historical record.[20]

While the party made their way west, Simpson wrote letters to McLoughlin and the McLeods offering them positions in the Hudson's Bay Company and "endeavoring to detach these young men who are respectably connected from such a disreputable enterprise." McLoughlin and Alexander McLeod accepted mid-level positions in the company and remained in Canada, loyal subjects of the British Empire. Martin McLeod rejected this path and returned to Saint Peters, establishing himself in the Pembina region as a fur trader and eventually marrying a Dakota woman. When Minnesota was organized as a territory, McLeod, assuming an identity as a free white citizen of the United States, became an elected member of the territorial legislature.[21]

For the mixed-race members of the Indian Liberating Army, the North American West, whether it be California or Rupert's Land, had seemed to offer the possibility of a Native polity that was independent of either Canada or the United States. Given the dominance of the Indigenous population and the absence of large numbers of white settlers, it was possible to imagine the Northwest as a place where Native peoples could rewrite their narrative trajectory. Perhaps this was the allure of the Indian Liberating Army: James Dickson promised a future where Native peoples survived and even reinvented their national identity as part of an Indigenous empire in North America. The Indian Liberating Army represented a political imaginary where at least part of North America remained Indigenous and independent of the continent's colonial powers. In this sense, the Indian Liberating Army offers a counterpoint to

20. Arthur, "General Dickson and the Indian Liberating Army," *Ontario History*, LXII (1970), 151–162.

21. Simpson to Pelly, Oct. 31, 1836, in Nute, "Documents Relating to James Dickson's Expedition," *Mississippi Valley Historical Review*, X (1923), 175.

the teleology of the vanishing Indian envisioned by Canadian and U.S. officials like Francis Bond Head and Lewis Cass.[22]

It is also productive to think about the motivations of these mixed-race Native men with ties to the fur trade and to the Northwest. Did they plan to filibuster California? Or was their goal the liberation of the Red River colony from the Hudson's Bay Company? Did the Indian Liberating Army foreshadow the 1869 Red River Rebellion that led briefly to the creation of an Indigenous province headed by the Métis political figure Louis Riel? Great Britain's Colonial Office wanted to transform Native allies into British subjects. But whether they would be considered equals or racial subordinates remained an open question. The Hudson's Bay Company never really accepted mixed-race employees, children of their own agents, as equal in judgment, leadership, and authority to the company's white employees. And the Red River Rebellion and the refusal of Canada to accept an Indigenous province into the nation at the birth of Confederation suggests that their national imaginary was not ready for this sort of racial inclusion. In this sense, postcolonial Canada was not so very different from the U.S. Republic. But examining the choices made by the Native people who joined the Indian Liberating Army and thinking through their political ambitions suggest that at least some Native people wanted a future independent of the colonial regime of British Canada. They did not seek a dual citizenship or dual identity as both members of Indigenous nations and subjects of the colonial settler state.[23]

The United States saw itself as a postcolonial republic, but it was, in reality, an ambitiously expansive settler colonial state that offered an even bleaker future for Native peoples than the one Head envisioned for Native peoples in British Canada. The political imaginary of the U.S. Republic called for western expansion at the expense of Native peoples on the

22. Anne Hyde has written regarding the North American West in the early nineteenth century, "It's very important to remember that this huge swatch of land did NOT belong to the United States." She concludes: "Even when it did, *belong* turns out to be a very capacious term. Throughout this period, any group could emerge as the one in control; it could be Native nations, it could be European invaders, it could be imperial Anglo-America, or it could be personally motivated pirates." See Hyde, *Empires, Nations, and Families: A New History of the North American West, 1800–1860* (New York, 2012), 17.

23. For the emergence of a Métis national identity, see Gerhard J. Ens, "The Battle of Seven Oaks and the Articulation of a Metis National Tradition, 1811–1849," in Nicole St-Onge, Carolyn Podruchny, and Brenda Macdougall, eds., *Contours of a People: Metis, Family, Mobility, and History* (Norman, Okla., 2012).

ground in the territories being organized into new states. The *Vermont Phoenix*, which printed the story of the arrest and detention of the Indian Liberating Army, also featured two stories that revealed a vision of the Republic centered on Black segregation and Indigenous elimination. One of the articles, titled "More Lynching," reported on the death by lynching of a Black man in Helena, Arkansas. "Monday evening after the election closed a man by the name of Bunch, was taken and hung by the citizens of that place." Mr. Bunch was lynched because "he claimed the right to vote, which was refused him by the judges, owing to his being a colored man." According to the newspaper, "Bunch took umbrage at this rejection and resorted to violent measures." During the conflict, he stabbed a white man, and, the paper reported, "This so incensed the citizens, that Bunch was taken up and hung."[24]

The second article, titled "Human Ferocity," told the story of a band of Creek Indians fleeing Georgia during the Second Creek War in an attempt to join the Seminoles in Florida and avoid forced removal to the Indian Territory. Georgia militia tracked down and killed all but two of the Creek men, who escaped during the confrontation and fled in the direction of Florida. Two teenage Creek girls who had been captured in this fight, fearing for their lives, begged the militia captain to protect them. He promised to do so and left the captured Creek women with a militia soldier to guard them while he pursued the two warriors who had escaped. In his absence, the guard beat the two girls to death.[25]

Martin McLeod, in the diary that he kept throughout his service with the Indian Liberating Army, wrote that he had read a newspaper that printed the story of his arrest outside Detroit. Did he also read the articles about lynching in Arkansas and the ethnic cleansing of the Creek nation in Georgia? Whether or not he read these specific stories, McLeod was reading newspapers that were chronicling the violent expansion of the U.S. Republic. By joining the Indian Liberating Army, he and his fellow Native soldiers signaled a desire to create a place in North America where

24. "More Lynching," *Vermont Phoenix*, Sept. 9, 1836, [2]. The *Indiana American* (Brookville, Franklin County), Oct. 7, 1836, [1], also reported the lynching of John Bunch in Chicot County, Arkansas, and noted "a life of Col. Johnson was found in his pocket." That he carried a biography likely indicated that John Bunch was literate.

25. "Human Ferocity," *Vermont Phoenix*, Sept. 9, 1836, [2]. Many Creeks desperately sought to avoid removal because of widespread atrocities committed by the militias charged with enacting this policy. See Christopher D. Haveman, *Rivers of Sand: Creek Indian Emigration, Relocation, and Ethnic Cleansing in the American South* (Lincoln, Nebr., 2016), 237–242.

Native peoples were not colonial subjects under threat of extinction. The Indian Liberating Army met with a failure that was both tragic and comical, and yet this largely forgotten moment in North America's history underscores Native peoples' desperation to preserve their homelands and their independence while the colonial powers that dominated the continent sought their subordination and destruction.[26]

26. Nute, ed., "Diary of Martin McLeod," *Minnesota History Bulletin*, IV (1922), 368.

Indian Country and the Origins
of the United States

On April 1, 1840, the state legislature of Michigan created Unwattin County out of 573 square miles in the middle of the Lower Peninsula. Unwattin was the name of an Odawa *ogimaa*, a chief, who signed the 1836 Treaty of Washington. This treaty between the United States and the Anishinaabe *doodemag*, bands of Odawa and Ojibwe people living in the Upper and northern Lower Peninsula of what had been designated by the United States as the Michigan Territory, ceded approximately thirteen million acres of land to the Republic. In return, the United States agreed to an annual payment or annuity of $30,000 for twenty years. This treaty also provided a one-time payout of $300,000 to traders who claimed the Anishinaabeg owed them money for goods provided on credit that they had failed to pay back through trade in processed animal peltry. Finally, it allocated $150,000 to mixed-race Anishinaabeg as compensation for their part of the land cession, offering them a cash payment instead of the creation of a land base reserved for them in their home territory.[1]

The 1836 Treaty of Washington was one of a large number of treaties that the United States negotiated with the Indigenous nations of the Northwest Territory, the name that the United States assigned to the

---

1. "Treaty with the Ottawa, Etc., 1836," in Charles J. Kappler, comp. and ed., *Indian Affairs: Laws and Treaties*, II, *Treaties* (Washington, D.C., 1904), 450–456. Anishinaabeg can be translated as human beings, original people, or even Indians; Anishinaabe is the singular form of this word. This term is a signifier of a collective identity shared by multiple Algonquian peoples. In the Great Lakes, people identifying as Anishinaabeg also belonged to doodemag, or bands, that used the national designations Odawa, Ojibwe, and Boudewaadamii. In the nineteenth century, these designations were Anglicized as Ottawa, Chippewa, and Pottawatomie. See John D. Nichols and Earl Nyholm, *A Concise Dictionary of Minnesota Ojibwe* (Minneapolis, Minn., 1995), vii; William W. Warren, *History of the Ojibway People* (1885; rpt. Saint Paul, Minn., 1984), 56–57.

region that would become the states of Ohio, Indiana, Illinois, Michigan, Wisconsin, and Minnesota. The treaty process in the Northwest Territory provided the United States with a largely peaceful means of forcing Native nations to cede their homelands to the Republic, even though the Republic already claimed dominion, or sovereignty, over them. The logic behind this claim derived from a semantic distinction; although the U.S. government recognized that Native people held title to their lands, it insisted that they had failed to take possession of these lands as property and therefore had never established sovereignty over them.[2] These treaties, which established U.S. dominion over the Northwest Territory, represented a massive transfer of wealth from Native peoples to the citizens of the United States. Native peoples ceded title to their lands to the federal government, which then converted this territory into the public domain of the United States. The federal government, acting as the sole proprietor over this land base, made it available for purchase as private property to settlers. These settlers were almost exclusively white, and they took possession of this land at a subsidized price in exchange for settling Native homelands and making them part of the U.S. Republic. In doing so, they entered into a social contract with the United States. They would not be colonists settling a foreign territory for the mother country; rather, they were citizens creating homesteads and settlements in Indian country, which their government had deemed unsettled land over which it exercised dominion.[3] Those settlements would be organized politically as territories administered by the federal government, and when

2. The Black Hawk War (1832) and the Dakota War (1862) were notable exceptions to a treaty process designed to extinguish Native title without forcing a violent confrontation with the Native peoples of the Northwest Territory. For the common law definition of "dominion," see Henry Campbell Black et al., *Black's Law Dictionary* . . . , abridged sixth ed. (Saint Paul, Minn., 1991), 338–339. See also Lauren Benton, *A Search for Sovereignty: Law and Geography in European Empires, 1400–1900* (New York, 2010), 11. The common law tradition also restricted heathens or infidels (non-Christians) from exercising dominion; see Robert A. Williams, Jr., *The American Indian in Western Legal Thought: The Discourses of Conquest* (New York, 1990), 41.

3. This phenomenon is described by political theorist Carole Pateman as the "settler contract," which "is a specific form of the expropriation contract and refers to the dispossession of, and rule over, Native inhabitants by British settlers in the two New Worlds." "Colonialism in general subordinates, exploits, kills, rapes, and makes maximum use of the colonized and their resources and lands. When colonists are planted in a *terae nullius,* an empty state of nature, the aim is not merely to dominate, govern, and use but to create a civil society. Therefore, the settlers have to make an

the population grew to sixty thousand white settlers, the territories could seek admission to the union as states.[4]

The treaty process in the Northwest Territory not only represented a massive transfer of wealth from Native peoples to white American settlers but also created a massive infusion of money in the form of specie into the regional economy. The federal government consistently spent more money meeting its treaty obligations than it allocated for the development of western territories. These treaties resulted in annuities or cash payments, which, though designated for Native peoples, mostly wound up in the hands of traders, territorial officials, and local merchants. Many of the white settlers, traders, and officials who claimed this money were able to do so because they had married into the Native communities that were being forced to bargain with the United States. These white interlocuters, who most often had Native wives and mixed-race children, facilitated the negotiation of treaties by acting as interpreters, counselors, and debt collectors to the leadership of Indigenous nations. Representatives of the federal government made it clear to Native leaders that these treaties were their only chance for compensation. In this sense, treaty making between Native nations and the federal government was an involuntary or coercive process. Together, the treaty process, the land cessions, the annuity payments, and the supply of goods and provisions to Native negotiators created a political economy of plunder.[5]

---

original—settler—contract." See Pateman, "The Settler Contract," in Pateman and Charles Mills, eds., *Contract and Domination* (Cambridge, 2007), 38.

4. The organization of territories and the establishment of states in the Northwest Territory was enacted according to the Northwest Ordinance; see article 5 for the requirement that sixty thousand "free inhabitants" were needed for admission to the union ("An Ordinance for the Government of the Territory of the United States, North-West of the River Ohio," July 13, 1787, Miscellaneous Papers of the Continental Congress, 1774–1789, Record Group [RG] 360: Records of the Continental and Confederation Congresses and the Constitutional Convention, 1765–1821, M332, roll 9, National Archives and Records Administration, Washington, D.C.).

5. The historian Robert Trennert, Jr., described the treaty process that facilitated the expansion of the Republic onto western territory claimed by the United States but occupied by Native peoples as "the Indian business." "With any practical regulation ruled out by the laissez faire philosophy of the age," he wrote, "traders developed the ability to earn a living from the federal subsidy for Indian welfare. After a while, the subsidy to the Indian became a subsidy to the trading profession." See Trennert, *Indian Traders on the Middle Border: The House of Ewing, 1827–54* (Lincoln, Nebr., 1981), 206–207. Similarly, Ethnohistorian Bruce M. White has described the treaty process in the Minnesota Territory as having a "multiplier effect." He argues:

The Political Economy of Plunder

This political economy of plunder became the means by which the United States expanded into the trans-Appalachian West, claimed by the Republic as federal territory but occupied and controlled by Native peoples. In the Old Northwest, through the creation of the 1787 land law known as the Northwest Ordinance, the federal government established a legal mechanism that linked state formation to economic production and Indigenous dispossession. The law used the power of the federal government to extinguish Native title to land and then enabled the development of that land as private property. This transfer of wealth from Native peoples to U.S. citizens was not a mutually beneficial, market-based transaction. It was theft, a plundering of Native land and Native wealth, orchestrated by the federal government of the United States. The plunder economy not only stripped Native peoples of their homelands, their most valuable resource, but also deprived them of just compensation for this loss. Cash payments for their land were systematically claimed as debt by traders, merchants, and Indian agents who maximized their profit by also supplying the manufactured goods and provisions of food that the government agreed to provide to Native peoples as part of their annuities.[6]

"Businessmen who contracted with the government or who dealt directly with Indian people used their money to invest in real estate, to build buildings and houses, to buy, sell, and hire. Each person they paid spread the money around to others, helping create a Minnesota economy, though little long-term benefit accrued to Indian people themselves." See White, "The Power of Whiteness; or, The Life and Times of Joseph Rolette, Jr.," *Minnesota History*, LVI (1998–1999), 186.

6. Both the Ordinance of 1784 and the Ordinance of 1787 (or Northwest Ordinance) provided the legal framework for the western expansion of the United States. See "An Ordinance," July 13, 1787, Miscellaneous Papers of the Continental Congress, RG 360, M332, roll 9. For a discussion of the land ordinance as a method of territorial expansion, see Robert F. Berkhofer, Jr., "Jefferson, the Ordinance of 1784, and the Origins of the American Territorial System," *William and Mary Quarterly*, 3d Ser., XXIX (1972), 231–262. Berkhofer also argued that the Revolutionary generation of American statesmen imagined western expansion as a form of colonization: "Full-fledged republican government would come to the frontier by itself, but the Continental Congress wanted to assure its eventuality by prior tutelage through subordination as a colony." See Berkhofer, "The Northwest Ordinance and the Principle of Territorial Evolution," in John Porter Bloom, ed., *The American Territorial System* (Athens, Ohio, 1973), 51. Peter S. Onuf argues similarly: "The real issue—for settlers and policy makers alike—was land. The enjoyment and productive use of the land depended on clear title, protection from 'savage neighbors'—Indian or white—and access to markets." See Onuf, *Statehood and Union: A History of the Northwest Ordinance* (Bloomington,

In the Northwest Territory, the political economy of plunder represented a mode of colonization that the United States masked as the physical expansion of the Republic onto "unsettled" western territory. According to historian Peter S. Onuf, "The Northwest Ordinance reflected
a new way of thinking about territorial expansion." Specifically, he argues
that a land system promoting economic development in the West would
simultaneously promote the wealth and power of the entire nation.[7] The
U.S. Republic relied on the sale of Indigenous land to generate revenue
for the federal government, and it relied on the economic development
of settler homesteads to boost the wealth of its citizens and increase the
economic productivity of the national economy. The political economy
of plunder created by the treaty process and implemented through the
Northwest Ordinance was the engine behind the economic growth that

---

Ind., 1992), 58. Legal scholar Denis P. Duffey writes, "Though the political scheme of
the Ordinance was not strongly imperialistic in the conventional modern sense, the
central government was nonetheless very actively involved in the process of expansion." He also argues that "the Ordinance was intended to increase settlers' wealth
by providing them with easy access to land." See Duffey, "The Northwest Ordinance
as a Constitutional Document," *Columbia Law Review*, XCV (1995), 957, 960. Historian and legal scholar Gregory Ablavsky contends that the land issue forced the
United States to confront the issue of autonomous Indigenous nations living within
the boundaries of the Republic, which resulted in the revision of the Articles of Confederation into the Constitution of 1787. He asserts that "using Indians to justify the
power of the new national state came with a cost: it elevated conquest of Indians to a
constitutional principle." The dispossession of Indians and the settlement of western
lands, he concludes, "became one of the central projects of the new federal state." See
Ablavsky, "The Savage Constitution," *Duke Law Journal*, LXIII (2014), 1008.

7. Onuf, *Statehood and Union*, 59. Andrew Shankman makes a similar argument:
"In North America, rural heads of household expected to acquire a 'competency.' By
'competency,' eighteenth-century small land holders meant acquisition of enough land
to sustain their families, to establish their sons with landed independence when they
married, and to see their daughters marry men who had achieved the same condition.
The expectation of competency pitted striving American colonists against Indians,
and further encouraged the dismissal of Indians' claims to land." See Shankman, "Introduction: Conflict for a Continent: Land, Labor, and the State in the First American
Republic," in Shankman, ed., *The World of the Revolutionary American Republic:
Land, Labor, and the Conflict for a Continent* (New York, 2014), 2. Similarly, Daniel
Vickers has argued that the drive to achieve competency, that is, a "comfortable independence," produced an insatiable demand for land in seventeenth- and eighteenth-
century Anglo-America that could only be developed by dispossessing Native people
(Vickers, "Competency and Competition: Economic Culture in Early America," *WMQ*,
3d Ser., XLVII [1990], 3–29).

made it possible to create and economically develop new states in the Northwest Territory. The United States acted as a colonial power, expanding onto new territory by systematically subjugating and exploiting Native people and their resources.[8]

As the United States expanded at the expense of Native peoples, Indigenous people remained outsiders within the Republic being created through their dispossession—that is, they were not citizens of the United States even when they lived within the boundaries of states and territories organized as part of the union. In the Old Southwest and in the southern tier of the Northwest Territory, where the agricultural value of Indigenous homelands was high and there was easy access to U.S. markets via river systems, the U.S. government began to focus on Indian removal, a strategy that literally eliminated Native peoples from the territory of the Republic and constituted an aggressive form of settler colonialism. In the middle and northern tier of the Northwest Territory, in contrast, Native people who remained on their land to cede additional territory and draw annuities at annual gatherings could be a boon to regional economic development. Merchants and territorial officials in this region wanted to preserve a politically subordinate Native population that received federal funds, which could then be siphoned off for their benefit.

No matter the modality of colonialism, however, expansion of the national domain was integral to the economic growth and political development of the United States, and this growth and development came at the expense of Native peoples and, where economically practical, proceeded with the coerced labor of enslaved Black people. The United States was not a postcolonial state settling an empty and uncharted wilderness. It

---

8. In the Northwest Territory, variations in climate resulted in different patterns of dispossession. In territories like Indiana and Ohio, for example, settlers sought farmlands already improved by Native farmers, leading to a more rapid displacement of the Indigenous population. Farther north, Native lands were not valued for timber, mining, and farming until the infrastructure allowed for the integration of these economic activities into the national economy; treaties and annuities thus created a source of income for non-Native peoples. See Susan Sleeper-Smith, *Indigenous Prosperity and American Conquest: Indian Women of the Ohio River Valley, 1690–1792* (Williamsburg, Va., and Chapel Hill, N.C., 2018), 13–66. In the Old Southwest, by contrast, the rapid conversion of Native farms to slave-labor camps designed for massive commercial production of cotton made land and land speculation the primary economic drivers of Indigenous dispossession and removal. See Claudio Saunt, "Financing Dispossession: Stocks, Bonds, and the Deportation of Native Peoples in the Antebellum United States," *Journal of American History*, CVI (2019), 315–337.

was a nation of settlers created through the systematic plunder of Native wealth and Native land. In effect, the United States operated as both a settler colonial state and as a traditional exogenous colonial power. In this sense, the national history of the United States, like the colonial history of British and French North America that preceded it, chronicles the ongoing colonization of Indigenous North America.[9]

Mixed-Race Natives and the Idea of Dual Citizenship

The political and social status of mixed-race Native peoples living in the Northwest Territory remained ambiguous and subject for negotiation as the Northwest Territory was organized into new states and incorporated into the union. Mixed-race Native peoples were often regarded by settlers from the East as nonwhite people, or, in the terminology of the nineteenth century, "half-breeds." For the most part, however, the traders and territorial officials whose cooperation made the expansion of the Republic onto Native homelands possible regarded this population as white. This recognition was part of the political bargain they made for facilitating the dispossession of their Native kin. Their Native wives and children would be treated as white citizens of the United States. Many mixed-race Native peoples asserted Native identities, but they also claimed identities as "civilized" people. In the early years of the Republic, being civilized was conflated with being white, and whiteness was conditional for exercising some of the privileges of citizenship, such as voting, holding public office, testifying in court, or serving on a jury. Conversely, Indianness was synonymous with being uncivilized and with living in a state of nature, which was interpreted as living on land that had not been converted into

9. Jack P. Greene has argued that the colonial process did not end with the formation of national states in North America. "In the United States and Canada," he argues, "it actually intensified with the colonization of vast new areas of the continent as swarms of settlers brought new areas under their hegemony, pushing out or confining to unwanted catchment areas thousands of indigenous peoples, . . . making extensive use of enslaved African Americans in doing so." See Greene, "Colonial History and National History: Reflections on a Continuing Problem," *WMQ*, 3d Ser., LXIV (2007), 235–250 (quotation on 240). Bethel Saler has made a similar argument, describing American expansion in the Old Northwest as an attempt to create "an expansive, settler republic and domestic empire." Like Greene, she believes that the United States was "at once a settler republic and a continental empire." See Saler, *The Settlers' Empire: Colonialism and State Formation in America's Old Northwest* (Philadelphia, 2015), 13, 15.

private property and was therefore deemed unsettled wilderness. Indians were thus excluded from the civil society of the U.S. Republic.

The half-breeds of the Old Northwest, the mixed-race Anishinaabeg, rejected this simplistic racial formulation and insisted on an identity that was rooted in the social worlds of both Indigenous and white people. In effect, they asserted what we would now recognize as dual citizenship. For example, many half-breed Odawa and Ojibwe people claimed a dual identity as Anishinaabe and as American citizens in petitions to the federal government and in the treaties that the federal government negotiated with their Indigenous kin.[10] Virtually all mixed-race Anishinaabeg were the children of the male voyageurs and traders who worked the fur trade. Because the Anishinaabeg were a patrilineal people, these mixed-race children, while clearly identified as kin, had no particular or clearly defined social role within the doodem and village communities of their mothers.[11]

U.S. officials frequently called upon mixed-race Anishinaabeg who were working in the fur trade or as translators or Indian agents to take

10. In contrast, Jacqueline Peterson has suggested that mixed-race Natives in the nineteenth-century Great Lakes experienced a "late-contact form of ethnogenesis" shaped by pan-Indian claims to sovereignty and the nationalism of emerging composite nation-states in the New World. See Peterson, "Red River Redux: Métis Ethnogenesis and the Great Lakes Region," in Nicole St-Onge, Carolyn Podruchny, and Brenda Macdougall, eds., *Contours of a People: Metis Family, Mobility, and History* (Norman, Okla., 2012), 39. For the ambiguous and changing political and legal status of mixed-race Native peoples, see Jameson Sweet, "Native Suffrage: Race, Citizenship, and Dakota Indians in the Upper Midwest," *Journal of the Early Republic*, XXXIX (2019), 99–109; Lucy Eldersveld Murphy, *Great Lakes Creoles: A French-Indian Community on the Northern Borderlands, Prairie Du Chien, 1750–1860* (New York, 2014), especially chapters 2 and 3, which deal with elections and jury trials, respectively; Susan Sleeper-Smith, *Indian Women and French Men: Rethinking Cultural Encounter in the Western Great Lakes Region* (Amherst, Mass., 2001); and White, "The Power of Whiteness," *Minnesota History*, LVI (1998–1999), 178–197.

11. For social organization among patrilineal Algonquian peoples, see Edward S. Rogers, "Band Organization among the Indians of the Eastern Subarctic Canada," in David Dumas, ed., *Contributions to Anthropology: Band Societies: Proceedings of the Conference on Band Organization, Ottawa, August 30 to September 2, 1965* (Ottawa, Canada, 1965), 21–55. For an examination of male leadership and social responsibility, see Cary Miller, *Ogimaag: Anishinaabeg Leadership, 1760–1845* (Lincoln, Nebr., 2010), 34–37. For an example of mixed-race Native children who were socialized within the fur trade as cultural insiders and whose status was defined by their fur-trader fathers, see Theresa M. Schenck, *William W. Warren: The Life, Letters, and Times of an Ojibwe Leader* (Lincoln, Nebr., 2007), 19–34.

advantage of their position as both insiders and outsiders to negotiate the treaties that transformed their homeland, Anishinaabewaki, into federal territories such as Michigan and Wisconsin. Unlike their mixed-race counterparts in the Old Southwest among matrilineal people such as the Creeks and Cherokees, the mixed-race Anisahinaabeg who aided the treaty process did not sign these documents except as witnesses or interpreters—that is, they were not parties to the treaty. They received some form of monetary compensation for land cessions, but they were not included in the annuity payments and were not granted separate jurisdictional territories, or reservations. In other words, these treaties marked their political exclusion from the nation-to-nation relationship between the federal government and their Indigenous or tribal communities. This marginalization was the cost of asserting an identity that was both Native and civilized, or both red and white, and was the result of an authenticity trap. From the perspective of nineteenth-century white Americans, any Native person acknowledging some degree of whiteness admitted that they were not a "real" Indian, even if they were also not accepted as genuinely white. To claim this dual citizenship in order to secure a place within the Republic was to be forced to erase a certain degree of one's Indigenous identity.[12]

Co-opting Indigeneity

There was a constant, if inconsistent, dialectic between erasure and inclusion in the nineteenth-century United States. The Republic seemed to struggle over how to think about Native people, valuing their legacy as the Indigenous inhabitants of North America while hating their presence as Indians, signifiers of savagery. This tension becomes visible in the naming and renaming of counties by the settler colonial state. As noted earlier, in 1840 the Michigan legislature organized a county named Unwattin after one of the Indigenous leaders who had ceded their country to the federal government. Several years later, the Michigan legislature reversed course and provided new Anglicized names to counties that had

12. John Ross, a mixed-race Cherokee leader, and William McIntosh, a mixed-race Creek leader, for example, signed treaties that led to the removal of their peoples to the Indian Territory. Not only did both men sign treaties for their people, but they did not assert a status as both Native and American. Rather, both men identified as citizens of the Cherokee and Creek nations, respectively. For Ross, see Tiya Miles, *Ties That Bind: The Story of an Afro-Cherokee Family in Slavery and Freedom* (Berkeley, Calif., 2005), 151–152. For McIntosh, see Christopher D. Haveman, *Rivers of Sand: Creek Indian Emigration, Relocation, and Ethnic Cleansing in the American South* (Lincoln, Nebr., 2016), 14–18.

originally been given Anishinaabe names. The county north of Unwattin, for example, originally named Rautawaubet, was renamed Wexford. Reflecting the dialectic of erasure and inclusion, Unwattin County was also later renamed Osceola, the identity of the Indigenous military leader behind the Second Seminole War. The Seminoles, refusing their forced removal from Florida, waged a war against the United States that humiliated the Republic, defeating the army and devastating American settlements. Osceola was captured under a white flag when he responded to a U.S. request for a parlay. He died in captivity in 1838, and the war came to an end in 1842, when the United States agreed to allow the Seminoles to remain in Florida.[13]

In both naming a county Unwattin and then changing that name to Osceola, the Michigan state legislature sought to co-opt the indigeneity of North American Native peoples. A county history of Osceola written in 1884 simply noted: "It was first laid off by an act of the Legislature approved April 1, 1840, and received the Indian name of Un-wat-tin. It retained this name until March, 1843, when it was changed by the Legislature to Osceola." This historical account of the county offers no additional information about the naming process, no thoughts on why a county created through the dispossession of the local Native population would take the name of a leader of that community. And it offers no explanation about why that name would subsequently be changed to the name of a leader who had just led a successful resistance to U.S. expansion in Florida. It did, however, note: "Osceola County [Michigan] has no special Indian history. A few of these uncivilized people roamed about the forests for awhile after the white settlers came in, and then went out."[14]

This county history at least attempted to create the illusion of erasure by stating that the Indigenous people went away following the arrival of

13. Lorenzo Veracini has argued: "If the demand . . . is to go away, it is indigenous persistence and survival that become crucial. Resistance and survival are thus weapons of the colonised and the settler colonised." See Veracini, "Introducing Settler Colonial Studies," *Settler Colonial Studies,* I (2011), 3–4. For the renaming of Unwattin County, see An Act to Change the Names of Certain Counties, *Acts of the Legislature of the State of Michigan, Passed at the Annual Session of 1843* . . . (Detroit, 1843), 146. For the Second Seminole War, see C. S. Monaco, *The Second Seminole War and the Limits of American Aggression* (Baltimore, 2018); and Laurel Clark Shire, *The Threshold of Manifest Destiny: Gender and National Expansion in Florida* (Philadelphia, 2016).

14. *Portrait and Biographical Album of Osceola County, Containing Portraits and Biographical Sketches of Prominent Citizens of the County* . . . (Chicago, 1884), 355, 360.

white settlers. The idea of the vanishing Indian was a common trope in the United States in the nineteenth century. An early-twentieth-century history of the names of counties in the state of Michigan, however, questioned the provenance of Unwattin / Osceola County: "Why such a name taken from an Indian chief of Michigan should be changed to Osceola, the name of a Seminole chief from Florida, even though the latter had a national prominence and his unfortunate experience with the whites and unhappy death in 1838 were then fresh in the mind, is difficult to see."[15]

But what the author of this later history missed was that in the mid-nineteenth century, approximately six decades after the founding of the Republic, the people of the United States understood that their country had been created on Native land. Any adult resident of Michigan would have known that both Unwattin and Osceola were not literary characters; they were real people whose homelands had been taken from them. This realization must have raised questions about how the United States came to possess this Indigenous land base. Was it stolen land? Or was it acquired in a fair and legal manner? The United States had not waged a war against the Anishinaabeg, so it could not rationalize their dispossession as the result of conquest following a just war. The United States had waged a war against the Seminoles, but although it managed to acquire possession of most of the state of Florida, the Republic had neither defeated nor removed the Seminoles from this territory. Americans, faced with a process of land acquisition that was morally ambiguous at best, often romanticized Native peoples in popular culture, particularly those who resisted their dispossession heroically. Idealizing the heroism of dead warriors reflected a cultural and political appropriation that obscured the reality of Indigenous dispossession. By incorporating Native figures into the national mythology, the citizens of the United States gave themselves an Indigenous past. Including the noble dead—heroic warriors and Indian princesses—into the story of America's creation obfuscated the exclusion of living Indians from the social contract that the Republic extended to white citizen-settlers.[16]

15. William L. Jenks, "History and Meaning of the County Names of Michigan," in *Historical Collections: Collections and Researches Made by the Michigan Pioneer and Historical Society* (Lansing, Mich., 1912), XXXVIII, 468.

16. For the Indian princess phenomenon, see Rayna Greene, "The Pocahontas Perplex: The Image of Indian Women in American Culture," *Massachusetts Review*, XVI (1975), 698–714. On co-opting the heroic Indian warrior figure, see Tiya Miles, "His Kingdom for a Kiss: Indians and Intimacy in the Narrative of John Marrant," in Ann Laura Stoler, ed., *Haunted by Empire: Geographies of Intimacy in North American History* (Durham, N.C., 2006), 163–188.

Romanticizing heroic Native resistance also fits within the trope of the vanishing Indian. Osceola's bravery could be admired by the average American because he was conveniently dead. He represented that "Live Free or Die" sentiment that emerged as a Revolutionary War motto, and his defiance could no longer cloud any admiration of his fight for the liberty and freedom of his people. He was, therefore, easy for the American public to co-opt. They could, in effect, claim him and his valor as their own, creating a true American hero. While in captivity, Osceola was painted by George Catlin, the famous painter of Indian peoples, who described his subject as "the fallen Prince and Hero of Florida." And historian C. S. Monaco wrote about the valorization of Osceola in nineteenth-century America: "Romanticism helped sustain a legitimating illusion, a diversion that drew national attention away from the country's core aggression toward Indigenous people by focusing on highly idealized and artistic creations." He also noted that the phenomenon of Native peoples' emerging as heroically iconic figures in popular culture had a parallel in treaty making because it allowed the government to define the terms of the Republic's interactions with and manipulation of Native peoples "while at the same time reinforcing Euro-American moral authority."[17]

The treaty process, though openly coercive, allowed the average U.S. citizen to imagine that Native peoples had been treated fairly by their government. They surrendered their land because they wanted to and because they received fair compensation. Of course, the underlying truth to this false narrative may also explain the change of the county name from Unwattin to Osceola. Unwattin was likely still alive when the county was named for him, and he had not lost his country in either a just or an infamous war. He was swindled out of his land, and the sight of his people living on tiny reservations while white settlers occupy their homeland was an omnipresent reminder of that swindle. Better to name the county after the dead war leader Osceola who fought valiantly to remain on his land as it was seized by the American state. One could take pride in settling the homeland of a brave, but now dead and gone, Indigenous warrior. Harder to take pride in stealing and settling the homeland of your living Indigenous neighbor. This problem, however, is not confined to the early years of the U.S. Republic. The settler colonial project of the United States is not complete but continues into the present.

17. Monaco, *The Second Seminole War*, 166 ("fallen Prince"), 167, 168.

When Is Indian Land No Longer Indian Land?

The stakes of ignoring the political and legal rights of one's living Indigenous neighbors has reemerged as a contested issue in twenty-first-century Michigan. In 2015, the non-Native citizens of Michigan's northern Lower Peninsula confronted a powerful reminder of the epic land swindle that created their state. In August of that year, the Little Traverse Bay Bands of Odawa Indians went to court to demand that the federal government recognize their jurisdiction over the territory of the original reservation granted to the bands in the 1836 Treaty of Washington.

That treaty established fourteen reservations for the Odawa and Ojibwe doodemag, whose leaders signed the document, or "touched the pen." The U.S. Senate arbitrarily altered the terms of this treaty during the treaty ratification process, introducing five-year time limits to the reservations. The Senate's move to alter the treaty terms reflected the passage of the Indian Removal Act, signed into law by President Andrew Jackson in 1830. The Senate expected that implementation of the removal policy would result in the relocation of the Indigenous population east of the Mississippi River. Removal, however, was not fully or immediately executed in the Michigan Territory. Some Native peoples, like the Anishinaabeg, managed to remain in their homelands. The Anishinaabe doodemag living in northern Michigan had agreed to the amended 1836 treaty because Michigan's Indian agent Henry Rowe Schoolcraft assured them that they would be allowed to remain on their lands beyond the five-year period. This understanding was codified in the Treaty of Detroit in 1855, which established permanent reservations in Michigan for the Anishinaabeg. By 1855, the United States had become a transcontinental nation-state, and there was no longer an unsettled West to organize as Indian country that existed outside the boundaries of the Republic. The injunction filed on behalf of the Little Traverse Bay Bands of Odawa on August 2015 noted that the 1855 treaty created a 337-square-mile reservation that stretched 32 miles north to south along the northern tip of Michigan's Lower Peninsula on the eastern shore of Little Traverse Bay.[18]

The 1855 treaty included a scheme that theoretically allowed Native peoples to select individual land allotments and permitted any remaining land to be purchased and settled by non-Natives. This scheme was

18. Little Traverse Bay Bands of Odawa Indians v. Rick Snyder, Court File No. 15–850 (W.D. Mich. Aug. 21, 2015), "Complaint for Declaratory and Injunctive Relief," 8, http://www.pora.org/Assets/LTBB-Complaint.pdf.

not properly effectuated, and although the Little Traverse Bay Bands of Odawa continued to live on their reservation, settlers acquired land not claimed as Indian allotments fraudulently. According to the injunction, "The federal government's inability to administer the allotment process resulted in title to much of the Reservation passing to non-Indians, but this did not operate to disestablish or diminish the Reservation." Although much of the Little Traverse Bay reservation passed into the possession of non-Natives, the tribe asked the federal government to recognize its legal jurisdiction and sovereignty over the territory established as a reservation in the 1836 and 1855 treaties, accepting this land as "Indian country," regardless of who now owned it.[19]

In effect, the Little Traverse Bay Bands of Odawa asked the U.S. federal government to acknowledge that its failure to administer land rights established through the treaty process resulted in their dispossession but that it did not diminish their legal jurisdiction. They did not suggest that this "history of swindle and dispossession" be reversed and non-Native citizens be dispossessed; they requested only that their jurisdiction over the original reservation territory be recognized. A brief filed in support of the tribe's lawsuit asserted that "'only Congress' can diminish a reservation." Accordingly, the brief argues that regardless of "the precise details of the swindle, timber trespass, and land frauds that plagued the Reservation. . . . it was not Congress who settled, stole, and sold parcels of land out from under the Predecessor Bands." The document concludes: "A defense that relies on proof of these private thefts to invalidate the United States' treaty promise defies justice and the U.S. Constitution."[20]

In an editorial published in the *Petoskey News*, Little Traverse Bay tribal chairwoman Regina Gasco-Bentley explained the impetus behind the lawsuit. "In the treaties, the tribe carried out its part of the bargain," she wrote. "The law suit asks the court to uphold the treaty promises made to the tribe by recognizing the treaty reservation boundary." In

19. Ibid., 9, 17.

20. Little Traverse Bay Bands of Odawa Indians v. Gretchen Whitmer, Court File No. 15-cv-850 (W.D. Mich. Mar. 18, 2019), "Brief in Support of Tribe's 'Historical Motion' for Partial Summary Judgment concerning Exemption-Diminishment and Title-Diminishment Defenses," 20 ("swindle and dispossession"), 29 ("diminish"), 32 ("precise details" and "relies on proof"), https://turtletalk.files.wordpress .com/2019/04/586-ltbb-motion-for-summary-judgment-historical.pdf. For a concise summary of the case and its attendant history, see Tom Beaman, "Hidden Reservation," *DBusiness Magazine*, Aug. 14, 2017, https://www.dbusiness.com/business-features /hidden-reservation.

an earlier article in the same newspaper, Jessica Intermill, the attorney representing the tribe stated: "It's totally workable, it's just another layer of jurisdiction. Sometimes it's a complication, but sometimes it's a good thing because it provides more resources to the people." The tribe sought expanded jurisdiction over its people and community throughout the territory of the original reservation, not an extension of its authority over non-Native people living on what they argued continues to be Indian country. In other words, they sought a restoration of the rights granted in a treaty ratified by the United States.[21]

Lance Boldrey, a lawyer representing a regional homeowner's association opposing the lawsuit, asserted that, "if the Tribe wins a decree that 337 miles is 'Indian Country,' governance of this land will be forever changed." He then demanded that the tribe drop the lawsuit and negotiate the issues it claimed to care about with the state or face defeat in court over its claims "that northern Michigan is an Indian reservation." Boldrey's statement underscores a fact that for many American citizens is a painful truth: at one point, all of North America was essentially an Indian reservation—that is, when Europeans began to arrive and make settlements in North America, the entire continent was the homeland of Indigenous peoples. The U.S. Republic was founded on land stolen from Native peoples. This theft has been rationalized through the doctrine of discovery, the natural law ideology that imagined Native peoples had failed to leave the state of nature, the condition of primitive humanity when mankind first left the Garden of Eden and all of the world existed as a commons. According to this ideology, civilization was created when humans began to transform this common land into private property, necessitating the creation of civil society and the rule of law through a process that consensually recognized a representative, sovereign authority designed to protect the property rights of individuals in that society. Following the logic of this ideology, Europeans rationalized that North America was in a state of nature when they began to arrive. Although

21. "Chairwoman: Tribe Seeks to Protect Own, Not Control Others," guest commentary by Regina Gasco-Bentley, *Petoskey News*, Feb. 21, 2017 (updated Sept. 19, 2019), https://www.petoskeynews.com/news/opinion/chairwoman-tribe-seeks-to-protect -own-not-control-others/article_a2f27652-444f-5a97-a6a4-ef9ba8f1b5b2.html; Jessica Intermill, quoted in Matt Mikus, "1855 Treaty in Spotlight: Federal Lawsuit between State and Tribe to Determine Jurisdictional Authority, Tribe's Attorney Says Lawsuit Deals with State Relationship," ibid., Jan. 25, 2016 (updated Sept. 19, 2019), https:// www.petoskeynews.com/featured-pnr/1855-treaty-in-spotlight/article_0154812e -4d22-5697-b6b5-9b9cffa45d5a.html.

it was occupied by Native peoples, North America was, in effect, an un-settled wilderness.[22]

Imagining that Michigan was an unsettled wilderness until people of European descent arrived and began to establish proper settlements, homesteads delineated as private property and organized into towns and counties, makes it easier to rationalize the theft of Indian land. A treaty like that of 1836, however, in which Indigenous leaders were removed from their communities as a condition of negotiation and were then pressured to mark an *X* on a document written in a language they could not speak or read that ceded thirteen million acres of territory, was an act of thievery. The treaty of 1855 that attempted to legally establish a dramatically reduced Odawa homeland as an Indian reservation but actually facilitated further theft of this remaining land base was evidence of the political economy of plunder that transferred Indigenous wealth in the Great Lakes to the white citizens of an expanding U.S. Republic.[23]

In August 2019, a federal court codified the work of the failed U.S. treaty process that produced this outcome, ruling: "The Tribe's predecessor bands bargained for—and received—permanent homes in Michigan in the form of individual allotments. They did not bargain for an Indian reservation, and no such reservation was created by the unambiguous treaty terms because the terms do not establish a federal set aside of land for Indian purposes or indefinite federal superintendence over the land." The court concluded that examining the treaty in "the relevant historical context, it cannot plausibly be read to have created an Indian reservation."[24]

22. "Attorney: Tribe Seeks to Reshape Governance of Region," guest commentary by Lance Boldrey, *Petoskey News*, Feb. 21, 2017 (updated Sept. 19, 2019), https://www.petoskeynews.com/news/opinion/attorney-tribe-seeks-to-reshape-governance-of-region/article_d3041f99-8cbd-5175-9110-4d471931de1b.html. For natural law, the state of nature, and the creation of private property and civil society, see John Locke, *Two Treatises of Government: A Critical Edition with an Introduction and Apparatus Criticus*, ed. Peter Laslett (Cambridge, 1960). For the doctrine of discovery and U.S. expansion, see Williams, *The American Indian in Western Legal Thought*, 228–231.

23. For the history of the 1836 and 1855 treaties, see Matthew L. M. Fletcher, *The Eagle Returns: The Legal History of the Grand Traverse Band of Ottawa and Chippewa Indians* (East Lansing, Mich., 2012), 2–83. See also Charles E. Cleland, *Rights of Conquest: The History and Culture of Michigan's Native Americans* (Ann Arbor, Mich., 1992), 225–230.

24. Little Traverse Bay Band of Odawa Indians v. Gretchen Whitmer, 398 F. Supp. 3d 201 (W.D. Mich. 2019). It is worth noting that in the same summer that the District Court of Southern Michigan decided this case against Little Traverse, the U.S. Supreme Court ruled in McGirt v. Oklahoma that the Muscogee (Creek) nation maintained

To read the treaty as the tribe asked would be to recognize the super-seding rights and authority of an Indigenous nation to claim all of its homeland in North America. For the settler colonial state that is the U.S. Republic, such a construction of the past would simply be inconceivable. The people of the United States, past and present, citizens and newly ar-riving immigrants, could never imagine Native North America before the Republic as anything other than an unsettled wilderness. To think of the continent as settled land, as a viable alternative to the United States—that is, to suppose that the self-determination of Indigenous peoples had resulted in permanent dominion over their North American homelands—would have been what the Haitian historian Michel-Rolph Trouillot has described as "unthinkable" history.[25] For European colonists and Ameri-can settlers, however, it was entirely conceivable that they had the right and the power to claim ownership of an entire continent controlled by the Indigenous peoples of North America. Contemporary American citizens

---

jurisdiction over the original territory of the reservation in Oklahoma established by treaty because Congress never disestablished the boundaries created by the 1856 treaty (McGirt v. Oklahoma, 591 U.S. [2020]).

25. For "unthinkable" history, see Michel-Rolph Trouillot, *Silencing the Past: Power and the Production of History* (Boston, 1995). Trouillot argues, "The ontological prin-ciples behind the colonialist enterprise" were "that the differences between forms of humanity were not only of degree but of kind, not historical but primordial." Accord-ingly, he observes, from the colonizer's perspective, "access to human status did not lead *ipso facto* to self-determination" (81). In this fashion, he asserts: "The Haitian Revolution did challenge the ontological and political assumptions of the most radical writers of the Enlightenment. *The events that shook up Saint-Dominque from 1791 to 1804 constituted a sequence for which not even the extreme political left in France or England had a conceptual frame of reference.* They were 'unthinkable' facts in the framework of Western thought" (82). Jürgen Osterhammel offers a similar analysis of the effects of modern colonialism on Indigenous societies in the Americas. Modern colonialism, he asserts, "is not just any relationship between master and servants, but one in which an entire society is robbed of its historical line of development." This theft "was justified by the existence of allegedly insurmountable 'racial' hier-archies." See Osterhammel, *Colonialism: A Theoretical Overview*, trans. Shelley L. Frisch (Princeton, N.J., 1997), 15–16. A similar category of unthinkable facts and un-thinkable history emerged following the American Revolution. That the country west of the Allegheny Mountains and east of the Mississippi was the unsettled property of the federal government was articulated by Alexander Hamilton in the Federal-ist Papers. "We have a vast tract of unsettled territory within the boundaries of the United States," he wrote. Several states in the newly formed union "have heretofore had serious and animated discussions concerning the right to the lands which were ungranted at the time of the Revolution, and which usually went under the name of

continue to find the idea that this continent already belonged to someone else to be an impossibility. This would be an unthinkable history.[26]

Seeing Red explores that unthinkable history. It examines the process and the ideology of dispossession that created a political economy of plunder—one that enabled the United States to forever change the governance of the region it identified as the Northwest Territory. The book is also the story of the Anishinaabeg (mixed-race or otherwise) and their attempt to shape their own history, to work the coercive system designed to rob them of all that they owned so that they could remain in their homeland and be recognized by the United States as a sovereign people.

------

crown lands." See Hamilton, "Federalist Paper No. 7," in Hamilton, James Madison, and John Jay, *The Federalist Papers*, ed. Clinton Rossiter (New York, 1961), 60. This idea also shaped the emergence of free-soil politics in the early Republic. In 1848, at the convention of the newly formed Free-Soil Party, one of the resolutions passed by the convention stated: "It is well known that during the war of the Revolution several of the States laid claim, under their respective charters, to the territory between the Alleghanies and Mississippi. It is also well known that the Federal Congress claimed the same territory as unoccupied lands, which originally belonged, not to the colonies, but to the Crown, and had been wrested from Britain by the common blood and treasure of all the States." See "Address of the Independent State Free Territory Convention . . . ," in *Addresses and Proceedings of the State Independent Free Territory Convention of the People of Ohio, Held at Columbus, June 20 and 21, 1848* (Cincinnati, 1848), 10. To see North America as already settled, to see it as Indian country, would be an "unthinkable" fact, outside the framework of Western or Enlightenment thought. To do so would be to acknowledge that the United States is a country created on stolen land. That this sentiment reflected a national consensus regarding the status of Native lands provided the federal government with the authority to take this land and sell it at a discount to its citizens. For this argument, see Andrew Shankman, "Toward a Social History of Federalism: The State and Capitalism to and from the American Revolution," *JER*, XXXVII (2017), 649.

26. In 1813, Thomas Jefferson wrote to Alexander von Humboldt about the "benevolent plan" of the United States to civilize the Indians, "to teach them agriculture and the rudiments of the most necessary arts, and to encourage industry by establishing among them separate property." For Jefferson, the path toward civilization necessarily meant the dismantling of Native homelands and the conversion of this territory into private property. Unfortunately, he wrote that British Canada had "seduced the greater part of the tribes within our neighborhood, to take up the hatchet against us, and the cruel massacres they have committed on the women and children of our frontiers taken by surprise, will oblige us now to pursue them to extermination, or drive them to new seats beyond our reach." See Jefferson to Humboldt, Dec. 6, 1813, in Jefferson, *Writings*, ed. Merrill D. Peterson (New York, 1984), 1312–1313.

CHAPTER 1

A Nation of Settlers

 On December 22, 1804, a delegation of Native leaders from the lower Missouri River region arrived in Washington D.C. Meriwether Lewis and William Clark, traveling into the country of the Louisiana Purchase, sent these men east to meet with Thomas Jefferson, the president of the United States. A significant part of the mission of the Corps of Discovery expedition would be diplomatic—not so much discovering an empty wilderness as introducing the Republic to the Indigenous nations of western North America. The United States purchased an enormous territory from the French Empire, approximately 828,000 square miles, stretching from the Mississippi River to the Missouri River and encompassing land that would eventually become all or parts of the states of Arkansas, Missouri, Oklahoma, Kansas, Nebraska, North Dakota, South Dakota, Montana, Wyoming, and Colorado. The man behind this land grab knew full well that the country he had just acquired was occupied and owned by dozens of Native American nations. Jefferson instructed Lewis and Clark, as part of their mission, to send "a few of their influential chiefs," whenever distance was practical, to visit the nation's capital and meet the president of the United States. On New Year's Day 1804, President Jefferson received "the Chiefs of the Osages, Missouris, Kanzas, Ottos, Panis, Ayowas, and Sioux" nations from the southern and central Great Plains at the White House.[1]

1. "[Thomas] Jefferson's Instructions to [Merriwether] Lewis," June 20, 1803, and Jefferson to the Indian Delegation, [Jan. 4, 1806], in Donald Jackson, ed., *Letters of the Lewis and Clark Expedition with Related Documents, 1783–1854*, 2d ed. (Urbana, Ill., 1978), I, 64, 280. For the expedition of the Corps of Discovery, see *History of the Expedition under the Command of Captains Lewis and Clark . . .* , ed. Paul Allen (Philadelphia, 1814), in Merriwether Lewis, *The Lewis and Clark Expedition*, introduction by Archibald Hanna, Keystone Western Americana Series, KB34-36 (Philadelphia, 1961), I; Peter J. Kastor, *William Clark's World: Describing America in an Age of Unknowns* (New Haven, Conn., 2011). For the Louisiana Purchase, see Kastor, *The Nation's Crucible: The Louisiana Purchase and the Creation of America* (New Haven, Conn., 2004).

Jefferson hoped to impress these Native leaders from the West with the modernity and the power of the United States. Americans imagined their relationship with Native allies in terms of kinship, following the diplomatic protocol first developed by the French. The chief executive of the United States, like the colonial regimes of France and Great Britain, assumed the role of a father presiding over a family of Native children. From the perspective of the colonial power, assuming the status of a parent and a patriarch made sense given the assumptions about its own political and cultural superiority.[2] Some Native nations resisted the implied subordination of assuming the role of a child and asserted their status as brothers, equal partners in the alliance. Many Native nations, however, managed their relationship with colonial regimes by accepting their status as children and then using that role to push the foreign power to act as a provider of trade goods and resources or as a political intermediary.

2. The governors of New France adapted the name and the social persona of Onontio, the French father; the title was a Mohawk translation of the surname of one of the early governors, Charles Huault de Montmagny. The various Indigenous nations allied to New France created a multi-ethnic kinship network based on the assumption of their identity as the children of Onontio. This relationship not only represented a form of fictive kinship, and therefore alliance, but also determined the obligations that the French father and his Native children owed to one another. Defining the terms of these kinship obligations would be a source of constant tension and negotiation. Neither the French nor their Native allies were able to completely enforce their understanding of the role and responsibilities of a father and his children, resulting in an alliance that blended Indigenous and French social and political norms, one that Richard White called the "middle ground." See White, *The Middle Ground: Indians, Empires, and Republics in the Great Lakes Region, 1650–1815* (Cambridge, 1991), xi, xiv, 36, 40. The presidents and agents of the federal government of the United States adopted the language identifying the chief executive of the Republic as a father to the Indian nations, who were identified as children, living on territory claimed by the United States. Unlike the French or British Empires, however, the United States was not making a claim to kinship but rather asserting cultural superiority over people deemed to be uncivilized and therefore primitive. The federal government did not, like the French father, wrestle with this role as a mediator who took on obligations to provide for his children; it instead imagined this patriarchal role as a means to control Native nations and demand their obedience. White contends that, from an American perspective, "Indians were not metaphorically but literally children. They were in the infancy of civilization." Accordingly, he argues, "Indians had lost control of the language of patriarchy, of the fiction of patriarchy, and the price they would pay would be a terrible one." See White, "The Fictions of Patriarchy: Indians and Whites in the Early Republic," in Frederick E. Hoxie, Ronald Hoffman, and Peter J. Albert, eds., *Native Americans and the Early Republic* (Charlottesville, Va., 1999), 83.

Regardless of the specific tactic, negotiating the relationship between Native nations and colonial powers was a constant struggle over the degree of obligation and kinds of responsibility the parties owed to one another.[3]

When Jefferson met with the Native leaders from the lower Missouri, he sought to activate the diplomatic protocol of past empires, establishing himself as their father. He also wanted to make certain they understood that their American father, and the American people, were different from the colonizers they had treated with in the past. "My friends and children," Jefferson began:

> We are descended from the old nations which live beyond the great water: but we and our forefathers have been so long here that we seem like you to have grown out of this land: we consider ourselves no longer as of the old nations beyond the great water, but as united in one family with our red brethren here. The French, the English, the Spaniards, have now agreed with us to retire from all the country which you and we hold between Canada and Mexico, and never more to return to it. And remember the words I now speak to you my children, they are never to return again. We are become as numerous as the leaves on the trees, and, tho' we do not boast, we do not fear any nation. We are now your fathers; and you shall not lose by the change.

Perhaps the visiting leaders took note of the language of accommodation, the idea expressed by Jefferson that Americans were "united in one family with our red brethren." Or, more ominously, maybe they noted that Jefferson claimed a Native or Indigenous identity for the United States—"we seem like you to have grown out of this land." Jefferson's claim was not necessarily exclusionary. After telling the visiting leaders that Americans wanted to live in peace "as brethren of the same family," however, he also warned these men, "My children, we are strong, we are numerous as the stars in the heavens, and we are all gun-men." The United States was a

3. The Iroquois imagined their alliance with the Dutch and later the English as the "covenant chain," a bond in which they were brothers of European powers rather than children. See Daniel K. Richter, *The Ordeal of the Longhouse: The Peoples of the Iroquois League in the Era of European Colonization* (Williamsburg, Va., and Chapel Hill, N.C., 1992), 134–142. See also Mary Druke Becker, "Linking Arms: The Structure of Iroquois Intertribal Diplomacy," in Richter and James H. Merrell, eds., *Beyond the Covenant Chain: The Iroquois and Their Neighbors in Indian North America, 1600–1800* (Syracuse, N.Y., 1987).

well-armed and fast-growing nation—an implicit threat. This new nation was descended from, but no longer part of, the "old nations . . . beyond the great water." The Republic, Jefferson proclaimed, was an American nation, a creation of the New World just like the Indigenous nations visiting the White House. The United States was not a foreign power. It was a nation of settlers claiming an American identity.[4]

The State of Nature

Jefferson's vision for the Republic and the continent was linked to a particular understanding of the relationship between Native peoples and the land. From his viewpoint, Native peoples could claim a title to their homelands, but they did not own that land as private property. Jefferson assumed a natural law legal perspective, derived from social contract theory, that Natives could claim aboriginal title, or right of occupancy, on their territory, but they did not exercise dominion over it. European powers, and later the United States, made this claim because they asserted that Native peoples lived in a state of nature—that is, they were not part of the civilized world. North America was terra nullius, a legal concept dating back to the Roman Empire designating territory as vacant or unoccupied. Declaring North America terra nullius implied that the land had never been properly cultivated or truly settled. It remained, in effect, in a state of nature, the condition in which it existed at the beginning of time.[5]

As early as the seventeenth century, these ideas about natural law and the state of nature informed Anglo-American understandings of private property. At the beginning of time, all the world was a commons whose resources were available to everyone. When human beings applied their labor to the things derived from this commons, the effort resulted in the creation of private property. A tree could be transformed into a table and chairs, making these items the possessions solely of their creator. A plot of

4. Jefferson to the Indian Delegation, [Jan. 4, 1806], in Jackson, ed., *Letters of the Lewis and Clark Expedition*, I, 281. Jefferson's speech provides a clear statement of the settler colonial ideology of the U.S. Republic. "Settler colonialism," Lorenzo Veracini has argued, "justifies its operation on the basis of the expectation of its future demise"; it *"extinguishes* itself" upon completion of the colonial project. See Veracini, "Introducing Settler Colonial Studies," *Settler Colonial Studies*, I (2011), 2–3.

5. For the history of terra nullius and its relationship to settler colonialism, see Carole Pateman, "The Settler Contract," in Pateman and Charles W. Mills, eds., *Contract and Domination* (Cambridge, 2007), 35–41. "The legitimacy of the states created in North America and Australia," she writes, "is ultimately based on the claim that, in

land, similarly, could be transformed into a farm—with built structures, plowed fields and planted crops, and fenced enclosures—and entailed as private property. The cultivation of land thus carved out parcels of this shared landscape as private property, transforming the commons into a built or improved environment, a process accelerated by the creation and circulation of currency. In this increasingly complex setting, men and women were compelled to leave the state of nature and enter into civil society in order to protect their property. This was the social contract articulated most clearly by the English philosopher John Locke. Individuals gave up a portion of their rights, creating a government or sovereign designated to act on behalf of all members of society to ensure the rule of law and to protect the individual right to property and the pursuit thereof. In forming civil society, humanity left the state of nature and entered a world of laws and civil institutions designed to protect their rights in property. Appropriating the resources of the commons, men, particularly male heads of household, created civilization.[6]

———

one or another sense of the term, they were created in a *terra nullius*," or unoccupied territory (37). For a similar argument, see David Armitage, *The Ideological Origins of the British Empire* (2000; rpt. Cambridge, 2007), 97–98. Lauren Benton and Benjamin Straumann offer a slightly different interpretation of terra nullius in "Acquiring Empire by Law: From Roman Doctrine to Early Modern European Practice," *Law and History Review*, XXVIII (2010), 1–38. They assert that the term was derived by analogy from the Roman law concept of "res nullius (things without owners)" (1). Res nullius signified possession, they argue, rather than occupation through a claim of *vacuum domicilium* (vacancy), which has been implied by historians who cite the use of terra nullius as a European justification for colonization. Instead, agents of empire "favored inclusion of both direct and indirect referencing of Roman legal language, in part precisely because they wanted their actions and words to be understood by European rivals" (3). In other words, describing colonized territory as terra nullius or res nullius was meant to signal possession, not a right of occupation.

6. This natural law conception of a commons and the creation of private property draws on John Locke's *Two Treatises of Government*. "God gave the World to Men in Common," he wrote, "but since he gave it them for their benefit, and the greatest Conveniencies of Life they were capable to draw from it, it cannot be supposed he meant it should always remain common and uncultivated." See Locke, *Two Treatises of Government: A Critical Edition with an Introduction and Apparatus Criticus*, ed. Peter Laslett (Cambridge, 1960), 309. In effect, labor established rights in property and transformed the commons, taking it out of a state of nature: "Thus *Labour*, in the Beginning, *gave a Right of Property*, where-ever any one was pleased to imploy it, upon what was common" (341). For Locke, the state of nature, and the formation of civil society, see Pateman, "The Settler Contract," in Pateman and Mills, eds., *Contract and Domination*, 54–61.

With this rhetorical sleight of hand, European powers claimed possession of North America by right of discovery. Existing in a state of nature, the continent was an uncultivated wilderness and therefore an unsettled land. Using the same legal logic, European powers established dominion over their new possessions by converting land and resources into private property that, in turn, became part of colonial settlements, effectively establishing sovereign governments where supposedly none had previously existed. From the European perspective, immigrant communities in North America represented civilization and human progress. Native communities represented the uncivilized; they were a primitive form of humanity that had failed to advance beyond the state of nature. North America was thus imagined as the New World, an uncivilized continent waiting to be settled, and colonial settlers saw themselves as bringing civilization to that world. The people of the United States envisioned the newly formed Republic to be the successor of this colonial project. American citizens and government officials uniformly regarded western expansion as the spreading of civilization across a New World wilderness.[7]

This cultural and legal logic informed Jefferson's actions and made the Louisiana Purchase possible, at least from the point of view of the United States and France. When the colonists arrived in North America, they found nothing that they recognized as private property. Of course, they encountered Native peoples with their own system of territoriality, distinct land-use practices, and political and social organization. By recognizing only concepts of property, property rights, and political self-determination specific to western Europe, however, they believed that North America remained in a state of nature. Part of this conceptual leap required that the colonizers see Indigenous peoples as less than fully human. They had not evolved socially and politically into a civilized people but instead remained in a state of nature where they lived as primitive

7. For the English idea of Native territory as "unimproved" and therefore unoccupied territory, see Patricia Seed, *American Pentimento: The Invention of Indians and the Pursuit of Riches* (Minneapolis, Minn., 2001), 14–23. Anthony Pagden similarly argues that European nations saw native peoples as uncivilized, which meant that, although they had usufruct rights, they did not possess their territory as property. See the chapter "Conquest and Settlement," in Pagden, *Lords of All the World: Ideologies of Empire in Spain, Britain, and France, c. 1500–c. 1800* (New Haven, Conn., 1995), 63–102. The acceptance of the political fiction that land inhabited by Indigenous peoples was an unsettled commons is a variation on Carole Pateman's notion of the "settler contract"; see Pateman, "The Settler Contract," in Pateman and Mills, eds., *Contract and Domination*, 38–41.

social beings, or, in the language of the era of discovery, "savages." By their very nature, the savage peoples of North America would be subordinate to the civilized peoples of Europe.[8]

The contention that Native peoples were uncivilized and therefore inferior or subordinate to peoples of European descent was thus based, not on empirical evidence, but on an ontology or political imaginary that assumed non-European peoples to be less than fully human while simultaneously presuming that European peoples represented the apex of humanity, civilization. To be of European descent and, more important, to live according to the social, political, and economic mores and traditions of western Europe was to be civilized. This reasoning constituted the ideology that shaped the political formation of the United States. For decades after its creation, the Republic, founded on the idea that all men were created equal, pursued policies predicated on the assumption that Native peoples were uncivilized savages. Their land was terra nullius, empty land, an unsettled wilderness. U.S. government officials, Indian agents, and countless settlers felt compelled to settle this land, to colonize it, to transform Native homelands into American homesteads—in fact, the identity of the United States as a political body depended on it.[9]

8. See, for example, Juliana Barr, "Geographies of Power: Mapping Indian Borders in the Borderlands of the Early Southwest," *William and Mary Quarterly,* 3d Ser., LXVIII (2011), 5–46; Paul W. Mapp, *The Elusive West and the Contest for Empire, 1713-1763* (Williamsburg, Va., and Chapel Hill, N.C., 2011); Walter D. Mignolo, "Colonial Situations, Geographical Discourses, and Territorial Representations: Toward a Diatopical Understanding of Colonial Semiosis," *Dispositio,* 14, nos. 36–38 (1989), 93–140. According to Richard White, "The idea of Indians as literally *sauvages,* or wild men embodying either natural virtue or ferocity, persisted among intellectuals and statesmen in France." For the French conception of Native peoples as *sauvage,* see White, *Middle Ground,* 50–51 (quotation on 51). Legal scholar Robert A. Williams, Jr., argues that political figures during the early Republic thought "the Indians of the New World were among the most primitive, savage peoples ever to live on the face of the earth. Lacking the civilizing institutions of property, law, government, or acceptable religious belief, the Indians' incontestable savage nature presented a challenge and an obstacle that the Founders sought to overcome by promoting white settlement of the Indian-held 'Western Country.'" See Williams, *Savage Anxieties: The Invention of Western Civilization* (New York, 2012), 211–212.

9. Williams, *Savage Anxieties,* 210–217; Ronald N. Satz, *American Indian Policy in the Jacksonian Era* (Norman, Okla., 2002), 246–279. For an explication of Native savagery as part of the political ideology of the early Republic, see [Lewis Cass], *Remarks on the Policy and Practice of the United States and Great Britain in Their Treatment of the Indians; from the North American Review, No. LV, for April, 1827*

Unthinkable History

The United States thus claimed possession of the Northwest Territory following the conclusion of the Revolutionary War. The 1783 Treaty of Paris, which ended the conflict, set the western boundaries of the United States at the east bank of the Mississippi River. This vast Trans-Appalachian region had been previously ceded to Great Britain by France after the Seven Years' War (1756–1763). All three of these colonial powers discovered that claiming possession of Indian country was not the same as exercising dominion over the territory. Notwithstanding the separate assertions of sovereignty over the territory by France, Britain, and the United States, the country between the Appalachian Mountains and the Mississippi River was occupied and controlled by a multitude of autonomous Indigenous nations. Indeed, the near-constant violence between Natives and settlers in the so-called backcountry west of the thirteen colonies during the Revolutionary War provided ample evidence of this Indigenous presence, belying claims by Anglo settlers that they were moving into an unsettled wilderness.[10]

Despite this contentious history, lawmakers in the United States began to formulate plans to settle the region as soon as the Revolutionary War was over. But the United States could not simply choose to ignore the presence of Native peoples or allow settlers to occupy land without

---

(Boston, 1827); see also James Monroe, Nov. 17, 1818, *Journal of the House of Representatives of the United States, at the Second Session of the Fifteenth Congress, in the Forty-Third Year of the Independence of the United States* (Washington, D.C., 1818). For the significance of violent conflict with Native peoples in the early Republic, see Peter Silver, *Our Savage Neighbors: How Indian War Transformed Early America* (New York, 2008).

10. Describing the 1783 Treaty of Paris that codified this land transfer, Alan Taylor has written that the treaty "abandoned most of Britain's Indian allies, including the Six Nations, by placing them on the American side of the new border. For the United States, a nation verging on financial collapse and unable to defend its long frontier against Indian raids, the peace treaty was a stunning diplomatic victory." See Taylor, *The Divided Ground: Indians, Settlers, and the Northern Borderland of the American Revolution* (New York, 2006), 111–112. For the transient nature of empire in the Trans-Appalachian West, see Michael Witgen, *An Infinity of Nations: How the Native New World Shaped Early North America* (Philadelphia, 2012), 213–222. For conflict between American settlers and Native people in the Ohio country before the formation of the Northwest Territory, see Susan Sleeper-Smith, *Indigenous Prosperity and American Conquest: Indian Women of the Ohio River Valley, 1690–1792* (Williamsburg, Va., and Chapel Hill, N.C., 2018), 210–242; and Rob Harper, *Unsettling the West: Violence and State Building in the Ohio Valley* (Philadelphia, 2018).

government regulation. On September 7, 1783, four days after the Treaty of Paris was signed, George Washington asserted in a letter to James Duane, chairman of the congressional Committee on Indian Affairs: "To suffer a wide extended Country to be run over with Land Jobbers, Speculators, and Monopolisers or even with scatter'd settlers, is, in my opinion, inconsistent with that wisdom and policy which our true interest dictates." Equally important, he noted, such a disorderly expansion "is pregnant of disputes . . . with the savages." Washington feared that rapid and unregulated expansion onto western lands occupied by Native peoples would lead to violent conflict. He understood that "savages" lived in this territory, but he also thought of it as an unsettled part of the public domain of the United States.[11]

In this same letter, the president informed Duane, who had written seeking policy advice, that Indian affairs would be closely tied to policies governing the expansion of the Republic onto western lands. Washington also warned the chairman that they needed to tell the Indians of the British cession of their lands to the Republic. At the heart of Washington's answer to Duane was the presumption that the West, Indian country, belonged to the Republic. This belief is not surprising, given that the movement of settlers onto Indian homelands west of the thirteen British colonies south of Canada had provided fuel to the fire that led to the Revolution. Following the Seven Years' War, the British Empire issued the royal Proclamation of 1763, which pledged to stop the expansion of colonial settlements west of the Appalachian Mountains. Many settlers defied the proclamation, resulting in widespread conflict with Native peoples, most of whom sided with Great Britain during the Revolution. The point was not lost on Washington. "The Indians . . . could not be restrained from acts of Hostility, but were determined to join their Arms to those of G Britain and to share their fortune," he noted. "But as we prefer Peace to a state of Warfare," he wrote, "we perswade ourselves that they

11. George Washington to James Daune, Sept. 7, 1783, in John C. Fitzpatrick, ed., *The Writings of George Washington from Original Manuscript Sources, 1745–1799; Prepared under Direction of the United States George Washington Bicentennial Commission and Published by Authority of Congress*, XXVII, *June 11, 1783–November 28, 1784* (Washington, D.C., 1938), 133. Colin G. Calloway argues that "when Washington and his peers talked about Indian land, they called it 'hunting territory,' which implied a more transient occupancy and a lesser value than farmland; with no deep attachment to the land, Indian hunters could, as Benjamin Franklin said, be easily persuaded to give it up as game diminished." See Calloway, *The Indian World of George Washington* (New York, 2018), 286.

are convinced, from experience, of their error in taking up the Hatchet against us, and that their true Interest and safety must now depend on *our* friendship." Washington knew that rapid and unregulated expansion would inevitably draw the Republic into wars with Native peoples.[12]

Accordingly, the president imagined a boundary between the United States and the Native nations living in the West, much like the one Britain had sought to create with its 1763 proclamation line. Crucially, he also understood this boundary to be temporary. The United States, he apprised Duane, would "establish a boundary line between them and us beyond which we will *endeavor* to restrain our People." He cautioned the congressman that, "in establishing this line, in the first instance, care should be taken neither to yield nor to grasp at too much." Instead, the United States should "endeavor to impress the Indians with an idea of the generosity of our disposition to accommodate them." The Republic needed to make clear to its Native neighbors "the necessity we are under, of providing for our Warriors, our Young People who are growing up, and strangers who are coming from other Countries to live among us." The Indians needed to be told, he concluded, that although they might be dissatisfied with this boundary line, they would nevertheless be compensated for their loss.[13]

Asked about the relationship of the U.S. Republic and Native peoples, Washington responded that this diplomatic issue was necessarily about the connection between U.S. citizens and land. "At first view," he wrote, "it may seem a little extraneous, when I am called upon to give an opinion upon the terms of a Peace proper to be made with the Indians, that I should go into the formation of New States; but the Settlemt. of the Western Country and making a Peace with the Indians are so analogous that there can be no definition of the one without involving considerations

12. Washington to Duane, Sept. 7, 1783, in *Writings of George Washington*, XXVII, 134. "During the Revolution," Colin Calloway writes, "the fears and realities of Indian warfare contributed to the development of an American racial consciousness. After the Revolution, westward expansion contributed to the development of a white American consciousness." See Calloway, *The Indian World of George Washington*, 285. The royal Proclamation of 1763 established the Ohio Valley as an Indian territory supposedly administered by the British military, and it forbade individuals from purchasing land directly from Indians. This policy quickly proved unenforceable as Anglo settlers moved into the region from the original thirteen colonies in British North America. See Taylor, *Divided Ground*, 40–42.

13. Washington to Duane, Sept, 7, 1783, in *Writings of George Washington*, XXVII, 134–135.

of the other." From the Revolution to the founding of the Republic, the political leadership of the United States believed the country would expand into the West, settling Indigenous territory and adding new states to the union.[14]

Although members of Congress thought of the West as unsettled wilderness, they also simultaneously understood it to be Indian country. This was the dilemma that George Washington warned them about: the creation of new states meant the dispossession of Native peoples. There was little reason to believe that they would abandon their homelands without a fight. Shortly after corresponding with President Washington, the Committee on Indian Affairs reported to Congress, "The hostile tribes in the ~~western districts~~ northern and middle departments . . . are not in a temper to relinquish their territorial claims, without further struggles." The report cautioned against war, for, if "repeated victories might produce retreat of the Indians," it would come at great financial cost. War also carried the risk that displaced Natives "would find a welcome reception from the British government in Canada, which by so great an accession of strength would become formidable in case of any future rupture." British alliances were not the only threat. American officials frequently worried that the Native peoples living in western territories claimed by the Republic might align themselves with a potentially hostile European empire.[15]

Establishing the U.S. Government in Indian Country

In order to truly take possession of Indian country, the United States would need to control the immigration of settlers onto Native lands. The report produced by the Committee on Indian Affairs warned against the hazards of the unauthorized settlement of the Northwest Territory, still occupied by "hostile tribes." The committee directed that commissioners of Indian affairs in the region be ordered to "obtain information of the

14. Ibid., 139. Colin Calloway argues that "Washington thought the precarious republic's security, prosperity, and future depended upon creating a strong government, creating a national market in Indian lands, and turning hunting territories over to commercial agriculture and economic development"; see Calloway, *The Indian World of George Washington*, 288. See also Andrew R. L. Cayton, *The Frontier Republic: Ideology and Politics in the Ohio Country, 1780–1825* (Kent, Ohio, 1986), 35–37.

15. Worthington Chauncey Ford et al., eds., *Journals of the Continental Congress, 1774–1789 . . .*, 34 vols. (Washington D.C., 1904–1937), XXV, 681–682 (hereafter cited as *JCC*).

numbers and places of residence of the citizens of the United States who have seated themselves on the northwest side of the Ohio; to signify to them the displeasure of Congress that they have taken this step." It warned Congress of the danger of "the increase of feeble, disorderly and dispersed settlements in those remote and wide extended territories." Such extralegal settlements would weaken the United States and involve the government in "frequent and destructive wars with the Indians." To avoid this fate, and to properly cultivate and settle the Northwest, the committee concluded with the resolution "that it will be wise and necessary, . . . to erect a district of the western territory into a distinct government." The Committee on Indian Affairs thus called for the creation of a new committee to devise a land law that would regulate the development of new settlements and facilitate their eventual incorporation into the union.[16]

In essence, James Duane and the Committee on Indian Affairs agreed with the president: the Republic needed a way to settle the West without provoking endless conflicts with Native peoples. Congressional leaders also wanted to prevent new settlements from forming that were independent of the United States or attached to one of the territories administered by a European empire along the nation's southern and northern borders. In their calculations, a failure to expand not only meant leaving Native land unsettled, it also carried the risk that a foreign power other than the United States would bring civilization to the wilderness of North America. From this perspective, devising a land policy that facilitated the expansion of the United States was a significant political imperative, one that had implications for both domestic and foreign policy. Duane and the Committee on Indian Affairs submitted their report to the Continental Congress on October 15, 1783. Following their recommendation, the Congress immediately formed a new committee, chaired by Thomas Jefferson, charged with setting a trade policy with the Indians and formulating a plan to settle western territory claimed by the United States.[17]

Their first attempt resulted in the short-lived Ordinance of 1784, which imagined the West divided into ten new districts that eventually would become states. Jefferson produced a map representing this scheme but showing fourteen new states (the Jefferson-Hartley map). The Ordinance created a standardized system for surveying, selling, and purchasing land in the public domain, and it established the federal government as the

16. Ibid., 692–693, 694. See also Calloway, *The Indian World of George Washington*, 291–294.

17. *JCC*, XXV, 680–695.

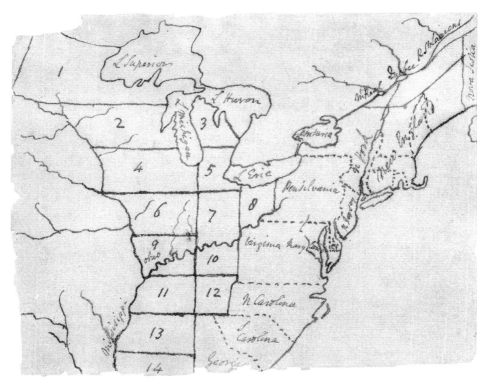

Figure 1. *A Map of the United States East of the Mississippi River in Which the Land Ceded by the Treaty of Paris Is Divided by Parallels of Latitude and Longitude into Fourteen New States* (Jefferson-Hartley map). By David Hartley. [1784]. William L. Clements Library, University of Michigan, Ann Arbor

sole agent authorized to make these sales. The law allowed settlers to govern themselves as long as they adopted the constitution of an existing state. The new settlement would elect a nonvoting member to represent the territory in Congress, and once the population reached twenty thousand free inhabitants, they could establish a permanent constitution of their own design consistent with and subordinate to the national government. The territory would enter the final stage of political development, statehood, once the population reached the size of the smallest of the original thirteen states. At this time, the new state would enter the union with all of the rights and privileges of every other state. The Ordinance, and the map drawn by Jefferson to illustrate the outcome of this policy, represented a complete erasure of Native peoples from the political landscape of North America. It was a reflection of the political imaginary that saw the continent as part of a New World, an unsettled and uncivilized space that remained trapped in a state of nature.[18]

The idea of North America as terra nullius, or empty wilderness, empowered the Continental Congress to imagine a republic that could quickly grow from a union of thirteen states to one of twenty-three states. The possession of a large public domain promised a source of income, an important asset for a country that emerged from war with significant debt. It also provided a land base for a growing republic of yeoman farmers. A citizenry composed of independent landowners was central to Jefferson's idea of a democratic republic. This same vision, however, also meant that a potential settler could look at the West and see, not the public domain of the United States, but simply an unsettled wilderness—that is, one could imagine, not public land owned by the Republic, but a commons waiting to be transformed into private property by those willing to work the land.[19]

American citizens, in fact, began to emigrate to the Northwest beyond the Ohio River in advance of the Ordinance of 1784. The report submitted by the Committee on Indian Affairs in 1783 urgently warned Congress of the need to account for these unregulated settlements. This task fell to the army of the United States, a drastically reduced version of the Continental army that had fought the Revolution. Because the United States had emerged from the War of Independence with a deep suspicion of standing armies and centralized political power, the newly organized First American Regiment was staffed by a small number of professional soldiers and a few hundred troops drawn from state militias. These men served under the command of Josiah Harmar and were deployed to the western territories to act as a form of national law enforcement.[20]

18. For the Ordinance of 1784, see *JCC*, XXVI, 275–279. For a history of the committee and the Jefferson-Hartley map, see "Plan for Government of the Western Territory: Editorial Note," in Julian P. Boyd et al., eds., *The Papers of Thomas Jefferson*, VI, *May 1781 to March 1784* (Princeton, N.J., 1952), 581–600. See also Robert E. Berkhofer, Jr., "Jefferson, the Ordinance of 1784, and the Origins of the American Territorial System," *WMQ*, 3d Ser., XXIX (1972), 231–262.

19. As Susan Sleeper-Smith has written, "The Ohio River valley was one of the most fertile landscapes in North America." It was, in fact, a densely settled and prosperous Indigenous territory; imagining it as an empty, uncultivated space was part of the frontier mythology of the U.S. Republic. See Smith, *Indigenous Prosperity and American Conquest*, 60–70 (quotation on 61); and Calloway, *The Indian World of George Washington*, 294–300.

20. Colin G. Calloway, *The Victory with No Name: The Native American Defeat of the First American Army* (New York, 2015), 18–26.

With no governments yet organized in the West, Harmar's forces were the only non-Indigenous political authority in the region at the time the Ordinance of 1784 was formulated and the only vehicle for removing unauthorized settlements. Policing and dismantling these illegal settlements immediately became the exclusive focus of the First American Regiment. Rather than soldiering, the armed forces of the Republic served as some combination of law enforcement and landlord. In April 1785, an officer, John Armstrong, reported to Harmar, "I proceeded with my party . . . as far as the mouth of the Little Beaver and dispossessed one family." Within four miles of this location, he found "three families living in sheds" who promised to return east of the Ohio. As Armstrong moved along watersheds northwest of the Ohio River, he "dispossessed," in his own words, another eight families. At a place called Mingo Bottom, he met opposition from a man with the last name of Raps who, according to Armstrong, "was determined to hold his possession." Raps threatened that "if I destroyed his house he would build six more in the course of a week." Armstrong arrested the man and sent him east. Armstrong's arrest and forced removal of Raps seems to have sent a clear message because the rest of the settlers who were his tenants dispersed, "promising that they would comply and that they would destroy their buildings."[21]

As Armstrong continued his journey, he found communities similar to the one established by Raps, those inhabited by people who believed they were exercising their rights as citizens of the Republic by organizing politically legitimate settlements in the unoccupied wilderness of the American West. On April 4, 1785, a few days after Armstrong "dispossessed" the settlers at Mingo Bottom, his encampment was visited by "a party of armed men," led by a man named Charles Norris. "I learnt from the conversation of this party," Armstrong reported to Harmar, "that at Norristown (by the inhabitants so called) seven miles far on down the river, a party of seventy or eighty men assembled with a determination to oppose me." He also learned that the community had selected Norris and another man, John Carpenter, to serve as justices of the peace. The officer informed his visitors that "it was my intention to treat any armed party I saw as enemies of my country." Armstrong visited the newly formed town the following day and "read them my instructions." In spite of their bluster, and their attempts to form a legal town complete with law

21. John Armstrong to Josiah Harmar, Apr. 12, 1785, Josiah Harmar Papers, 1681–1937, II, 55, William L. Clements Library, University of Michigan, Ann Arbor.

enforcement officials, the settlers accepted the authority of the U.S. army. They agreed to move back east of the Ohio in three days.[22]

Armstrong encountered and dispossessed a wide array of settlements, from hastily constructed shacks to communities that named their town and elected political officials. As he traveled through the Ohio country, he left behind copies of his instructions issued by the U.S. commissioner of Indian affairs, requiring the removal of settlers from the country northwest of the Ohio River. Armstrong, however, seemed to recognize that he had been tasked with a futile mission. "It is the conclusion of many sensible men (with whom I conversed on my return from a late expedition down the Ohio)," he wrote to Harmar, "that if the honorable Congress, don't fall on some speedy method to prevent people from settling on the lands of the United States, west of the Ohio that country will soon be inhabited by a banditi whose actions are a disgrace to human nature." In this sentiment, Armstrong echoed George Washington, who had written to the head of the Committee of Indian Affairs about his fear of an influx of "Land Jobbers" and "Monopolisers" onto land inhabited by Native peoples. Armstrong's letter concluded: "Notwithstanding they have seen and read those instructions, they are moving to the unsettled country, by forties and fifties."[23]

Give Them Federal Law

A weak federal government made it difficult to control western migration and, as a consequence, increased fears of lawlessness within unauthorized settlements. Another soldier under General Harmar's command reported from the Ohio country: "While men who wish to act orderly and under good government anxiously await for arrangements being made, others of speculative and enterprising genius step forward and there is little doubt but most of the valuable spots will be seized . . . a few may be

---

22. Armstrong to Harmar, Apr. 4, 1785, ibid. American settlers not only saw Indian country as unsettled wilderness, they also believed that the Revolution and the creation of the U.S. Republic established their right to settle this territory. Honor Sachs argues that "men who migrated to the greater Ohio River Valley after the American Revolution anticipated that a virtuous and enlightened government would secure the conditions of domestic happiness for all white men equally, both as national policy and as individual right." See Sachs, *Home Rule: Households, Manhood, and National Expansion on the Eighteenth-Century Kentucky Frontier* (New Haven, Conn., 2015), 73–74.

23. Armstrong to Harmar, Apr. 13, 1785, Harmar Papers, II, 56.

dislodged but they will soon become too numerous for this to be easily effected." This officer, William Irvine, worried about his ability to stop and dislodge the influx of settlers squatting on what he and Congress considered land owned by the federal government. At the same time, however, he sympathized with the settlers. In the same letter that expressed his concern, Irvine wrote, "Yet tis hard to look tamely on and see people of all ranks acquire property, which is or ought to be equally in my power—This world or at least this new part of it, is in almost a state of nature." Irvine, like so many American settlers, believed they had a right to transform Native homelands into American homesteads. This was the idea that led to the creation of the United States, the promise of easily acquired unsettled land.[24]

In this sense, the ideology that imagined Native territory as "unsettled country" created a politically volatile environment in the absence of any recognizable political authority. Following Armstrong's return, Harmar sent yet another expedition into the Ohio country with the order, "The grand object of the public is to prevent lawless men from settling on their lands." He elaborated on this phenomenon in a letter describing the unregulated Ohio settlements to Secretary of War Henry Knox: "These men on their frontiers have hitherto been accustomed to seat themselves on the best land, making a tomahawk light or improvement as they term it, supposing that to be sufficient title. I believe them in general to be averse to federal measures, and that they would wish to throw every obstacle in the way to impede the surveying of the Western Territory, agreeably to the ordinance of Congress." The "tomahawk light" was a hatchet mark carved into a tree meant to signify that a particular plot of land had been altered or "improved," thus removing it from the state of nature and transforming it into private property. Creating homesteads and settlements in this fashion ignored the law that required land in the West to be surveyed and sold by the federal government after its representatives formally extinguished Native title. Harmar promised Secretary Knox he would put

24. William Irvine to Harmar, May 31, 1785, ibid., 77. Following the Revolution, American settlers migrating to the Trans-Appalachian West assumed that abundant land and property ownership were the keys to political and economic independence for white males in the newly created Republic. See Sachs, *Home Rule*, 41–70; Bethel Saler, *The Settlers' Empire: Colonialism and State Formation in America's Old Northwest* (Philadelphia, 2015), 26–29; Calloway, *The Indian World of George Washington*, 283–318.

an end to such practices. "I shall endeavor to apprehend them," he wrote, "and give them *federal law*."[25]

In spite of this promise, the American army continued to find and evict illegal settlers who sought to stake their claim on what they saw as the unimproved territory of the American West. The Ohio country afforded settlers access to the confluence of the Ohio and Mississippi River systems, which in turn offered access to markets in Saint Louis and New Orleans and to the larger U.S. economy. Harmar posted a soldier at the rapids of the Ohio River near the junction with the Muskingum. Between October 10, 1786, and May 12, 1787, the officer recorded the passing of "177 boats, 2689 souls, 1333 horses 766 cattle and 102 wagons." The message was not lost on Harmar, who added to this account, "You will be pleased to judge what a flourishing country this must be in the course of a few years from the number of emigrants to it." The Ohio country would rapidly be converted to a settled territory. The only problem would be whether the United States could maintain control over the region. Two days after reporting that the Northwest Territory was fast becoming "a flourishing country," Harmar described these eager settlers as illegal squatters. "Twelve cabins by the intruders, have lately been destroyed by order of Major Hamtramack in Mingo Bottom and its vicinity. Mingo Bottom is a fertile spot," he wrote "and very much attracts the attention of these fellows who wish to live under no government."[26]

Illegal settlements also provoked the Native peoples in the Ohio country and jeopardized legal settlements recognized by the United States. Harmar proposed establishing a post at the rapids at the edge of the Ohio boundary, to be called Fort Harmar. "The ostensible object for establishing troops at the rapids," he wrote to Secretary Knox, "I shall hold out to the probability of the Indians attacking the settlements there." Indeed, he noted, "as the western Indians have never been treated with, and are avers to the idea of their lands being forfeited from the adherence to the King of Britain, I conceive it will require marching into their country to conciliate and reconcile them to movement." Harmar concluded by informing the secretary, "You may rest assured sir, that no endeavors shall be wanting on my part to promote the federal interest in the western Territory." Obediah Robbins, a fur trader operating in the Ohio country,

25. Orders to Captain John Doughty, Oct. 3, 1785, Harmar Papers, Letter Book A: Jan. 9, 1784–Nov. 6, 1786, XXVIII, 96–97; Harmar to Major General Henry Knox, Aug. 4, 1786, ibid, 145.

26. Harmar to Knox, May 14, 1787, ibid., Letter Book B: Nov. 6, 1786–Jan. 29, 1788, XXVIII, 79–80.

expressed a similar fear in a letter he wrote to Harmar: "It is the opinion of several people that I conversed with that there will never be a solid peace with the Shawnee while there is so many vagabonds among them." The fur trader's warning was a reminder to the general that a confederacy of Native peoples led by Shawnee and Wyandot leaders constituted a serious and rival source of political power in the Northwest, a region that was settled almost exclusively by Native peoples before 1784. Although men like Washington, Harmar, and Robbins feared that unauthorized settlements could lead to conflict with Native peoples, they nevertheless saw Indian country as an unsettled wilderness, not unlike the illegal settlers they hoped to stop.[27]

The experience of the U.S. army in the West made it increasingly clear to members of Congress that settling the region peacefully and in a regulated fashion would require a stronger federal presence. The committee that formulated the Ordinance of 1784 was reconstituted and began working on a revision to the land law. The result was the Northwest Ordinance, a new law passed by Congress in 1787 that concentrated the political authority of the federal government in newly formed western territories through the appointment of a territorial governor, secretary, and three judges. The new Ordinance organized the Northwest into a territory that would be further divided into no less than three and no more than five districts, or states. Once the population reached five thousand free white males, the new territory would elect a General Assembly that would govern in consultation with appointed officials. The Northwest Ordinance stipulated that "the states which may be formed therein, shall forever remain part a of this confederacy of the United States." When the population reached sixty thousand free inhabitants, the territory would be authorized to draft a state constitution and request admission to the union on an equal footing with the original states. Significantly, all states created by the Northwest Ordinance would be free states, and all state constitutions must contain a fugitive slave clause.[28]

27. Harmar to Knox, June 7, 1787, ibid., 101; Obediah Robbins to Harmar, May 17, 1785, ibid., II, 66. In the newly created Northwest Territory, Colin Calloway argues, "Indian power stood squarely in the way of the new nation's ability to turn real estate into revenue and alleviate the postwar tax burden on its citizens"; see Calloway, *The Indian World of George Washington*, 314.

28. "An Ordinance for the Government of the Territory of the United States, North-West of the River Ohio," July 13, 1787, Miscellaneous Papers of the Continental Congress, 1774–1789, Record Group (RG) 360: Records of the Continental and Confederation Congresses and the Constitutional Convention, 1765–1821, M332, roll 9, National

The Northwest Ordinance shifted the focus of western settlement away from the establishment of new, fully enfranchised sovereign states. Instead, it sought to establish an effective territorial government that could secure property rights, enforce the rule of law, and manage relations with Native peoples. Section 8 of the law stipulated that the governor "shall proceed from time to time, as circumstances may require, to lay out the parts of the district in which the Indian titles shall have been extinguished, into counties and townships." The Ordinance also guaranteed the right of inheritance for the estates of both residents and nonresidents, asserted the right of habeas corpus and the right to a trial by jury, and ensured the sanctity of contracts as well as freedom of religion. It also specified that all navigable waterways leading to the Mississippi and Saint Lawrence Rivers "shall be common highways, and forever free."[29]

In sum, the provisions of the Northwest Ordinance were designed to facilitate the sale and settlement of land in the public domain under a legal regime recognizable by the United States. In creating the legal mechanism for the orderly transfer of Native land to white property holders, federal authorities hoped to attract a steady flow of immigrants to western territory claimed by the United States.[30] Because the system was organized politically by the federal government, it also minimized the possibility that settlers would seek to form a new nation-state independent of the Republic.[31]

————

Archives and Records Administration, Washington, D.C.; Paul Finkelman, "Slavery and Bondage in the 'Empire of Liberty,'" in Frederick D. Williams, ed., *The Northwest Ordinance: Essays on Its Formulation, Provisions, and Legacy* (Lansing, Mich., 1989); Peter Onuf, "The Empire of Liberty: Land of the Free Home of the Slave," in Andrew Shankman, ed., *The World of the Revolutionary American Republic: Land, Labor, and the Conflict for a Continent* (New York, 2014), 195–217.

29. "An Ordinance," July 13, 1787, Miscellaneous Papers of the Continental Congress, RG 360, M332, roll 9.

30. For the history of the Ordinance of 1784 and the Northwest Ordinance as policies for managing the sale and settlement of public lands, see Onuf, *Statehood and Union: A History of the Northwest Ordinance* (Bloomington, Ind., 1987), 58–60; Patrick Griffin, *American Leviathan: Empire, Nation, and the Revolutionary Frontier* (New York, 2007), 197–211; Denis P. Duffey, "The Northwest Ordinance as a Constitutional Document," *Columbia Law Review*, XCV (1995), 929–968; Berkhofer, "Jefferson, the Ordinance of 1784, and the Origins of the American Territorial System," *WMQ*, 3d Ser., XXIX (1972), 231–262; R. Douglas Hurt, "Historians and the Northwest Ordinance," *Western Historical Quarterly*, XX (1989), 261–280.

31. As Honor Sachs writes, "State and national leaders alike recognized that many alienated Kentucky settlers harbored precariously fragile loyalties to the new

In providing for the possible creation and settlement of up to five free states, the Northwest Ordinance also offered a solution to the rapid expansion of power for slaveholders and slave states in the Southwest. The Ordinance designated the vast public domain of the Northwest Territory as a subsidized land base for white settlers. In exchange for this transfer of wealth to white settlers, the new free states created out of the Northwest Territory would guarantee the property rights of white southerners. The fugitive slave clause required in each new state constitution secured their right to hold enslaved people as chattel property and to recover this property if enslaved individuals sought to obtain freedom by moving to northern free states. At the same time, article 6 of the Ordinance theoretically prohibited slavery in the Northwest Territory, stating, "There shall be neither slavery nor involuntary servitude in the said territory," creating a clear North-South divide over the issue of the expansion of slavery in the Trans-Appalachian West.[32]

This regional distinction regarding slavery proved to be less sharp than the Ordinance implied. Arthur St. Clair, the first governor appointed to the Northwest Territory, made it known publicly that he regarded the elimination of slavery in the region as aspirational, a law that would only be fully implemented at some unspecified date. Indeed, the labor of enslaved people had been part of the fur trade since its inception during the colonial era, and most of the prominent fur-trading families in the region owned enslaved Indigenous people, designated as "Panis," as well as enslaved Blacks. Article 6 of the Ordinance was thus put to the test five years after the creation of the Michigan Territory in a freedom suit brought by the parents of three enslaved children. Their owner, Catherine Tucker, a British subject who was a resident of Detroit, asserted that she

---

American state." The same could be argued for settlers migrating anywhere in the Northwest Territory. See Sachs, *Home Rule*, 93.

32. "An Ordinance," July 13, 1787, Miscellaneous Papers of the Continental Congress, RG 360, M332, roll 9. Legal scholar Denis Duffey has argued that the Northwest Ordinance was designed to create and increase the wealth of settlers as a means of promoting national economic development and securing western settlements. See Duffey, "The Northwest Ordinance as a Constitutional Document," *Columbia Law Review*, XCV (1995), 959–960. Paul Finkelman has argued that nineteenth-century slaveholders believed the article affirmed their right to own the enslaved and through the fugitive slave laws strengthened slavery in the South. See Finkelman, "Slavery and the Northwest Ordinance: A Study in Ambiguity," *Journal of the Early Republic*, VI (1986), 343–370. See also Eugene H. Berwanger, *The Frontier against Slavery: Western Anti-Negro Prejudice and the Slavery Extension Controversy* (Urbana, Ill., 1967).

acquired the enslaved children when the city was part of British Canada. She claimed that the Jay Treaty guaranteed her property rights when the city passed into the jurisdiction of the United States. Augustus Woodward, the chief justice of the Michigan Supreme Court, anxious to affirm the sovereignty of the Republic represented by this treaty, acknowledged Tucker's right of possession according to the dictates of international law. A treaty ratified by the U.S. Congress, he ruled, superseded the quasi-constitutional text of the Northwest Ordinance, and Tucker and other prominent Detroit trading families continued to employ enslaved labor during the territorial period.[33]

Slavery survived in similar fashion, and even expanded in the southern tier of the Northwest Territory. Not only had French habitants in the Illinois country held enslaved laborers, but once it was formed as a territory, Illinois became home to a large slaveholding southern diaspora seeking affordable western land. Under the influence of this powerful block of settlers, the territorial legislature passed in 1807 An Act concerning the Introduction of Negroes and Mulattoes into This Territory, which provided a legal framework for turning the enslaved into servants who would serve lifelong indentures. Similar to the case in Detroit, lawmakers in Illinois created a new category, "French Negroes," to designate individuals enslaved under the regime of French Louisiana who were therefore exempt from the emancipation provision of the Northwest Ordinance. Indiana, like Illinois, had a large enslaved population held by families whose residence in the region predated the existence of the United States. These influential citizens also used their newly established territorial legislature to adapt laws that effectively transformed enslaved persons into indentured servants or they created "rental contracts" that similarly codified and regulated the involuntary servitude of enslaved Black persons either resident or brought into the Indiana Territory. In both Illinois and Indiana, federal officials allowed planters and merchants to manipulate and control the legal conventions regarding slavery and involuntary servitude because their presence in newly formed territories gave the United States political power in a region of the Northwest that had been dominated by

33. Tiya Miles, *The Dawn of Detroit: A Chronicle of Slavery and Freedom in the City of the Straits* (New York, 2017), 148, 178–180 ("Panis" on 179); Edward J. Littlejohn, "Slaves, Judge Woodward, and the Supreme Court of the Michigan Territory," *Michigan Bar Journal*, XCIV, no. 7 (July 1015), 22–25. The Godfroy family, also living in Detroit, owned enslaved laborers during the American period. Gabriel Godfroy, for example, was deeded two slaves by his father on June 15, 1795. See Samuel W. Beakes, *Past and Present of Washtenaw County Michigan . . .* (Chicago, 1906), 540.

independent Native nations willing to resist U.S. expansion. The federal government and territorial officials prioritized the recruitment of a settler population, particularly wealthy individuals whose estates included the enslaved, as a counterweight to the political and economic power of Native villages in the newly organized territories. Allowing for a flexible interpretation of antislavery laws not only enticed economically powerful settlers but also enhanced a regional economy that was not tied to the fur trade and Native hunters. The ultimate goal of the political project envisioned by the Northwest Ordinance was the dispossession and displacement of the Native population, and this project occasionally required the inclusion of slave labor within the legal regime of an ostensibly free state.[34]

Indeed, Native dispossession underpinned this system of property rights, land transfers, and the eventual extension of the full franchise for white men willing to move to Indian country. Section 8 of the Ordinance of 1787 required federally appointed governors to work to extinguish Native title on the Indigenous homelands that would be part of any newly organized territory or state. This provision of the Ordinance reflected the presumption that Native peoples maintained too much uncultivated land. These unproductive or underutilized lands, according to the Ordinance, would then be converted into "counties and townships" by the governor. Yet article 3 of the Ordinance stated, "The utmost good faith shall always be observed towards the Indians; their lands and property shall never be taken from them without their consent." This seeming pledge, though, came with a caveat: Natives "never shall be invaded or disturbed, unless in just and lawful wars authorised by Congress." Embedded in this contradiction—that governors were tasked with extinguishing Native title and that Natives were not to be "disturbed"—was the unthinkable history that sovereign Native nations could have produced Native homelands that were permanent settlements as opposed to unsettled wilderness. The contradiction, written into the law, expressed the ideology that

34. An Act concerning the Introduction of Negroes and Mulattoes into This Territory, in *Laws of the Indiana Territory; Comprising Those Acts Formerly in Force, and as Revised by Messrs. John Rice Jones, and John Johnson, and Passed (after Amendments) by the Legislature; and the Original Acts Passed at the First Session of the Second General Assembly of the Said Territory* . . . (Vincennes, Ind., 1807), 523–526; M. Scott Heerman, *The Alchemy of Slavery: Human Bondage and Emancipation in the Illinois Country, 1730–1865* (Philadelphia, 2018), 60 ("French Negroes"), 78–81 (1807 act); Paul Finkelman, "Evading the Ordinance: The Persistence of Bondage in Indiana and Illinois," *JER,* IX (1989), 21–51 (quotation on 22).

informed the social contract established by the Republic. Like the U.S. Constitution, also drafted in 1787, the Northwest Ordinance was a legal document designed to create and preserve a politically legitimate settlement on territory that was part of the public domain of the United States but that remained unsettled from the standpoint of the common law tradition of the Republic. The Northwest Ordinance essentially provided a legal mechanism for reproducing the original thirteen states of the union in the West.[35]

The Ohio Company and the
Expansion of American Democracy

In 1788, the Ohio Company, the first land company to acquire property in the Northwest, held a celebration in the town of Marietta to commemorate the passage of the Northwest Ordinance. Located at the confluence of the Ohio and Muskingum Rivers next to the newly established Fort Harmar, Marietta was the first American town in the Northwest Territory, as opposed to French settlements like Detroit or Vincennes and Indigenous settlements like Mackinac and Sault Sainte Marie. In the political imaginary of the U.S. Republic, Marietta was thus the first civilized settlement in the Northwest. "The subduing [of] a new country, notwithstanding its natural advantages, is alone an arduous task, a task however that patience and perseverance will surmount," proclaimed James Varnum, former general in the Continental army and justice of the Supreme Court of the Northwest Territory. "Neither is the reducing a country from a state of nature to a state of cultivation so irksome," he declared. Varnum told the gathered crowd, "The gradual progress of improvement fills the mind with delectable ideas.—Vast forests converted into arable fields, and cities rising in the places which were lately the habitations of wild beasts." The U.S. government, the Ohio Company, and American settlers

35. "An Ordinance," July 13, 1787, Miscellaneous Papers of the Continental Congress, RG 360, M332, roll 9. For the Northwest Ordinance as a constitutional document, see Duffey, "Northwest Ordinance," *Columbia Law Review*, XCV (1995), 940–943. Patrick Wolfe called this inherent contradiction of asserting fair and just treatment for Native peoples while expecting that they would peacefully cede their lands or suffer a just war an "intentional fallacy." See Wolfe, "Against the Intentional Fallacy: Logocentrism and Continuity in the Rhetoric of Indian Dispossession," *American Indian Culture and Research Journal*, XXXVI, no. 1 (2012), 3–45. See also Jeffery Ostler, "'Just and Lawful War' as Genocidal War in the (United States) Northwest Ordinance and Northwest Territory," *Journal of Genocide Research*, XVIII (2016), 1–20.

Map 1. Northwest Territory, circa 1780–1812. Drawn by Rebecca Wrenn

all insisted that they were engaged in an effort to transform a continent from a state of nature into a civilized and cultivated country.[36]

For many of the settlers moving to the Ohio country, the Northwest Ordinance was more than a mechanism for creating private property and establishing a government; it was a fuller realization of American

36. James M. Varnum, *An Oration, Delivered at Marietta, July 4, 1788 . . .* (Newport R.I., 1788), 10. Jack P. Greene has described this "deeply internalized ideology" as the belief that Anglo settlers and their American successors "were engaged in a noble

democracy. "Never, probably, in the history of the world, did a measure of legislation so accurately fulfil, and yet so mightily exceed the anticipations of the legislators," wrote Salmon P. Chase. Originally from New Hampshire, Chase immigrated to Ohio, where he became a prominent jurist, politician, and abolitionist. "When the settlers went into the wilderness, they found the law already there," he wrote in an 1833 publication *The Statutes of Ohio and of the Northwestern Territory Adopted or Enacted from 1788 to 1833.* "The purchaser of land became, by that act, a party to the compact, and bound by its perpetual covenants," Chase asserted. The social contract created by the Northwest Ordinance, according to Chase, was uniquely American. Comparing the Ordinance to the U.S. Constitution of 1787, he wrote, "The principles established by the articles of compact are to be found in the plan of 1784, and in the various English and American bills of rights." He continued, "Of this number are the clauses in relation to contracts, to slavery, and to the Indians." Summarizing the effect of the Ordinance, Chase proclaimed, "On the whole, these articles contain what they profess to contain, the true theory of American liberty. . . . They are indeed the genuine principles of freedom, unadulterated by that compromise with circumstances, the effects of which are visible in the constitution and history of the union."[37]

The compromise Chase referred to, of course, was slavery. From his perspective, the institution was a stain on the national honor. It was a sin of the American past and a vestige of the Old World. Ohio, the Northwest

___

enterprise: bringing improperly exploited territories into a cultivated state, rendering their resources productive, and reorganizing the wilderness into settled and bounded spaces where property and labor could be acquired and secured by local political and judicial institutions designed to achieve these ends." See Greene, "Colonial History and National History," *WMQ*, 3d Ser., LXIV (2007), 247–248. Osterhammel makes a similar argument about the "universal mission" of European colonial projects in the Americas; see Osterhammel, *Colonialism: A Theoretical Overview,* trans. Shelley L. Frisch (Princeton, N.J., 1997), 15–16. Susan Sleeper-Smith overturns the mythology of an unsettled wilderness by demonstrating that the Indigenous Ohio country was a densely settled and intensively developed agricultural territory. See Sleeper-Smith, *Indigenous Prosperity and American Conquest,* 13–66.

37. Salmon P. Chase, ed., *The Statutes of Ohio and of the Northwestern Territory Adopted or Enacted from 1788 to 1833 Inclusive; Together with the Ordinance of 1787; the Constitutions of Ohio and of the United States, and Various Public Instruments and Acts of Congress; Illustrated by a Preliminary Sketch of the History of Ohio . . .* (Cincinnati, Ohio, 1833), 17, 18.

Territory, and the Northwest Ordinance represented the future. They signified human progress, the promise of a modern democratic republic. Chase was one of many Ohio politicians at the center of an emergent free-soil politics in the northern states. In 1838, shortly after Chase wrote his legal history of the Northwest, James Perkins, a scholar delivering an address to the Ohio Historical Society argued, "The principle of life in the west, and in Ohio emphatically, is self-rule." The social contract of republican democracy, he asserted, had been perfected in this northwestern state. "In the old world, self-rule, political and social, unembarrassed by feudal or servile habits of life, has not been seen to this day; and in all our Atlantic states, more or less of the feudal spirit was ever found before the revolution ... and through the whole south, the servile element prevented the full operation of the principle of self-rule." Perkins concluded his speech with a bold statement about perfecting the Republic in the Northwest: "In Ohio, then, was first founded a nearly true democratic community."[38]

The institution of slavery, according to the politics of the free-soil movement, compromised the social contract. The compact of self-rule required by a true democratic republic required free men to work free land. This construct, free land, represented a version of the idea of a state of nature. A reviewer evaluating Salmon Chase's *Statutes of the Northwestern Territory* described the Northwest Ordinance as "a national compact, forbidding slavery, securing civil and religious freedom, and all those privileges that others had struggled for through ages of blood and turmoil." Free-soil thinkers linked slavery, like feudalism, to the past, one defined by the inequalities of Europe. The United States represented something new, a rejection of empire and landed aristocracy and a revitalization of the ancient idea of a republic. This republican rebirth, however, had been tainted by slavery—"the servile element," that "compromise with circumstances" in the American South. In the Northwest Territory, men like Salmon Chase and James Perkins argued, Americans had forged a new civil society based on equality and freedom from the continent's unsettled wilderness. But this critique of southern slave power ignored the complicity of free states in preserving this institution through the fugitive slave clause required by the Northwest Ordinance in state constitutions. It discounted that northern states and territories such as Illinois, Indiana, and

38. James H. Perkins, "A Discourse: Delivered Before the Ohio Historical Society," in Historical and Philosophical Society of Ohio, *Transactions*, part 2 (Cincinnati, Ohio, 1839), I, 282.

Michigan carved out legal exceptions to allow slave labor when it proved politically advantageous to some portion of the settler population.[39]

The Northwest Ordinance, as noted above, also provided the legal means for taking Indigenous land and transferring it to the public domain of the United States. This denial of Native rights, equality, and self-determination was justified because most Americans, from George Washington to Salmon Chase, regarded Native peoples as savages—that is, they represented a human past that failed to evolve or become civilized. They remained, like the territory they inhabited, in a state of nature. At the 1788 Ohio Company celebration of the Northwest Ordinance at Marietta, James Varnum spoke of the Ohio country as if it were an unsettled wilderness, and yet he also acknowledged the presence of Native peoples: "You have upon your frontier, numbers of savages." Varnum admonished the new settlers: "Run not into their customs and habits, which is but too frequent with those who settle near them; but endeavor to induce them to adopt yours. . . . They will soon become sensible of the superior advantages of a state of civilization." This idea, the inevitability of Native assimilation, represented one strand of thought in the early Republic regarding the fate and future of Native peoples.[40]

The Confederacy of Northwest Indians

In imagining that Native peoples, confronted with civilization, would seek to become civilized themselves, Justice Varnum offered an inclusive vision of American expansion—one that also presumed that Native peoples would accept a cultural and political death as independent peoples. He confidently assumed U.S. customs and culture would replace those of Native peoples either through force or assimilation because it was impossible to envision a Native North America successfully challenging the advance

39. Review of Salmon P. Chase, *The Statutes of Ohio and of the North Western Territory . . .* , *North American Review*, XLVII, no. 100 (July 1838), 2. For a concise description of free-soil ideology, see Jonathan H. Earle, *Jacksonian Antislavery and the Politics of Free Soil, 1824–1854* (Chapel Hill, N.C., 2004), 13–16. For the importance of linking free labor to "free soil," see Eric Foner, *Free Soil, Free Labor, Free Men: The Ideology of the Republican Party before the Civil War* (New York, 1995), xxv. See also Onuf, "The Empire of Liberty," 195–217, and Reeve Huston, "Land Conflict and Land Policy in the United States, 1785–1841," 324–345, both in Shankman, ed., *The World of the Revolutionary American Republic*.

40. Varnum, *An Oration*, 10; Ostler, "Just and Lawful War,'" *Journal of Genocide Research*, XVIII, no. 1 (March 2016), 1–20; Calloway, *The Indian World of George Washington*, 316.

of civilization. Yet Native peoples in the Northwest had a long history as a confederacy, resisting the expansion of non-Indigenous settlements on their territory. In July 1787, the month that Congress passed the Northwest Ordinance, Secretary of War Henry Knox informed General Josiah Harmar that "certain Indians" had sent a message to the U.S. Congress. The Iroquois, Wyandot, Delaware, Shawnee, Odawa, Ojibwe, Bodewaadamii, Miami, Cherokee, and "Wabash Indians" had formed a confederacy, he told the general, and "they request a treaty be held in order to adjust all differences." He also wrote, "'It is very evident, that they mean to dispute the boundaries that have been marked out by the treaties that have been made since the peace." Knox instructed Harmar to preserve the peace if at all possible but concluded that if "it should appear that nothing but a blow at the savages, would prevent their depredations, and incline them to peace, you will take the steps pointed out by congress."[41]

In fact, the United States had already been forced to grapple with Indigenous confederacies. In 1784, the United States negotiated the Treaty of Fort Stanwix with the Haudenosaunee, or the Iroquois confederacy of six nations (the Mohawks, Oneidas, Onondagas, Cayugas, Senecas, and Tuscaroras). The Haudenosaunee had largely sided with the British during the Revolution, and the treaty restored peace and established a boundary line that ceded the Ohio country to the Republic. In 1785, the United States signed the Treaty of Fort McIntosh with the Wyandots, Delawares, Odawaag, and Ojibweg, which was also intended to restore peace, but, in addition, it ceded lands in the Ohio east of the Cuyahoga and Muskingum Rivers as well as territory around Detroit and Mackinac. Much of the leadership of the larger Northwest confederacy, including *doodemag*, or bands, among the Odawa and Ojibwe people north of the Ohio River and the various nations on the Wabash, believed the signers of both treaties lacked the political authority to make these agreements. By the time that Knox wrote to Harmar about the Natives' request to revisit boundaries, the newly formed Republic was already on a collision course with the Indigenous confederacy that dominated the Northwest Territory.[42]

In this divisive political climate, the U.S. settlement at Marietta raised the political anxiety among the Indigenous peoples of the Northwest, who

41. Knox to Harmar, July 24, 1787, Harmar Papers, VI, 37.

42. For disputes among the Northwest confederacy regarding these treaties, see Sleeper-Smith, *Indigenous Prosperity and American Conquest*, 216–219. For the Treaty of Fort Stanwix and Fort McIntosh, see Calloway, *The Indian World of George Washington*, 301–313; Taylor, *Divided Ground*, 154–166, 237–241; and White, *Middle Ground*, 436–448.

believed that they had not been properly represented in past negotiations with the officials of the Republic. In January 1788, less than a year after the passage of the Northwest Ordinance, Governor St. Clair warned Secretary of War Knox that "the intelligence respecting the disposition of the Indians that I was able to obtain at Fort Pitt was not very satisfactory." "Indeed," he reported, "it amounted to little more than that they had been extremely anxious to see some person with authority from the United States to treat with them." In fact, the leadership of the Northwest confederacy, including the Haudenosaunee, sought a treaty council with government officials because they wanted to halt U.S. settlement at the Muskingum River.[43]

St. Clair called for a treaty council at the falls of the Muskingum in the summer of 1788. "The proposed establishments in the country north-west of the Ohio," he informed Knox, "and the further sale of lands there for the discharge of the public debt, depends entirely on a solid peace with the Indians." St. Clair expressed concerns about his ability to preserve the peace: "Though we hear much of the injuries and depredations that are committed by the Indians upon the whites, there is too much reason to believe that at least equal, if not greater injuries are done to the Indians by the frontier settlers." In April, a month before the council called by the governor, Harmar reported to Knox "that Indians will be late in assembling and that they are determined not to give up their lands." The nations preparing to negotiate with St. Clair and Harmar gathered at Brownstown on the Detroit River, the council grounds of their confederacy, and proceeded to the Miami village at Sandusky in the Ohio country. They awaited the arrival of Joseph Brant, a prominent Mohawk leader, who would be speaking for the Haudenosaunee. Before he arrived, a party of Ojibwe and Odawa warriors attacked the American troops sent to prepare the council grounds at the falls of the Muskingum River, killing two soldiers. The Americans took six of the attacking warriors captive and withdrew to Fort Harmar. "After such an insult," St. Clair wrote to Knox,

43. Governor Arthur St. Clair to Secretary of War Henry Knox, Jan. 27, 1788, in William Henry Smith, ed., *The St. Clair Papers: The Life and Public Services of Arthur St. Clair, Soldier of the Revolutionary War; President of the Continental Congress; and Governor of the North-Western Territory, with His Correspondence and Other Papers* . . . , 2 vols. (Cincinnati, Ohio, 1882), II, 40. For the confederacy argument against the Treaty of Fort McIntosh and the attempt to halt U.S. expansion, see White, *Middle Ground*, 444–445.

"to meet the Indians at that place, should they be inclined to come, I thought inconsistent with the dignity of the United States."[44]

In response to this provocation, St. Clair sent word to the nations of the Northwest confederacy that he would meet only at Fort Harmar. Brant, in turn, demanded that the treaty be held at the council grounds designated by Congress at the falls of the Muskingum. He also insisted that the border for U.S. settlements be established at the junction of the Ohio and Muskingum Rivers. St. Clair responded that the nations of the confederacy would not "be discharged from the obligation of former treaties." Brant withdrew from the treaty process and returned to Haudenosaunee territory by way of Detroit, bypassing Fort Harmar. The Shawnees, Delawares, and some of the Wyandots followed his lead and refused to attend the treaty. The remainder of the Wyandots, joined by some of the Odawaag, Ojibweg, and Boodewaadamiig from Detroit River villages and the Delawares from Ohio, met with St. Clair and eventually signed the Treaty of Fort Harmar. St. Clair crowed to Knox "that their confederacy is broken." The governor's optimism was premature; the confederacy remained a potent political force within the Northwest Territory.[45]

With the withdrawal of the Haudenosaunee from the treaty, however, the confederacy was in disarray. At council, T'Sindatton, a prominent Wyandot, addressed the governor. "He began by telling their origin," one American soldier recorded, "and how the Thirteen Fires had gotten possession of their country; how we had, in two instances, cheated them." T'Sindatton then presented the governor with a wampum belt that had a solid purple line down the middle representing the Ohio River, and he declared "that all the nations present had determined to grant no more of the country, but were willing to abide by the treaty which established the Ohio River as the boundary line." St. Clair refused to accept their demands "and told them he could not possibly make the least deviation from the treaties which had been concluded at Fort Stanwix, at Fort McIntosh,

44. St. Clair to Knox, Jan. 27, 1788, July 13, 1788, in Smith, ed., *St. Clair Papers*, II, 41, 50–51; Harmar to Knox, Apr. 24, 1788, Harmar Papers, Letter Book C: Jan. 30–July 6, 1788, XXVIII, n.p. For the attack at Muskingum, see Harmar to Knox, July 16, 1788, ibid., Letter Book D: July 16–Nov. 28, 1788, XXVIII, 6.

45. St. Clair to Knox, Sept. 14, 1788, Dec. 3, 1788, Jan. 18, 1789, all in Smith, ed., *St. Clair Papers*, II, 87–88, 99 ("discharged"), 109 ("broken"). For Brant's role in the Northwest confederacy and its relation to Haudenosaunee politics, see, Taylor, *Divided Ground*, 253–264. For St. Clair, see Calloway, *Victory with No Name*, 58–60; and White, *Middle Ground*, 445.

and at the Miami River; that at these treaties the several boundaries had been fixed, and were unalterable." T'Sindatton refused to sign the treaty, and his refusal along with the departure of Brant severely undermined the legitimacy of the treaty among the Indigenous peoples of the Northwest. The governor produced a signed document, but the treaty signers were not recognized leaders of the confederacy. The perception of bad faith on the part of the U.S. officials had the effect of reuniting the Native peoples of the Ohio country and the Detroit and Wabash River villages around the militant leadership of the Miami and Shawnee warriors who had stayed away from the treaty conference.[46]

War and Peace in the Northwest Territory

The result of this botched treaty process was a series of crushing military defeats for the American army in the Northwest Territory. Violence plagued the region in the aftermath of the council at Fort Harmar. Warriors from the Ohio villages began to raid American settlements, and the settlers responded in kind, failing to distinguish between Native communities that participated in the raids and those that refrained. In October 1790, Josiah Harmar marched his army west into the Ohio country with the intention of chastising the warriors of the confederacy. His force of approximately fifteen hundred men, consisting mostly of militia, advanced on the principal Miami village of Kekionga, which they found abandoned. Setting fire to the village, Harmar divided his forces in pursuit of the Miami. The detachments stumbled into a series of ambushes where they suffered significant losses—well over one hundred men—eventually forcing Harmar to leave the field and return to Fort Washington in eastern Ohio.[47]

The following year, Governor St. Clair, who had risen to prominence as an officer in the Continental army, led the U.S. army back into the Ohio country. Two thousand men, again consisting mostly of militia, marched to the head of the Wabash River. A Native army of Miami, Shawnee,

46. "Account of the Indian Treaties from the Diary of Major Ebenezer Denny," in Smith, ed., *St. Clair Papers*, II, 109–111. See also White, *Middle Ground*, 445–448.

47. For Harmar's destruction of the Ohio villages and his disastrous retreat from the Ohio River valley, see Sleeper-Smith, *Indigenous Prosperity and American Conquest*, 232–242; Calloway, *Victory with No Name*, 61–68; Gregory Evans Dowd, *A Spirited Resistance: The North American Indian Struggle for Unity, 1745–1815* (Baltimore, 1992), 106; White, *Middle Ground*, 448–468; and Harper, *Unsettling the West*, 154–156.

Delaware, Odawa, Ojibwe, Boodewaadamii, Wyandot, and Mingo warriors struck St. Clair's encampment at dawn on November 4, 1791, and killed or captured more than half of the U.S. forces. The conflict saw the highest casualty rate ever sustained by the armed forces of the young Republic, which had fought a bloody Revolution. In spite of this victory, the politics among members of the Northwest confederacy remained contentious. Leaders continued to argue about whether to seek peace and where to accept a western boundary for the United States. In 1794, General Anthony Wayne marched into the Northwest Territory leading the Legion of the United States, a three-thousand-man force that was a reorganization of the Continental army. Fighting with a professional army, Wayne engaged the warriors of the confederacy in a series of battles that continued through the summer of 1794.[48]

This protracted fight for control of the Northwest Territory forced both the United States and the Native peoples of the confederacy to rethink the nature of their relationship. The warriors of the confederacy proved to be formidable fighters, superior to conscript soldiers and equal to the professional army fielded by the United States. The villages of the Ohio and Great Lakes had to feed the equivalent of a standing army of their own for an extended military campaign. The agricultural villages of the Wabash and Ohio River valleys had been numerous and prosperous enough to sustain the warriors and the noncombatants of the confederacy in spite of the American invasion. War with the United States, however, amplified by the constant raiding by backcountry settlers, caused considerable social and political disruption in the village communities of the Ohio country. Warriors, traditionally restricted to tactical military decisions, found themselves at the center of village life. They began to make strategic decisions about war and diplomacy, ignoring or bypassing the council of village women who dominated the economy and trade in the Ohio country.[49]

The aggressive military posture assumed by the warriors of the confederacy made them increasingly dependent on the British for arms and ammunition. But when the successful negotiation of the Jay Treaty in the middle of Wayne's campaign resulted in the sudden withdrawal of British support, they lost this crucial source of supplies. Unable to replenish their ammunition or retreat behind British fortifications, the warriors of the

48. For St. Clair's defeat, see Sleeper-Smith, *Indigenous Prosperity and American Conquest*, 271–282; Calloway, *Victory with No Name*, 68–91, 115–128.
49. Sleeper-Smith, *Indigenous Prosperity and American Conquest*, 309–310.

Northwest were defeated by Wayne and the Legion of the United States in the Battle of Fallen Timbers in August 1794. This military defeat forced the confederacy to surrender and seek peace with the United States.[50]

The Americans also reevaluated their relationship to Native peoples as well as the nature of the authority of the federal government and its relationship to the western territories. Congress recognized the necessity of overcoming its aversion to a professional standing army. More important, U.S. officials had to give up the conceit that in winning the Revolutionary War they had conquered the Native peoples who sided with Great Britain. They might claim possession of the Trans-Appalachian West, but they did not gain title to this land by right of conquest. The United States would need to negotiate a cession of Native title to any lands it claimed as part of the public domain of the Republic. This conflict also underscored the advice that President George Washington had provided to the Committee on Indian Affairs as early as 1783. Western expansion and the governing of new western territories could not be disentangled from relations with Native peoples. Pursuing expansion through military action, moreover, would be too costly. "In a word there is nothing to be obtained by an Indian War," Washington argued, "but the Soil they live on and this can be had by purchase at less expence."[51]

Following the Battle of Fallen Timbers, the United States negotiated the Treaty of Greenville in 1795, reestablishing peace with the Native peoples of the Northwest confederacy. This treaty marked a major turning point in the Indian policy of the Republic. The government demanded and received cession and title to all of the land that would make up Ohio except for the northern quarter of the state. However, the United States recognized Native title to all the land north of the Ohio River through the Great Lakes to the east bank of the Mississippi River. More significant, the government agreed to an annuity, an annual payment of ninety-five hundred dollars in perpetuity, as compensation for ceded Native land. This annuity would be divided among the various nations of the

50. For the significance of the Battle of Fallen Timbers, see Sleeper-Smith, *Indigenous Prosperity and American Conquest*, 311–314; and White, *Middle Ground*, 448–468. For the importance of the Jay Treaty in isolating the Northwest Indians and the battle for control of the Northwest Territory, see François Furstenberg, "The Significance of the Trans-Appalachian Frontier in Atlantic History," *American Historical Review*, CXIII (2008), 647–677. For the significance of the Jay Treaty in the battle of Fallen Timbers, see White, *Middle Ground*, 469–476.

51. Washington to Duane, Sept. 7, 1783, in Fitzpatrick, ed., *Writings of George Washington*, XXVII, 140; Calloway, *The Indian World of George Washington*, 314–318.

confederacy and dispensed through the civil leadership of those nations. With the treaty process linked to a substantial payout, federal officials created a politically subordinate client relationship with Native leaders. The commitment to annuities departed from the symbolic gift exchanges that established alliances between two sovereign nations, and it signaled the creation of a patronage relationship with Native leaders, who would be turned into political dependents of the Republic.[52]

The Treaty of Greenville thus simultaneously allowed the United States to peacefully transfer Indigenous land into the public domain and to create an effective form of political leverage over Native leaders in the Northwest. This leverage would be extended through article 5 of the treaty, which explained the significance of the land cession and recognition of remaining land under Native title: "The Indian Tribes who have a right to those Lands, are quietly to enjoy them; hunting planting and dwelling thereon so long as they please without molestation from the United States." The article also stipulated, however, that "when these Tribes, or any of them shall be disposed to sell their lands or any part of them, they are to be sold only to the United States." The federal government would act as the sole proprietor of any land that Native peoples wanted or needed to sell. The United States would use this leverage, combined with the promise of annuities, time and time again to expand the public domain of the Republic onto Indigenous lands in the Northwest Territory.[53]

The treaty also formalized the idea that the United States would help Native peoples become civilized. Article 4 established the annuity for land ceded in the Ohio country, but it also stated that any nation that signed the treaty could request "that a part of their annuity should be furnished in domestic animals, Implements of Husbandry and other utensils convenient for them, and in compensation to useful artificers who may reside near them." The goal was to shift social relations of production for

52. Historian Gregory Evans Dowd argues that federal officials "cultivated clients among native leaders"; see Dowd, *A Spirited Resistance*, 115. In addition to creating a client relationship with Native leaders, Sleeper-Smith contends that the annuities created a political and social wedge between leadership and the warriors. Militant warriors like Tecumseh associated the annuities with a reversal of traditional gender roles and the adoption of American-style commercial agriculture. See Sleeper-Smith, *Indigenous Prosperity and American Conquest*, 314–319.

53. "A Treaty of Peace between the United States of America and the Tribe of Indians Called the Wyandots, Delawares, Shawoenoes, Ottawas, Chipewas, Putawatames, Miamis, Eel River, Weeas, and Kickapoas," in *Collections and Researches Made by the Michigan Pioneer and Historical Society*, XX (Lansing, Mich., 1912), 414.

Figure 2.
*A Map of the
North Western
Territory.* By
Jedidiah Morse.
1796. Minnesota
Historical
Society, Saint
Paul

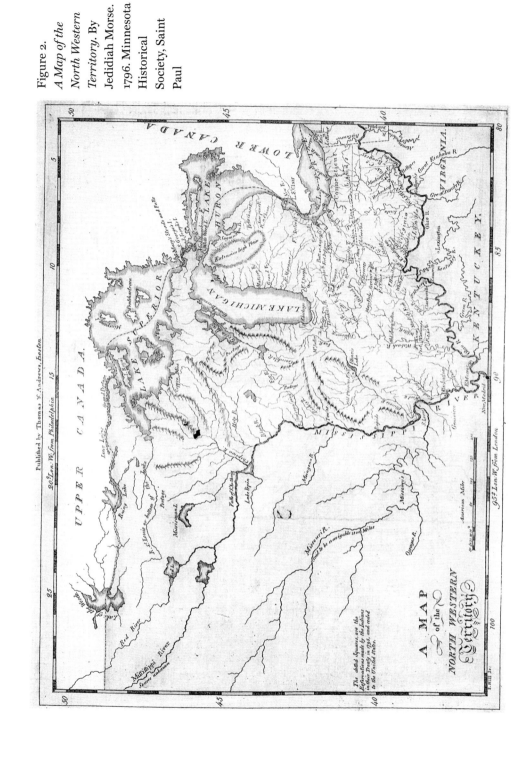

Indigenous peoples in the Northwest to commercial agriculture. By taking a portion of their annuity in "domestic animals" and "Implements of Husbandry," Natives would begin the transition out of the state of nature and into a civilized life of cultivating and improving their land. This was the ideology, and the methodology, behind America's civilizing mission, the descriptor for the Republic's Indian policy.[54]

The United States might have pursued this civilizing mission in good faith, but that good faith also reflected an ulterior motive. In 1803, Thomas Jefferson, as president, wrote to William Henry Harrison, the governor of the Indiana Territory, offering "a more extensive view of our policy respecting the Indians." Jefferson described an inclusive vision for Native peoples in the Republic not unlike his speech in 1804 to the Native leaders from the lower Missouri visiting the White House. "Our system," he wrote, "is to live in perpetual peace with the Indians, to cultivate an affectionate attachment from them." To accomplish this, "we wish to draw them to agriculture, to spinning and weaving." Jefferson then explained the logic behind this shift to agriculture and the expected outcome that might result from this transformation of the political economy of Native peoples in the Northwest. "When they withdraw themselves to the culture of a small piece of land," he wrote, "they will perceive how useless to them are their extensive forests, and will be willing to pare them off from time to time in exchange for necessaries for their farms and families." He went on to reveal the benefit that the United States might expect from this change in political economy. "To promote this disposition to exchange lands," he declared, "which they have to spare and we want, for necessaries, which we have to spare and they want, we shall push our trading uses, and be glad to see the good and influential individuals among them run in debt, because we observe that when these debts get beyond what the individuals can pay, they become willing to lop them off by a cession of lands."[55]

Jefferson's good faith attempt to civilize Native peoples and incorporate them into the Republic would result in the conversion of Native homelands into American homesteads. Ceded Native land, under the provisions of the Northwest Ordinance, would be sold to white settlers at

54. "A Treaty of Peace," *Collections and Researches*, XX, 413. For the civilizing mission, see Nicholas Guyatt, *Bind Us Apart: How Enlightened Americans Invented Racial Segregation* (New York, 2016), 87–111.

55. Jefferson to Governor William Henry Harrison, Feb. 27, 1803, in Thomas Jefferson, *Writings*, ed. Merrill D. Peterson (New York, 1984), 1117, 1118.

a subsidized rate resulting from the government monopoly in acquiring Indigenous territory. "In this way," Jefferson informed Harrison, "our settlements will gradually circumscribe and approach the Indians, and they will in time either incorporate with us as citizens of the United States, or remove beyond the Mississippi." The president shared the same inclusive vision of the future for Native peoples as expressed by Justice Varnum celebrating the founding of Marietta by the Ohio Land Company. Jefferson described this evolution of Native peoples into U.S. citizens as "the termination of their history most happy for themselves." In other words, they could have a future as citizens of the United States. Their history as Native peoples, however, would come to an end. For President Jefferson, like most Americans, it was simply unthinkable to imagine Native peoples living as discrete Indigenous nations in perpetuity within the boundaries of the United States.[56]

The Northwest Ordinance and the Treaty of Greenville reflected this assumption about the future of Native peoples. Both documents contained provisions that promised to allow Native peoples to live peacefully in their homelands, but they also contained measures designed to facilitate the purchase of these homelands and the termination of Native title on all land claimed by the Republic. The United States was and is a settler colonial state, and the plan embodied in the Ordinance of 1787 was to convert the Northwest Territory—all of it—into public domain that would eventually become American homesteads forming American towns and counties that would be part of newly formed American states. This settler colonial state did not seek permanent dominance over a subordinate Indigenous population. Rather, it demanded the elimination of Native peoples—through assimilation, removal, or destruction in a just war.[57]

A mere eight years after the signing of the Treaty of Greenville, Jefferson instructed Harrison to plan for the acquisition of additional Native territory, for, as he put it, "We are entitled to their country by our paramount

56. Ibid., 1118. George Washington shared this idea that Native people might become civilized and be incorporated into the Republic; see Calloway, *The Indian World of George Washington*, 316. For the civilizing mission and its ideological overlap with the trope of the vanishing Indian, see Jeffery Ostler, *Surviving Genocide: Native Nations and the United States from the American Revolution to Bleeding Kansas* (New Haven, Conn., 2019), 4–5.

57. This is a phenomenon specific to settler colonialism that Patrick Wolfe has identified as the "logic of elimination." According to Wolfe, settler colonialism has both positive and negative dimensions. "Negatively, it strives for the dissolution of native societies," he writes; "Positively, it erects a new colonial society on the expropriated

sovereignty." The governor was to begin talks with the Wabash villages to acquire their land. Jefferson told him that the "Cahokias" were "extinct" and that the Peorias had been "driven off from their country." "The Kaskaskias being reduced to a few families," he stated, "I presume we may purchase their whole country for what would place every individual of them at his ease." Jefferson proposed to leave the remaining Kaskaskias "as much rich land as they could cultivate" and added, "We might take them also under the protection of the United States." They would be compensated with an annuity for this cession. "Thus possessed of the rights of these tribes," Jefferson informed Harrison, "we should proceed to the settling their boundaries with the Poutewatamies and Kickapoos; claiming all doubtful territory, but paying them a price for the relinquishment of their concurrent claim." This, he concluded, was "the system which we suppose will best promote the interests of the Indians and ourselves, and finally consolidate our whole country to one nation only."[58]

Native Savagery, the Civilizing Mission, and American Expansion

The political fantasy of an empty Northwest Territory must have been compelling for immigrants seeking affordable land, even as they adjusted to the more complicated reality that they were settling in a region that still had a significant Native population. In places like Ohio, Indiana, and Illinois—with easy access to the Mississippi and the market economy of the Republic—the demography flipped rapidly, allowing these territories to reach statehood shortly after they opened for settlement.[59] Settlers who

---

land base—as I put it, settler colonizers come to stay: invasion is a structure not an event." See Wolfe, "Settler Colonialism and the Elimination of the Native," *Journal of Genocide Research*, VIII (2006), 388. See also Wolfe, "Against the Intentional Fallacy," *American Indian Culture and Research Journal*, XXXVI, no. 1 (2012), 3–45; Frederick E. Hoxie, "Retrieving the Red Continent: Settler Colonialism and the History of American Indians in the US," *Ethnic and Racial Studies*, XXXI (2008), 1153–1167.

58. Jefferson to Harrison, Feb. 27, 1803, in Jefferson, *Writings*, ed. Peterson, 1119, 1120.

59. The non-Native population of Ohio grew so quickly under federal authority that it entered the union as a state in 1803 without needing to go through a separate territorial period. Indiana made the transition from territory to state in sixteen years, becoming a state in 1816. The state of Illinois made a similar transition; it was organized as a territory in 1809 and admitted to the union as a state in 1818. For the transition from territory to state in Ohio, see Cayton, *Frontier Republic*, 68–80. For the transition from territory to state in Indiana, see Cayton, *Frontier Indiana* (Bloomington, Ind., 1996), 252–260. For the transition from territory to state in Illinois, see Berwanger, *Frontier against Slavery*, 7–29.

migrated to territory north and west of the Ohio River, however, faced a different reality. Michigan was organized as a territory in 1805 but did not enter the union as a state until 1837. Wisconsin was organized as a territory that same year but did not become a state until 1848. Minnesota, the last so-called unsettled region of the original Northwest Territory, was not organized until 1849 and was admitted to the union in 1858, shortly before the Civil War. In truth, throughout most of the Northwest Territory, Native peoples constituted the majority of the population on lands claimed by the United States in the first half of the nineteenth century. In 1820, although the southern tier of the Northwest Territory had been transformed into the states of Ohio, Indiana, and Illinois with their requisite population of sixty thousand or more white settlers, the majority of the territory remained a homeland for a multitude of Indigenous peoples. Fewer than nine thousand white settlers lived in the Michigan Territory, which stretched from the Detroit River in the east to the Mississippi River in the west. Twenty-three years after the creation of the Northwest Ordinance, the majority of the Northwest Territory was, in reality, Native territory—or the Native New World, a composite landscape of Indigenous peoples living in their homelands and connected to the global market economy through trade carried out with European, American, and Canadian traders and trading companies.[60]

In the Michigan Territory, for example, Native peoples felt no pressure to adapt to commercial agriculture. Indeed, there was no commercial agriculture northwest of the Ohio when the territory was organized. There was no local market and no easy way to move bulky commodities to American cities to the south and east. The British traders of the Hudson's Bay Company and the North West Company, operating out of posts north of the Great Lakes and on the northern Great Plains, expanded the possibilities and rewards of participating in the fur trade during the late eighteenth and early nineteenth centuries. In this highly competitive market, Native peoples with homelands in the Northwest Territory ranged at will across an unenforceable border in pursuit of economic opportunity. This competition also resulted in greater political independence for Native peoples living in a region where the United States struggled to project power. In other words, Native peoples continued to live and thrive in

60. Federal Population Census, 1820 Michigan, transcribed by Ruby Wiedman and Larry C. Bohannan, U.S. Census Office, 4th Census, 1820, Bentley Historical Library, University of Michigan. For an expanded explanation of the Native New World, see Witgen, *An Infinity of Nations*, 111–115.

what Americans thought of as a state of nature. In reality, this space was not pristine wilderness, nor was it an Indigenous North America void of non-Native influence. Instead, the Northwest interior of the continent emerged as a Native New World, a social world transformed by the process of mutual discovery that resulted when the people, things, and ideas of European empire began to interact with the people, things, and ideas of Indigenous North America. Unlike the New World created along the Eastern Seaboard, however, this Native New World remained the political domain of Indigenous peoples.[61]

This reality posed a problem politically, economically, and militarily for the United States. Native peoples from the Great Lakes and the Ohio country sided with and fought for the British during the War of 1812. British success in taking Detroit and Mackinac early in the war could be attributed to their alliance with Native peoples. In an 1828 letter to the Senate Committee on Indian Affairs, thirteen years after the conclusion of the war, the governor of the Michigan Territory, Lewis Cass, articulated the tenuous nature of American power in the Northwest. "Most of our Indians are migratory tribes," he wrote, "roaming through the forests and prairies, and occupying a border country, divided partly by a natural and partly by an imaginary boundary, between the United States and Great Britain." Further complicating this situation, he noted, "along this boundary and in many cases upon our side of it, the British traders are stationed, with ample supplies for the Indians." As long as the nations of the Northwest freely traded with the British, he concluded, they could potentially fall under the influence of the British Empire. They could become, according to Cass, an "interior enemy."[62]

61. For the significance of the fur trade in the Lake Superior country of the Anishinaabeg, see Brenda J. Child, *Holding Our World Together: Ojibwe Women and the Survival of Community* (New York, 2012), 31–62. For an overview of the fur trade in the Great Lakes and Rupert's Land, see Harold A. Innis, *The Fur Trade in Canada: An Introduction to Canadian Economic History*, with a new introductory essay by Arthur J. Ray (1970; rpt. Toronto, 1999). For a firsthand account of this world at the zenith of the fur trade, see George Nelson, *My First Years in the Fur Trade: The Journals of 1802–1804*, ed. Laura Peers and Theresa Schenck (Saint Paul, Minn., 2002).

62. W[illia]m Clark and Lew[is] Cass to the Hon. Thomas H. Benton, Dec. 27, 1828, in *Public Documents Printed by Order of the Senate of the United States, at the Second Session of the Twenty-First Congress, Begun and Held at the City of Washington, December 6, 1830 . . .* , I (Washington, D.C., 1831), document 39, 27. For the significance of Native allies fighting with the British in the War of 1812, see Alan Taylor, *The Civil War of 1812: American Citizens, British Subjects, Irish Rebels, and Indian Allies* (New York, 2010), 203–234.

Cass believed that British Canada indulged the savage nature of their allies. In an essay published in the *North American Review* in 1827 comparing the Indian policy of the United States and Great Britain, Cass asserted that during the War of 1812, the British "availed themselves of the passions and wants of the Indians to harass their enemies, and employed them without scruple, wherever their services were useful." He complained that "the Indians were employed with a full knowledge of their habits and propensities." These propensities included a fierce cruelty and fondness for war. "The Indians," Cass wrote, "are impelled to war by passions, which acknowledge no control, and death and desolation are the objects of their military expeditions." Unlike Thomas Jefferson, Cass believed that Native people were unredeemable savages, unprepared and incapable of leaving the state of nature for civilized society. "When we look back upon the long interval of Indian intercourse," he wrote, "which elapsed between the first settlement on the shores of the Atlantic, and the final consolidation, of the British power, nothing but a dreary waste meets the eye." In contrast, Cass asserted, "remote and feeble colonies had become important and flourishing provinces," and "aboriginal inhabitants, had disappeared, or receded, before the mighty tide of population." He described this Anglo-American population as "spreading with exterminating force over the forests and prairies of the west." The demise of Native North America, while sad, was inevitable. "We hold no fellowship," he concluded, "with those, to whom the sound of an Indian's rifle is more attractive than that of the woodman's axe, nor are we believers in that system of legal metaphysics, which would give to a few naked and wandering savages, a perpetual title to an immense continent."[63]

Cass came by this understanding of Native peoples and their homelands by virtue of serving as the governor of the Michigan Territory. In his experience, Native peoples stubbornly refused to adopt a civilized way of life, and thus the section of the Northwest Territory under his administration remained an unsettled wilderness. Like Justice James Varnum or Thomas Jefferson, Lewis Cass believed in the political imaginary that insisted North America was an unsettled wilderness. Like these men, he, too, felt that the American people had been called to settle this untamed land, to bring it out of the state of nature. However, he did not believe that Native peoples could be included in this project. "There are but two serious occupations, connected with the ordinary business of life, to which an

63. [Cass], *Remarks . . . from the North American Review, No. LV, for April, 1827,* 4, 6, 10.

Indian willingly devotes himself," Cass wrote; "These are *war* and *hunting*." As a result, "he is perhaps destined to disappear with the forests, which have afforded him food and clothing, and whose existence seems essential to his own." Like others before him, Cass conflated forested land with unimproved land. Natives' failure to clear forests, and in the process carve out private property from the commons to make individual homesteads with fenced fields and permanent built infrastructure, was a refusal to embrace civilization. And because Natives could not embrace civilization, they were doomed to disappear as it advanced across the interior. Civilization was an "exterminating force" in the face of which Native peoples could only disappear. Two strands of thought, one that conceives Native assimilation as inevitable and the other that anticipates Native people will vanish from the face of the earth, shaped the Indian policy of the United States.[64]

The ideas conveyed by Lewis Cass in 1827 expressed a familiar discourse about the future of Native peoples and the expansion of the U.S. Republic. In many ways, he simply rehashed ideas advanced decades earlier by George Washington and Thomas Jefferson. Unlike these presidents, however, Cass did not believe that Native peoples belonged in the Republic—either as citizens or as assimilated savages. Cass's views gained purchase because of his experience. Serving as the governor of the Michigan Territory required him to treat frequently with Native peoples, the majority population living within his jurisdiction. Accordingly, he acquired a national reputation as an expert on Native peoples, and in this capacity he became one of the leading advocates for Indian removal. In an article written for the *North American Review* in 1830, a publication with a national circulation, the governor argued that Native people, by their nature, were uncivilized. "As civilization shed her light upon them, why were they blind to its beams?" Cass asked the reader. "Existing for two centuries in contact with a civilized people," he lamented, "they have resisted, and successfully too, every effort to meliorate their situation, or to introduce among them the most common arts of life." The reason for this resistance, Cass concluded, was that "there must then be an inherent

64. Ibid., 11, 29. This thinking reflected the natural law ideology that equated unimproved wilderness with "waste" or "desert." See Pateman, "The Settler Contract," in Pateman and Mills, eds., *Contract and Domination*, 48–49; Seed, *American Pentimento*, 14–23. The argument articulated by Cass expresses the idea of the "logic of elimination" voiced by Patrick Wolfe; see Wolfe, "Against the Intentional Fallacy," *American Indian Culture and Research Journal*, XXXVI, no. 1 (2012), 4.

difficulty, arising from the institutions, character, and condition of the Indians themselves."[65]

Indian Removal and the Settlement of the Trans-Appalachian West

At the time Lewis Cass was publishing lamentations about the savagery and unassailability of Native peoples, Indian removal was also being debated by the U.S. Congress. Andrew Jackson, elected president of the United States in 1828, famously presented the argument for removal in his second inaugural address to Congress by describing North America west of the Appalachian Mountains as unsettled territory. Echoing the natural law construct of the Enlightenment and the more recent argument for removal articulated by Cass, Jackson proclaimed, "What good man would prefer a country covered with forests and ranged by a few thousand savages, to our extensive republic, studded with cities, towns, and prosperous farms[?]" His vision, he assured his listeners, would be facilitated by the conveniently vanishing Indians. "The tribes which occupied the countries now constituting the eastern States," he declared, "were annihilated, or have melted away, to make room for the whites." Removal would save the Indians remaining in North America from this fate. As the tide of Native peoples receded, he claimed, "waves of population and civilization are rolling to the westward."[66]

Jefferson, Cass, and Jackson all told the same story, one that endowed the United States with a purpose and gave the nation a destiny that justified the dispossession of the continent's Indigenous peoples. These men, prominent political figures in the early Republic, shaped popular discourse about the fate and future of Native peoples. They understood the United States to be a nation of settlers and imagined a future without Native peoples. From their political perspective, it was unthinkable to imagine autonomous Native nations existing within the boundaries of the U.S. Republic.[67]

65. Review of [Lewis Cass], *Documents and Proceedings Relating to the Formation and Progress of a Board in the City of New York, for the Emigration, Preservation, and Improvement of the Aborigines of America, North American Review,* XXX, no. 66 (January 1830), 72–73.

66. *Journal of the House of Representatives of the United States; Being the Second Session of the Twenty-First Congress, Begun and Held at the City of Washington, December 6, 1830 . . .* (Washington, D.C., 1830), XXI, 26.

67. "The Jeffersonian civilizing mission," writes Adam Rothman, "began with an idea about the proper relation between land, people, and self-government." This made

For Andrew Jackson, especially, realizing this vision was a matter of political necessity. The United States was a nation of settlers. And settlers in a democracy lived in a world defined by political rights. The problem with the Indian, Jackson told Congress in his second inaugural address, was that "he is unwilling to submit to the laws of the States, and mingle with their population." Indian removal, he asserted, was "part of the compact" that individual states made with the federal government. Explaining this compact, Jackson asked members of Congress, "Why, in authorizing Ohio, Indiana, Illinois, Missouri, Mississippi, and Alabama, to form constitutions, and become separate States, did Congress include within their limits extensive tracts of Indian lands, and, in some instances, powerful Indian tribes?" "Was it not understood . . . that . . . with all convenient despatch, the General Government should extinguish the Indian title, and remove every obstruction to the complete jurisdiction of the State Governments over the soil?"[68] Jackson concluded by asserting that federal territories had been organized in the West with the implicit expectation of Indian removal. In essence, new territories were created for the purpose of settling western lands so that they could be incorporated into the union as new states. This process required the transfer of a non-Native population onto the public domain in the Trans-Appalachian West, lands that the federal government created by transforming Native homelands into American homesteads. On May 28, 1830, Jackson signed the Indian Removal Act, which authorized the president to grant unsettled lands west of the Mississippi to Native peoples in exchange for their lands within the borders of the states of the union east of the Mississippi.[69]

---

western expansion integral to the success of the American experiment. "The continual addition of new land," from Jefferson's perspective, "would allow the United States to remain a nation of industrious, commercially oriented farmers." See Rothman, *Slave Country: American Expansion and the Origins of the Deep South* (Cambridge, Mass., 2005), 38.

68. *Journal of the House of Representatives of the United States*, XXI, 27. As historian Christina Snyder explains, "Andrew Jackson believed that Indian treaties, many of which he had negotiated, were a relic of his nation's birth, when the United States had been too weak to conquer Native nations." More to the point, she argues, "Jackson feared that Indian nations, like European empires that claimed land in North America, represented a challenge to US sovereignty, one that might prevent territorial expansion." See Snyder, *Great Crossings: Indians, Settlers, and Slaves in the Age of Jackson* (New York, 2017), 132.

69. An Act to Provide for an Exchange of Lands with the Indians Residing in Any of the States or Territories, and for Their Removal West of the River Mississippi, May 28, 1830, in *Acts of the Twenty-First Congress of the United States, Passed at the First*

Indian removal was a controversial policy, but a policy with enough public support to become the law of the land. That said, it was enforced unevenly. In the Southeast, where U.S. settlers desperately sought Native lands for the expansion of cotton production, removal occurred in a brutal fashion that would now be recognized as ethnic cleansing. In the Northwest, in contrast, particularly in the Michigan Territory, while some Native peoples were forced to remove to the Indian Territory west of the Mississippi, many other communities managed to remain on their homelands. Those who resisted removal would be locked in a desperate struggle to hold on to some portion of their homelands throughout the nineteenth century.[70]

Native Peoples in the Past and Future of the U.S. Republic

The politics of passing and implementing the Indian Removal Act represented a fraught national conversation about the future of Native peoples in the Republic and in North America. In the early nineteenth century, there was no escaping the reality of Native peoples. Their presence in the United States, and the fact that the country had been established on their homelands, shaped what it meant to be a citizen of the world's newest democracy. Thomas Jefferson had advocated for the assimilation of Native peoples into the body politic of the United States. A quarter century later, policies pursued by Lewis Cass and Andrew Jackson reflected a decisive shift away from this inclusive vision for Native peoples in the Republic. Cass and Jackson were leading figures in the first generation that worked,

------

Session, Which Was Begun and Held at the City of Washington, in the District of Columbia, on Monday, the Seventh Day of December, One Thousand Eight Hundred and Twenty Nine, and Ended on the Thirty-First Day of May, 1830, https://www.loc .gov/law/help/statutes-at-large/21st-congress/session-1/c21s1ch148.pdf. Regarding the trans-Mississippi West and the government of the early Republic, Walter Johnson writes, "Administering this vast domain for the cultivation of independent and equal white men was the central business of federal governance in the 1830s." See Johnson, *River of Dark Dreams: Slavery and Empire in the Cotton Kingdom* (Cambridge, Mass., 2013), 34.

70. For Indigenous dispossession in the Old Southwest, see Claudio Saunt, "Financing Dispossession: Stocks, Bonds, and the Deportation of Native Peoples in the Antebellum United States," *Journal of American History*, CVI (2019), 315–337. For the logic of removal pursued by the Jackson administration and overseen by Lewis Cass, see Snyder, *Great Crossings*, 132–135. For northern removal, see John P. Bowes, *Land Too Good for Indians: Northern Indian Removal* (Norman, Okla., 2017).

on the ground, to incorporate western lands outside the original thirteen colonies into the union. For these men, the inclusion of Native peoples, and especially Native nations, within the social, political, and geographic boundaries of the Republic was inconceivable. They could not be part of the social contract between the American nation-state and its citizens.

At the very moment when politicians like Cass and Jackson sought to drive Native peoples from their homelands and expel them physically from the Republic, however, the United States embraced Native peoples as part of the public imagination of what it meant to be an American. As Congress debated the merits of Indian removal, the federal government completed construction of the Capitol Rotunda, the centerpiece of the re-constructed congressional buildings of the United States. The British had set fire to the Capitol and the White House during the War of 1812. The Capitol was rebuilt and completed with the building of the Rotunda in 1824. The Rotunda was decorated with a series of bas-relief murals com-missioned by President John Quincy Adams between 1824 and 1829. At the time of their completion, they were the sole decorative elements built into the Rotunda. Congressmen and visitors entering the building looked upon a four-sided interior, each side carved with a bas-relief sculpture chronicling the national mythology of the United States: *Preservation of Captain Smith by Pocahontas, 1606,* above the west entrance; *Landing of the Pilgrims,* over the east entrance; *William Penn's Treaty with the Indians, 1682,* over the north entrance; and *Conflict of Daniel Boone and the Indians, 1773,* over the south entrance.[71]

The national mythology imagined by President Adams in the artwork he commissioned for the Rotunda was inseparable from the history of Native peoples. In the decades following the creation of the United States, most Americans would have regularly encountered Native peoples, par-ticularly in areas such as the Michigan Territory, where settlers, territorial officials, and representatives of the federal government frequently inter-acted with them. Indigenous people were commonly subjects in the presi-dent's State of the Union address, and debates over removal was part of a national political conversation. Native characters featured prominently in popular literature and cultural productions such as James Fenimore Cooper's novel *Last of the Mohicans* (1826), John Augustus Stone's play *Metamora; or, The Last of the Wampanoags* (1829), and Joseph Dod-dridge's novel *Logan, the Last of the Race of Shikillemus, Chief of the*

---

71. Vivien Green Fryd, *Art and Empire: The Politics of Ethnicity in the United States Capitol, 1815–1860* (Athens, Ohio, 2001), 19–41.

Figure 3. *Preservation of Captain Smith by Pocahontas, 1606.* By Antonio Capellano. 1825. Relief sculpture, sandstone. Architect of the Capitol

Cayuga Nation (1821). In effect, the national mythology that linked American identity to the history of American Indians in the murals of the Capitol Rotunda represented the lived experience of the American people.[72]

The first two murals commissioned, *Preservation of Captain Smith by Pocahontas* and the *Landing of the Pilgrims*, represent moments of

72. For American Indians in the American political imaginary, see Philip J. Deloria, *Playing Indian* (New Haven, Conn., 1999). See also Cristina Stanciu, "'The Last Indian' Syndrome Revisited: Metamore, Take Two," *Intertexts*, X (2006), 25–49.

Figure 4. *Landing of the Pilgrims, 1620.* By Enrico Causici. 1825.
Relief sculpture, sandstone. Architect of the Capitol

encounter, but also moments of transfer. Pocahontas, the Indian princess, saves John Smith from the savagery of her father. Later she marries an English colonist and converts to Christianity, signifying a joining of the fate of English settlers and the Native people of North America. Her story reflects the settlers' triumph over Native savagery and the English assimilation of Native nobility. Pocahontas embodies the civilizing mission of English colonization and, by extension, the U.S. Republic. In the second mural, the Wampanoag welcome the Pilgrims, who are seeking refuge in North America. They share their corn and teach the colonists to plant

Figure 5. *William Penn's Treaty with the Indians, 1682.* By Nicholas Gevelot. 1827. Relief sculpture, sandstone. Architect of the Capitol

Figure 6. *Conflict of Daniel Boone and the Indians, 1773.* By Enrico Causici. 1827. Relief sculpture, sandstone. Architect of the Capitol

their own food crops—a sharing of the knowledge needed to survive in the New World. In both of these historic moments, Americans have found meaning. These mythological representations of the past, both the murals and the stories themselves, do important ideological work. They signal an Indigenous acceptance of European settlement. More important, they suggest an Indigenous complicity with the forging of these New World settlements by European empires and their successor, the United States.[73]

The murals of William Penn and Daniel Boone represent the other face of European empire. The histories imagined by these murals depict Indigenous dispossession. The murals of Pocahontas and the Pilgrims focus less on the dispossession that followed English colonization than on the peaceful assimilation of Native North America through the advance of civilization. In both stories, we can see savagery yielding to civilization. *William Penn's Treaty with the Indians* tells a similar story, but it more explicitly emphasizes the European acquisition of Indigenous land. The mural represents another peaceful transfer, Native peoples yielding their land to English colonists.

In the mural, William Penn the Quaker, the embodiment of peace and nonviolence, shakes hands with Delaware chiefs, holding a signed treaty dated 1682. This representation alludes to the account of Penn and his relationship with the Delawares. In 1681, Charles II gave Penn a charter designating him as the sole proprietor of a forty-five-thousand-square-mile territory west of New Jersey in compensation for a debt owed to Penn's father. This grant made Penn the single largest landholder in British America. Charles claimed possession of this territory by right of discovery, and he transferred this sovereignty claim to Penn. In truth, as Penn soon learned, this land was the homeland of the Delawares, or Lenni Lenape, whose descendants would assume a leadership role in the Northwest confederacy. Arriving in his newly acquired territory in 1682, Penn traveled to the village at Shackamaxon, where he negotiated a treaty with the Delawares. Penn not only affirmed peace between his colony and the Delawares but also paid twelve hundred pounds for the land he planned to sell to settlers. There is no surviving text for this treaty, and it was subsequently violated in the eighteenth century as Pennsylvania expanded deeper into the West, a recurring theme in the United States' history of treaty making. Nevertheless, this act of diplomacy became part of the mythology of William Penn, the man who treated Native peoples fairly and as equals. Although the

73. For an analysis of the production of these two murals, see Fryd, *Art and Empire*, 25–28.

mural offers a vision of European expansion and the transfer of land from Natives to European settlers, it also suggests the potential for this process to unfold diplomatically and peacefully. But one could also argue that there is a hidden and darker meaning to this mural. Angered at English expansion onto their lands in violation of the 1682 treaty, the Delawares fought against the English in the Seven Years' War, and later against Americans during the Revolution, and again in the Northwest Indian War (1785–1795) and in the War of 1812. These conflicts produced bitter violence in the Pennsylvania backcountry, which was also part of American popular culture, perhaps presented most famously in Cooper's *Last of the Mohicans*. In other words, *William Penn's Treaty with the Indians* foreshadowed a history of diplomatic failure, violence, and Native dispossession.[74]

The representation of frontier violence in American mythology, in which settlers seeking a better life in the western territories faced armed resistance from bloodthirsty savages, is also prominently reflected in the legend of Daniel Boone. And, indeed, the final mural, *Conflict of Daniel Boone and the Indians*, presents an account of violent conquest. In this mural, Daniel Boone engages in hand-to-hand combat with a shirtless warrior, rifle in one hand, long knife in the other. They both stand on top of a dead Indian. Popularized by John Filson's autobiography published in 1784, the narrative of Daniel Boone is the story of American expansion into the West. "Thus we behold Kentucke," Filson wrote, "lately an howling wilderness, the habitation of savages and wild beasts, become a fruitful field; this region, so favourably distinguished by nature, now become the habitation of civilization."[75]

Daniel Boone the Indian fighter, defender of frontier settlements, represents America's story as one of conquest, a triumph over a wild and

74. For the significance of backcountry violence, particularly in Kentucky and the Ohio River valley, see Sachs, *Home Rule*, 22–40; and Sleeper-Smith, *Indigenous Prosperity and American Conquest*, 210–242.

75. "Appendix: The Adventures of Col. Daniel Boone; Containing a Narrative of the Wars of Kentucke," in John Filson, *The Discovery, Settlement, and Present State of Kentucke (1784): An Online Electronic Text Edition*, ed. Paul Royster, 39, Electronic Texts in American Studies, Digital Commons@University of Nebraska–Lincoln, 2006, https://digitalcommons.unl.edu/cgi/viewcontent.cgi?article=1002&context=etas. Unlike the violence depicted in Cooper's *Last of the Mohicans*, which focused on captivity and redemption, Daniel Boone's story centered on the American homestead and the need to protect women and children from the violence of Native savages; see, for example, Sachs, *Home Rule*, 24–25. For the production of these two murals, see Fryd, *Art and Empire*, 28–34. For Penn and the Lenni Lenape, see Richter, *Ordeal of the Longhouse*, 272–275.

unsettled North American wilderness populated by bloodthirsty savages. American pioneers push into the West to fulfill their destiny and settle the continent. In a sharp counterpoint to the story of William Penn, this mural suggests that there would be no place for Native peoples in the U.S. Republic. The *Conflict of Daniel Boone* marks a temporal as well as a thematic shift in the murals. This relief moves from the seventeenth to the eighteenth century and from the colonial era to the early national period in North American history. The other murals hold out the possibility of Indigenous assimilation; Boone's mural seems to foreclose such incorporation. In this sense, the mural represents the shift from the Revolutionary generation to the post-Revolutionary generation. Political leaders like Thomas Jefferson and George Washington envisioned the possibility of some form of inclusion or assimilation for Indigenous peoples, even if they imagined the demise of autonomous Native nations. Leaders like Lewis Cass and Andrew Jackson saw no future for Indigenous peoples in the United States—as nations, unenfranchised subjects, or as citizens. In effect, the murals of the Capitol Rotunda, commissioned to chronicle the history of the United States, depict the two strands of thought about the future of Native peoples in the Republic. Whatever the future, however, to vanish or assimilate, the founding of the United States is told as a story about the encounter with the Indigenous peoples of North America. Americans, like their imperial predecessors, imagined their national project as the colonization of Native North America. This was the civilizing mission of the United States.[76]

In other words, the civilizing mission of the United States was a totalizing ideological project. It was not merely aimed at civilizing Native people but was about the transformation of a continent, and that transformation never imagined a political future for Native peoples. For citizens of the new Republic, the idea that a burgeoning United States would yield to the territorial sovereignty of Native nations would have been unthinkable. Treaty making, however, was a diplomatic process. It allowed the United States to acquire Native land peacefully, and the negotiation itself offered the possibility of a political future for Indigenous peoples to continue existing as Indigenous nations.

When Native nations signed treaties with the United States, they either attempted to limit American expansion and maintain some measure of their homeland and their freedom or they accepted the political bargain of inclusion promised by the American settler state. Whatever path a Native

76. For a standard art history of the Rotunda reliefs, see Fryd, *Art and Empire*.

nation chose represented an attempt to preserve an Indigenous future. The idea of the civilizing mission, central to America's Indian policy, represented a promise of inclusion—eliminate the Native through assimilation or through removal with the promise of eventual assimilation and incorporation within civil society. This bargain played out in dramatic fashion as America expanded into the Old Southwest, removing Indians through coercion and establishing new territories that were incorporated into the Republic. In the Old Northwest, in contrast, the United States had to act as a colonial state, an exogenous power driven into an ongoing relationship with a permanently subordinated Indigenous population—non-citizens forced to live as colonial subjects on homelands claimed by the federal government. The history of this colonial project in the Old Northwest is poignantly revealed in the struggle to organize the states of Michigan and Wisconsin in the heart of the Great Lakes. The economic development of these states in particular, and the Northwest Territory in general, forged the path and made possible the western expansion of the Republic.

The U.S. Republic was a nation of settlers struggling to colonize Native North America. Accepting this fact, that America has always been a colonial power, reveals American expansion for what it was—and for what it was not. It was not a nation of immigrants settling a savage or untamed wilderness. Thinking through the mechanics of western expansion—the Northwest Ordinance, the Ohio Company, the Treaty of Greenville—or the iconography of the Capitol Rotunda, we see the United States locked in a fight with Indigenous people about the meaning of place and belonging in North America. We see the U.S. Republic as a colonial power, doing what colonial powers do, subordinating Native peoples while plundering their land and resources and, wherever it was politically possible and financially profitable, using enslaved African Americans to do so.

In the Northwest Territory, particularly in the country north and west of the Ohio River, the American story is also that of the Anishinaabe people and their fight to remain in their homeland, Anishinaabewaki. Like Native peoples throughout North America, the Anishinaabeg were coerced into engaging in a battle for their freedom. The arrival of American settlers, along with their ideology and government, resulted in a struggle, one that continues to this day, to preserve their right to self-determination, their sovereignty. We cannot disentangle American history and Indigenous history, nor can we separate the history of Native dispossession from the history of slavery, western expansion, and the emergence of free-soil politics.

CHAPTER 2

Indigenous Homelands and American Homesteads

 In the summer of 1802, a young Ojibwe man named Zhaazhaawanibiisens, or the Swallow, set out on the northern plains along the Assiniboine River to recover a horse that had been stolen from him the previous year. The young man had brooded about the stolen horse for a year. His friends and family had begged him to forget about the theft. Any attempt to retake the animal, they feared, would simply be too dangerous and not worth the risk. In the early spring, however, when his people came together to make maple sugar, Zhaazhaawanibiisens learned that the man who stole his horse continued to boast about it. Angered by this humiliation, the young man left his village at the mouth of the Assiniboine River and made his way toward the Turtle Mountain region of the northern Great Plains. He knew the identity of the thief, a senior male Assiniboine with a bad reputation among his own people as a quarrelsome troublemaker. The Assiniboine were allies of the Ojibweg, and so marching off into their territory on the northern plains was not dangerous in and of itself. However, the Sioux, deadly enemies of both the Assiniboine and the Ojibweg, also came into this country to hunt, trade, and raid. That was the risk, the danger, the thing that made his friends and family worry.[1]

After traveling four days, Zhaazhaawanibiisens approached an Assiniboine village located near the Souris River trading post of the North West

1. John Tanner, *A Narrative of the Captivity and Adventures of John Tanner, (U.S. Interpreter at the Saut* [sic] *de Ste. Marie,) during Thirty Years Residence among the Indians in the Interior of North America; Prepared for Press by Edwin James* (London, 1830), 142. The Assiniboine were a Siouan-speaking people who called themselves Nakoda, a dialect variation of the word Dakota, signifying "allied." Though linked linguistically with people identified as the Sioux, the Nakoda were a distinct Native people occupying the region between Lake Winnipeg and the Saskatchewan River. See Douglas R. Parks, "Synonymy," in Raymond J. De Mallie and David Reed Miller, "Assiniboine," in William C. Sturtevant, gen. ed., *Handbook of North*

Company. There he learned that the thief had passed the winter among the Mandan people in the upper Missouri, that he had returned to his people, but that now his whereabouts were unknown. Zhaazhaawanibiisens made his way to the trading post to explain his mission and seek additional information. The North West Company traders outfitted the young man with gunpowder and musket balls as well as knives and other trade goods to facilitate his passage among the Assiniboine. They then gave him directions to the closest village and sent the young man on his way.[2]

Zhaazhaawanibiisens arrived at a wide and treeless expanse of prairie. Halting at the edge of this open space he observed a lone hunter lying prone in the middle of the prairie. He approached the man quietly, keeping himself hidden. Unaware of his presence, the hunter emptied his gun at a passing flock of geese. Zhaazhaawanibiisens rushed the hunter. Jangling hawk bells and silver ornaments gave him away, but he smothered the hunter and trapped him in his arms. "When he saw himself captured," Zhaazhaawanibiisens later recalled, "he cried out 'Assinneboine' and I answered 'Ojibbeway.' We were both glad to find that we could treat each other as friends."[3]

Zhaazhaawanibiisens released the man, and they sat side by side recovering from the adrenaline rush of their brief struggle. They quickly ascertained that neither man spoke the other's language. Even without the ability to speak to each another, both men knew the thing that had provoked the attack: fear of the Sioux, their common enemy. A chance encounter with an unknown person was a perilous moment. Was the stranger an enemy, a Sioux traveling to the north to hunt or raid? Shouting their identities while they wrestled on the ground—"Assinneboine,"

American Indians, 13 vols. to date (Washington, D.C., 1978–), XIII, part 1, 590–592 (hereafter cited as HNAI). For conflict between the Assiniboine and the Sioux, see Pekka Hämäläinen, Lakota America: A New History of Indigenous Power (New Haven, Conn., 2019), 143–144, 158–159. For an ethnohistorical narrative account of the Assiniboine and their relationship with the Cree and the Sioux, see Dale R. Russell, Eighteenth-Century Western Cree and Their Neighbors, Archaeological Survey of Canada, Mercury Series Paper 143 (Hull, Quebec, 1991), 172–186. For analysis of Indigenous warfare on the Great Plains and the impact of the adaptation of the horse and guns, see Frank Raymond Secoy, Changing Military Patterns on the Great Plains (17th Century through Early 19th Century) (New York, 1953). For Ojibwe migration into the Assiniboine and Red River regions, see Laura Peers, The Ojibwa of Western Canada, 1780 to 1870 (Saint Paul, Minn., 1994).

2. Tanner, Narrative of the Captivity, 145.
3. Ibid., 145–146.

"Ojibbeway"—they realized they were not strangers but allies. Zhaa-zhaawanibiisens, the aggressor and intruder, gave the man a goose he had killed earlier in the day. With this gift, a gesture of both apology and alliance, the Assiniboine signaled for the Ojibwe to follow him to his lodge in a nearby village.[4]

The Assiniboine and Ojibweg had been trading partners and allies since the late seventeenth century. Their alliance had been facilitated over the years by their mutual ties to the Cree. Lowland Cree bands ranging inland from the Hudson Bay coast and upland Cree bands that migrated between the boreal forests north of the Great Lakes and the northern Great Plains acted as intermediaries in a transregional trade network. Exchange—ritualized gift giving, trade, and intermarriage—bound the Assiniboine, the Cree, and the Ojibweg together as allies. With the arrival of Europeans and the evolution of the fur trade, these connections took the form of a wide-ranging and loosely structured political alliance and exchange network.[5] Their alliance proved critical to the development of French, English, and, later, American and Canadian trading operations

4. Ibid. In the Great Plains and northern prairies, territory is rarely the exclusive domain of a single Indigenous people. Indigenous peoples followed the seasonal migration pattern of the game they hunted, and as a result the territories of Native nations on the plain remained porous and flexible. See Donald L. Hardesty, *Ecological Anthropology* (New York, 1977), 186. See also Patricia Albers and Jeanne Kay, "Sharing the Land: A Study in American Indian Territoriality," in Thomas E. Ross and Tyrell G. Moore, eds., *A Cultural Geography of North American Indians* (Boulder, Colo., 1987), 47–91. In an environment of shared or overlapping territoriality, such as on the Great Plains, Albers asserts that social connections between different Indigenous social formations "emerged under relationships based on war (competition), merger (cooperation), and symbiosis (complementarity)." In effect, social relations and diplomacy operated along a continuum producing violent or peaceful encounters and exchange that drew Native peoples into ongoing social relationships that shaped enduring patterns of cooperation, alliance, and warfare on the plains. See Albers, "Symbiosis, Merger, and War: Contrasting Forms of Intertribal Relationship among Historic Plains Indians," in John Moore, ed., *The Political Economy of North American Indians* (Lincoln, Nebr., 1993), 99 (quotation).

5. Cree is the English-language designation for people who identified themselves as Winnipeg-athiniwick or Muskekowuck-athiniwick. Athiniwick was a designation that signified "original person" or "human being." Winnipeg and Muskekowuck were place designations. Thus, lowland Cree bands living in the coastal tundra zone identified as Winnipeg-athiniwick, and bands living in the marshlands inland from the coast self-identified as Muskekowuck-athiniwick. See David H. Pentland, "Synonymy," in John J. Honigmann, "West Main Cree," *HNAI*, VI, 227. Upland Cree bands

that relied on commerce with the peoples of the Northwest interior. This commerce, in turn, created a political and diplomatic structure that provided a veneer of truth to British and American claims of sovereignty over the territory. These claims, however, rested entirely upon the willingness of Native peoples to incorporate Europeans and Americans into their own political and economic systems, which were connected to the British Empire, the U.S. Republic, and the global market economy but remained autonomous. The encounter between Zhaazhaawanibiisens and the Assiniboine hunter occurred in an Indigenous space—the contested borderland between the territories of the Sioux, or the Oceti Sakowin (People of Seven Council Fires), and the Assiniboine, Cree, and Ojibwe peoples. This was the Native New World, the western interior of the North American continent where Native peoples continued to exercise political dominion over their homelands.[6]

---

living in the prairie parkland, north of the Great Plains, called themselves Nehiyaw-athiniwick, with Nehiyaw designating "those who speak the same language"; see Pentland, "Synonymy," in James G. E. Smith, "Western Woods Cree," *HNAI*, VI, 267–268. For the alliance between the Cree, Ojibwe, and Assiniboine peoples, see Michael Witgen, *An Infinity of Nations: How the Native New World Shaped Early North America* (Philadelphia, 2012), 223–232. For the best history of the early contact history of the Cree and Assiniboine, see Russell, *Eighteenth Century Western Cree*. See also Victor P. Lytwyn, *Muskekowuck Athinuwick: Original People of the Great Swampy Land* (Winnipeg, Canada, 2002).

6. For an early history detailing the establishment of the fur trade in Hudson Bay, see John Oldmixon, "The History of Hudson's-Bay . . . ," in J. B. Tyrrell, ed., *Documents Relating to the Early History of Hudson Bay* (Toronto, 1931); E. E. Rich, ed., *James Isham's Observations on Hudsons Bay, 1743 and Notes and Observations on a Book Entitled 'A Voyage to Hudsons Bay in the Dobbs Galley, 1749'* (London, 1949); and Glyndwr Williams, ed., *Andrew Graham's Observations on Hudson's Bay, 1761–91* (London, 1969). For the French fur trade, see Richard White, *The Middle Ground; Indians, Empires, and Republics in the Great Lakes Region, 1650–1815* (New York, 1991), 142–185. For the Native New World, see Witgen, *An Infinity of Nations*, 1–21. The Oceti Sakowin, a designation signifying "People of Seven Council Fires," consisted of seven *oyate*, a term meaning people—Mdewakanton, Sisseton, Wahpeton, Wahpekute, Yankton, Yanktonai, and Teton. The peoples of these oyate referred to themselves as the Dakota and, in the Teton dialect, Lakota. See James Warren Springer and Stanly R. Witkowski, "Siouan Historical Linguistics and Oneota Archaeology," in Guy Gibbon, ed., *Oneota Studies* (Minneapolis, Minn., 1982), 69–83. See also Hämäläinen, *Lakota America*, 15–21; Parks, "Synonymy," in Raymond J. DeMallie, "Sioux until 1850," *HNAI*, XIII, part 2, 749–760; Guy Gibbon, *The Sioux: The Dakota and Lakota Nations* (Malden, Mass., 2003), 292–299.

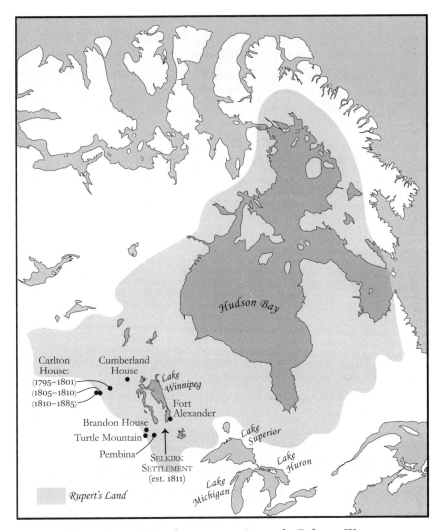

Map 2. Rupert's Land, 1790–1820. Drawn by Rebecca Wrenn

At the dawn of the nineteenth century, politically independent, or sovereign, Native peoples controlled the western interior of North America. The chance encounter between Zhaazhaawanibiisens and the Assiniboine hunter underscored this fact. Identifying himself as an Assiniboine, the hunter gambled that the man he wrestled with was an ally. He also asserted his right to be on the prairie, in Assiniboine territory. And, as luck would have it, the man who ambushed him was an Ojibwe. They immediately recognized each another as friends because they lived in a world shaped by the politics of Native North America. This was a world where alliance signified kinship, and kinship represented a system of mutual obligation and responsibility that determined access to territory and resources. Alliance also demanded a shared commitment to confronting enemies, like the Sioux. Zhaazhaawanibiisens and the Assiniboine hunter accepted each another as allies because they lived in a social world shaped by the alliance between their two peoples.[7]

Worlds Collide:
The Fur Trade and the U.S. Republic

Native peoples, however, were not the only source of political power in the western interior of North America. The fur trade, and its association with various colonial powers, also influenced life on the plains and connected this region to the upper Mississippi Valley, the Great Lakes, and the northern boreal forest that drained into the marshy lowlands of Hudson Bay. Great Britain, via Canada and the Hudson's Bay Company, claimed much of this space as Rupert's Land. These claims of possession and sovereignty were based on the right of discovery, recognized in international law, which resulted in a crown charter for the Hudson's Bay Company. But international law did not translate into political power on the ground. Neither the empire nor the company possessed the capacity to govern in this region. They might influence alliances and shape trading practices, but the region that the British called Rupert's Land remained an Indigenous space.[8]

7. For the Indigenous West as an autonomous space, see Michael Witgen, "The Native New World and Western North America," *Western Historical Quarterly*, XLIII (Autumn 2012), 292–299.

8. For the English claim to possession of Hudson Bay by right of discovery, see *The Royal Charter for Incorporating the Hudson's Bay Company, Granted by His Majesty King Charles the Second, in the Twenty-Second Year of His Reign, A.D. 1670* (London, 1816). For French dependence on Native allies and trading partners in claiming possession of the Great Lakes and the Hudson Bay region, see "Premier extrait d'une lettre de Jean Talon à Colbert," Nov. 10, 1670, in Pierre Margry, *Découvertes et etablissements des Français dans l'Ouest et dans le Sud de L'Amérique septentrionale (1614–1754): Mémoires et documents originaux* (Paris, 1876), I, 83–84; "Extrait d'une lettre de Jean Talon da Roy," Nov. 2, 1671, ibid., I, 92–93; "Memoire general sur les limites de la Baye d'Hudson," C 11E 2, Archives Nationale, Pierrefitte-sur-Seine, France. For the inability of the Hudson's Bay Company to enforce British law in the Northwest interior, see Hamar Foster, "Long-Distance Justice: The Criminal Jurisdiction of Canadian Courts West of the Canadas, 1763–1859," *American Journal of Legal History*, XXXIII (1990), 1–48. For trade and the evolution of the Ojibwe, Cree, and Assiniboine alliance, see Peers, *The Ojibwa of Western Canada.*

Similarly, the upper Mississippi Valley, the homeland of the Dakota peoples and the Great Lakes homeland of the Ojibweg, were claimed by the United States following the Treaty of Paris in 1783, which brought an end to the Revolutionary War. The U.S. Republic organized these Native homelands along with those of Native peoples in the Ohio country, the Wabash River basin, and the Illinois country into the Northwest Territory in 1787. The Republic administered this space as a federal territory, but at the time of its creation the government exercised only limited political control over the region. Much like Rupert's Land, the Northwest Territory was dominated by a large multiethnic alliance of Native peoples.

If the Northwest interior, the regions identified by Anglo-America as Rupert's Land and the Northwest Territory, was for all practical purposes an Indigenous space, it was hardly a timeless Eden. The fur trade boomed in this region when Great Britain assumed control of Canada and the monopolies that New France and the Hudson's Bay Company struggled to maintain gave way. Scottish traders operating out of Montreal and Americans working out of Saint Louis brought fierce competition and breathed new life into trade in the Northwest. Toward the end of the eighteenth century, many Anishinaabe peoples from the Great Lakes, in particular the Odawaag and Ojibweg, migrated west to take advantage of the bounty of the upper Mississippi and the Great Plains. Some people migrated seasonally or for extended periods of time. Others made a more permanent move west, ranging as far as Turtle Mountain in the border region of present-day North Dakota and Manitoba. Reoriented toward the western interior, the Anishinaabe population expanded significantly during a time when the population of Native peoples on the East Coast began to contract and the Ohio country faced pressure from immigrant settlers.[9]

The violence of the Seven Years' War and the American Revolution took a toll on Native peoples living east of the Mississippi. While Canada and

9. For population growth, see Jeanne Kay, "The Fur Trade and Native American Population Growth," *Ethnohistory*, XXXI (1984), 265–287. For Ojibwe migration, see Peers, *Ojibwa of Western Canada*, 27–62. For the Ohio country during the fur-trade boom, see Susan Sleeper-Smith, *Indigenous Prosperity and American Conquest: Indian Women of the Ohio River Valley, 1690–1792* (Williamsburg, Va., and Chapel Hill, N.C., 2018), 67–104. Sleeper-Smith presents a revision of Richard White's middle ground concept, arguing instead that the Great Lakes and Ohio country were an Indigenous landscape where the French played a minor political role. "The fur trade," she writes, "created a prosperous Indian world and encouraged diverse people to band together and form the first Northwestern Indian confederacy that resisted intrusion

the British Empire provided a refuge and source of political support for many northern Indians, American expansion into Kentucky and the Ohio country brought the potential for conflict and dispossession throughout the Trans-Appalachian region. The Americans pushing west onto lands ceded to them by the British following the Revolution did not come in search of trade. They came as settlers seeking to expand the boundaries of their Republic by creating homesteads on lands they believed to be unsettled.[10] The natural law ideology of the United States recognized Native title as imperfect and temporary. True possession, understood as dominion (possession) and sovereignty (political order or control), could only follow improvement—the transformation of land recognized as a commons into private property, or homesteads. The western expansion of the U.S. Republic through the creation of new territories and states required this transformation, which necessitated the elimination of the Native population. In contrast, the fur trade, which also brought Americans and Canadians into the Northwest, required the continued existence of Native North America. In other words, the expansion of the United States was predicated on the dispossession of Native peoples, a process that could only result in the dismantling of the fur trade.[11]

The presence of Zhaazhaawanibiisens on the northern Great Plains, searching for his stolen horse, was a manifestation of the push and pull created by a booming fur trade in the West and the western expansion

---

on their lands" (10). For a history of the Canadian fur trade, see Harold Innis, *The Fur Trade in Canada: An Introduction to Canadian Economic History*, with a new introductory essay by Arthur J. Ray (1970; rpt. Toronto, 1999); Arthur J. Ray and Donald Freeman, *'Give Us Good Measure': An Economic Analysis of Relations between the Indians and the Hudson's Bay Company before 1763* (Toronto, 1978); W. J. Eccles, "The Fur Trade and Eighteenth Century Imperialism," *William and Mary Quarterly*, 3d Ser., XL (1983), 341–362.

10. Honor Sachs argues persuasively that American settlers moving into the Trans-Appalachian West immigrated in search of "mastery and personal independence." That many settlers found only landlessness and a life of economic subservience resulted in a reorientation of civic culture that privileged a highly racialized articulation of white manhood. This ideological development not only perpetuated inequality and social stratification but also exacerbated violence against Native peoples. See, Sachs, *Home Rule*, 39 (quotation). For the violent struggle over the possession of the Trans-Appalachian West, see Peter Silver, *Our Savage Neighbors: How Indian War Transformed Early America* (New York, 2008).

11. The Supreme Court under chief justice John Marshall ruled that the United States came into possession of North America from the Mississippi to the Eastern Seaboard by right of discovery, passed to the Republic from Great Britain following

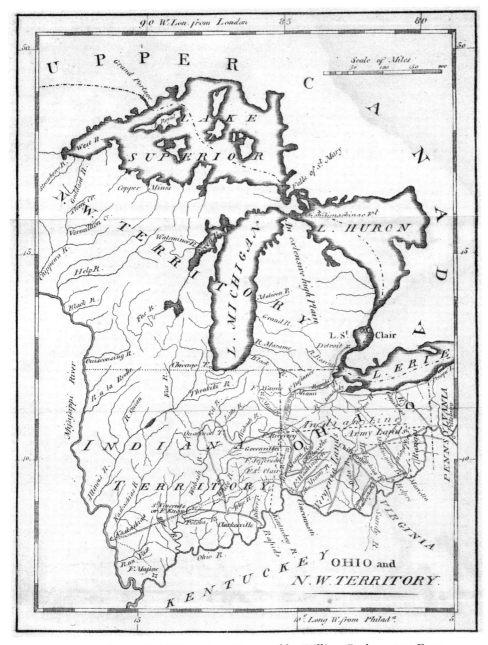

Figure 7. *Ohio and N. W. Territory.* Engraved by William Barker. 1805. From [Mathew Carey], *Carey's American Pocket Atlas . . .* (Philadelphia, 1805), 76. William L. Clements Library, University of Michigan, Ann Arbor

of the United States from the East. Zhaazhaawanibiisens had originally made his way into the West from the colony of Virginia in 1780, traveling with his father and namesake John Tanner when the older man moved his family to Boonesborough (present-day Boonesboro), Kentucky. Boonesborough was one of a growing number of white settlements established west of the proclamation line of 1763, the country beyond the Appalachian Mountains that Great Britain recognized as Indian Territory following the Seven Years' War. These communities were regarded as illegal settlements by the British and met with violent resistance from Native peoples. When the British ceded this territory to the United States following the Revolution, settlers poured into the Kentucky and Ohio country, and violence and raiding between Natives and settlers became part of the fabric of life along the western frontier. In this contentious environment, John Tanner, the son, was taken captive by Native peoples. In 1795, five years after his capture, John, renamed Zhaazhaawanibiisens, moved west to the Red River Valley with his Native family.[12]

The story of Zhaazhaawanibiisens provides a provocative look at the Native New World, the Indigenous social world that emerged in the heartland of North America following the establishment of European colonies on the Eastern Seaboard. Zhaazhaawanibiisens experienced this world at

---

the Treaty of Paris in 1783 (Samuel A. Worcester v. Georgia, 31 U.S. 515 [6 Pet.] 515 [1832]). For the distinction between dominion and sovereignty, see Carole Pateman, "The Settler Contract," in Pateman and Charles W. Mills, eds., *Contract and Domination* (Cambridge, 2007), 53–58. For the right to occupy uncultivated land, see Richard Tuck, *The Rights of War and Peace: Political Thought and the International Order from Grotius to Kant* (Oxford, 1999), 49–50. For the idea that English common law provided the legal basis for English claims of possession in North America, see Patricia Seed, *Ceremonies of Possession in Europe's Conquest of the New World, 1492–1640* (Cambridge, 1995).

12. For the Tanner family homestead, see Tanner, *Narrative of the Captivity*, 23–29. For violence in the Ohio country, see Sleeper-Smith, *Indigenous Prosperity and American Conquest*, 67–104. For the raiding of the Northwest Territory by Kentucky militia, see ibid., 248–277; and White, *Middle Ground*, 413–333. Many historians mistakenly attribute Tanner's captivity to the Shawnees who lived in the Ohio Valley and Kentucky region, but he was taken by the Saginaw Ojibweg. For the capture, adoption, and naming of Tanner, see John T. Fierst, "A 'Succession of Little Occurences': Scholarly Editing and the Organization of Time in John Tanner's Narrative," *Scholarly Editing: The Annual of the Association for Documentary Editing*, XXXIII (2012), 1–29.

its zenith and witnessed its rapid disintegration in the face of the expansion of the U.S. Republic. When the Tanner family arrived in Kentucky, the region was at a crossroads. The Ohio country north of Kentucky settlements like Boonesborough was an intersectional space, a pathway to the Indigenous West via the Maumee and Ohio Rivers. These watersheds connected Native peoples to the Great Lakes, creating a network of lakes and rivers linked to the boreal forest of the north and the plains and prairie parklands of the western interior. These same rivers also connected the Ohio Valley to important market cities like New Orleans and Saint Louis. Kentucky represented the western edge of Anglo-American colonial settlement and the eastern edge of territory inhabited by the confederation of northwestern Indians.

The Origin of Zhaazhaawanibiisens

This confederacy of northwestern Indians had evolved from the Indigenous alliance network of Wyandot and Algonquian peoples linked to colonial New France. Following the Seven Years' War, many *doodemag*—or bands—left their Great Lakes homelands to join a reimagined alliance in the Ohio country led by the Shawnee and their Delaware allies. This expanded alliance was increasingly animated by a new pan-Indian Nativism that rejected any form of assimilation to the new world of European empires and their colonies. The Nativists called for a rejection of European social and material cultures, and they encouraged violent opposition to the western expansion of colonial settlements. This confederacy was also linked through the diplomacy of the Shawnees with a coalition of Nativists among the Creek and Cherokee peoples in the Southeast. Kentucky thus sat at a crossroads between the expansion of Anglo-America and a broad transregional Nativist alliance linking northern and southern Indian confederations.[13]

John Tanner, the son, was taken captive from his father's homestead in 1790 during a time when warriors from the Northwest confederacy regularly raided settlements throughout the Kentucky and Ohio country. That same year, the United States army, under the command of Josiah Harmar, suffered a devastating loss to the coalition of Northwest Native peoples led by the Miami leader Little Turtle. This defeat followed the

13. For Nativists and the Northwest confederacy, see Gregory Evans Dowd, *A Spirited Resistance: The North American Indian Struggle for Unity, 1745–1815* (Baltimore, 1992), xx, 20–21.

divisive and failed Treaty of Fort Harmar (1789) that ultimately culminated in the Treaty of Greenville in 1795.[14]

For Native peoples in the Trans-Appalachian West, raiding settlements was a form of resistance designed to halt the trajectory of American expansion. It was also a response to the immediate problems of violence and land seizure committed by settlers who mistakenly thought of the western lands claimed by the Republic as unsettled territory. But raids could also be a way to counter population loss. When Native families suffered a loss, they often sought to replace the departed loved one with a captive taken from their enemies. This practice weakened their foes while rebuilding their own community. In the spring of 1790, two men, Manidoogiizhig and his son Giishkako, from the Saginaw Ojibwe village below the southern shore of Lake Huron, led a party of five Anishinaabe warriors into the Ohio country. Manidoogiizhig had recently lost another son through illness, and his wife had begged the warrior to bring her a child to take his place. Tanner, aged nine, was taken by the warriors, renamed Zhaazhaawanibiisens, and brought to live among the Saginaw Ojibweg. Manidoogiizhig, however, would not accept Zhaazhaawanibiisens as his son and treated him cruelly. As a result of this ostracism, he was never truly integrated into his adoptive family or the Anishinaabe community at Saginaw.[15]

After two difficult years at Saginaw, Zhaazhaawanibiisens met with good fortune when Manidoogiizhig decided to sell him to another Anishinaabe *ogimaa*, or leader, who had also lost a son. This ogimaa, Naadinookwa, was an extraordinary figure. She was an Odawa woman who was both a leader and prominent trader from the village of L'Arbre Croche, located in the straits of Mackinac. Saddened by the loss of her son, Naadinookwa provided Manidoogiizhig with a significant quantity of trade goods in order to take Zhaazhaawanibiisens into her family. She treated

14. For Harmer's defeat, see Colin G. Calloway, *The Victory with No Name: The Native American Defeat of the First American Army* (New York, 2015); Dowd, *A Spirited Resistance*, 106; White, *Middle Ground*, 420; *The Proceedings of a Court of Enquiry, Held at the Special Request of Brigadier General Josiah Harmar, to Investigate His Conduct, as Commanding Officer of the Expedition against the Miami Indians, 1790: The Same Having Been Transmitted by Major General St. Clair, to the Secretary of the United States, for the Department of War* (Philadelphia, 1791).

15. Tanner, *Narrative of the Captivity*, 23–37. For captive adoption and mourning-war rituals, see Daniel K. Richter, "War and Culture: The Iroquois Experience," *WMQ*, 3d Ser., XL (1983), 528–559. For the practice of raising and covering the dead among Algonquian peoples, see White, *Middle Ground*, 79–82.

her adopted son with great affection and kindness and began socializing him to be Anishinaabe. Although Zhaazhaawanibiisens readily adapted to his new life, Naadinookwa worried that American traders or settlers might attempt to return him to his family. Accordingly, she decided to move for a time to the Red River valley. Tagaweninne, her husband, was an Ojibwe from this region, and the couple resolved to join his extended family farther west. Because she was well regarded as a trader and political leader, several other families from L'Arbre Croche and Mackinac decided to join her. The move promised to provide economic opportunity while removing Naadinookwa and her people from the fighting with the Americans. It would also take Zhaazhaawanibiisens away from any American traders who had contacts in the Ohio and Kentucky settlements.[16]

The Great Lakes and the Western Trade
When Naadinookwa and Tagaweninne moved from Mackinac to the Red River valley with their adopted son, they followed a pattern of long-term seasonal migration practiced by Anishinaabe peoples from the Great Lakes that stretched back to the very origins of the fur trade. The French produced a record of this pattern of migration from the Great Lakes onto the plains and then overland by river to the Hudson Bay coast as early as 1660, when Jesuit missionaries began to explore the possibility of expanding their missions beyond the Saint Lawrence River valley into the Pays d'en Haut, or upper country. The Pays d'en Haut, which to the French signified all of the interior northwest of the Saint Lawrence River valley, remained largely a mystery to Europeans in the first decades after colonization. Few traders ventured into the region, and the French instead relied on Native traders, who both hunted and traded for pelts, to bring the pelts down to French settlements in exchange for manufactured goods.[17]

In 1660, the Jesuit Gabriel Druillettes met a Native man named Awatanik, who had just completed such a journey. Druillettes was working to compile a map of the Pays d'en Haut and its peoples in the hope of expanding the Jesuit mission system into the West. As part of this project, he traveled up the Saguenay River, making his way toward Hudson Bay. Approximately ninety miles above Tadoussac, the oldest trading post in New France, he wrote, "I encountered eighty Savages; and among them was one named Awatanik, a man of importance because he was a Captain

16. Tanner, *Narrative of the Captivity*, 34–44.

17. For the French fur trade, see Witgen, *An Infinity of Nations*, 124–127; White, *Middle Ground*, 94–124; and Innis, *The Fur Trade in Canada*, 9–118.

in rank." In effect, Awatanik was an ogimaa traveling with his doodem. Druillettes identified this doodem as Algonquians from "the country of the Nipisiriniens," meaning that Awatanik and his people were Nipissing-Anishinaabeg from the territory north of Lake Huron. Awatanik boasted deep connections to New France. According to Druillettes, he had been baptized and had taken the Christian name Michael, a sign that he maintained an ongoing relationship with the Jesuits, and, by extension, with New France. More important from Druillettes's perspective, he made his way to the French settlements after a two-year journey through the Northwest interior, and he willingly provided the missionary with a description of his travels.[18]

In the summer of 1658, Awatanik and his doodem left their homeland north of Lake Huron and made their way to Bow-e-ting, known as the falls of Saint Mary, or Sault Sainte Marie to the French. Bow-e-ting was an important Anishinaabe village and a gateway to the West. After portaging the falls, which connected Lake Huron to Lake Superior, the Nipissing doodem made their way west along the southern shore "lined with Algonkin Nations." Algonkin or Algonquian was the general designation that the French applied to the multitude of Indigenous peoples who spoke an Algonquian language and lived in the region they identified as the Pays d'en Haut. These peoples included the Anishinaabeg—the Boodewaadamiig, Odawaag, and Ojibweg who resided in the Great Lakes—and other speakers of Anisahinaabemowin, such as the Nipissing. Awatanik's doodem, "advancing by short stages," reached the end of Lake Superior, where they traded with peoples from the headwaters of the Mississippi River. From the west end of the lake, they then made their way northeast by river until they reached the mouth of the Nelson River at the top of Hudson Bay. Awatanik and his band "procured a great abundance of Beavers in exchange for hatchets, cleavers, knives, and other like commodities, which they carried thither," as they moved south along the shoreline to James Bay. Druillettes concluded: "After our Algonkin had visited all the Nations surrounding the Bay, and had laden himself with various presents sent by those peoples to the French and Algonkins of these regions,—to attract them to their Bay, . . . he left the seacoast to

---

18. Reuben Gold Thwaites, ed., *The Jesuit Relations and Allied Documents*, 73 vols. (Cleveland, Ohio, 1896–1901), XLV, 217 (hereafter cited as *JR*). For baptism and the significance of taking a Christian name among the Native allies of New France, see Witgen, *An Infinity of Nations*, 104–107.

proceed inland and seek a road to Tadoussac," a French settlement at the confluence of the Saint Lawrence and Saguenay Rivers.[19]

Awatanik and his people brought manufactured goods into the Northwest, trading with Native peoples without direct access to the French. This circuit took two years, but it allowed the Nipissing to return to their homeland with an ample supply of beaver pelts, which they could trade for European merchandise. In the first decades following European colonial settlement, a destructive war between the Dutch-allied Iroquois confederacy, based in the Hudson and Mohawk River valleys, and the French-allied Huron confederacy interrupted trade throughout the Northeast. A temporary peace between the Iroquois and New France and its network of Native allies made it safe to resume long-distance travel. The Nipissing-Anishinaabeg, experts at making and piloting birch bark canoes, took advantage of this opportunity to resume trading in the Northwest interior, where the thickest and most-valued beaver pelts could be harvested.[20]

Many Anishinaabe people began to make a similar calculation in the decades following the British takeover of New France. In the aftermath of the Seven Years' War, British Canada's more liberal policy regarding the fur trade spurred competition across the region. The North West Company, the short-lived XY Company, and various American and Canadian traders worked hard to attract Native hunters to new posts throughout the region. During the French era, Rainy Lake, northwest of Lake Superior, had been at the edge of Anishinaabe country. In 1793, however, the trader at the Hudson's Bay Company post at Rainy Lake complained about a reduction of trade. "Much could not be expected," he reported "as these lands was in a manner ruined . . . that the major part of the Indians that belonged to this place has since gone to the red river a place more suitable for the support of their families." Similarly, the Hudson's Bay Company trader at the Dauphine River post reported on the presence of "Red Lake Indians" from the upper Mississippi Valley trading

19. *JR*, XLV, 219 ("lined"), 225 ("advancing"), 229 ("great abundance"), 233 ("presents"). For a concise explanation of the role and authority of the ogimaa among the Anishinaabeg, see Carry Miller, *Ogimaag: Anishinaabeg Leadership, 1760–1845* (Lincoln, Nebr., 2010), 65–112.

20. For the Beaver Wars, see White, *Middle Ground*, 29–34; and Daniel K. Richter, *Ordeal of the Longhouse: The Peoples of the Iroquois League in the Era of European Colonization* (Williamsburg, Va., and Chapel Hill, N.C., 1992), 50–74. The Jesuits would make a similar journey to Hudson Bay in 1667 (*JR*, LVI, 149–217).

with North West Company traders north of the Assiniboine River in the summer of 1795.[21]

Tagaweninne, the adoptive father of Zhaazhaawanibiisens, would have been part of this pattern of western migration among the Ojibweg. Anishinaabe doodemag from the Great Lakes moved into the headwaters region of the upper Mississippi Valley in the late eighteenth century. During this same period, British and Canadian traders began to establish posts inland along the Assiniboine and Red Rivers. Many Anishinaabeg from the upper Mississippi and the Great Lakes began to make extended forays into this region, expanding the beaver pelt trade to include buffalo hunting. The northern Ojibweg from Rainy Lake and Lake of the Woods, identified as Muskego by Anishinaabeg, had been shifting their trade and hunting between English posts associated with the Hudson's Bay Company and French posts in the Great Lakes since the early colonial period. They, too, sought out new trade opportunities among the many trading posts in the Red River valley and along the Assiniboine River as far west as Turtle Mountain. Extended trading voyages, as in the time of Awatanik, could last for one to two years. With the increased competition among rival traders, many Anishinaabe people, like the family of Tagaweninne, began to reside in the region permanently.[22]

Farther to the west, at Brandon House on the Assiniboine River north of Turtle Mountain, Hudson's Bay Company traders remarked on the presence of Ojibwe hunters from the Lake Superior country during the time when Naadinookwa and Zhaazhaawanibiisens arrived in the region. Traders at this post, like the trader at Rainy Lake, lamented their competition with "Canadians," or North West Company traders. Native hunters

21. John McKay, Lac La Pluie Journal, Dec. 12, 1793, B.105/a/1, Hudson's Bay Company Archives (HBCA), Archives of Manitoba, Winnipeg, Canada; John Best, River Dauphin Journal, Aug. 9, 1795, HBCA, B.51/a/1. For the movement of the fur trade into Rupert's Land, see Peers, *Ojibwa of Western Canada*, 63–98; Arthur J. Ray, *Indians in the Fur Trade: Their Roles as Trappers, Hunters, and Middlemen in the Lands Southwest of Hudson Bay, 1660–1870* (Toronto, 1998); and E. E. Rich, *The Fur Trade and Northwest to 1857* (Toronto, 1967).

22. For the movement of Anishinaabe peoples into the upper Mississippi, see Harold Hickerson, *Chippewa Indians II: Ethnohistory of Mississippi Bands and Pillager and Winnibigoshish Bands of Chippewa* (New York, 1974), 97–98. For an account of the history and origin of the Muskeego, see William W. Warren, *History of the Ojibway People* (1885; rpt. Saint Paul, Minn., 1984), 45, 85. For migration of Anishinaabe people into the Northwest, or Rupert's Land, see Peers, *Ojibwa of Western Canada*, 14–21.

frequently split their trade, even when they received goods on credit from the Hudson's Bay Company. In the winter of 1795, for example, the post trader reported: "Two of the Coterays came in with my horses brot a good many skins at night they paid their credit and got drunk, they are much in want of wampum beads, silver works and steel traps, we cannot get any of them." Coterays was a designation for the Ojibweg from Lac Courte Oreilles, an important Ansihinaabe village south of Lake Superior in the heart of the Northwest Territory claimed by the United States. The Co-terays frequented the Brandon House post throughout the summer and into the winter of 1796, at times bringing "made," or processed, beaver pelts that they hunted on credit. At other times, they hunted buffalo, which they sold to the post traders in direct one-off transactions. As the company trader noted, these Coteray Indians sought high-status goods for their peltry. They demanded items such as wampum, silver jewelry, and steel traps, and the trader fretted that without these goods he would lose their trade to the North West Company. This Hudson's Bay Company trader's description of Ojibwe hunters in the Assiniboine River valley as relatively affluent matches the account of Zhaazhaawanibiisens, who re-marked that his silver bracelets and ornamental jewelry gave him away during his ambush of the Assiniboine hunter.[23]

The Lac Courte Oreilles Ojibweg visiting Brandon House were part of a flourishing community that had evolved over centuries of alliance between the Anishinaabeg, the Assiniboine, and the Cree. These Coteray Indians visited the Brandon House post and ventured out onto the plains to hunt with people that the Hudson's Bay Company employees identified as Assiniboine, Cree, and "Soetis." Soetis, like Coteray, was a mangled Anglicized version of the French name Saulteaux, referring to Ojibwe-speaking peoples who had migrated permanently to the Red River valley during the late eighteenth century. (Saulteaux was a variation of the word "sauteur" (people of the rapids) which had been applied to the Anishi-naabeg residing at Sault Sainte Marie in the seventeenth century). In ad-dition to trading at Brandon House and at the North West Company post during the winter of 1795–1796, the Lac Courte Oreilles hunters, along

23. John Linklater, Brandon House Journal, Dec. 9, 1795, HBCA, B.22/a/3; Victor Lytwyn, *The Fur Trade of the Little North: Indians, Pedlars, and Englishman East of Lake Winnipeg, 1760–1821* (Winnipeg, Canada, 1986); Lytwyn, "The Anishinabeg and the Fur Trade," in Thorold J. Tronrud and A. Ernest Epp, eds., *Thunder Bay: From Rivalry to Unity* (Thunder Bay, Canada, 1995), 16–35. For the western migration and rising affluence of Anishinaabe traders, see Peers, *Ojibwa of Western Canada*, 63–98.

with the Saulteux, Cree, and Assiniboine, made a brief sojourn deeper into the plains to raid the Mandan.[24]

The following summer, the company trader reported interactions with "Cordonee Indians" from "Michliamackinac." Cordonees was likely a variation on Courte Oreilles, and this time the trader linked this Ojibwe designation to the Anishinaabe village and trading post in the straits of Mackinac dominated by the Odawaag. In May 1796, he recorded that "the Cordonees arrived nine in number in two buffalo skin canoes, brought plenty of furs which they intend to carry to Montreal with them, there being neither liquor or goods here to trade it with." They took no credit, but over the course of the summer they made a small number of direct trades with both the Hudson's Bay Company and the North West Company. They reserved most of their peltry, however, believing they would do better to trade it in Canada. They also joined the Cree and Assiniboine on a summer raid, most likely against the Sioux.[25]

During the subsequent trading season in 1797 and 1798, the traders at Brandon House north of Turtle Mountain recorded a similar mix of Native trading partners. In addition to the Assiniboine and Cree, the traders again noted the presence of Mackinac Indians at the post. In late May, one trader, Thomas Miller, wrote that "the Makinac Indians came in with about one hundred prime beaver skins, they paid twenty beaver of their debt and traded 12." He also lamented that "the Canadians will get the rest as I have no brandy." In addition to luxury items, Anishinaabe hunters in the Northwest demanded hospitality, food, and alcohol in exchange for entering into an ongoing relationship with a trader. Once again, however, the Mackinac hunters, most likely a combination of Odawa and Ojibwe people, announced their intent to return to the Great Lakes with the majority of their peltry. On June 3, 1797, Miller recorded, "They mean to set off tomorrow, one of them a young man remains here called Wapo by name." Miller was referring to Wabooz, or the Hare, who received credit at Brandon House and hunted beaver throughout the summer and into the winter months. He periodically delivered processed pelts even after he paid off his debt and was frequently at the post along with Cree and Assiniboine bands that were following a similar pattern of hunting and trading. In November, Miller documented the arrival of twenty "Chippeway" Indians who took on debt and then left to

24. John Linklater, Brandon House Journal, Aug. 15, 1795, HBCA, B.22/a/3. For the Native peoples engaged in this trade, see J. M. Bumstead, *Fur Trade Wars: The Founding of Western Canada* (Manitoba, Canada, 1999), 35–48.

25. Thomas Miller, Brandon House Journal, May 25, 1796, HBCA, B.22/a/4.

hunt for the winter. This seemed to be a different band of Ojibwe hunters because the trader distinguished them from the Mackinac Indians. This description—"Chippeway" rather than Saulteux—also marked them as from the Great Lakes, as opposed to the Red River valley. Indeed, a multitude of Ansihinaabe doodemag from the Great Lakes converged on the Red River region at the end of the eighteenth century. The expansion of multiple American and Canadian trading outfits inland from Hudson Bay and Great Lakes posts resulted in a fierce competition and a booming fur trade.[26]

The Education of Zhaazhaawanibiisens

The trading ledger at Brandon House during the late 1790s mirrored the experience of Zhaazhaawanibiisens during this same period. He wrote about the moment when he arrived in the Northwest with Naadinookwa: "We started to go up the Red River and in two days came to the mouth of the Assinneboin, where we found great numbers of Ojibbeways and Ottawwaws encamped." They found the family of Tagaweninne, gathered with other Ojibwe and Odawa families preparing to disperse for the winter hunting season. Their arrival and reunion, however, was marred by tragedy. Tagaweniine and his oldest son, Giiwedin, had both died during their journey into the Northwest, leaving Naadinookwa's family without their senior male hunters. One of Tagaweninne's relatives agreed to hunt for Naadinookwa's family, and they ascended the Assiniboine onto the plains to pass the winter with two other Ojibwe families. They settled near a trader and were soon joined by four lodges of Cree hunters and their families. They immediately began to hunt buffalo and trap beaver, with Naadinookwa and the kin of Tagaweninne teaching her two surviving sons—Wamegonabiew and the adopted Zhaazhaawanibiisens—how to hunt and trap.[27]

After a successful fall hunting season, the game began to grow scarce,

---

26. Ibid., May 30, June 3, Nov. 9, 1797, HBCA B.22/a/5. On exchange and gift giving in the fur trade, see Bruce M. White, "The Trade Assortment: The Meanings of Merchandise in the Ojibwa Fur Trade," in Sylvie Dépatie et al., eds., *Vingt ans aprés Habitants et marchands: lectures de l'histoire des XVIIe et XVIIIe siècles canadiens/ Habitants and Marchands, Twenty Years Later: Reading the History of Seventeenth- and Eighteenth-Century Canada* (Montreal and Kingston, 1998); White, "A Skilled Game of Exchange: Ojibway Fur Trade Protocol," *Minnesota History*, L (1987), 229–240; E. E. Rich, "Trade Habits and Economic Motivation among the Indians of North America," *Canadian Journal of Economics and Political Science*, XXVI (1960), 35–53.

27. Tanner, *Narrative of the Captivity*, 50–53 (quotation on 50).

and the Cree departed to winter in their home country. Naadinookwa and her family moved their camp to the post of the trader who had accompanied them from Red River. With her husband and oldest son dead, Naadinookwa remained vulnerable, but she received an offer to move her family to the camp of Peshaube, a prominent Odawa war chief originally from Lake Huron. He had heard of the plight of Naadinookwa and sought her out as kin to aid her family until she and her sons could establish themselves on their own. In the Red River valley, far from the extended kinship networks of their village communities, both Peshaube and Naadinookwa needed each another. Peshaube offered to hunt for Naadinookwa and her family, but he needed their labor as well in order to be successful. Peshaube hunted with three Odawa men in the country to the northwest of Lake Winnipeg. The men were in the Northwest without their wives and families, so taking on Naadinookwa and her children—especially her daughter and daughter-in-law—greatly enhanced their ability to process peltry and generally maintain their camp. Male hunters were entirely dependent on the fur-processing skills of women, and these Odawa men were on their own. After a successful winter hunt in the Souris River country, Peshaube, Naadinookwa, and their companions made their way back to the Assiniboine River valley with the intention of returning to Lake Huron.[28]

Like Wabooz, the Mackinac Indian who took credit at Brandon House, Peshaube and his hunting companions decided to put off their return to the Great Lakes and remain in the West. Making their way toward the Grand Portage, Peshaube and his people stopped at a large Assiniboine-Cree village at a rapids on the Assiniboine River. Both the North West Company and the Hudson's Bay Company had established posts at this location. While they stopped to trade, reprovision, and make birch bark canoes, the Odawa hunters learned that the village was preparing for a raid into the Missouri country. The Mandan had invited the Cree and Assiniboine to join them on a raid against the Hidatsa. One of the Odawa men, a distinguished warrior named Waasese, decided to join the raid, and the others could not dissuade him. Reluctant to leave their companion

28. Ibid., 54, 56–57. Susan Sleeper-Smith has argued that in the Northwest interior, "the region's ability to export peltry depended on the processing skills of women, who were increasingly the center of the households." See Sleeper-Smith, *Indigenous Prosperity and American Conquest*, 96. See also Lucy Eldersveld Murphy, *A Gathering of Rivers: Indians, Métis, and Mining in the Western Great Lakes, 1737–1832* (Lincoln, Nebr., 2000), 24–25.

behind, Peshaube and the two other Odawa men accompanied the raiding party in order to visit the Mandan. As a result, Naadinookwa decided to forego her return to the Great Lakes and remained in the Red River valley with her children. They rejoined Peshaube and his companions in the fall and resumed their hunting in the Souris River region, where they had access to both beaver and buffalo—and to traders from the Hudson's Bay and North West Companies.[29]

Fierce competition among traders in the Northwest combined with the opportunity to trade and raid into the Missouri River valley drew many Anishinaabe peoples into the region for extended periods at the end of the eighteenth century. They moved between hunting territory in the western Assiniboine River valley and a shifting array of trading posts from the junction of the Assiniboine and Red Rivers to the Grand Portage leading back to the Lake Superior country. In the winter of 1797–1798, when Wabooz, the Mackinac Indians, and twenty "Chippeway Indians" took credit at Brandon House, the Ojibweg from Rainy Lake also visited the post for the first time. On December 22, 1797, the post commander wrote in his ledger that "Brother . . . Grand Chief from Lac la Pluie . . . visited me after taking a dram and making a pipe of tobacco, the Old man said, my friend, the account I heard of you from the Canadians made me believe you was a perfect devil." Brother, it seems, had taken credit with North West Company traders and been warned to stay away from the Hudson's Bay Company post. The ogimaa, however, traded twenty made beaver pelts at Brandon House.[30]

Competition between the Hudson's Bay and the North West Companies allowed Anishinaabe hunter-traders like Brother, Wabooz, Peshaube, and Naadinookwa—from Rainy Lake, Lac Courte Oreilles, Lake Huron, and Mackinac—to split their trade between different posts in order to maximize their return. In the fall of 1798, the post commander at Brandon House complained that "two houses of Canadians is to be here and will hurt us much, also two houses only six miles above me also two houses at the burnt carrying place so I shall have seven houses to contend with this year more than was the last." Brother returned to Brandon House again during the 1798–1799 trading season. Wabooz remained year-around in the Red River valley for six years, taking credit at Brandon

29. Tanner, *Narrative of the Captivity*, 58–59.

30. Thomas Miller, Brandon House Journal, Dec. 22, 1797, HBCA, B.22/a/5. For a history of Ojibweg in the Rainy Lake region, see Hickerson, *Chippewa Indians II*, 75–103.

House through the spring of 1801. He returned in the company of "Mackinac Indians" to trade at the Hudson's Bay Company's Red River post in the winter of 1804. Peshaube and his Odawa companions had been hunting and trading in the Red River and Assiniboine valleys "several years" before the arrival of Naadinookwa. They came to the Northwest from Lake Huron at the same time as Ojibweg from Leech Lake and Red Lake in 1790. These Great Lakes and upper Mississippi doodemag remained in the region for more than a decade, generally hunting and trading with the North West Company, as did Naadinookwa and her extended family. Accordingly, their paths frequently overlapped, as they did during the winter of 1800–1801 when they hunted for the North West Company's Alexander Henry at Pembina on the Red River.[31]

Odawa and Ojibwe peoples from the upper Mississippi and Great Lakes prospered in the Northwest interior region that the British called Rupert's Land in the decade before the turn of the century. Whether entering the region as permanent migrants or commuting between the Northwest and their homelands, extended families of hunters joined other families to form temporary winter bands and to harvest maple sugar in the spring. They came together with their allies the Cree, Assiniboine, and Saulteaux to create summer raiding parties and to take goods on credit at a shifting number of temporary posts erected each fall. This was the social world in which John Tanner entered adulthood as Zhaazhaawanibiisens, the son of Naadinookwa. He received added instruction in hunting and trapping from Peshaube and later from another well-regarded Odawa ogimaa, Wagetoat, who also acted as a father figure. These relationships were important, but Naadinookwa shaped the development of her adopted son as an Anishinaabe person. She began to teach him to track and read the land for signs of animals the moment they arrived in the Northwest. Like the male hunters Peshaube and Wagetoat, Naadinookwa earned a reputation among the traders as a provider and "was in the habit of receiving every year a chief's dress and ornaments, and a ten gallon keg of spirits."

31. Rob Goodwin, Brandon House Journal, Sept. 22, 1798, HBCA, B.22/a/6 ("two houses"). For Brother, see ibid., Dec. 25, 1798, B.22/a/6. For Wapo (Wabooz), see ibid., Mar. 19, 1799, HBCA, B.22/a/6; ibid., Jan. 2, 5, Feb. 26, Apr. 8, 1800, HBCA, B.22/a/7; ibid., Feb. 28, Apr. 24, 1801, HBCA, B.22/a/8; John McKay, Red River Journal, Jan. 2, 5, Mar. 6, 1804, HBCA, B.22/a/11. See also Tanner, *Narrative of the Captivity*, 54 ("several years"). For the Leech Lake and Red Lake Ojibweg in the Northwest, see Barry M. Gough, ed., *The Journal of Alexander Henry the Younger, 1799–1814*, I, *Red River and the Journey to the Missouri* (Toronto, 1988), 25. For Naadinookwa's trading with Henry at Pembina, see Tanner, *Narrative of the Captivity*, 79–80.

Zhaazhaawanibiisens thus grew up the son of an ogimaa at the zenith of the fur trade in the Northwest.[32]

Zhaazhaawanibiisens's complete immersion in this world was evident when he wrestled with the lone Assiniboine hunter on the prairie in the early 1800s. His language, his dress, and the claims of kinship he made all signaled his identity as an Ojibwe in a way that the Assiniboine recognized immediately. He did not look at the man shouting "Ojibbeway" and see a white man. Instead, he saw the Ojibwe son of Naadinookwa, a young man on a quest to recover his stolen horse. This quest came to a distinctly Ojibwe conclusion. After this encounter, Zhaazhaawanibiisens discovered that the Assiniboine who had stolen his horse had sold it. He responded to this turn of events as an Ojibwe warrior, by stealing a horse from the thief. Zhaazhaawanibiisens emerged as a leader among the Red River Ojibweg, on at least one occasion accepting the chief's robe and keg of rum on his mother's behalf. His right to do so was accepted by the Ojibweg gathered at Pembina and by the North West Company trader granting credit for the winter hunt. Zhaazhaawanibiisens gained a reputation as a prodigious hunter and a man capable of conducting a medicine hunt in times of want—that is, he sang to the trickster figure Nanabozho, asking for his intercession with the earth mother, and was rewarded with *mazinibii'iganan*, drawings of game animals that came to the hunter after prayer and allowed the dreamer / drawer to track and kill his prey. Zhaazhaawanibiisens forgot English and became a fluent speaker of Anishinaabemowin, the language of the Odawaag and Ojibweg. Some ten years after his capture, he entered adulthood as an Anishinaabe-inini, an Anishinaabe man.[33]

The Disillusion of Zhaazhaawanibiisens

Although Zhaazhaawanibiisens accepted and even reveled in his immersion in the social world created by the Anishinaabeg in the Northwest, he understood that he once belonged in the white world created by the settlers of the U.S. Republic. When he became old enough to live independently of his mother, one of the North West Company traders tried to persuade him to stop living among the Indians and remain at the post

32. Tanner, *Narrative of the Captivity*, 102 (quotation). Women occasionally assumed the leadership status usually reserved for men; for this phenomenon, see Bruce M. White, "The Woman Who Married a Beaver: Trade Patterns and Gender Roles in the Ojibwa Fur Trade," *Ethnohistory*, XLVI (1999), 109–147. For the political roles of women, see Miller, *Ogimaag*, 66–69.

33. Tanner, *Narrative of the Captivity*, 192–193, 209.

working for the trading outfit. Zhaazhaawanibiisens thought about it, but in the end found the idea of such a sedentary way of life unappealing. Shortly after making this decision, however, he refused to marry the daughter of Wagetoat. Although the ogimaa and his mother agreed on the match, Zhaazhaawanibiisens rejected the proposal, hesitant about his long-term future among the Anishinaabeg. "I had as yet thought little of marriage among the Indians," he later recalled, "still thinking I should return before I became old, to marry to the whites." Yet a little more than a year later, Zhaazhaawanibiisens, now in his early twenties, began to court a young woman named Miskwabunokwa. The match was of their own design and not negotiated by the elders of their respective families. At first, Naadinookwa objected, but eventually she consented, and the couple married. Even though he had earlier spurned an arranged marriage with the thought of possibly returning to live in the United States, Zhaazhaawanibiisens now chose to begin his married life and raise a family with an Ojibwe woman.[34]

For years, Zhaazhaawanibiisens prospered in the Northwest. He had three children, and he was well regarded as a hunter. He shifted his residence among the multitude of Anishinaabe doodemag that gathered at trading posts in the spring and fall and that dispersed in smaller numbers for winter hunts. His decisions each season reflected his opinions about what hunting grounds would prove most profitable and which ogimaa he most respected. After 1800, however, the fur trade in the Northwest became increasingly volatile, and a series of unfortunate events radically disrupted the life Zhaazhaawanibiisens had made for himself.[35]

North West Company traders operating in the Red River region had long maintained a base of operations at Pembina. The Hudson's Bay Company usually established posts farther north and west, but they, too, eventually established a post at Pembina. When they did, the North West trader feared the competition would raise exchange rates. To prevent price gouging, he refused to offer credit in the fall to the many Anishinaabe hunters who regularly traded with the company. In spite of this disadvantage, Zhaazhaawanibiisens had a successful hunt, and midway through the winter he sought and received credit from the Hudson's Bay Company trader. In the spring when he brought in his peltry, the North West Company trader attempted to claim them. Zhaazhaawanibiisens

34. Ibid., 96, 100 (quotation), 115–118.

35. For the allocation of hunting territories among the Ojibweg, see Miller, *Ogimaag*, 93–94.

refused to hand over his furs and announced his intent to make good his debt to the Hudson's Bay Company. A physical altercation ensued with the North Western trader pulling a gun and yelling, "You have always . . . belonged to the north west." Zhaazhaawanibiisens disarmed the man and vowed to trade exclusively with the Hudson's Bay Company because of his ill-treatment.[36]

Zhaazhaawanibiisens eventually repaired his relationship with the North West Company, but this violent confrontation reflected the increasing volatility of the fur trade in the Northwest. The beaver population declined sharply in the aftermath of a deadly epidemic affecting the animals in 1797, with lasting consequences for at least two decades. This scarcity forced hunters from Red River to venture more frequently to the south into Sioux territory, which resulted in an escalation of conflict as the rival Indigenous alliance networks competed for the same resources. During this atmosphere of increasing economic uncertainty and social unrest, the message of the Shawnee prophet Tenskwatawa, which had been animating Native resistance to American expansion all along the frontier of the U.S. Republic, reached the Red River valley.[37]

The prophecy of Tenskwatawa called for Native peoples to unite and separate themselves from the social world and material culture of white settlers. Multiple emissaries carried this message to the Anishinaabeg in the Northwest, including Manidoogiizhig, the Saginaw Ojibwe man who took Zhaazhaawanibiisens captive as a child. "As long as I remained among the Indians, I made it my business to conform," Zhaazhaawanibiisens later recalled, but he regarded the Shawnee prophecy with overt skepticism. Although he appreciated the call for temperance and an end to violence among Native peoples, he could not abide the admonition to give up practical things such as flint, steel, dogs, and other objects believed to have originated with white people. This defiance undermined his social standing. "I found," he later wrote, "that though my skepticism might not be offensive to the Great God, . . . still it was highly so to those who were pleased to stile themselves his messengers."[38]

When an Ojibwe man who wintered with Zhaazhaawanibiisens began to claim that he, too, received a message from Gichi-Manidoo, or the Great

36. Tanner, *Narrative of the Captivity,* 183.

37. Ibid., 39, 89. For the decline in the beaver population, see Peers, *Ojibwa of Western Canada,* 39.

38. Tanner, *Narrative of the Captivity,* 157 ("conform"), 178 ("skepticism"). For Tenskwatawa and his message, see Dowd, *A Spirited Resistance,* 129–131.

Spirit, Zhaazhaawanibiisens met these claims with derision. This new prophet, Aiskawbawis, was a widower and a poor hunter, but his alleged spiritual power elevated his social status. By assuming the role of shaman, he also exempted himself from the social relations of production—hunting, fishing, gathering—by asserting that he contributed to the life of the doodem through prayer and visions. Confronted by the open hostility of Zhaazhaawanibiisens, the new shaman poisoned the minds of his enemy's family. When the siblings of Miskwabunokwa died from illness, the shaman convinced her mother-in-law that Zhaazhaawanibiisens caused their death through bad medicine. Eventually, Miskwabunokwa herself came to believe this story, and she left her husband, resulting in the estrangement of Zhaazhaawanibiisens from her extended family, the kinship unit he had lived with since becoming an independent adult.[39]

The life that Zhaazhaawanibiisens had built for himself in the Red River valley began to slowly unravel. Feeling unwelcome within the doodem he had wintered with for the past decade, he accepted an invitation to hunt for the Hudson's Bay Company. In 1812, Thomas Douglas, the earl of Selkirk, acquired a controlling interest in the company in order to establish a settler colony at the junction of the Assiniboine and Red Rivers. This was an ill-conceived scheme to create a permanent European settlement in Rupert's Land that could provide a new home for Highland Scots immigrants displaced by land enclosures in their own country. The settlers were not prepared to survive in the Native New World that ordered the social relations and political economy of Rupert's Land. Recognizing this fact, Selkirk hired Indigenous hunters to provide for the colony, which was never successful as a self-supporting agricultural settlement. Zhaazhaawanibiisens, who had remained on good terms with the Hudson's Bay Company, was thus hired as a hunter.[40]

Zhaazhaawanibiisens, although shunned by his in-laws, was still living with his wife and managed to pass a profitable year as a hunter for the company. After his wife left, however, he struggled to provide for himself and his children. He wintered near Leech Lake in the upper Mississippi, but without a partner he was forced to spend a great deal of time performing domestic tasks, limiting his ability to hunt and trap. The ogimaa of this village urged him to take another wife among his people, but

39. Tanner, *Narrative of the Captivity*, 212.
40. For Selkirk and the Red River colony of the Hudson's Bay Company, see Peers, *Ojibwa of Western Canada*, 89–91; Bumstead, *Fur Trade Wars*, 153–170.

Zhaazhaawanibiisens refused and began to contemplate a return to the United States.[41]

Even as he imagined leaving the Northwest and returning to his old life, out of necessity Zhaazhaawanibiisens returned to the village of his wife's people at Lake of the Woods in the spring. His skill as a hunter, especially in a time of growing scarcity, enabled him to preserve some social connections in spite of the ill will of his in-laws. While Zhaazhaawanibiisens sorted out his options, however, the conflict between the North West Company and the Hudson's Bay Company escalated. The governor of the Red River colony, supposedly to ensure a food supply for his settlers, issued a proclamation prohibiting the trade in pemmican—meat from large game animals such as buffalo, elk, or moose, dried and pounded until pulverized, then mixed with dried fruit and the rendered fat of the animal. This food staple was also an important trade item, especially for the mixed-race Canadian traders of the North West Company. They regarded this attempt at prohibiting its trade as a thinly veiled attempt by the Hudson's Bay Company to monopolize the fur trade in the Red River region. Moreover, they did not recognize the authority of the colony's governor, as they believed the colony itself was a violation of the royal Proclamation of 1763 barring British settlement in the West.[42]

In this charged atmosphere, the conflict between the two rival fur-trading companies turned into a violent confrontation. Once again living among the Ojibweg at Lake of the Woods, Zhaazhaawanibiisens recalled, "The traders of the North West Company sent messengers and presents to all the Indians, to call them to join in an attack on the Hudson's Bay establishment at Red River." Zhaazhaawanibiisens ignored the call. "For my own part," he wrote, "I thought these quarrels between relatives unnatural . . . though I had long traded with the people of the North West Company, and considered myself in some measure belonging to them." His statement revealed the extent to which the Indigenous people of the Northwest interior—Assiniboine, Cree, Ojibweg, Saulteaux,

41. Tanner, *Narrative of the Captivity*, 200–201, 214.

42. For the pemmican proclamation, see Bumstead, *Fur Trade Wars*, 93–108; and Peers, *Ojibwa of Western Canada*, 90. For the growing tension between the trading companies, colonial officials at Red River, and the Métis, see Gerhard J. Ens, "The Battle of Seven Oaks and the Articulation of a Metis National Tradition, 1811–1849," in Nicole St-Onge, Carolyn Podruchny, and Brenda Macdougall, eds., *Contours of a People: Metis Family, Mobility, and History* (Norman, Okla., 2012), 93–119; Peers, *Ojibwe of Western Canada*, 89–95.

and the mixed-race traders, both half-breed (Anglophone) and Métis (Francophone)—regarded themselves as connected through kinship to one another and to the trading outfits where they took credit. As a result, this rapidly escalating conflict would prove to be extremely divisive not only for the fur trade but also for the social relations that made the trade possible.[43]

Following the pemmican proclamation, a series of armed conflicts broke out culminating in a defeat of the Hudson's Bay forces at the Battle of Seven Oakes, which ended with the governor of the Hudson's Bay Company's Red River colony dead and the North West Company traders in control of Fort Douglas on the Red River and Brandon House on the Souris. In response, Lord Selkirk led a force into the Northwest and captured Fort William, the main base of operations for the North West Company, located on the Kaministiquia River, near the Grand Portage. He then sent his men to take the North West Company post at Rainy Lake. At this post, the officer in charge of Selkirk's forces met with Zhaazhaawanibiisens and persuaded him to help them capture the North West Company forts on the Red River. "About this time," Zhaazhaawanibiisens later wrote, "I made up my mind to leave the Indian country, and return to the States" because of the "many difficulties" with his in-laws. The officer and a Hudson's Bay Company interpreter "succeeded in convincing me that the Hudson's Bay Company was that which, in the present quarrel, had the right on its side."[44]

With Zhaazhaawanibiisens acting as a guide, the Hudson's Bay Company forces captured the North West Company posts at Pembina and on the Assiniboine River, reasserting their control over the fur trade in the Northwest. The armed conflict between the two companies, the capturing and recapturing of posts, devolved into an inconclusive legal battle. Selkirk insisted that the North West Company men responsible for the governor's death be brought up on charges. They were, but they were acquitted. Shortly thereafter, Selkirk died, and in 1821 the companies merged,

43. Tanner, *Narrative of the Captivity*, 216.

44. Ibid., 217, 218 ("about this time"), 219 ("succeeded"); Ens, "The Battle of Seven Oakes," in St-Onge, Podrunchny, and Macdougall, eds., *Contours of a People*, 93–119; Peers, *Ojibwa of Western Canada*, 91–92; *Statement respecting the Earl of Selkirk's Settlement upon the Red River in North America* ... (1817; rpt. New York, 1968); Lyle Dick, "The Seven Oakes Incident and the Construction of a Historical Tradition, 1816–1970," *Journal of the Canadian Historical Association*, II, no. 1 (1991), 91–113. For the reconquest of Fort William by Selkirk, see Bumstead, *Fur Trade Wars*, 157–164.

ending the competition and restoring a monopoly to the fur trade in the Northwest interior region identified as Rupert's Land by the British.[45]

Converting Native Land into Private Property

While the rival companies battled over the future of the fur trade in court, Zhaazhaawanibiisens attempted to secure a future for himself and his children by returning to the United States. He made his way to Mackinac and from there traveled to Detroit by schooner with a letter of introduction written by the Indian agent to Lewis Cass, the governor of the Michigan Territory. After landing at Detroit in the summer of 1818, twenty-eight years since he had been taken captive at his family farm in Kentucky, Zhaazhaawanibiisens ventured onto the city streets and promptly encountered a number of Saginaw Ojibweg, including Giishkako, the son of Manidoogiizhig, and one of the men who took him captive in 1790. He eventually made his way to the governor's house and presented his letter to the soldier guarding the residence. Governor Cass read the letter, and, after calling for an interpreter, interviewed Zhaazhaawanibiisens about his life story. The governor knew Giishkako, and he sent for the ogimaa and asked him to confirm the story as it related to the capture and relocation of Zhaazhaawanibiisens to Saginaw and then to the Red River valley.[46]

Cass took an interest in Zhaazhaawanibiisens perhaps because his story was not unique. There were a number of white people living among the Native peoples of the Northwest Territory, some like Zhaazhaawanibiisens living as Natives. There were also white people, mainly men, married to Native people and living in Indigenous communities. And, of course, there were mixed-race individuals—some living as Indians residing in villages and wintering in the bush, and some living among the white people who worked in the fur trade. Among Native peoples, identity, like that of Zhaazhaawanibiisens, was a lived cultural experience.

45. Great Britain, Colonial Office, *Papers Relating to the Red River Settlement: viz: Return to an Address from the Honourable House of Commons to His Royal Highness the Prince Regent, Dated 24th June 1819* . . . , (London, 1819), https://www.canadiana.ca/view/oocihm.18595; Ens, "The Battle of Seven Oakes," in St-Onge, Podrunchny, and Macdougall, eds., *Contours of a People*, 93–119; Peers, *Ojibwa of Western Canada*, 91–92; *Statement respecting the Earl of Selkirk's Settlement upon the Red River*; Dick, "The Seven Oakes Incident," *Journal of the Canadian Historical Association*, II, no. 1 (1991), 91–113; Bumstead, *Fur Trade Wars*, 175–214.

46. Tanner, *A Narrative of the Captivity*, 238–244.

Among Americans, in contrast, phenotype, or "race," marked a person as white or colored. The status of a person's racial identity—Native, African American, or mixed-race—however, was fluid in the Northwest Territory. Americans linked race and identity, and they privileged whiteness—white people could not be enslaved, and they could vote, testify in court, and hold public office. Native peoples, in contrast, used kinship and culture to determine identity, belonging, and privilege. Zhaazhaawanibiisens, by virtue of his relationship with Naadinookwa and Tagaweninne, claimed an Ojibwe identity. This identity allowed him to make kinship claims with other Anishinaabe peoples. He could, in effect, reside in Anishinaabe villages and hunt on Anishinaabe lands at places like Red River, Leech Lake, or Mackinac.[47]

Detroit was a city that straddled both of these social worlds, the Native New World and the expanding social world of the U.S. Republic. The city had undergone a significant transformation since its founding. European settlement at this locale began in 1701, when the French established a military post along the strait *(detroit)* of the river connecting two lakes, later named Erie and Saint Clair. The post was created by the colony of New France to manage the fur trade and alliance with Native peoples in the Great Lakes, many of whom occupied seasonal villages along the strait. The settlement at Detroit came under British control following the

47. Tanner's status as a male captive adoptee is most likely what piqued the interest of Lewis Cass, who would have regarded him as white no matter how he lived or dressed. Women, however, particularly mixed-race women, more easily moved between racial categories. Historian Lucy Eldersveld Murphy writes that, "although Creoles were frequently scorned for their perceived cultural, ethnic, racial, and economic differences, some Creole women succeeded in reaching across the cultural divides by navigating the intersections of gender ideals." See Murphy, *Great Lakes Creoles: A French-Indian Community on the Northern Borderlands, Prairie du Chien, 1750–1860* (New York, 2014), 185–186. Murphy applies the term "Creole" to persons of mixed ancestry from the Great Lakes region. For a description of how race, particularly mixed-race identity, functioned in Anishinaabe communities, see Brenda J. Child, *Holding Our World Together: Ojibwe Women and the Survival of Community* (New York, 2012), 37–43. See also Bruce M. White, "The Power of Whiteness; or, The Life and Times of Joe Rolette Jr.," in *Making Minnesota Territory, 1849–1858*, special issue of *Minnesota History*, LVI (1998–1999), 178–197; Jennifer S.H. Brown, *Strangers in Blood: Fur Trade Company Families in Indian Country* (Vancouver, 1980); Sylvia Van Kirk, *Many Tender Ties: Women in Fur-Trade Society, 1670–1870*, 1st American ed. (Norman, Okla., 1983); Tiya Miles, *Ties That Bind: The Story of an Afro-Cherokee Family in Slavery and Freedom* (Berkeley, Calif., 2005); Claudio Saunt, *Black, White, and Indian: Race and the Unmaking of an American Family* (New York, 2005).

Seven Years' War and then American jurisdiction following the Revolution. During this time, the fort and surrounding settlement evolved into a trading entrepôt linking the fur trade and the Northwest interior to the settlements and cities on North America's Eastern Seaboard. When Michigan was organized as a territory in 1805, Detroit, by then the largest non-Native settlement north of the Ohio River, became the capital. It was also the home of the territorial governor.[48]

When Zhaazhaawanibiisens arrived in Detroit, Cass was preparing for a treaty council of enormous political significance. He was negotiating a series of treaties that would remake Native homelands in the Northwest Territory and determine how race, identity, and belonging worked on the frontier of the Republic. After meeting Zhaazhaawanibiisens, Cass provided him with a stipend and sent him to live with his interpreter; "He told me I must wait till he should assemble many Indians and white men, to hold a council at St. Mary's, on the Miami, whence he would send me to my relatives on the Ohio." The year before, in the fall of 1817, Cass had negotiated a treaty with the Wyandot, Seneca, Delaware, Shawnee, Boodewaadamii, Odawa, and Ojibwe peoples that ceded 3,880,320 acres to the United States. Of these acres, 3,360,000 had been the territory of the Wyandots, and they were demanding that the boundaries of their territory, and the extent of their land cession, be renegotiated. At the heart of this disagreement was the struggle over the future of Native peoples with homelands on territory claimed by the United States. From the governor's perspective, Zhaazhaawanibiisens was a piece of this puzzle. What would be the place of Native peoples and those with an identity that did not fit neatly into the binary that defined race in the Republic? These questions would need to be resolved in order for the United States to claim, populate, and incorporate the western territories within the union.[49]

48. For Detroit, see Miles, *The Dawn of Detroit: A Chronicle of Slavery and Freedom in the City of the Straits* (New York, 2017); Catherine Cangany, *Frontier Seaport: Detroit's Transformation into an Atlantic Entrepôt* (Chicago, 2014). For the founding of Detroit, see White, *Middle Ground*, 83–87.

49. Tanner, *Narrative of the Captivity*, 240 (quotation); "Amendments Proposed to the Treaty with the Wyandots, Senecas, Delawares, Shawanees, Pattawatamies, Ottowas, and Chippewas," Dec. 29, 1817, in *American State Papers: Documents, Legislative and Executive, of the Congress of the United States, from the First Session of the Fourteenth to the Second Session of the Nineteenth Congress, Inclusive: Commencing December 4, 1815, and Ending March 3, 1827 . . . ,* Class II, *Indian Affairs,* 2 vols. (Washington, D.C., 1834), II, 149 (hereafter cited as *American State Papers, Indian Affairs*). For the national debate about Native peoples and removal, see John P. Bowes,

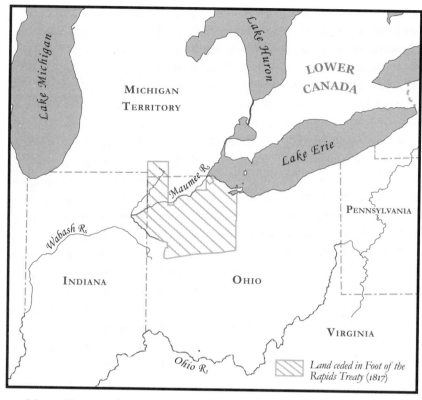

Map 3. Treaty at the Foot of the Rapids, 1817. Drawn by Rebecca Wrenn

The negotiations for the 1817 treaty, known as the Treaty at the Foot of the Rapids, had occurred at Fort Meigs, an American fort located on a stretch of rapids near the mouth of the Miami River on Lake Erie. The council had been fiercely contentious, and although the stakes were high for all of the Native peoples in attendance, the Wyandots had been asked to make the greatest sacrifice. As the Ohio Indian agent John Johnston later wrote in his memoir: "All Northwestern Ohio was at this time ceded to the United States. The greatest opposition was experienced from the Wyandots." They were left with a small territory in the interior of Ohio sixty miles from the lakeshore. According to Johnston: "The attachment

Land Too Good for Indians: Northern Indian Removal (Norman, Okla., 2016), 50–77; Ronald N. Satz, *American Indian Policy in the Jacksonian Era* (1975; rpt. Norman, Okla., 2002), 97–125.

of the Wyandots was ardent for their native country. The night they agreed to give it up many of the chiefs shed tears." The treaty was regarded as a stunning success for the United States. At the conclusion of the treaty council, the U.S. acting secretary of war, George Graham, wrote to Cass and General Duncan McArthur, the officer in charge of the army of the Northwest, "This treaty may be considered, in its fiscal, political, and moral effects, as the most important of any that we have hitherto made with the Indians."[50]

With this treaty, the American government sought to bring an end to autonomous Native communities in the Ohio country. The goal was to either remove Native peoples from the state or to incorporate them into the Republic as settlers. Graham sent instructions to Cass ordering him "to make an effort to extinguish the Indian title to all the lands now claimed by them within the limits of the State of Ohio." This negotiation, he wrote, "should be founded on the basis that each head of a family who wishes to remain within the limits ceded should have a life estate in a reservation of a certain number of acres, which should descend to his children in fee." Anyone who rejected these terms "should have a body of land allotted to them on the west of the Mississippi." In other words, Native peoples who remained in Ohio would live on land that they owned as individuals in fee simple title.[51]

By the terms of the treaty, the Wyandots received a twelve-square-mile reserve, the equivalent of four townships under the Northwest Ordinance. This land was to be divided into 144 sections, each a one-mile-square settlement consisting of 640 acres. The Wyandot headman Deunqod and six subchiefs were allotted two sections each. Additional sections were set aside for a mission, a school, and a blacksmith's forge, and the remaining land, 80,000 acres, was to be divided among the 187 Wyandots listed on the treaty schedule. The Senecas, Delawares, and Odawaag also ceded land, but their cessions were smaller, and they received similar, albeit correspondingly smaller, grants of land in Ohio. The Odawaag along with the Boodewaadamiig and Ojibweg also made a land cession to the Catholic Church Sainte Anne de Détroit. This land would be sold and the funds

50. Leonard U. Hill, *John Johnston and the Indians in the Land of the Three Miamis, with Recollections of Sixty Years by John Johnston* (Piqua, Ohio, 1957), 179 ("greatest opposition"); George Graham to Governor Lewis Cass and General Duncan McArthur, Oct. 17, 1817, *American State Papers, Indian Affairs*, II, 140 ("most important"); Bowes, *Land Too Good for Indians*, 121–124.

51. Graham to Cass, Mar. 23, 1817, *American State Papers, Indian Affairs*, II, 136.

used to found a school that would include Native students and constituted the original land grant for the University of Michigan.[52]

The Native nations that signed the Treaty at the Foot of the Rapids refused to accept the idea of removal, but they were dispossessed of almost all of their territory in Ohio. This land would be converted to the public domain of the United States and made available for sale at a subsidized rate to white settlers. For Graham, the conversion of Native land into private property represented the significant "moral effect" of this treaty. He regarded Native land-use practices as an immoral failure to improve the land. This treaty, like every treaty negotiated in the Northwest since the Treaty of Greenville, allowed Native peoples to continue to hunt and harvest on ceded lands as long as the lands remained in the public domain. Unlike the earlier treaty at Greenville, it also attempted to change the way Native peoples lived by confining them to individual parcels of property as opposed to territory held collectively by the band or nation. That the individual allotments were clustered in "compact settlements," however, mitigated the intended effects of this policy. "The only objection," Graham informed Cass and McArthur, "is, that it will have a tendency to preserve their customs and manners for a longer period than if they had made their locations more diffusively."[53]

Creating the conditions that would terminate Indigenous custom was important from a moral perspective for U.S. policymakers, but it was also a national security issue. Cass explained the "political value" of the land cession made in this treaty to the secretary of war: "This tract of country, in its present situation, renders the Territory of Michigan an insulated point upon the map of the nation." Northwest Ohio, he noted, could only be approached by water, and Lake Erie was frozen for months at a time. This region was equally inaccessible by land as it was surrounded by an enormous wetland known as the Great Black Swamp. These barriers, Cass argued, made Northwest Ohio practically indefensible in the event of a war with British Canada, which would deploy Native forces who could travel this terrain. The governor concluded by arguing that only the construction "of a good road" would secure this newly acquired

52. "Treaty with the Wyandot, etc., 1817," Sept. 29, 1817, in Charles J. Kappler, comp. and ed., *Indian Affairs: Laws and Treaties*, II, *Treaties* (Washington, D.C., 1904), 145–155. The land grant used to establish the University of Michigan was, not a land transfer, but an allotment sold, and the proceeds were used to purchase land in Detroit.

53. Article 11, "Treaty with the Wyandot," in Kappler, comp. and ed., *Indian Affairs*, II, 149; Graham to Cass and McArthur, Oct. 17, 1817, *American State Papers, Indian Affairs*, II, 140 (quotations).

territory: "Such a road would remove the barriers which nature has interposed, and would, in effect, approximate this country to the western portion of the Union, and, connected with the natural advantages it possesses, would insure it a steady settlement and an active and enterprising population." In effect, the Treaty at the Foot of the Rapids would allow the United States to connect the state of Ohio to the Michigan Territory, thus facilitating the rapid settlement of a region inhabited exclusively by Native peoples. Without such a road, Cass feared the British could block American expansion and take control of the Northwest Territory.[54]

From the perspective of the federal government, the Northwest was American territory to which Native peoples still retained title. Cass considered the process of extinguishing that title and replacing the Indigenous population with a settler population vital to the national security of the United States. "From the settlements in Ohio to Detroit, nearly the whole country is the property of the United States," he wrote, and "every consideration, either of a fiscal or political nature, demands the immediate sale and settlement of this land." This was the significance of the 1817 treaty: it would convert Native homelands in Ohio into the public domain of the U.S. Republic, allowing settlers to purchase this land as private property and making this territory part of the United States. The rapid settlement of Ohio should be "considered as the means of increasing the national strength, and of securing the possession of an important frontier." Cass considered the ceded territory as "the great connecting link which binds together our northwestern frontier."[55]

Breaking the Northwest Confederacy

Without a steady stream of settlers buying land, American possession of northern Ohio and the Michigan Territory remained, like Native title, an imperfect thing. Cass recognized that the key to spurring settlement was infrastructure, like the road he proposed to cut a path through the Great Black Swamp and connect Ohio to Detroit. The other key to claiming this space for the Republic was the destruction of independent Indigenous polities that were occupying land claimed by the United States. In fact, Indian nations, acting like sovereign powers, would serve as a deterrent

54. Cass and McArthur to Graham, Sept. 29, 1817, *American State Papers, Indian Affairs*, II, 137.

55. Ibid., 138 ("From the settlements"); Cass and McArthur to Graham, Sept. 30, 1817, ibid., 139 ("binds together"). For the significance of opening this land to U.S. settlers, see Bowes, *Land Too Good for Indians*, 123–125; Mary Stockwell, *The Other Trail of Tears: The Removal of the Ohio Indians* (Yardley, Pa., 2016), 88–95.

to settlers who wanted cheap land but feared "Indian depredations." Cass believed the 1817 Treaty at the Foot of the Rapids would facilitate these policy goals, spurring white settlement and deconstructing Native sovereignty in a space that was supposed to be part of the Republic.

The Native leaders who negotiated with the United States at Fort Meigs in 1817, however, were aware of the strategic significance and economic value of their land. "A large portion of the country is beautiful and valuable, fertile, well watered, and handsomely situated," Cass informed the secretary of war. And foreshadowing the need to reconvene the Native parties to a second treaty in 1818, he noted: "Its acquisition was also rendered more difficult, because it is the last tract of land in possession of the Wyandots—once a powerful, and still a high-spirited people. Its cession to the United States will make it necessary for those Indians to change the manners and customs of their whole nation." The Wyandots had been at the heart of every Native coalition in the Northwest since the French era. They were given the highest rank and the first right to speak at any council. The same was true for political gatherings among Native peoples as well as councils held by the confederacy with Canada and the United States. Their villages in the Ohio country situated them in the heartland of the confederacy of the Northwest Indians. It also exposed them to pressure from the United States in a way that the Indigenous peoples of the Michigan Territory had yet to feel.[56]

American expansion not only threatened to dispossess Native peoples in Ohio; it also undermined their ability to survive as autonomous nations. "In fact," Cass wrote, "the whole of the Wyandots and all the Shawanees and Senecas in this quarter have made the last attempt to preserve the inheritance of customs and of land transmitted to them by their ancestors." He noted, however, "They feel that our settlements are surrounding them," and, he concluded, "they will cease to be hunters, and will, we trust, become farmers." From an American perspective, this was the fate that awaited all Native peoples in the face of western expansion. Because of the desire of Native peoples to preserve their customs and land, Cass conceded, "we have experienced much difficulty in adjusting the quantity, tenure, and conditions of the reservations to their and our satisfaction."[57]

56. Cass and McArthur to Graham, Sept. 30, 1817, *American State Papers, Indian Affairs*, II, 139. For the significance of the Wyandots in the Northwest confederacy, see White, *Middle Ground*, 436–448; and Eric Hinderaker, *Elusive Empires: Constructing Colonialism in the Ohio Valley, 1673–1800* (New York, 1997).

57. Cass and McArthur to Graham, Sept. 30, 1817, *American State Papers, Indian Affairs*, II, 139.

One of these adjustments was that Americans were forced to recognize non-Native and mixed-race peoples as members of the Native nations negotiating the Treaty at the Foot of the Rapids. "We have been compelled to admit the claims of a number of individuals," Cass reported, "and to stipulate that patents shall be granted to them. Almost all these persons are Indians by blood. Some have been taken prisoners in early life, have married Indian women, and have identified themselves in feelings, manners, and interest with the Indians." In the 1817 treaty, the federal government acknowledged both mixed-race and captive adoptees as Natives or Indians. "Under these circumstances," Cass wrote, "we judged it expedient to consider these persons as the heads of Indian families, and to make for them the provision which is found in the treaty." Article 8 of the 1817 treaty, "at the special request of the said Indians," reserved land in fee simple title for a number of individuals designated by name and "connected with the said Indians, by blood or adoption." The refusal to accept American categories of racial and national identity signaled the failure of the treaty negotiators to extinguish Native sovereignty, even as they forced Indigenous nations to cede land against their will.[58]

The Treaty at the Foot of the Rapids granted land sections to seven non-Native adoptees who continued to live among the Ohio Indians as adults and who had married Native wives or husbands. Article 8 also recognized four women as "heads of Indian families" who deserved a land grant; they included two white women adoptees and two Native women who had married white men. The treaty also granted land sections to at least four mixed-race children, including Alexander and Richard Godfroy. The treaty listed these two individuals as "adopted children of the Potawatomy tribe," but in truth they were mixed-race children of the Indian agent Gabriel Godfroy and a Boodewaadamii woman. Their identification as "adopted" seemed to signal their whiteness—at least in the eyes of territorial officials. Officials like Governor Cass recognized the mixed-race children of their Indian agents as white but were willing to stipulate that they were adopted by their mother's people and therefore Native enough to receive a land grant through treaty deliberations with the United States.[59]

58. Ibid. ("compelled"); "Treaty with the Wyandot," in Kappler, comp. and ed., *Indian Affairs*, II, 148 ("special request").

59. "Treaty with the Wyandot," in Kappler, comp. and ed., *Indian Affairs*, II, 148 ("adopted children"). This ambiguity around the racial identification of the mixed-race Native children of fur traders and Indian agents was common in the Northwest Territory. See White, "The Power of Whiteness," in *Making Minnesota Territory*,

This concession regarding the status of the Godfroy children reflected the ambiguous understanding of race among Native peoples in the Northwest and the importance of kinship in determining rights. It might have also reflected a political calculation on the part of Governor Cass. During the council for the 1817 treaty, the Wyandot leaders remained steadfast in their refusal to sell land or sign the treaty. In the face of this refusal, Godfroy and Whitmore Knaggs, Indian agents for the Boodewaadamiig, Odawaag, and the Ojibweg, threatened to sell the Wyandot lands. They asserted that their Anishinaabe clients could also lay claim to this territory and that they would sell it to the United States government on their behalf. Cass and McArthur, acting as treaty commissioners, "declared that if the Wyandots would not sell their lands, they would buy them of the others—the Chippewas, Pottawatomies and Ottawas." With the Indian agents of their allies threatening to sell their land out from under them, the Wyandots signed the treaty. As their agent John Johnston later recorded, "the chiefs shed tears" over this deception. Immediately following the council, however, the Wyandot leader Tauyaurontoyou (Between-the-Logs) led a delegation of disgruntled treaty signers to Washington, D.C., to demand that the terms of the 1817 treaty be renegotiated.[60]

Tauyaurontoyou left Ohio without seeking the permission of agent Johnston and surprised Washington officials when he showed up at the American capital. Heading a delegation of Wyandot, Shawnee, and Seneca leaders, he met with the newly appointed secretary of war, John Calhoun, and with President James Monroe. Calhoun complained that he had not been informed of their desire to meet with government officials. "We got up and came of ourselves," Tauyaurontoyou responded; "We believed the great road was free for us." After meeting with the secretary and the president, Tauyaurontoyou testified before the Senate's Committee on Public Lands, stating that their land grant was "too small . . . to

<hr />

special issue of *Minnesota History*, LVI (1998–1999), 178–197; Anne F. Hyde, *Empires, Nations, and Families: A History of the North American West, 1800–1860* (Lincoln, Nebr., 2011), 274–275; Theresa M. Schenck, *William W. Warren: The Life, Letters, and Times of an Ojibwe Leader* (Lincoln, Nebr., 2007), 1–34; Karl S. Hele, "The Anishinabeg and Métis in the Sault Ste. Marie Borderlands: Confronting a Line Drawn upon the Water," in Hele, ed., *Lines Drawn upon the Water: First Nations and the Great Lakes Borders and Borderlands* (Waterloo, Canada, 2008), 65–84.

60. For the details of this land swindle, see *The History of Wyandot County, Ohio, Containing a History of the County; Its Townships, Towns, Churches, Schools, etc. . . .* (Chicago, 1884), 269 (quotation). For Tauyaurontoyou's resistance to the 1817 treaty, see Stockwell, *The Other Trail of Tears*, 64 ("shed tears"), 85–91.

afford them subsistence in the mode of life and occupation they intend to pursue—that of pasturage, for rearing and feeding of cattle." The committee also reported that "the grant appears in disproportion to the cession of land they have made, when compared with the cessions of other tribes, and the grants made to them."[61]

As a result, the Committee on Public Lands proposed a series of amendments to the 1817 Treaty at the Foot of the Rapids. These included expanding the Wyandot land grant from twelve square miles to sixteen. The total land ceded by the Wyandots would thus be reduced from 3,360,000 to 3,231,560 acres. The committee recommended regranting land to the other treaty signers as well, decreasing the total land cession of the Wyandot, Shawnee, Delaware, Boodewaadamii, Odawa, and Ojibwe peoples in Ohio from 3,880,320 to 3,694,540 acres. The 1817 treaty had also stipulated that individuals could sell their allotments "in complete title to any person whatever." Fearing that this provision exposed the treaty signers to fraud, the committee recommended that the treaty be amended so that the sale or transfer of Indian lands could be made only to other Indians and would require "the approbation of the President, or some agent specially appointed for that purpose." This provision provided the federal government with a monopoly over the sale of Indian land, making the treaty consistent with the Northwest Ordinance. It also had the effect of codifying the rejection of individual landownership by the Indigenous treaty signers. They would hold on to what was left of their land as Indian nations, not as individual settlers who happened to be identified racially as Native. The revisions thus reversed the attempt to deconstruct the sovereignty of Ohio's Indigenous nations.[62]

In spite of these revisions, the secretary of war made clear to the Wyandots, Senecas, and Shawnees who accompanied Tauyaurontoyou to Washington, D.C., that the end goal of the civilizing mission was, in fact, the eventual termination of Indigenous sovereignty. Shortly after their arrival, the secretary delivered a speech to the visiting delegation, declaring, "It is the wish of your father the President that the reservations which have been made for you should be sufficient to afford to every Indian family a tract of good land of not less than 640 acres." Each Indian

61. *History of Wyandot County*, 269 ("We got up"); "Amendments Proposed to the Treaty with the Wyandots, Senecas, Delawares, Shawanees, Pattowatomies, Ottowas, and Chippewas," Dec. 29, 1817, *American State Papers, Indian Affairs*, II, 148 ("too small").

62. "Amendments Proposed to the Treaty," Dec. 29, 1817, *American State Papers, Indian Affairs*, II, 149.

family would "be protected by the laws of the United States, in the same manner and in every respect as his white children are; and he will make no difference between them." Designating Native allies as the children of a white father extended back into the French era when the governor of New France claimed this role. American presidents took on this mantle following the Revolution and used this claim of kinship as a form of patriarchy to signal the subordination of Native nations allied to the United States. With the 1817 treaty, however, the United States had sought to transform Native peoples from allied Indigenous nations into individual settlers whose only claim to their homeland in Ohio was possession of a homestead as private property. Senate deliberations about the need to restrict the sale of Native lands asserted a guardianship role on the part of the federal government. Native peoples would not actually be citizens, but they would be "protected by the laws of the United States." Accordingly, Native peoples could purchase their ceded land once it was surveyed and made part of the public domain. "At the public sales any of you," the secretary declared, "will have the same right to purchase as the white people." Forced to relinquish title to their homeland in Ohio, they could buy it back as private property, one homestead at a time.[63]

Even with the slightly more generous settlement proposed by the Senate, the United States retained the goal of eventually extinguishing all Native title in the state of Ohio. The United States intended to transfer this land to its citizens, but it also sought to politically dismantle the Native nations with homelands in the Northwest. In Ohio, American settlers recognized the political and economic significance of this treaty. During the negotiation of the 1817 treaty, the *Liberty Hall and Cincinnati Gazette* reported: "The cession made by the Indians on this occasion nearly extinguishes their title to this state. The small reservations are but little consequence to us. The two great objects gained; the security of the North Western Frontier and an opportunity for an immediate settlement of the country." This land transfer, the newspaper argued, "will soon compel the few remaining Indians to adapt to the habits of civilization, or to migrate to situations more congenial to savage life." The ideology underlying this sentiment conflated Native homelands with unsettled territory. It also

---

63. George Graham, "Talk Addressed to the Wyandot, Seneca, and Delaware Nations," Nov. 18, 1817, ibid., 140. For the lethal patriarchy of the American father, see Richard White, "The Fictions of Patriarchy: Indians and Whites in the Early Republic," in Frederick E. Hoxie, Ronald Hoffman, and Peter J. Albert, eds., *Native Americans and the Early Republic* (Charlottesville, Va., 1999), 62–84.

refused to imagine a world where independent Indigenous nations and the U.S. Republic could coexist. The new terms secured by Tauyaurontoyou represented only a temporary solution to the threat to Indigenous sovereignty posed by American expansion.[64]

The "Search for an Efficient White Population"

Tauyaurontoyou's desperate appeal to the president and Congress thus forced the United States to renegotiate the terms of the 1817 Treaty at the Foot of the Rapids. Before Lewis Cass left for the council grounds on the Saint Mary's River to hammer out this new treaty, however, he received instructions from the secretary of war. "The great object," the secretary's office informed Cass, "is to remove, altogether, these tribes beyond the Mississippi. . . . there then ceases to be any question about the tenure by which the Indians shall hold lands." His instructions also stated that if he could not negotiate removal, "make the best contract you can for the territory, granting small reservations to families or to individuals, with the right of pre-emption to the United States." In other words, in spite of the new terms negotiated by Tauyaurontoyou in the capital, the American government wanted Cass to pressure the Native peoples of Ohio to leave the state. Failing that he needed to transfer their collective title into private property through fee simple title and secure a right of preemption for the federal government. Thus, the goal of the new treaty was not only the transfer of Native land wealth to the Republic; it was the destruction of Native people's collective identity as Indigenous nations. The instructions to Cass concluded by asserting, "An efficient white population will supply the place of their feeble society, and will give strength and vigor to our frontier, as well as develop, by the progress of improvement, many resources which will largely contribute to the power and safety of our institutions."[65]

The council that Cass called to the Saint Mary's River in the summer of 1818 was even larger than the one he called at the Foot of the Rapids. In addition to the Wyandot, Shawnee, Seneca, Delaware, Boodewaadamii, Odawa, and Ojibwe peoples living in Ohio and the Michigan Territory, the Boodewaadamiig, Miami, and Wea who lived on the tributaries of the Wabash in Indiana attended. Following the council, Cass wrote to

64. *Liberty Hall and Cincinnati Gazette,* Oct. 15, 1817, [1], Ohio History Connection, Columbus.

65. Christopher Van Deventer, to Cass, June 29, 1818, *American State Papers, Indian Affairs,* II, 175.

Secretary of War Calhoun, "The time has not yet arrived for them voluntarily to abandon the land of their fathers." He assured Calhoun, however, that "as our settlements gradually surround them, their minds will be better prepared to receive this proposition, and we do not doubt but that a few years will accomplish what could not now be accomplished." The Wyandot reservation on the Upper Sandusky in Ohio was increased by 55,680 acres, and they would receive an extra five hundred dollars a year in annuity payments. In total, the American government returned 100,000 acres to the signatories of the 1817 Treaty at the Foot of the Rapids.[66]

After restoring land to the Native parties to the 1817 Treaty at the Foot of the Rapids, however, Governor Cass negotiated a new series of treaties designed to strip land from their relatives living in the state of Indiana. The Boodewaadamiig ceded their remaining lands south of the Wabash River as well as a stretch of land south of the Tippecanoe River for an annuity of twenty-five hundred dollars. The payments would be split between Chicago and Detroit, the two cities closest to their remaining territories in the Northwest. The Wea ceded all of their land "within the limits of the states of Indiana, Ohio, and Illinois" in exchange for a seven-by-seven-mile reservation between Raccoon Creek and the Wabash River in Indiana. For this cession, their annuity would be doubled to three thousand dollars. The Miami ceded millions of acres, approximately one-third of the land in Indiana as well as the western edge of Ohio in exchange for an extra fifteen thousand dollars in annuities. The Delawares ceded all their land in the state of Indiana and accepted a land grant west of the Mississippi in exchange for a four-thousand-dollar annuity and material assistance for their relocation.[67]

Following the 1818 treaty council at Saint Mary's, the vast majority of the Indigenous land base in Indiana and Ohio had been ceded to the federal government. The Miami retained five reservations in the state of Indiana, ranging from two square miles to ten square miles. They also received twenty-three land sections in fee simple title, designated for Jean Baptiste Richardville, their principal leader, and several other headmen.

66. Cass and McArthur to John C. Calhoun, Sept. 18, 1818, ibid., 177; "Treaty with the Wyandot, etc., 1818," Sept. 17, 1818, in Kappler, comp. and ed., *Indian Affairs*, II, 162–163.

67. "Treaty with the Potawatomi," Oct. 2, 1818, in Kappler, comp. and ed., *Indian Affairs*, II, 168–169; "Treaty with the Wea," Oct. 2, 1818, ibid., II, 169–170; "Treaty with the Delawares, 1818," Oct. 3, 1818, ibid., II, 170–171; "Treaty with the Miami," Oct. 6, 1818, ibid., II, 171–174; Andrew R. L. Cayton, *Frontier Indiana* (Bloomington, Ind., 1996), 261–276.

François and Louis Godfroy, the two Miami children of the agent for the Boodewaadamiig, Gabriel Godfroy, each received six sections of land. The Miami treaty awarded land grants to several other mixed-race individuals described as "being Miami Indians by birth." Similar land grants were allotted to mixed-raced individuals identified by the treaty commissioners and Native leaders as members of the Boodewaadamii, Wea, and Delaware nations. Most, though not all, of these individuals had English or French surnames, and they accepted land grants alongside the reservations and land grants allotted to their respective nations. Unlike the Treaty at the Foot of the Rapids, the series of treaties negotiated at Saint Mary's did not include land grants for captive adoptees.[68]

With the exception of the Delawares, Cass failed to persuade the Native peoples of the Northwest living in Ohio to accept removal west of the Mississippi. Although their homelands had been radically reduced, these nations maintained a foothold in the region. Maintaining their place within the boundaries of the Republic, however, came at a steep political cost. About the 1818 treaty negotiations, the *Liberty Hall and Cincinnati Gazette* reported: "To the states of Ohio and Indiana these acquisitions are of immense importance. In a few years these almost interminable forests will be converted into flourishing towns and villages and cultivated farms." The newspaper concluded, "The silent footsteps of the savage will give way to the resounding of the axe, the din of industry, and the bustle of commercial enterprise." This vision of an uncultivated Indigenous landscape giving way to the farms, towns, and industry of the settler state echoed the sentiments of Cass and Andrew Jackson. But this was also the expression of an American ideology that refused to see Native farms, villages, and industry as part of the American political economy, or part of the modern world. From this perspective, Native peoples had no place in a modern republic because they existed outside the boundaries of civilization.[69]

68. "Treaty with the Miami," Oct. 6, 1818, in Kappler, *Indian Affairs*, II, 172–173. For dispossession of the Ohio nations, see Bowes, *Land Too Good for Indians*, 122–144.

69. "Treaties with the Indians," *Liberty Hall and Cincinnati Gazette*, Oct. 11, 1818, [1], Ohio History Connection. The Ohio River valley was, in fact, a flourishing agrarian village world; see Sleeper-Smith, *Indigenous Prosperity and American Conquest*, 13–66. Peter S. Onuf asserts that "the foundational premise of American exceptionalism, the new national mythology, was newness"; see Onuf, "Empire of Liberty," in Andrew Shankman, ed., *The World of the Revolutionary American Republic: Land, Labor, and the Conflict for a Continent* (New York, 2014), 206; Reeve Huston, "Land Conflict and Land Policy in the United States, 1785–1841," ibid., 324–345.

This set of beliefs about American Indians, modernity, and civilization seemed to be the motivating factors in Cass's attempt to reunite Zhaazhaawanibiisens with his American family. Just as the governor believed that Native land, Indian country, must inevitably become the private property of white settlers, he also believed captive adoptees must abandon their Indian identity and resume their true identity as white citizens of the Republic. Zhaazhaawanibiisens traveled to the council at Saint Mary's in advance of the American delegation led by Cass. Anxious to return to his relations, he left early with Binesi, one of the sons of Manidoogiizhig, and remained at the council grounds until the treaties were concluded. En route to Kentucky, however, he learned that his brother Edward had heard of his return and was searching for him. Zhaazhaawanibiisens changed course and made his way to Detroit hoping to reunite with his brother. On the road, he passed a man "with a Sioux pipe in his hand, whose strong resemblance to my father immediately arrested my attention." Unable to speak English, he could not communicate with the man, who ignored him and continued traveling in the opposite direction. Zhaazhaawanibiisens arrived in Detroit and within a few days was joined by his brother Edward, the man with the Sioux pipe.[70]

John Tanner, though taken as a young boy, recognized his brother on the road to Detroit. His transformation into Zhaazhaawanibiisens, however, rendered him unrecognizable to Edward. Of course, they could speak to each other only with the assistance of a translator. But for Edward, as for Lewis Cass, phenotype served as a marker of race, and John's physical appearance served as a barrier to his reintegration into civilized society. Accordingly, as John later recalled, the first thing Edward did was "cut off my long hair, on which, till this time, I had worn strings of broaches, in the manner of the Indians." Long hair shorn and wearing, in his words, "the dress of a white man," John and his brother visited Governor Cass, who "expressed much satisfaction at my having laid aside the Indian costume." In spite of the expectation that he now dress like a white man, John Tanner / Zhaazhaawanibiisens found such attire uncomfortable and was "compelled to resume my old dress for the sake of convenience." Resuming a white identity, it turned out, would not be as easy as changing clothes.[71]

After a short stay in Kentucky among his white relatives, John Tanner / Zhaazhaawanibiisens returned to Lake of the Woods to reunite with

70. Tanner, *Narrative of the Captivity*, 251.
71. Ibid., 251, 252.

his children. He then brought three of them back with him to Kentucky, where he lived for two years with his white family. "In the spring of 1822," he wrote, "I started to go again to the north, not finding that I was content among my friends in Kentucky." John Tanner / Zhaazhaawanibiisens moved with his children to Mackinac Island in the Michigan Territory, returning to live in the Indian country, or Anishinaabewaki. In 1822, the population of Michigan was dominated demographically by Native peoples. The Anishinaabeg inhabited northern Michigan almost exclusively, with small populations of non-Natives and mixed-race Native peoples living at trading posts associated with important Native villages. Mackinac was a community like this, a mixture of Native village and fur-trading outpost. It was perhaps the most important village and trading post in terms of Native diplomacy and politics in the Northwest—and in terms of the fur trade. John Tanner, in fact, moved to the island to work for the American Fur Company.[72]

72. Ibid., 261. For an explication of Tanner's life as an Anishinaabe, see Fierst, "A 'Succession of Little Occurences,'" *Scholarly Editing*, XXXIII (2012), 1–29. For Tanner's return to Indian country, see John T. Fierst, "Return to 'Civilization': John Tanner's Troubled Years at Sault Ste. Marie," *Minnesota History*, L (1986), 23–36. Fierst makes a convincing argument that although Tanner's autobiography is usually read within the tradition of captivity narratives, it should not be thought of as part of this genre. Rather, the autobiography is "an Anishinaabe account rendered in English," as told by Tanner and written by the Mackinac surgeon Edwin James (Fierst, "A 'Succession of Little Occurrences,'" *Scholarly Editing*, XXX, [2012], 3). I, too, have used this narrative as an accurate reflection of Anishinaabe life in the Northwest Territory at the end of the eighteenth century. The book has a complicated history, first published in 1830 by New York publisher G. & C. & H. Carvill as *Narrative of the Captivity and Adventures of John Tanner, (U.S. Interpreter at the Saut* [sic] *de Ste. Marie,) during Thirty Years Residence among Indians in the Interior of North America. . . .* A London edition (cited throughout this chapter) was published as well in 1830 by Baldwin & Cradock. Alexis de Tocqueville purchased the narrative and published it in France as, *Mémoirs de John Tanner, ou Trente anées dans les déserts de L'Amerique du Nord,* trans. Ernest de Blosseville, 2 vols. (Paris, 1835). Tocqueville interviewed Tanner and used that information along with Tanner's published narrative to inform the sections of *Democracy in America* that focus on Native peoples (Tocqueville, *Democracy in America,* trans. and ed. Harvey C. Mansfield and Delba Winthrop [Chicago, 2000], 317–318). In 1940, the anthropologist Paul Radin directed the reprinting, *An Indian Captivity (1789–1822): John Tanner's Narrative of His Captivity among the Ottawa and Ojibwa Indians,* ed. Edwin James, Occasional Papers, reprint series no. 20, part 1 (San Francisco, Calif., 1940). Many other reprints followed, most recently, *The Falcon: A Narrative of the Captivity and Adventures of John Tanner,* with an introduction by Louise Erdrich (New York, 1994).

"Surrounded by a People,
in the Rudest State of Barbarism"

For all practical purposes, John Tanner/Zhaazhaawanibiisens could return to his old life among the Indians because Michigan Territory remained a largely Indigenous space. Lewis Cass, however, had ambitions to bring "civilization" to Michigan, much as he had to Ohio, and so he proposed a treaty with the Michigan Indians to the secretary of war John C. Calhoun. In January 1819, approximately three months after treaty negotiations at Saint Mary's in Ohio, Cass wrote to the secretary: "Sir, Information, which has recently reached me from different quarters, induces me to believe, that an attempt to procure from the Chippeways a cession of the Country upon the Saginaw bay in this Territory would be successful." He described the land in the Saginaw region as "of the first quality" and asserted that it "would undoubtedly settle with great rapidity." The secretary of Michigan Territory, William Woodbridge, echoed this sentiment in a letter to Calhoun in February. He informed the secretary, "I also conversed with the President on the subject of the value to our Country of the lands possessed by the Saguina Indians and the probability of being able by treaty to procure those lands." The president, he suggested, asked him to convey this information to his secretary of war, the man responsible for treating with the Indians.[73]

Acquiring land "of the first quality" was not Cass's sole concern in seeking a treaty with the Saginaw Ojibweg. "Those Indians have always been troublesome and discontented, and even now commit almost daily depredations upon the exposed settlements of this Territory," he told Calhoun. Cass noted that he understood the goal of the government was removal west of the Mississippi or confinement to small reservations. "Favourable moments," he wrote, "must be embraced for this purpose as they occur." For Cass, 1819 represented not so much a favorable moment as one of necessity. His January letter to the secretary of war warned darkly: "The contiguity of these Indians to the British possessions in Canada, and the use, which might be made of them, in the event of any future difficulties upon this frontier furnish additional reasons in favour of this attempt." And he concluded by remarking, "I take the liberty of again calling your attention to the propriety of procuring a cession of land from the Indians at the Falls of St. Marys."[74]

73. Cass to Calhoun, Jan. 6, 1819, in Clarence Edwin Carter et al., eds., *The Territorial Papers of the United States*, 28 vols. (Washington, D.C., and New York, 1934–), X, 808; William Woodbridge to Calhoun, Feb. 19, 1819, ibid., X, 816.

74. Cass to Calhoun, Jan. 6, 1819, ibid., X, 808, 809.

There was, however, a significant difference between the state of Ohio and the Michigan Territory. Forty thousand non-Native settlers were living in the Ohio Territory in 1800, and that population grew to sixty thousand three years later, allowing Ohio to enter the union as a state. By the mid-1820s, there were more than eight hundred thousand American settlers living in Ohio. The Michigan Territory, in contrast, had a sparse population and had not experienced the rapid growth of states such as Ohio, Indiana, and Illinois. Without access to watersheds linked to the Mississippi and economically important cities such as Saint Louis and New Orleans, Michigan remained isolated. In another letter to the secretary of war in May 1819, Cass noted, "There are not more than eight thousand Inhabitants in this Territory, and they are not formed into compact settlements, mutually supporting and supported by each other, but thinly scattered upon the margins of the principle streams and presenting one Continued frontier to the Indians."[75]

Cass complained that the U.S. settler population remained vulnerable to Indian depredation because of the low number of soldiers stationed at Detroit. He catalogued a number of assaults, murders, and thefts of cattle, hogs, and horses committed by Native peoples against Americans. The governor concluded this list of offenses by stating, "I have myself no fear of Indian hostilities, but aggressions like those may be attended with evils, almost as much to be deprecated as a state of open war." This environment, he warned, "will check if not entirely prevent migration to the Country and stop our progress in improvement and population." Drawing on a recent census, Cass estimated that there were more than eight thousand Natives living in the Lower Peninsula of Michigan alone, with easy access to the "British Indian head quarters" at Fort Malden, located at the mouth of the Detroit River. He told Secretary Calhoun that "the Indians east of Lake of Michigan, many west of that Lake, and those upon the Wabash and Miami rivers and their tributary streams make an annual journey to receive the presents, which are distributed to them, and to confer, as they express it, with their British father." He described the Michigan Territory as "an exposed and defenceless frontier" and pleaded with Calhoun to station more soldiers at Detroit. "We are," he wrote, "exposed to and in fact surrounded by a people, in the rudest state of barbarism, brave ferocious and vindictive." Cass concluded, "These people are much influenced by the agents of a foreign and rival

75. Cass to Calhoun, May 27, 1819, ibid., X, 828. For population growth in Ohio, see Stockwell, *The Other Trail of Tears*, 72.

power, who view with jealousy the increase of our power, and the development of our resources."[76]

Violent encounters between Anishinaabe people and American settlers continued into the summer of 1819. In early June, Cass informed Calhoun, "Joseph Wampler and his party employed in Surveying the publick lands were driven in by the violence and menaces of the Indians." Cass repeated the assertion that he had "no fear of Indian hostilities. . . . But the effect of these repeated acts of violence will be felt upon our emigration, and will keep the Country in some alarm." That same month, Cass wrote a complaint to the commissioner of the General Land Office, Josiah Meigs, that "publick lands in this Territory . . . intended by the Secretary of the Treasury to be brought into market," had yet to be surveyed. The Indian agent at Mackinac, George Boyd, then wrote to Cass, "A Body of between 6 and seven hundred Indians, principally from the contiguous settlements, took their departure from hence three days ago for Drummond's Island." They met with British officials, "receiving large disbursements of Indian presents . . . with a view to influence their attendance on the Treaty to be held by your Excy the ensuing fall at Saganah bay." Forced to leave Sault Sainte Marie to the Americans following the Revolutionary War, the British established a post at Drummond Island where the Saint Mary's River drains into the Georgian Bay of Lake Huron. Like Fort Malden opposite Detroit, this post was an important point of contact with British-Canadian officials for Anishinaabeg who lived, hunted, and traded along this largely meaningless border.[77]

The Anishinaabeg, including the Saginaw Ojibweg, continued to cultivate their alliance with British Canada. This fact alarmed Governor Cass, and it might also have contributed to the intermittent violence between the Anishinaabeg and American settlers. Why, then, did Cass tell the secretary of war that he believed the Saginaw Ojibweg wanted to

76. Cass to Calhoun, May 27, 1819, in Carter et al., eds., *Territorial Papers of the United States*, X, 827, 828, 830. For U.S. concerns about the British and the northern border, see Alan Taylor, "The War of 1812 and the Struggle for a Continent," in Shankman, ed., *The World of the Revolutionary American Republic*, 246–267.

77. Cass to Calhoun, June 5, 1819, Cass to Josiah Meigs, June 12, 1819, George Boyd to Cass, June 18, 1819 (enclosed in Boyd to Calhoun, June 18, 1819), all in Carter et al., eds., *Territorial Papers of the United States*, X, 833, 836, 840. For Anishinaabe border crossing, see Phil Bellfy, "Cross-Border Treaty-Signers: The Anishnaabeg of the Lake Huron, Borderlands," in Hele, ed., *Lines Drawn upon the Water*, 21–42; Janet E. Chute, *The Legacy of Shingwaukonse: A Century of Native Leadership* (Toronto, 1998).

cede territory to the United States? Why would he claim that ceded territory would be settled quickly when he could not even survey Native lands ceded by the 1817 treaty? If anything, he might have hoped that making even more land available would entice settlers, thus restricting the ability of Native peoples to maintain themselves in traditional fashion in their homelands. It seems more likely, however, that it was not the Anishinaabe ogimaag who signaled a willingness to make land concessions. The only people associated with the Anishinaabeg eager for these negotiations to occur were the subagents, such as Whitmore Knaggs and Gabriel Godfroy, who had sold out the Wyandots in 1817, and the fur traders, such as Louis Campau, who hoped to claim portions of the annuity payments as recompense for unpaid debt. Cass needed the cooperation of these men. He needed them to exploit their kinship connections and trade ties to force the Anishinaabeg to the council. As an added incentive, these same men would be paid to provide the provisions and trade goods offered in addition to annuity payments as part of the treaty process.[78]

In spite of his claim to the contrary, Governor Cass knew that the Saginaw Ojibweg were not eager to cede their land to the United States. In August 1819, he summoned Louis Campau to Detroit. Campau had been trading at Saginaw since 1816. "He asked me how Indians would feel about a treaty," he later wrote in a memoir; "I told him they would not be pleased with it." According to Campau, "That was what inclined him to bring troops with him." Unlike the treaty cessions in Ohio held at American forts, Cass would have to travel to the Anishinaabe village at Saginaw Bay in order to force the Ojibweg to negotiate with him. As a result, he sent two ships with trade goods and supplies, along with a company of soldiers under the command of his brother Charles Cass. Governor Cass also told Campau that Henry Conner and Louis Beaufait, two interpreters working for the governor, would advise Campau about "what preparations to make."[79]

Bringing the Political Economy of Plunder to Michigan

The subagents working for the U.S. government but intermarried among the Anishinaabeg thus reassured Governor Cass that the Saginaw Ojibweg could be pressured to make a land cession. They were in favor

78. Charles E. Cleland, *Rites of Conquest: The History and Culture of Michigan's Native Americans* (Ann Arbor, Mich., 1992), 212–218.

79. Louis Campau, Biographical Statement, Draper Manuscript Collection, Wisconsin Historical Society, Madison.

of the treaty process because they stood to gain the most from a land cession made to the American government. Moreover, as Louis Campau understood, the fur trade was in decline and would only diminish further as settlers continued to alter the landscape with new farms and towns. Campau sought to make the most of the treaty negotiations and "hired two large Mackinac boats to bring my goods . . . dry goods and everything" from Detroit to his post at Saginaw. He then returned to the bay and "built the council house, rolled in logs for seats, crossed it over with elm and cedar bark."[80]

As Cass began to prepare for a treaty council with the Saginaw Ojibweg, he realized that the U.S. government had not paid their annuities for land ceded in the 1807 Treaty of Detroit. "It would be hopeless to expect a favorable result to the proposed treaty," he wrote to Secretary Calhoun, "unless the annuities previously due are discharged." When the government failed to send him the appropriate funds, he was forced to arrange a loan through a Detroit bank. At least one Detroit merchant, Abraham Wendall, learning about the impending treaty negotiations, solicited Cass: "Supposing there would be goods wanting, I take the liberty and hope you will consider me an applicant a part or the whole of these goods which may be wanted for the Indians." While Cass acquired cash money and trade goods to facilitate what he must have known would be a tense negotiation, virtually all of the traders, subagents, and interpreters rushed to join him at Saginaw with the hope of claiming as much of the cash as possible in the form of unpaid debt and through the sale of provisions and trade goods they knew the government would offer as part of the treaty settlement.[81]

While the soldiers and provisions made their way to Saginaw by boat, Cass and his interpreters made their way overland, by horse and canoe, to the bay. They arrived to find a gathering of approximately four thousand Anishinaabeg, mostly Ojibwe but also some Odawa and Boodewadaamii peoples. By Cass's reckoning, the Native peoples gathered at Saginaw represented as much as half of the settler population in Michigan's Lower Peninsula. In Ohio, when he pressed Native peoples to cede land, they could feel the presence of a settler population of approximately two hundred thousand people and easily imagine losing their land, without

80. Ibid.

81. Cass to Calhoun, Sept. 11, 1819, *American State Papers, Indian Affairs*, II, 198; Abraham Wendell to Cass, Apr. 10, 1819, Lewis Cass Papers, reel 32, Bentley Historical Library, University of Michigan, Ann Arbor.

compensation, to squatters. At this council, it was the American delegation that must have felt surrounded and in danger of losing their land or lives to their Indigenous neighbors.

Cass arrived at Saginaw on September 10, 1819, and he called for the Anishinaabeg to gather at the council house built by Louis Campau the following morning. At this first council meeting, speaking through the interpreters Henry Conner and Whitmore Knaggs, the governor "endeavored to impress upon them the paternal regard which their Great Father at Washington had for their welfare." He then "reminded them of their condition as a people, the swelling of the wave of civilization towards their hunting grounds, the growing scarcity of game, the importance and necessity of turning their attention more to agriculture, and relinquishing the more uncertain mode of living by the chase." He concluded by stating that they would be better off "confining themselves to reservations" and ceding "the residue of the territory" to the American government. Or, as Louis Campau later recalled, "The first Council was to let them know that he was sent by the great father to make a treaty with them, that he wanted to buy their lands."[82]

By all accounts, the Anishinaabeg gathered at the council responded with shock and anger to the opening remarks of Governor Cass. They were not at an American fort surrounded by a rapidly growing settler population that regarded them with contempt. They came together at the mouth of the Saginaw River at one of the most important village sites in Anishinaabewaki. Other than the governor and his company of soldiers, the only non-Native peoples at the council were the handful of fur traders and subagents whose livelihood depended on their relationship to the Anishinaabeg. Three men had been designated to speak for the Anishinaabeg at this council—Ogamawkeketo, Giishkako, and Mishenenanonequet. These ogimaag were civil leaders of the doodemag that

82. Charles P. Avery, "The Treaty of Saginaw of 1819: Indian and Pioneer Incidents of the Saginaw Valley," in James M. Thomas and A. B. Gallatin, comps., *Indian and Pioneer History of the Saginaw Valley, with Histories of East Saginaw, Saginaw City, and Bay City, from Their Earliest Settlement, also Pioneer Directory and Business Advertiser, for 1866 and 1867* (East Saginaw, Mich., 1866), 6 ("paternal regard"); William L. Webber, "Indian Cession of 1819, Made by the Treaty of Saginaw," *Historical Collections: Collections and Researches Made by the Michigan Pioneer and Historical Society*, XXVI (Lansing, Mich., 1896), 525–526 ("first Council") (hereafter cited as *MPHC*). The 1866 account of this meeting by Avery, an amateur historian, was based on interviews with both Native and non-Native participants.

lived in the villages on the Saginaw River and its tributaries that flowed into the bay.[83]

Ogamawkeketo delivered the response to Cass, and he offered a stern rebuke. "You do not know our wishes," he began; "Our people wonder what has brought you so far from your homes." Then he offered an elaborate rebuttal to Cass's presumptions:

> Your young men have invited us to come and light the Council fire. We are here to smoke the pipe of peace, but not to sell our lands. Our American Father wants them. Our English Father treats us better. *He* has never asked for them. Your people trespass upon our hunting grounds. You flock to our shores. Our waters grow warm. Our land melts like a cake of ice. Our possessions grow smaller and smaller. The warm wave of the white man rolls in upon us and melts us away. Our women reproach us. Our children want homes. Shall we sell from under them the spot where they spread their blankets? We have not called you here. We smoke with you the pipe of peace.

According to Louis Campau, "Cass arose to his feet—and said stop that language." Speaking in anger, the governor informed the council that the United States had defeated "their father the English King and the Indians too, that the land was forfeited by their fighting, and he could hand it over without payment."[84]

To the many Anishinaabeg who saw Cass negotiate treaties in Ohio, his threat to take their land and "hand it over" to American settlers would not have seemed like an idle one. Although in the Michigan Territory they were not surrounded by settlers, any expansion of American settlement beyond Detroit would necessarily spread along the river valleys of the Saginaw region north of the city. According to Charles Avery, historian and Michigan settler who wrote the earliest account of the treaty negotiations, after this confrontation the council broke up, and the interpreters, subagents, and the governor "all retired to their lodgings disappointed and anxious, while the Chiefs and head-men of the natives retired to their wigwams in sullen dignity, unapproachable and unappeased." Expecting a fraught negotiation, Cass included an immense quantity of alcohol among the provisions he brought to Saginaw. He began to dispense

---

83. Cleland, *Rites of Conquest*, 213.

84. Avery, "The Treaty of Saginaw," in Thomas and Gallatin, comps., *Indian and Pioneer History*, 7, 8; Campau, Biographical Statement, Draper Manuscript Collection.

brandy and whiskey liberally, targeting in particular Giishkako, who adamantly opposed ceding territory to the United States.[85]

In this tense atmosphere, formal negotiations came to a close, but the Anishinaabeg and the American delegation remained encamped at the council grounds. As Campau later recalled, "They then worked at private business for three or four days." In other words, the American delegation attempted to persuade individual ogimaa to sign off on a land cession. Cass called a second meeting of the council, but he once again failed to secure a consensus among the ogimaag. According to Campau, "At the second Council there was great difficulty, hard words; they threatened General Cass among the rest." Giishkako, who continued to oppose the idea of a land cession, remained intoxicated and refused to participate in the second council.[86]

With negotiations at a standstill, Neome, an influential Saginaw Ojibwe ogimaa from the Flint River basin, began a collaboration with trader Jacob Smith. The two men had a close relationship. Smith operated a trading post on the Flint River, and Neome and his family were his principal trading partners. Known as Wabeshins (The Swan) among the Ojibweg, Smith had a Native family at his Flint River post and a white family in Detroit. In his account, Avery described Smith as the "power behind the throne greater than the throne itself" and asserted, "So nearly had he identified himself with the good old chief, Ne-ome, that each ever hailed the other as brother." According to Avery, Smith was the mastermind while "Ne-ome was honest and simple minded . . . easy to be persuaded by any benefactor who should appeal to his Indian sense of gratitude."[87]

Whoever took the lead, Jacob Smith and Neome started down a path that would benefit themselves at the expense of the larger Saginaw Ojibwe community. The two men entered into a complicated scheme to secure additional land grants beyond those set aside for reservations and the fee simple sections for mixed-race children. Neome's grandson Naugunnee would later testify that Smith visited his grandfather in his tent at night and that "Neome requested Smith to assist him in trying to get a reservation for his children, and Smith agreed." Neome then visited the tent of

85. Avery, "The Treaty of Saginaw," in Thomas and Gallatin, comps., *Indian and Pioneer History*, 8.

86. Webber, "Indian Cession of 1819," *MPHC*, XXVI, 526 (quotations); Kim Crawford, *The Daring Trader: Jacob Smith in the Michigan Territory, 1802–1825* (East Lansing, Mich., 2012), 148–149; Cleland, *Rites of Conquest*, 215.

87. Avery, "The Treaty of Saginaw," in Thomas and Gallatin, comps., *Indian and Pioneer History*, 11, 12.

Governor Cass with Smith acting as interpreter and asked for land for his children. Mixenene and Tondogane, two Saginaw ogimaag, saw Neome meet privately with Cass, and they, too, sought an audience with the governor. Again, Smith acted as an interpreter. After these private meetings, all of the ogimaag began to meet with Cass individually (with Smith and other traders serving as interpreters). Eventually, even Giishkako sought a private meeting with the governor, and he also secured a land grant.[88]

The refusal to cede land quickly gave way to a scramble to secure land grants in addition to the reserved territory that would be assigned to the Saginaw Ojibweg. The possession of land was power in the U.S. Republic, and, in the face of this reality, the Ojibwe ogimaag met separately and decided that they would submit a list of eleven names to the governor, requesting that each receive a 640-acre land grant. This list was compiled by Jacob Smith and amended to include his Ojibwe daughter, but the list also contained the names of the two daughters, the son, and a grandson of Neome. Smith told Governor Cass, however, that the eleven children on the list were his own with his Ojibwe wife, thus making them eligible for the land sections the United States usually granted to mixed-race individuals. The logic was that the mixed-race children of traders and agents were nominally white, or civilized, but also Native and therefore deserving of compensation for any land cession by the Anishinaabeg. In order to secure his treaty, Governor Cass conceded these claims to dual identity.[89]

The land cession negotiated by Lewis Cass cut an enormous swath across the heart of Anishinaabewaki in the Michigan Territory. The Saginaw ogimaa signed away 4.3 million acres of land, stretching from Kalamazoo County in the western part of the territory northeast to Thunder Bay and then south to Saginaw Bay on the shores of Lake Huron. In addition to the private reserves set aside for the children and grandson of Neome and Smith's daughter, land sections were set aside for the mixed-race children of several other traders. Inexplicably, the treaty also provided land grants to the interpreters Henry and James Conner, Peter and George Knaggs (the brothers of Whitemore), and Jacques Godfroy, the brother of trader Gabriel Godfroy, all non-Natives. The Senate did not recognize or ratify these non-Native land grants, but the traders,

88. Webber, "Indian Cession of 1819," *MPHC*, XXVI, 522, 528 (quotation). For Smith's role in the Saginaw Treaty, see Crawford, *The Daring Trader*, 148–156.

89. Webber, "Indian Cession of 1819," *MPHC*, XXVI, 522–228. For a detailed explanation of how the list of Smith's Native children was produced, see Crawford, *The Daring Trader*, 150–156.

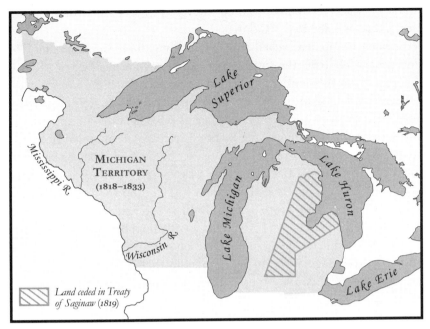

Map 4. Treaty of Saginaw, 1819. Drawn by Rebecca Wrenn

subagents, and interpreters, including Smith and Campau, were all generally compensated in cash payments at a time when specie was hard to come by in the West. Ultimately, fully 10 percent of the land reserved for the Saginaw Ojibweg following the treaty was granted to the mixed-race children of traders and agents.[90]

The Saginaw Ojibweg insisted that their annuity be paid in full and in specie, avoiding a delayed payment, as happened after the Detroit Treaty of 1807, but also making them vulnerable to traders eager to take their cash. Campau insisted the Saginaw Ojibweg owed him fifteen hundred dollars in trade debt and made an agreement with Cass to be repaid directly out of the annuity. According to Campau, "Ten Eych, Wendell, Godfroy and Jake Smith were there with Goods and it did not please them to see so much of the money go to me." These traders hoped to induce the newly paid Ojibweg to purchase their goods, and a large payout to Campau potentially reduced their profit. They roused Giishkako, urging him to object, and he did so, admonishing the governor: "They want their money in hand. They are your children." Faced with this stern objection

90. Cleland, *Rites of Conquest*, 215–216.

from an influential ogimaa who began negotiations in opposition to the treaty, Cass refused to pay Campau.[91]

Furious, Campau attacked Smith, punching him in the face twice. He then proceeded to put the entire American delegation at risk. To celebrate the treaty after the signing, Governor Cass opened five barrels of whiskey. After being denied his payment, Campau opened ten barrels of whiskey and began to give away as much alcohol as possible. Copious amounts of alcohol and the tension created by the forced land cession led to an increasingly hostile atmosphere. Once again, the Saginaw Ojibweg began to threaten the Americans. At this point, Cass feared for his life and begged Campau: "Louis, Louis, we shall all be killed. Stop the Liquor." In response, Campau later wrote, "I told Godfroy and Beaufait and Cass you have plundered me and robbed me but I will stand between you and my honor." In the end, the American delegation was able to quell the growing hostility of the Saginaw ogimaag, who knew that, in spite of their numbers, violence against the Americans would come at too high a price.[92]

"Our Land Melts Like a Cake of Ice"

The Treaty of Saginaw, and to a similar extent the treaties in Ohio in 1817 and 1818, represented the emergence of a political economy of plunder that would come to define American expansion in the Old Northwest. With the extinction of Native title, vast tracts of Indigenous land were transferred into the public domain, creating a market monopoly in western land for the federal government and subsidizing the expansion of white property ownership in the form of homesteads. This process would also require the dispensing of trade goods and cash payments, which in turn offered American settlers and officials the opportunity to lay claim to this money by selling goods and provisions, receiving cash payments for supposedly unpaid debt, and procuring additional payments for services rendered in facilitating the treaty negotiations. If Native peoples resisted the request for land cessions, the governor or his Indian agents openly and publicly threatened to take and sell their land anyway. The message conveyed at council was negotiate now or forfeit your land with no compensation. This political economy of plunder benefited white settlers, but it particularly enriched government officials, traders, and Indian agents

---

91. Campau, Biographical Statement, Draper Manuscript Collection.
92. Ibid.; Cleland, *Rites of Conquest*, 216.

with kinship and business ties to Native peoples or political and legal jurisdiction over them.[93]

On September 29, 1819, at Saginaw the federal government acquired 4.3 million acres of Anishinaabewaki for an annuity of one thousand dollars per year. The Saginaw Ojibweg retained the right to hunt and fish on ceded lands, but doing so would become increasingly difficult when the land became more densely settled. Following the treaty signing, Cass wrote to Secretary of War Calhoun, informing him that although he believed it was in the best interest of the Indians to "migrate to the country west of the Mississippi, . . . it was impossible to give effect to that part of your instructions." As he explained the situation to the secretary: "An indisposition to abandon the country so long occupied by their tribe, an hereditary enmity to many of the western Indians, and a suspicion of our motives, are the prominent causes which, for the present, defeat this plan." However, he concluded, "when they are surrounded by our settlements, and brought into contact with our people, they will be more disposed to migrate." The *Detroit Gazette*, reporting on the successful conclusion of this treaty, seemed to agree with Governor Cass. In an article dated October 1, 1819, days after the treaty was signed, the paper asserted, "We anticipate speedy migration to this tract and a great increase of population and wealth to the Territory."[94]

In his letter to Calhoun, Cass also made a vague effort to explain the exceptional nature of the land grants offered to the mixed-race and non-Native treaty beneficiaries at Saginaw. "Reservations have also been made for a few half-breeds," he asserted; "It was absolutely necessary to our success that these should be admitted into the treaty." Cass insisted that the Saginaw Ojibweg demanded the grants to white traders be included

93. This phenomenon, the overlap of diplomacy, politics, and financial transactions, has been labeled the "Indian business" by historian Robert A. Trennert, Jr., who noted, "These merchants viewed themselves as public benefactors, serving the needs of both government and Indians in a high-risk business." See Trennert, *Indian Traders on the Middle Border: The House of Ewing, 1827–54* (Lincoln, Nebr., 1981), 206. Similarly, Peter S. Onuf argues that the Northwest Ordinance, the legal mechanism for converting Native homelands into American homesteads, was designed to promote economic development; see Onuf, *Statehood and Union: A History of the Northwest Ordinance* (Bloomington, Ind., 1987), 59.

94. "Treaty with the Chippewa, 1819," Sept. 24, 1819, in Kappler, comp. and ed., *Indian Affairs*, II, 185–187; Cass to Calhoun, Sept. 30, 1819, *American State Papers, Indian Affairs*, II, 199; *Detroit Gazette*, Oct. 1, 1819, [1].

in the treaty. And, he noted, "The private debts conditionally assumed are *bona fide* due by the Indians." Although Cass lamented the refusal of the Anishinaabeg to move west, in reality the political economy of plunder necessitated the continued presence of Native peoples in their homelands as the state negotiated the terms of their colonization. The business of the Northwest Territory was shifting from the fur trade to colonization— the management and exploitation of a subordinated population of Indigenous, noncitizen subjects was becoming the economic engine of the Michigan Territory.[95]

With the Hudson's Bay Company monopoly restored in the British Northwest, or Rupert's Land, competition diminished and the fur trade declined in that region. Extended periods of migration onto the Great Plains became less profitable for the Anishinaabeg in the Michigan Territory. They faced a similar decline in their home territory, exposing them to greater pressure from traders all too willing to begin cashing out of the fur trade at their expense during treaty negotiations. As they negotiated their place in the U.S. Republic, they suffered devastating land losses. Increasingly tied to the federal government through annuity payments rather than alliance, the political leadership of Native nations in the Northwest saw their influence eroded. And with their annuities plundered, they saw their people become impoverished.

With the Saginaw Treaty, U.S. officials continued their attempt to reorganize Native nations into communities of individual landholders with a fee simple title to their property. The Anishinaabeg, however, resisted this attempt at social engineering and maintained their communities on reservations where they collectively insisted on their right as a people to hunt, fish, and harvest seasonal resources in their ceded homelands. The status of mixed-race peoples remained liminal; their Indigenous status earned them land grants but also made them wards of the state when it came to the ability to control or sell this property. In 1835, for example, when Richard Godfroy, the mixed-race son of Indian agent Gabriel Godfroy, sought to sell land granted to him in the 1817 Treaty at the Foot of the Rapids to his son James, he had to obtain permission from Steven Mason, the governor of Michigan Territory at the time of the sale. The connections of mixed-race individuals like the Godfroys to white traders and agents, often their parents or uncles, seemed to allow the government to recognize in them some measure of a civilized identity. The Godfroys were enumerated as white in the 1830 census of the Michigan Territory.

95. Cass to Calhoun, Sept. 30, 1819, *American State Papers, Indian Affairs*, II, 199.

They also owned two people enumerated on the census as slaves, in spite of the prohibition against slavery in the constitution of the territory.[96]

The status of white captive adoptees like John Tanner seemed more precarious. The state recognized people like Tanner/Zhaazhaawanibiisens as white and identified them as citizens of the United States. Their standing as Indigenous people with legitimate claims to land grants and treaty rights, however, was uncertain. U.S. treaty negotiators, and Congress, seemed willing to recognize captive adoptees when negotiating treaties with the Native nations in Ohio in 1817. By the time of the Saginaw Treaty two years later, however, this recognition would give way to the subterfuge of white men claiming land rights through their association with Native peoples. Traders, Indian agents, and other federal officials relied on Indigenous understandings of kinship and identity to integrate themselves into the political economy of the Native New World in order to make a profit in the fur trade. Increasingly, they would use these same kinship ties, identities, and their attendant obligations to profit from the political economy of plunder that facilitated the American colonization of the Northwest Territory.

96. Richard Godfroy to Gov. Steven T. Mason, June 10, 1835, *MPHC*, XXXVII, 351; United States, Census Office, "Population Schedule for Michigan, 1830" (Wayne County, not including Detroit), microfilm, Bentley Historical Library. On the issue of slavery in the Northwest Territory, see Paul Finkelman, "Slavery and the Northwest Ordinance: A Study in Ambiguity," *Journal of the Early Republic*, VI (1986), 343–370.

CHAPTER 3

The Civilizing Mission, Women's Labor, and the Mixed-Race Families of the Old Northwest

Alexis de Tocqueville arrived in Detroit on July 20, 1831. He had departed Buffalo, New York, the day before on the steamship *Ohio* with his traveling companion Gustave de Beaumont. They had been in the United States for about two months when they decided to head to the western frontier in their "search for savages and wilderness." The roughly eight months Tocqueville traveled America would make him famous, memorialized with the publication of *Democracy in America*. The first two volumes of this highly influential work, an exploration of the United States and the function and meaning of democracy in the first decades of the U.S. Republic, were published in 1835, with an additional two volumes published in 1840. Absent from these original publications, however, was the essay *Quinze jours dans le désert*, or *Two Weeks in the Wilderness*. The essay was written in the United States immediately after Tocqueville and Beaumont embarked on an overland journey from Detroit to the village of Saginaw on the Lower Peninsula of Michigan. Tocqueville traveled to the Michigan Territory in search of Indians, who, he believed, were vanishing—"an ancient people, the original and rightful masters of the American continent melting away daily like snow in sunshine and disappearing before our eyes from the face of the earth."[1]

Tocqueville fully accepted the idea of the vanishing Indian, a trope he encountered in his day-to-day interactions with people everywhere

1. Alexis de Tocqueville, *Two Weeks in the Wilderness*, in Tocqueville, *Democracy in America and Two Essays on America*, trans. Gerald E. Bevan, ed. Isaac Kramnick (London, 2003), 876. For the trope of the vanishing American Indian in U.S. popular culture and policymaking in the nineteenth century, see Christina Snyder, *Great Crossings: Indians, Settlers, and Slaves in the Age of Jackson* (New York, 2017), 190–193.

he went in the United States—despite the fact that Native peoples were omnipresent in the early-nineteenth-century Republic. "As for the Indians," he wrote, in a quote attributed to a generic citizen, "you'll see too many of them in our public squares and streets, you do not need to go very far to see that." Yet this same generic citizen encountered by Tocqueville time and again assured him: "Every day the numbers of Indians decrease. . . . God, by his refusal to grant its first inhabitants the art of civilization, doomed them to an inevitable destruction. The true owners of this continent are those who are able to take advantage of its wealth." From this perspective, the true owners of the continent were the settlers who brought civilization to the untamed American wilderness. Tocqueville and Beaumont thus traveled to Detroit, "to the furthest limits of European civilization," in order to see wilderness and Native peoples before they disappeared.[2]

Upon arriving in Detroit, they sought the official in charge of selling public land and inquired what part of the territory experienced the least immigration. The country northwest of Pontiac, a city a few miles north of Detroit, they were told, "is covered with almost impenetrable forest stretching endlessly toward the northwest where only wild animals and Indians are to be found." Tocqueville and Beaumont rented two horses and set out for Saginaw, an Ojibwe village, fur-trading post, and the only settlement north of Pontiac in Michigan's Lower Peninsula. Two days travel brought them to the Flint River, where they passed the night in a log cabin with an American settler. The next day, this man, acting as an interpreter, helped the two French men hire Native guides to take them to Saginaw. They traveled through a forest that Tocqueville compared to "the measureless expanses of the sea." After seven hours, they reached a small Native settlement with a few wigwams, and their guides indicated it was time to stop for the night. Tocqueville and Beaumont felt uneasy spending the night in the village, however, and paid their guides to continue on in spite of the setting sun.[3]

Tocqueville and his companions reached the Saginaw River after nightfall, where they had an encounter that should have upended all their expectations about vanishing Indians and the advance of European civilization. As they approached the river, their guides cried out and were

2. Tocqueville, *Two Weeks in the Wilderness,* in Tocqueville, *Democracy in America,* trans. Bevan, ed. Kramnick, 875 ("furthest limits"), 878–879 ("Every day"), 883 ("too many").

3. Ibid., 884 ("impenetrable"), 907 ("measureless").

answered in kind from some indeterminate location in the darkness ahead. In a few moments, a Native boat, ten feet long and hewn from a single tree, appeared on the shore. The pilot addressed the guides in Anishinaabemowin, the Ojibwe language, and they unsaddled the horses in preparation for crossing the river. Seeing this, Tocqueville made to board the canoe when the pilot, "the so-called Indian," in Tocqueville's words, "said to me in a Norman French accent which startled me: 'Don't move too quickly, sometimes people drown.'" In his essay, Tocqueville recorded his response, "I would not have been more astonished if my horse had addressed me." He asked the man who he was. "He replied that he was a half-breed Indian—that is, the son of a Canadian man and an Indian woman." With Tocqueville on board, the man then piloted the canoe across the river, humming a French tune, with the horse in tow swimming.[4]

Tocqueville woke up the next morning in Saginaw, and, in spite of his encounter the previous night, perceived that he had landed in a place without a history. He described Saginaw as "an embryo in its earliest stages and a burgeoning seed entrusted to the wilderness." "No common link existed between them and they were profoundly different from each other. You encountered there Canadians, Americans, Indians, and half-castes." He understood the non-Native inhabitants of this village as distinct peoples, settlers descended from the French and English. Make your way to the cabin of the Francophone, he wrote, and "you will perhaps take him for an Indian; in his submission to life in the wild, he has assumed his clothes, ways, and, to a degree, his customs." Tocqueville insisted that, in spite of this adaptation, "this man has no less remained a Frenchman." Yet, like the Natives, the French settler "has become the worshiper of life in the wilds," preferring hunting to agriculture. "A few yards from this man lives another European," Tocqueville wrote. He "is cold, stubborn, mercilessly argumentative. He clings to the land and rips from the life in the wilds everything he can snatch from it. He engages in a neverending struggle against it; everyday, he strips it of a few more of its spoils. Bit by bit, he transports his own laws, ways, customs, and, wherever possible, even the smallest benefits of advanced civilization into the wilderness." This man was Tocqueville's American. "The United States immigrant," he wrote, "values only the results that stem from his victory."[5]

Americans waged war against the wilderness in order to conquer it, Tocqueville argued. In contrast, "for nigh on three hundred years, the

4. Ibid., 912.
5. Ibid., 915 ("embryo"), 916 ("common link"), 917 ("worshiper").

savage of America has struggled against this civilization which has been encroaching and surrounding him." This resistance was the result of a false pride. "Lying upon his coat, surrounded by the smoke of his hut, the Indian casts a scornful glance at the European's comfortable dwelling. For himself, he proudly derives pleasure from his wretchedness and his heart swells and is uplifted by the sight of his primitive independence." Tocqueville envisioned the "half-caste" to be stranded between these two worlds. "At the confines, so to say, of the old and new worlds, stands a rustic cabin, more comfortable than the savage's wigwam and cruder than the house of the civilized man." In this dwelling, both real and metaphorical, Tocqueville encountered a young woman. He asked her if she was French, and she replied no. He then asked whether she was English. "Not that either," she responded, and informed him that she was "only a savage." Tocqueville described the woman as "a child of two races, brought up in the tradition of two languages." He concluded that, "nourished upon different beliefs and reared upon contradictory prejudices, the half-caste constitutes a mixture which is as inexplicable to others as it is to himself."[6]

Tocqueville would have us believe that these "so-called Indians," the "half-castes" speaking perfect Norman French, remained a mystery even to themselves. This sentiment, however, more clearly reflected his own sense of confusion about what to make of mixed-race Indigenous peoples who spoke his own language as fluently as their Indigenous tongue. From Tocqueville's perspective, Native peoples represented a timeless past, like the wilderness itself. On his journey back to Detroit, he marveled at the "uninhabited" parts of the "district of Michigan," writing, "The wilderness was probably just as it appeared six thousand years before to our first ancestors' eyes—a delightful and scented solitude festooned with flowers; a magnificent dwelling, a living palace constructed for man but into which the master had not yet made its way." In this particular construction of the wilderness, Native peoples have failed to realize their full humanity because they insist on living as savages, as forest primitives inhabiting a state of nature. They were not men, or at least they were not the masters of the house—that "living palace" that was actually their homeland. Because he deemed Native peoples as primitive beings who had not evolved culturally or socially, Tocqueville could conceive of Native North America as uninhabited wilderness. Encountering mixed-race people who seemed Indigenous in appearance yet spoke a civilized language destroyed this construct of Native peoples as unchanging and

6. Ibid., 918 ("nigh," and "nourished"), 919 ("only a savage").

North America as unsettled. Rather than confront this contradiction, Tocqueville regarded this Indigenous adaptation to a postcontact world as "inexplicable," a mystery. He could imagine a talking horse before he could imagine an Indian, even a half-caste, as a civilized, fully human, being, living in a forested homeland. Instead, Native peoples were part of a primitive wilderness destined to fade away, like the forest itself, when the master of the house (the American settler) finally made his way home.[7]

The figure of the settler in Tocqueville's narrative is always a man, and the social contract that reproduced the Republic in the West was between the state and the white male head of household. Curiously, he seemed to perceive the French settler as childless, writing, "In order to come to the wilderness, he seems to have broken all ties which linked him to life; you do not see him with wife or children." He made this observation in spite of his two recorded conversations with individuals who were clearly the offspring of French men. He described the American settler, in contrast, as "an adventurer surrounded by his family." In effect, Tocqueville considered the "half-caste" children of the fur trade as outside the social and political boundaries of a republic that was being re-created or extended into the wilderness by Anglo-Americans.[8]

Like Thomas Jefferson, Tocqueville believed that the western expansion of the United States was inevitable. Both men also assumed that American settlers would replace Native peoples as they extended the nation-state onto lands that they refused to see as Indigenous homelands. Jefferson viewed the West as an eighteenth-century naturalist; Tocqueville reveled in the romanticism of what he saw as unspoiled nature. Jefferson thought that some Native peoples, those willing to assimilate, could become citizens. Tocqueville held that Native peoples could not make this transformation but must remain forever outside the social and political boundaries of the Republic. The Great Lakes region of the Northwest Territory would challenge these assumptions, commonly held by settlers and government officials alike. When Tocqueville traveled to Michigan, some forty years after the American Revolution, he

7. Ibid., 883 ("district of Michigan"), 922 ("living palace").

8. Ibid., 916 ("wilderness"), 917 ("adventurer"). The fur trade, in fact, was a family business. As historian Anne F. Hyde described the trade in the nineteenth century, "This flexible and stable system, based in families who had the ability and desire to make powerful kinship links to other families, solidified over the entire period, protecting people against change and insulating them for a very long time against the rigid demands of American conquest." See Hyde, *Empires, Nations, and Families: A History of the North American West, 1800–1860* (Lincoln, Nebr., 2011), 29.

did so because the territory was still an Indigenous space. The Anishinaabeg, the Indigenous people Tocqueville encountered when he visited the western frontier, were no strangers to ambitious colonial powers. They would seek an accommodation with the expanding Republic that sought to maintain both their Indigenous identity and some portion of their national homeland, while simultaneously claiming a place in the civil society of the United States. Mixed-race Anishinaabeg, particularly mixed-race women, would emerge as crucial figures in this struggle for Indigenous inclusion and "survivance."[9]

The Search for Civilization

In *Democracy in America*, Tocqueville argued that Native peoples had the capacity to become civilized, potentially entering into the same social contract as white settlers. They would never get the chance, however, because the United States, and the American people, were moving west with ruthless efficiency. "But the misfortune of the Indians," he wrote, "has been to come into contact with the most civilized and, I may add, the most avaricious people on the earth at a time when they themselves are still half-barbarian." If greedy Americans spelled doom for Native peoples, Native peoples also bore some responsibility for their own demise. "Living freely in the depths of the forests," he maintained, "the North American Indian was wretched but felt himself inferior to no man." Native peoples willing to become American citizens "can only occupy the lowest rank for he arrives uneducated and poor into a society endowed with knowledge and wealth." In short, because Native people were unwilling to accept a subordinate social status, they preferred autonomy and freedom—even if that stance meant living a "wretched" (read "uncivilized") life. When Native peoples did attempt to cultivate the land, they faced "disastrous competition" from their white neighbors, who had already mastered commercial agriculture. Doomed to failure in this sedentary life, Native peoples would always choose the independent life of the migratory hunter. Native pride doomed the American Indian to oblivion.[10]

9. Gerald Vizenor writes that "survivance, in the sense of native survivance, is more than survival, more than endurance or mere response; the stories of survivance are an active presence. . . . Survivance is an active repudiation of dominance, tragedy, and victimry." See Vizenor, *Fugitive Poses: Native American Indian Scenes of Absence and Presence* (Lincoln, Nebr., 1998), 15.

10. Tocqueville, *Democracy in America*, trans. Bevan, ed. Kramnick, 387 ("misfortune"), 388 ("disastrous").

Figure 8. *North America Sheet V : The Northwest and Michigan Territories.* Engraved by J. & C. Walker. 1833. Published by the Society for the Diffusion of Useful Knowledge. William L. Clements Library, University of Michigan, Ann Arbor

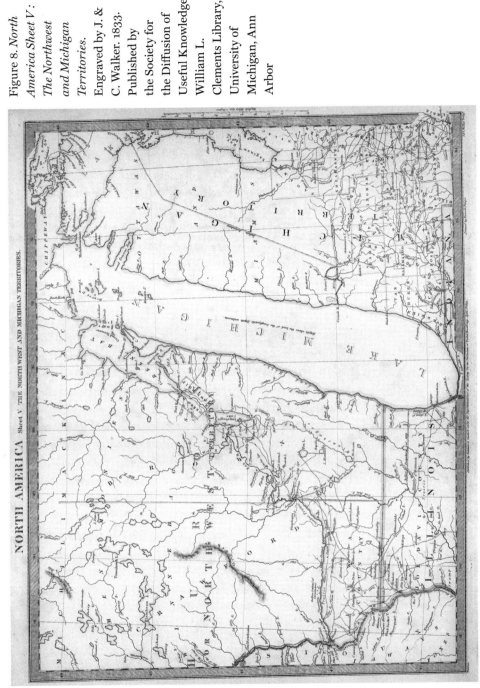

NORTH AMERICA Sheet V THE NORTH-WEST AND MICHIGAN TERRITORIES.

Tocqueville's model for understanding the perspective of Native peoples was John Tanner, or Zhaazhaawanibiisens. Tocqueville met Tanner at Mackinac and, referring to the conversation in the footnotes to *Democracy in America,* he wrote, "He seemed to me to resemble more a savage than a civilized man." Tanner's autobiography, he asserted, "paints a vibrant picture" of Native life. "There is in the adventurous life of these hunting peoples a certain irresistible charm that takes hold of a man's heart." Indeed, Tocqueville's *Two Weeks in the Wilderness* was narrated as a lark and an exciting undertaking, although one from which Tocqueville gladly returned to civilization. Tanner, he noted in contrast, struggled to make this return and frequently left Mackinac for brief periods to live among his Native relatives. Living as a Native, Tocqueville writes, was tempting and even glamorous, living off the bounty of the unspoiled wilderness. Drawn to the freedom of the hunt and its escape from the toil of working the land, Native peoples refused to leave the state of nature. This was their defining characteristic and the thing that condemned them to disappear from the face of the earth. It was also an unproductive and unpredictable life, a perspective he shared with or perhaps adopted from the governor of the Michigan Territory, Lewis Cass.[11]

In his reflections on Native peoples, Tocqueville drew heavily from the writings of Cass. In another footnote, he cited a report Cass submitted to Congress in 1829 in which the governor declared that "the time when the Indians generally could supply themselves with food and clothing, without any of the articles of civilized life, has long since passed away." Native peoples had grown dependent on manufactured goods like guns and traps to hunt animals that grew more and more scarce as American settlers advanced into the West. Cass himself had predicted this phenomenon when he negotiated treaties in Ohio in 1817 and 1818 and at Saginaw in 1819. A decade later, he could write, "The Indians have no wish to live like Europeans and yet they cannot do without them nor are they able to live exactly as their fathers did." Although the idea that Native peoples could not survive without access to manufactured goods was an exaggeration, the fur trade did decline in the parts of the Northwest Territory with significant American settlement, resulting in economic hardship and an increasing dependence on land sales and annuities from the U.S. government. Cass attributed this cycle to their "improvidence," which he

11. Ibid., 388, n. 18. For John Tanner's authobiography, see Tanner, *A Narrative of the Captivity and Adventures of John Tanner, (U.S. Interpreter at the Saut* [sic] *de Ste. Marie,) during Thirty Years Residence among the Indians in the Interior of North America; Prepared for Press by Edwin James* (London, 1830).

described as "habitual and unconquerable." Tocqueville was more critical in his observations about the relations between Native peoples and the United States, citing the greed of American citizens and the complicity of the federal government in accommodating their hunger for Native land. However, he shared the vision of men such as Cass who regarded North America as an unsettled wilderness and Native peoples as primitive nomads fading away in the face of an advancing civilization.[12]

The reality in Michigan, however, was much more complicated, and many of the territory's more influential residents remained intimately involved with Native peoples and the fur trade. In fact, traders and the mixed-race population that evolved around the trade became one of the principal means by which the government, federal and territorial, could influence the largely Indigenous population northwest of Detroit. In July 1830, one year before Tocqueville's visit to Saginaw, the American Board of Commissioners for Foreign Missions (ABCFM) acknowledged a request from the American Fur Company for missionaries to be sent to the Lake Superior country. The ABCFM was deeply involved with the civilizing mission of the U.S. government and informed Jedediah Stevens, a missionary at the Mackinac Island mission school, that "the committee regard[s] the state of feeling manifested by the traders during the last year or two as remarkable and especially providential." Board corresponding secretary David Greene noted, "They have therefore for the last two years been making inquiries for one or two well qualified and devoted missionaries." Missionaries sent to the Great Lakes would "strengthen the traders and give them further instruction, acquire the language of the natives, make translations into it, give them religious instructions . . . and thus open the way for making the gospel known extensively in that quarter."[13]

12. Tocqueville, *Democracy in America*, trans. Bevan, ed. Kramnick, 377, n. 3 ("passed away"), 381, n. 7 ("improvidence").

13. David Greene to J. D. Stevens, July 20, 1830, American Board of Commissioners for Foreign Missions, Correspondence, 1827–1878, box 1, Gale Family Library, Minnesota Historical Society (MHS), Saint Paul (hereafter cited as ABCFM). For Jedidiah Morse and the civilizing mission, see Hyde, *Empires, Nations, and Families*, 281–289. In 1819, Congress voted to allocate ten thousand dollars annually to promote the civilization of Native peoples in the United States. Churches and missionaries such as the ABCFM were invited to apply for these funds. As Nicholas Guyatt argues, U.S. politicians such as Secretary of War John Calhoun "saw missionaries as go-betweens (and sometimes stooges) in the effort to reconcile Native Americans to territorial expansion"; see Guyatt, *Bind Us Apart: How Enlightened Americans Invented Racial Segregation* (New York, 2016), 281–282.

The following year, the ABCFM successfully recruited two Andover graduates, Sherman Hall and William Boutwell, to take on this mission work. The board operated missions at Mackinac and at Sault Sainte Marie, important Anishinaabe villages with nearby American forts and American Fur Company posts. Hall and Boutwell would represent the ABCFM and the American government in the region between the west end of Lake Superior and the headwaters of the Mississippi River, known in the trade as the Fond du Lac, Lac Courte Oreilles, and Saint Croix Departments. The two missionaries were informed by Greene that their mission would be unique. The board's other missions "have been mostly among Indians who were surrounded by white settlements, limited to a comparatively small territory, easy of access, and whose character and habits had been much modified by their intercourse with more civilized communities." In contrast, he wrote, "you are to go among Indians who are remote, occupying the unlimited wilderness, difficult of access, and but little effected by intercourse with white men." As a result, "your mission must, in many respects, be conducted in a different manner from any other mission, which the board has established among the Indians."[14]

In August 1831, a newly married Sherman Hall departed Mackinac with his wife Betsey. Traveling west with the American Fur Company flotilla, they carried supplies for the coming winter season. Although the ABCFM identified Sherman as the missionary, Betsey's presence was deemed vital to the project they were undertaking. Securing a domestic partner for male missionaries would prove to be the key to successfully establishing missions in the western Great Lakes because women performed the domestic labor that sustained the mission families. The ABCFM intended for Hall to establish a mission at La Pointe on Madeline Island. This post was comparable to Mackinac and was the last major settlement on the route to the Ojibwe villages south of Lake Superior and west in the upper Mississippi Valley. Hall's party traveled in thirty-foot-long birch bark canoes capable of hauling three tons of goods as well as

14. Greene to Sherman Hall and William Boutwell, June 10, 1831, ABCFM, box 1. As Keith R. Widder has argued, because the missions established at Sault Sainte Marie and Mackinac "were part of the westward advance of American settlement and institutions, they brought more than the word of Christ with them. Whether they recognized it or not, they were agents of the American republic." See Widder, *Battle for the Soul: Métis Children Encounter Evangelical Protestants at Mackinaw Mission, 1823–1837* (East Lansing, Mich., 1999), 27.

even larger wooden bateaux fitted with masts for sailing. The vessels were filled up to the rowing benches with trade goods and provisions, and the passengers were perched on top along with the voyageurs. "Most of the traders of the interior and their clerks have Indian families," Hall wrote in his journal. "Most of those with us except our own family," he observed, "the principle traders, and some of their clerks and a part of the oarsmen are Indians or half breeds." The board sent Hall west to serve the Native peoples of La Pointe, but the mixed-race families of the fur trade would become his most important and consistent students.[15]

Beyond the Limits of Civilization

When Sherman Hall referenced "our own family," he meant those associated with the mission. Included in this mission family were John Campbell, a mixed-race Anishinaabe who would serve the mission as blacksmith, along with his mixed-race Anishinaabe wife, Elizabeth, and their five children, as well as Hester Crooks, a young mixed-race Anishinaabe woman who would work as a domestic servant. Hester was the daughter of a prominent Sault Sainte Marie trader and had been educated at the Mackinac mission school. Both Hester Crooks and Elizabeth Campbell would prove vital to the mission as translators. Hall understood these mixed-race people attached to the mission to be white because they were Christian and lived a civilized life as opposed to residing in the wilderness among their charges. That most everyone associated with the mission was, in fact, Native or connected by blood or marriage to Native people undoubtedly added to Hall's sense that he had left the United States and entered a foreign land. Or, as he wrote in his journal on the seventh day of travel, "We are now beyond the limits of civilization in this part of the world." They paddled along the southern shore of Gichigamiing, or Lake Superior, "on one side a boundless wilderness, on the other an expanse of water extending beyond the ken of man, and with no house or any other mark of civilization." Hall imagined his journey in much the same

15. Journal of Rev. Sherman Hall, Aug. 8, 1831, ABCFM, box 1. Laurel Clark Shire argues that women's work was a vital component of American expansion: "Americans treated women's work for settlement as they did the rest of their labor. It was vital to the reproduction and survival of society but completely discounted as work. Unlike women's domestic work elsewhere, however, their labor on frontiers supported not only their households and the growth of the middle class and modern capitalism but also the expansion of national territory." See Shire, *The Threshold of Manifest Destiny: Gender and National Expansion in Florida* (Philadelphia, 2016), 17.

romantic way as Tocqueville, as if he moved through a timeless and unsettled wilderness.[16]

Hall arrived at La Pointe, much like Tocqueville at Saginaw, to discover a community of Anglo-Americans, Canadian Americans, and mixed-race and Indigenous peoples. But whereas Tocqueville had Native guides with whom he could not communicate and made his observations over the course of a few days, Hall was introduced to the Indigenous Northwest by the traders and their families who acted as intermediaries for a missionary who intended to make the post his home. Hall and his wife moved into the house of Lyman Warren, the principal trader for the American Fur Company at La Pointe. Warren had taken over the trading business of Michel Cadotte in 1824 after marrying his daughter Mary. Michel, in turn, had been brought up in the business by his father Jean-Baptiste Cadotte, who began trading in the Lake Superior region in 1742. The men who conveyed Hall, the mission family, and their supplies to La Pointe were also company traders married to Native women. One of these men, Charles H. Oakes, married Julia, the daughter of French trader Bazil Beaulieu and Ogenaw-gizzhigokwe (Respected Sky Woman), the daughter of a Lac du Flambeau *ogimaa*, or civil leader.[17] Julia had attended the Mackinac mission school. The other trader who helped transport the missionaries was William Aitkin. Originally from Great Britain, Aitkin migrated to Canada and then to the Fond du Lac Department, where he married Magdalene Ermatinger, also named Beshibiiaanakwad (The Striped Cloud). She was the daughter of a Canadian trader and an Ojibwe woman who was the daughter of Katawbidai (Broken Tooth), the ogimaa of Sandy Lake, where Aitkin based his trading operations. Four of Aitkin's children attended the Mackinac mission school. In establishing the mission at La Pointe, Hall and the ABCFM embedded themselves in a village

16. Journal of Rev. Sherman Hall, Aug. 11 ("beyond the limits"), 14 ("boundless wilderness"), 1831, ABCFM, box 1; Hester Crooks Boutwell, Life Memoranda, American Board of Commissioners for Foreign Missions Archives, ABC 6.5.3, I, 183, Houghton Library, Harvard University, Cambridge, Mass.; Widder, *Battle for the Soul*, 32–34.

17. Hall to Greene, Sept. 17, 1831, ABCFM, box 1. For Lyman Warren, see Theresa M. Schenck, *William W. Warren: The Life, Letters, and Times of an Ojibwe Leader* (Lincoln, Nebr., 2007), 1–15. For the connections between the fur trade, mixed marriages, and the mission at Mackinac, see Widder, *Battle for the Soul*, 4–7. For the significance of intermarriage in the fur trade of the Lake Superior country, see Brenda J. Child, *Holding Our World Together: Ojibwe Women and the Survival of Community* (New York, 2012), 31–62.

world with deep ties to the fur trade, with fur–trading families stretching back multiple generations.[18]

It immediately became clear to Sherman Hall that the traders were keenly interested in his mission. Writing to board member David Greene, he noted, "The Lord appears to be inclining all of the principle traders to favor our missions to these Indians." The Natives who lived in the village at La Pointe, however, seemed more ambivalent. "With regard to our prospects for immediately benefiting the Indians, I hardly know what to say," Hall wrote. "It will be difficult to keep children long at school among these Indians, unless they are fed, on account of their migratory habits and the difficulty of obtaining provision. Many of them reside at several different places during the year." The traders called a council to enable Hall to address the assembled village. At the council, Hall outlined the board's goals for his listeners and "explained to them the benefits they would derive from having schools and in receiving the gospel, and told them of the advantages of their cultivating their land." One of the ogimaag responded that Hall's words were "all true, and very good" but cautioned that "they should not compel their children to attend school, but if any of them were disposed to attend, they should not hinder them."[19]

Indeed, although Hall and the ABCFM supposed that the traders wanted the missionaries among them to bring the civilizing mission of the United States to their Native kin and trading partners, in truth the traders primarily wanted the missionaries to educate their own children. Shortly after establishing his school at La Pointe, Hall reported that "Mr. Aitkins is desirous to have a school at his post at Sandy Lake" and urged the board to accommodate the trader. Moreover, traders' interest in the educational opportunities afforded by mission schools transcended religious divides. Initially, Hall feared opposition to the ABCFM missions from the Francophone traders, who were "nearly all Catholics," but he found that not to be the case. He wrote in his letter to Greene the summer after his arrival at La Pointe: "The Cadotte family which resides at this

18. For the marriages of Oakes and Aitkins, see "Register of the Post of Michilimackinac Begun and Opened by James Gruet, Notary, June 1st, 1785," Mackinac County Courthouse, Saint Ignace, Michigan. See also Alan Knight and Janet E. Chute, "In the Shadow of the Thumping Drum: The Sault Métis—the People In-Between," in Karl S. Hele, ed., *Lines Drawn upon the Water: First Nations and the Great Lakes Borders and Borderlands* (Ontario, Canada, 2008), 91–92. For a record of the children who attended the Mackinac mission school, see "Appendix 1: Children at Mackinaw Mission," in Widder, *Battle for the Soul*, 137–143.

19. Hall to Greene, June 14, 1832, ABCFM, box 1.

place and constitutes a large part of the civilized inhabitants here, has been very kind to us and favored our mission." The missionaries established a school and Sunday religious services, though, Hall reported, "our Indian meeting has been attended only by a few, except the children who belong to the school." "The Indians when here, have not felt much interest in coming to hear. The hearers have been principally females which belong to the civilized families here."[20]

Ostensibly, Hall served the Lake Superior Anishinaabeg, or, more specifically, the people associated with the Ojibwe village at La Pointe on Madeline Island where his mission was located. Most of his interactions, however, were with the employees of the American Fur Company, who were the only year-round residents at the post—a situation that would also prove true for the other missions the ABCFM would establish at Anishinaabe villages between Lake Superior and the Mississippi. The traders and their English-speaking mixed-race children were the only people the missionaries could communicate with directly. These interactions, however, were also understood to be vital to the success of the missionary project. Hall and the other ABCFM missionaries worked hard to cultivate social and political relationships with the mixed-race families who were attached both to the fur trade and to the Native population that made the fur trade possible. These communities represented the only pockets of civilized settlement, as opposed to Indian villages, in the Michigan Territory outside Detroit, Green Bay, and Prairie du Chien.[21]

The missionaries thus worked to foster a sense of national identity among these nascent citizens who lived at the American Fur Company posts which, by necessity, meant dealing with multiracial communities. This effort was part of the civilizing mission, the social contract between the American state and the multiracial families that dominated the fur trade and the politics of the Northwest Territory. The fur traders, often French Canadian or British immigrants, would be recognized as settler-citizens. Similarly, the Indigenous and mixed-race wives and children of American Fur Company employees were also recognized as American citizens. They would be counted as civilized, meaning they would be

20. Ibid.
21. Anne F. Hyde writes: "These men were the good fathers of the fur trade. They worried about the future of Native nations and the fur trade because their children came from this world and would have to make their own lives there"; see Hyde, *Empires, Nations, and Families*, 317–318. See also Widder, *Battle for the Soul*, 21–23, for the argument that mixed-race fur traders sought missionaries and their schools for their children as agents of Americanization.

enumerated by the federal government as white. The civilizing mission, as it applied to fur traders and their families, promised inclusion within the social and legal boundaries of the Republic. In exchange for this modification of the color line in the Northwest Territory, the fur traders and their families would help engage in the political work of reshaping the social and physical boundaries of the United States.[22]

The Civilizing Missions of William Boutwell and Henry Schoolcraft

The missionaries and the ABCFM accepted their role as an extension of the U.S. government in the Northwest Territory. William Boutwell, the missionary who had traveled west with Sherman and Betsey Hall, fully embraced the intersection of the ABCFM's civilizing mission and U.S. policy. When the Halls departed for La Pointe, Boutwell remained behind at the Mackinac mission to study Anishinaabemowin. The following winter, he learned that he would accompany Henry Rowe Schoolcraft, the Indian agent for the Michigan Territory, on a voyage deeper into the West. Writing to David Greene of the ABCFM, Boutwell reported the contents of Schoolcraft's letter regarding the proposed expedition. "The last mail brought me information from Washington," Schoolcraft informed Boutwell, "that it is the intention of the War Department to send me to the heads of the Mississippi the ensuing spring." Schoolcraft then asked Boutwell "whether you will accept a seat in my canoe." He explained that making this voyage together would make it clear to the Natives that the government of the United States sanctioned the missionary project among

22. The Supreme Court of Michigan Territory granted U.S. citizenship and the associated rights to vote and serve on a jury to French-speaking Canadian-born men residing in the territory on the basis of article 2 of the Jay Treaty. See "Notes of Trials, Arguments, Decisions, and Proceedings in the Supreme Court of the Territory of Michigan—September Term, 1821," Sept. 18, 1821, in William Wirt Blume, ed., *Transactions of the Supreme Court of the Territory of Michigan, 1805–1836*, 2 vols. (Ann Arbor, Mich., 1935–1940), I, 483–484. For mixed-race or Métis communities and the relation of Native peoples and the fur trade, see Chris Andersen, "*Moya `Tipimsook* ('The People Who Aren't Theie Own Bosses'): Racialization and Misrecognition of 'Métis' in Upper Great Lakes Ethnohistory," *Ethnohistory*, LVIII (2011), 37–63. "One of the first lessons of the fur trade for European men," historian Brenda J. Child writes, "was that their success depended on conducting business with Ojibwe women"; see Child, *Holding Our World Together*, 32. Lori J. Daggar argues that the mission, as a political and economic enterprise, was central to U.S. expansion; see Daggar, "The Mission Complex: Economic Development, 'Civilization,' and Empire in the Early Republic," *Journal of the Early Republic*, XXXVI (2016), 467–491.

the Anishinaabeg. In a separate letter to the board, Schoolcraft explained why he wanted Boutwell to accompany him on his voyage to the western edge of the Michigan Territory: "I am quite satisfied that their *political,* must result from their *moral* melioration. And that our attempts in the way of agriculture, schooling and the mechanic arts, are liable to miscarry and produce no permanent good, unless the Indian mind can be purified by the gospel truth." Schoolcraft, like Hall and Boutwell, believed that conversion to Christianity was vital to the eventual success of the civilizing mission.[23]

Boutwell left Mackinac for the upper Mississippi Valley on June 5, 1832. The thirty-four-man expedition led by Schoolcraft made the journey in two barges and two canoes, and, like the flotilla carrying Hall and the mission family, they paddled west along the southern shore of Lake Superior. In addition to the missionary, Schoolcraft's party included a ten-man squad of U.S. soldiers under the command of Lieutenant John Allen along with George Johnston, who served as interpreter. Johnston was the son of a prominent British-born trader named John Johnston and an Anishinaabe woman, Ozhaawshkodewikwe (Green Prairie Woman). He was also Schoolcraft's brother-in-law and a subagent at La Pointe. Johnston's mother was the daughter of Waabojig (The White Fisher), an ogimaa also from the Ojibwe village at La Pointe. They met several parties on their way to Mackinac, including Ojibweg from Lac Court Oreilles and Lac du Flambeau as well as a number of canoes belonging to the Warren and Cadotte families. When they arrived at La Pointe, they visited the mission but found most of the Natives absent, either working their gardens or en route to Mackinac.[24]

Schoolcraft's party pressed on toward the Fond du Lac village and trading post, where they would begin their overland route to the Mississippi via an interconnected series of rivers and lakes. Passing the Brule River, an alternate route into the interior, they met a party of Ojibweg from Red Cedar Lake. They learned that a war party of one hundred "Pillagers," the epithet Americans ascribed to Ojibweg from the Leech Lake village, were raiding into the country of the Dakota, more widely

23. Boutwell to Greene, Mar. 7, 1832, Henry Rowe Schoolcraft to Greene, Feb. 25, 1832, both in ABCFM, box 1. The political leadership of the ABCFM, Alisse Portnoy argues, "encouraged this coupling of Christianity and government"; see Portnoy, *Their Right to Speak: Women's Activism in the Indian and Slave Debates* (Cambridge, Mass., 2005), 23.

24. The Diary of William T. Boutwell (hereafter cited as Boutwell Diary), June 7, 1832, William T. Boutwell Papers, 1832–1881, Gale Family Library, MHS.

known as the Sioux in nineteenth-century North America. Boutwell and his companions arrived at the Fond du Lac post, at the mouth of the Saint Louis River, on June 23, 1832. "On arriving here I was a little surprised to find nearly 400 souls," Boutwell wrote to the board, "French half breeds, Inds. and white men." "Nor was I less surprised in witnessing the scene which presented itself," he continued, "yelling of Indians, barking of dogs, crying of children, running and shouting of the multitude, and flourishing of flags, all combined to make me feel that I was no longer among civilized beings."[25]

Tocqueville had marveled at the juxtaposition of French, Anglo-Americans, "half-castes," and Natives, which he imagined as part of an embryonic community of civilized and savage people at Saginaw. Boutwell, in contrast, imagined the community at Fond du Lac as something beyond the pale of civilization. "But my feelings were indescribable," he wrote, "when I came to my senses and felt that on myself devolved the duty of preaching to this motley group the only salvation of J. Christ." He despaired, however, "when I remembered that they neither understood my language, nor I theirs." Throughout this voyage, Boutwell frequently found himself unable to communicate with the people of the Michigan Territory because they did not speak or understand the English language. This experience underscored the extent to which he understood the Anishinaabe homeland to be a foreign territory rather than a part of the United States.[26]

The following day, a Sunday, Boutwell preached a sermon, the first ever conducted at Fond du Lac, according to the trader William Aitkin. In the morning, Boutwell wrote, "We repaired to the messroom, where I preached to 30 or 40 souls, French, half-breeds, Americans, and a few Indians, who came in through curiosity." He preached in English to an impromptu congregation that spoke mostly French and Anishininaabemowin. "At 4 P.M.," he wrote, "I met the Indians, half-breeds, and French, in the same place. More than twice the number assembled that were present in the morning." This time Boutwell spoke through an interpreter, George Johnston. According to the missionary, his audience "listened with attention and apparent interest" while he read from the gospels and recited the Ten Commandments. However, he concluded the day with the more realistic observation: "There is no Sabbath with these

25. Ibid., June 22, 23 ("yelling"), 1832; Boutwell to Greene, June 25, 1832, ABCFM, box 1 ("400 souls").

26. Boutwell to Greene, June 25, 1832, ABCFM, box 1 ("motley group"); Boutwell Diary, June 23, 1832, Boutwell Papers ("language").

Indians." Underscoring this sentiment, Maangozid (Loon's Foot), a *gechi-medewid*—a high-ranking member of the Midewiwin (the Anishinaabe medicine society)—asked Schoolcraft for permission to dance. "From 5 P.M. till midnight," Boutwell wrote, "my ears were filled with the monotonous sound of their drum, which was the first thing heard in the morning."[27]

If Boutwell despaired at his inability to communicate with savage Indians, he seemed equally distressed about the Francophone traders. "There is no Sabbath with the Indians," he wrote, "nor is there any with the French half-breed voyageurs." They played the violin and danced throughout the night on Saturday and into the afternoon on Sunday. They only stopped the music and dancing, he noted, to play cards. "These men are more hopeless than the Indians," Boutwell concluded, "whose example before, and influence upon them, is most pernicious. There are few exceptions, where they were not as degraded in intellect, and as disgusting with filth, as the Indians themselves." On Monday morning, before Schoolcraft departed for the interior, the warriors of Fond du Lac came to the American Fur Company post. Thirty men marched in two columns, each led by a man carrying an American flag. Watching the procession, Boutwell wrote, "The drums beat, and the dancers began their perpendicular motion, up and down, up and down, holding their muskets in their hands at the same time." The missionary observed that with "their muskets, paints, feathers, bells, war-clubs, knives," it "looked more like what I can imagine as a war dance than a dance of respect." After the warriors made their entry, a senior warrior gave an oration to the young men extolling their victories over their enemies. The traders produced tobacco and flour, and after receiving this gift, the warriors produced a pipe, which was presented to Schoolcraft, George Johnston, and Boutwell. Once the visitors had smoked, the pipe was passed to every warrior from the procession. The ceremony was an affirmation of the friendship and alliance between the Fond du Lac Ojibweg and the United States. Boutwell, in both his journal and his letter to the board, recounted the ceremony as a spectacle and as a signifier of the uncivilized world into which he traveled with the hope of impressing upon the Natives the need for additional Christian missions.[28]

27. Boutwell Diary, June 23, 1832, Boutwell Papers. For Maangozid and the gechi-medewid, see Cary Miller, *Ogimaag: Anishinaabeg Leadership, 1760–1845* (Lincoln, Nebr., 2010), 72–73.

28. Boutwell Diary, June 24, 25, 1832, Boutwell Papers (quotations); Boutwell to Greene, June 25, 1832, ABCFM, box 1. The ABCFM missionaries, Keith R. Widder

If Boutwell came west on behalf of the ABCFM in order to establish missions among the Anishinaabeg, Schoolcraft traveled west to represent the federal government. In the summer of 1826, Governor Lewis Cass wrote a series of letters to James Barbour, the secretary of war, asserting: "It is also important that the power and authority of the United States should be displayed upon Lake Superior. That region is subject to British influence. . . . and the hostile attitude assumed by the Indians evince the necessity of exhibiting the physical force of the government." Cass wrote this letter following the negotiation of the Treaty of Prairie du Chien in 1825 with most of the Native nations of the Northwest Territory. The United States did not demand land cessions at this meeting but rather a recognition of American sovereignty and the promise that each nation would remain within their territorial boundaries. The latter pledge was meant to end warfare between nations that often fought over access to hunting territories. He also asked for additional Indian agents as a countermeasure designed to diminish the influence of British Canadian traders.[29]

The War Department sent Schoolcraft to the headwaters of the Mississippi in 1832 because of conflict between the Dakota and the Ojibweg, which was in violation of the 1825 treaty that both nations signed with the United States. In addition to the rumor about a Pillager raid against the Dakota, Schoolcraft learned from Charles Oakes at Fond du Lac that the people at Lac du Flambeau had formed a war party "to go against the Sioux" but had subsequently abandoned the raid. In other words, the threat of conflict remained a constant, in spite of the treaty signed in 1825. Fifteen of the twenty voyageurs who departed with Schoolcraft continued the

---

argues, "condemned the behavior of most people in the fur-trade society as incompatible with a way of life based upon book learning, agriculture, artisanry, or business." "Similarly, the traditional seasonal rounds of the Chippewa and Odawa, when coupled with what appeared to be strange religious practices, verified in the missionary mind that these people were indeed 'uncivilized.' Since the Roman-Catholic French-Métis seemed to have adopted or accepted much of what they found in Indian society, the missionaries often relegated many of them to an 'uncivilized' status as well." See Widder, *Battle for the Soul*, 44.

29. Lewis Cass to James Barbour, May 19, 1826, Michigan Superintendency, 1824–1851, Letters Received, 1824–1880, Record Group (RG) 75: Records of the Bureau of Indian Affairs, 1793–1999, M234, roll 419, 484–489 (quotation on 485), National Archives and Records Administration (NARA), Washington, D.C.; "Treaty with the Sioux, etc.," Aug. 19, 1825, in Charles J. Kappler, comp. and ed., *Indian Affairs: Laws and Treaties*, II, *Treaties* (Washington, D.C., 1904), 250–255.

journey west carrying supplies for the inland posts and escorting the agent, missionary, interpreter, and the squad of U.S. soldiers as they pressed on from Fond du Lac hoping to head off the war party rumored to be gathering at Leech Lake.[30]

Leaving Fond du Lac, Schoolcraft and his party endured a series of grueling portages as they made their way toward Leech Lake, an experience that would make it all too clear that the United States was barely an idea in this region let alone an actual presence. After leaving the mouth of the Saint Louis River, they came to the Grand Portage, where they would need to unpack and carry their supplies and canoes overland for nine miles. Reentering the river, they ascended a series of rapids. "Often," Boutwell wrote, "the men are obliged to spring into the water and lighten the canoe, which they at the same time steady by hand." They frequently stopped to mend their canoes, battered by rapids. When they at last reached the Ojibwe village and post at Sandy Lake, the missionary wrote, "Our men look like renegades, covered with mud from head to foot, some have lost one leg of their pantaloons, others, both." They arrived at the home village of Beshibiiaanakwad, the wife of William Aitkin, and were greeted by "a salute of musketry." The trader maintained a large two-story house, a storehouse, and a cabin for his *engagés*, or fur-trade employees. The following day, on July 4, Schoolcraft called the people of the village to council. He presented gifts and a string of wampum, a gesture signifying peace and alliance. "Mr S. then made a few remarks to them," Boutwell wrote, "touching on the object of my visit and commending myself to their friendship as I was a friend of his." Lt. Allen called his men to stand for inspection and to offer the village a salute "and reminded us of its being the fourth of July."[31]

This was the extent of American power in the upper Mississippi Valley in the summer of 1832, exactly one year after Tocqueville's visit to Saginaw. Eleven soldiers covered in mud, some without an intact pair of pants, carried west by voyageurs and hosted by one of the principal traders of the American Fur Company. They were meant to represent the authority of the U.S. government. Schoolcraft and Boutwell traveled to Sandy Lake to project American power and to sell the idea of civilization. Instead, they suggested the very thing Governor Cass worried about in

30. Boutwell to Greene, June 25, 1832, ABCFM, box 1.

31. Boutwell Diary, June 28 ("obliged"), July 2–3 ("renegades"), 4 ("friendship"), 1832, Boutwell Papers.

his letter to the secretary of war: the weakness of the American state in the remote Northwest of the Michigan Territory.

The absence of federal authority in the Illinois country, a more densely settled part of the Northwest, had already resulted in clashes between settlers and a Sauk, Mesquakie, and Kickapoo band led by Blackhawk earlier that year in April 1832. Not wanting to appear weak in the face of Indian depredations, the United States sent federal troops from Saint Louis to bolster local militia. The result was a short, unnecessary war that decimated Blackhawk's band and terrorized both white and Indigenous inhabitants of northwestern Illinois. Schoolcraft's party began to ascend the Mississippi just as this conflict came to a violent end. Making their way toward Leech Lake, they met an engagé who worked for William Aitkin. This man informed them that Eshkibagikoonzh (Bird with the Green Bill), also known as Flat Mouth, had just returned to Leech Lake after leading a successful raid against the Dakota. Eshkibagikoonzh was an important ogimaa, and he had signed the treaty, or touched the pen, at Prairie du Chien in 1825.[32]

Thus, not only had the Leech Lake Ojibweg violated the treaty in raiding the Dakota, but they had been led by the distinguished ogimaa Eshkibagikoonzh. Most raids were led by younger men, which made this recent raid politically significant. In a letter to the superintendent of Indian Affairs, Schoolcraft explained politics and warfare in Anishinaabewaki. "All of the Indians permanently located within this agency," he wrote, "speak the Chippeway language, and pronounce themselves *Ojibways*. They are dispersed over an immense surface of country, and separated into small independent bands, each of which has some distinct appellation, and obeys its own village chiefs." These leaders "are hereditary, their power as magistrates is feeble and doubtful." "The war chiefs of this tribe are popular, and whatever authority they exercise, begins and ends with the expeditions which called them forth. It is comparatively rare, that the powers of a village and a war chief unite in the same person." The Treaty of Prairie du Chien in 1825 and a subsequent treaty with the Ojibweg of Fond du Lac in 1826 were meant to hold all of the Ojibwe *doodemag*, or

32. Boutwell Diary, July 8, 1832, Boutwell Papers; Patrick J. Jung, *The Black Hawk War of 1832* (Norman, Okla., 2007); Lucy Eldersveld Murphy, *Great Lakes Creoles: A French-Indian Community on the Northern Borderlands, Prairie du Chien, 1750–1860* (New York, 2014), 190–191; Bethel Saler, *The Settlers' Empire: Colonialism and State Formation in America's Old Northwest* (Philadelphia, 2015), 118–120.

Figure 9. *Ne gon e bin ais (Flatmouth)*. Circa 1905.
Minnesota Historical Society, Saint Paul

bands, collectively responsible for the maintenance of peace with the Dakota. The raid led by Eshkibagikoonzh was a sign that something had gone wrong and that U.S. diplomacy had failed.[33]

Schoolcraft, an Indian agent married to a Native woman and living among the Anishinaabeg, was well positioned to recognize the significance of the raid led by Eshkibagikoonzh. Most representatives of the U.S. government, in contrast, tended to perceive Native warfare, not as strategic, but rather as a reflection of their savage nature. In a letter to the secretary of war explaining the necessity of the 1826 Fond du Lac treaty, Cass observed that "the Sioux and the Chippewas have been at war for ages." He attributed this ageless conflict to "the rash young men, who are always turbulent and vindictive." The treaty Council held at Fond du Lac in 1826 was intended to disrupt this pattern and to reinforce the provisions of the 1825 Treaty of Prairie du Chien, negotiated at a council that many of the Lake Superior Ojibweg had not attended. "They must have some object before them to attract their attention," Cass informed the secretary, "to divert the tedious monotony of savage life. A general convention of the tribe would ensure this object." This, in effect, was also the purpose behind Schoolcraft's expedition in 1832. Describing his mission to the commissioner of Indian Affairs, Cass wrote, "Annual messages to them and remonstrances, with appeals to the calamities impending over them, we may have to make for some time." But, he noted, "eventually these checks will produce the desired effect, and by destroying the habit, will likewise destroy the wish for war."[34]

Two days after learning about the raid led by Eshkibagikoonzh, Schoolcraft's party encountered evidence of its aftermath when they arrived at the American Fur Company post at Red Cedar Lake. "There I witnessed the first scalp dance," Boutwell wrote in his diary. Some young men from the village joined the Pillager's raid against the Dakota, and one of them had been killed. Three scalps had been taken from the Dakota, however, and "three young women, each holding one of them in the air, led the dance this evening, while men, women and children accompanied the drum with their voices." After the dance, the voyageurs gifted the widow of the slain warrior with tobacco. "I visited their lodge before the dance

33. Schoolcraft to Thomas McKenny, Aug. 4, 1824, Michigan Superintendency, RG 75, M234, roll 419.

34. Cass to the Barbour, May 19, 1826, Michigan Superintendency, RG 75, M234, roll 419, 484–489 (quotations on 485); Cass to Samuel Hamilton, Dec. 4, 1830, ibid., roll 420.

began," Boutwell noted, "and read the ten commandments, and sang a few hymns, with two of our men. All listened with astonishment, never before having heard them." "As I had no interpreter," he concluded, "I could not address them." Time and again, Boutwell would experience this sort of cognitive dissonance, recording in his journal that his preaching had been met with interest and astonishment and then lamenting that his audience could not understand his English. This was a different version of the disconnect experienced by Tocqueville, who marveled at the ability of mixed-race Natives, living in what he perceived as unsettled wilderness, to communicate with him, fluently, in his own language. Boutwell marveled at his inability to communicate altogether with Native peoples living in what was supposed to be the United States. Such cognitive dissonance was an inherent feature of the ideology represented by the civilizing mission that Boutwell, Schoolcraft, and other U.S. officials believed in so thoroughly.[35]

Schoolcraft's party continued, stopping at upper Red Cedar Lake, where they discovered that they had, once again, been preceded by warriors from Leech Lake. They witnessed another scalp dance ceremony the night of their arrival. The following day, the American party called the village to council. "Mr. S. addressed them," Boutwell wrote, "and made them presents of ammunition, lead knives, tobacco, Calico, cloth, beads, thread, needles, beads, feathers, ribbons, awls flints. A medal and flag were presented to Ozonshtiguan, Yellow Head." Boutwell asked the ogimaa if he wanted a missionary to "come and instruct your children." He demurred and said he could not answer because too many of their senior people were not present. Nevertheless, when they left for Leech Lake, Boutwell wrote in his diary: "They must now feel that our government is exercising paternal care for their interests. Their presents will long keep awake the kind feelings which they have called into exercise, and which they received with marked expressions of gratitude." Even in the face of a subtle rejection by Ozaawinishtigwaan, Boutwell expressed confidence in

---

35. Boutwell Diary, July 10, 1832, Boutwell Papers. Powerful preaching and public worship were the cornerstones of the evangelical movement, and Boutwell's willingness to repeatedly confess his faith, read from the Bible, and explain the main tenets of Christianity were a reflection of this tradition. For the significance of public worship and the power of public preaching, see Curtis D. Johnson, "The Protracted Meeting Myth: Awakenings, Revivals, and New York State Baptists, 1789–1850," *JER*, XXXIV (2014), 349–383.

the power of U.S. paternalism, another aspect of the ideology underlying the civilizing mission.[36]

The ensuing confrontation between Schoolcraft and Eshkibagikoonzh would shake the missionary's confidence, but it also revealed that both the United States and the Ojibweg needed to rethink the nature of their relationship. When the American delegation arrived, they were asked to join Eshkibagikoonzh in his house for breakfast. The ogimaa lived in a large log cabin with a stone chimney. They entered the house to find Eshkibagikoonzh with his face painted black in mourning over the death of his son killed by the Dakota. Warriors lined the walls of his house, their faces painted red, signaling their determination to seek revenge against the Dakota. "Their countenances were full of a wildness such as I never saw before," Boutwell wrote. According to the missionary, the ogimaa offered a litany of complaints, "especially against Mr. Aitkins." Schoolcraft asked the ogimaa to listen to the Reverend Boutwell. "I addressed them on the subject of my visit," he wrote. After listening, Eshkibagikoonzh announced "that he would speak a few Words." Addressing Schoolcraft rather than the missionary, he began by saying "that he was sorry Mr. S. considered them as children, and not as men." Rejecting the diplomatic language of the subordinate and obedient Native child, Eshkibagikoonzh declared his people the equals of their American allies. He also affirmed the legitimacy of the conflict with the Dakota. "The promise was, when they smoked the pipe with the Sioux, that the first one who crossed the line, should be flogged." They had broken their promise, the ogimaa declared, "their Great Father, the President of the United States, had not stretched out the long arm which he had promised." This broken promise cost Eshkibagikoonzh the life of his son, and he was determined "not to lay down arms as long as he saw the light of the sun."[37]

Eshkibagikoonzh made no attempt to conceal that he had led the retaliatory attack against the Dakota, but he did offer Schoolcraft a way

36. Boutwell Diary, July 15–16, 1832, Boutwell Papers. Laurel Clark Shire has noted that many of the cultural and political elite in the Jacksonian era "embraced a cultural delusion called paternalist racism." "Their sincere commitment to that ideology meant that they were collectively convinced of their own racial superiority, but not humane or innocent, because, after all, that ideology enabled them to justify taking land from Indigenous peoples and stealing life and labor from Africans and African Americans." See Shire, "Sentimental Racism and Sympathetic Paternalism: Feeling Like a Jacksonian," *JER*, XXXIX (2019), 115.

37. Boutwell Diary, July 17, 1832, Boutwell Papers.

to move forward. After his speech, the ogimaa took his seat, according to Boutwell, "with as much dignity as if he was king of an empire." He then asked Schoolcraft to give him a white shirt, "that he might lay aside his mourning." The following day, the American delegation began their return voyage, and when they reached the lake shore, they found Eshkibagikoonzh waiting for them. Douglass Houghton, the surgeon traveling with Schoolcraft, recorded the encounter in his journal. "He was dressed in a military frock coat and hat and made altogether [an] imposing appearance," he wrote, and he was accompanied by Gichiaya'aa nisayehn (Elder Brother) and Maajigaabaw (Stirring Man), the second and third ogimaag of Leech lake. According to Houghton, Eshkibagikoonzh informed Schoolcraft "that since he had come to visit him he would wash away his mourning." Under his frock coat, the ogimaa wore the white shirt Schoolcraft gave him. Eshkibagikoonzh chastised the Indian agent at council, but he also reaffirmed the alliance between his people and the United States, wearing the gifted shirt along with formal attire that the Indian agent would recognize as civilized dress.[38]

Eshkibagikoonzh greeted the Americans in the morning, having put aside his grief with the help of his American allies. And although he ignored Boutwell's offer at council, the Leech Lake village allowed the missionary to live among them and establish a mission school. Boutwell returned to Leech Lake in the summer of 1833. Accepting the missionary made strategic sense for the people at Leech Lake. An additional American presence in the village, one tied to the U.S. government as opposed to the fur trade, could prevent additional hostilities with the Dakota. "The second chief (Kiji Osaie), the Elder Brother, as he is called," Boutwell wrote the board, visited the missionary as soon as he arrived. "I said to him, I have come to pass the winter with your trader, and I thought I would teach some of the chil. to read and I don't think an Ind. in the whole band can be displeased or say a word against it replied he." A few days later, leaving with his family for the winter hunt, Gichiaya'aa nisayehn "came and asked me if I should be pleased to have his little boy, a lad of ten years, remain with me." Aitkin agreed to feed the boy, and Boutwell agreed to teach him. "If you will learn him to read and as

38. Ibid. "The Manuscript Journal of Douglass Houghton, June 23 to August 25, 1832," July 8–17, in "Appendix D: Journal, Letters, and Reports of Dr. Douglass Houghton," in Philip P. Mason, ed., *Schoolcraft's Expedition to Lake Itasca: The Discovery of the Source of the Mississippi* (Lansing, Mich., 1993), 260. For another account of this council, see Michael Witgen, *An Infinity of Nations: How the Native New World Shaped Early North America* (Philadelphia, 2012), 1–7.

the whites do, I should be glad," the ogimaa informed the missionary, seeing the advantage in having his child learn the skills needed to navigate a future that necessarily included relations with the United States. Gichiaya'aa nisàyehn was one of the few ogimaa to grasp, like the traders, the value of mission schools in preparing their children for the coming encounter with the peoples and institutions of the Republic.[39]

The U.S. government, of course, also saw the advantage of placing missionaries among the Ojibweg. Schoolcraft wrote to the ABCFM regarding their plans for Boutwell, Hall, and other missionaries: "As yet the Chippewa of this quarter are (with one exception) without annuities." As a consequence, the United States was without direct influence over their leaders other than through the traders, who placed their own interests first. Governor Cass complained about this dependency, using traders to represent the interests of the United States. Schoolcraft likewise saw the value of using the missionaries to influence the Ojibweg. He, like the missionaries of the ABCFM, was deeply influenced by the Second Great Awakening and understood the United States to be God's chosen nation. Accordingly, he and the missionaries advocated for an Indian policy that linked Christian evangelism and government intervention in the daily lives of Native peoples.[40]

"Surrounded by a Nation of Barbarians"

William Boutwell's success with Gichiaya'aa nisayehn was the exception rather than the rule. After their first year in the field, Sherman Hall and Boutwell reported that "few among the uncivilized Indians have come to be instructed." They cautioned against any idea of rapid progress, for "on our arrival to this country, we found ourselves surrounded by a nation of barbarians who know nothing of the Christian religion or civilization." They ignored the fact that the Anishinaabeg had been exposed to Catholicism for more than two centuries, just as they ignored the similarly long history of Anishinaabe peoples trading among and living alongside Europeans. If Hall and Boutwell's report represented the Anishinaabeg as living in isolation in the wilderness, they also found an additional need for their mission in the most tangible evidence that this representation was a fiction. "The character and condition of the mixed population," they wrote, "with some exceptions, is such as to call for Christian benevolence

39. Boutwell to Greene, Dec. 18, 1833, ABCFM, box 1.
40. Schoolcraft to Greene, Nov. 2, 1833, ABCFM, box 1. See Portnoy, *Their Right to Speak*, 22–25.

and missionary effort no less than the Indian itself." Arriving at Yellow Lake in the fall of 1833 to establish a new mission in the Saint Croix Department, ABCFM missionaries Frederick and Elizabeth Ayer attended a council called by the trader. "I made known to them the object of our coming to Y.L. and the design of the board relative to the Chippeways generally," he wrote. "On the 24th or 5," he continued, "we opened our school with eight scholars all except 2 half breeds." He also noted that Hester Crooks, the mixed-race Anishinaabe who had initially provided domestic help to Hall, was "well fitted to teach on this plan. . . . She has entered upon her work with zeal, and appears to have the welfare of those who are her kindred according to the flesh at heart." Similarly, Hall reported from La Pointe: "Most of the scholars are of mixed breed. A few are full Indian. They were generally attended to English and Indian Studies." And, as noted previously, he relied on the domestic servant Elizabeth Campbell, married to a mixed-race Anishinaabe man, as an interpreter for his school and mission.[41]

Rather than make distinctions according to race, the missionaries consistently used the concepts of "civilized" and "uncivilized" to serve as markers of identity. The definition of civilized behavior or character was expressed inconsistently by both the missionaries and territorial officials. Mixed-race people, almost always the children of traders, clerks, and voyageurs who spoke a European language, were often identified as civilized. The missionaries identified the Cadotte family at La Pointe, for example, as civilized. Such a designation, however, was also often conflated with class status. William Aitkin's mixed-race wife Magdalene, or Beshibiiaanakwad, did not speak English, but the missionaries identified her as civilized and did not refer to her as Ojibwe or even as an Indian when they wrote about her in their diaries. Nor did the designation of civilized correlate with living arrangements. The families of the American Fur Company proprietors lived like Europeans or Americans in log cabins associated with trading posts. Voyageurs and clerks, however, often lived among their Native relatives in Native fashion. When Boutwell returned

41. Hall and Boutwell to the Prudential Committee, May 1833 ("instructed"), Frederick Ayer to Greene, Oct. 4, 1833 ("made known"), Hall to Greene, Oct. 17, 1834 ("scholars"), all in ABCFM, box 1. By "Indian Studies," Hall meant instruction with religious texts written in Anishinaabemowin. Elizabeth Campbell had served as an interpreter for William and Amanda Ferry, who founded and administered the Mackinac mission; see Widder, *Battle for the Soul*, 73.

to Leech Lake, he spent his first night in the home of François Brunet, a "half-breed" clerk. In his diary, Boutwell noted that "he, like the Indians, lives in a lodge which is about 30 feet by 15." The missionary dined with Brunet's family in their wigwam and stayed the night: "The lodge was filled with noisy Indians, laughing, talking, singing, etc. while we ate."[42]

In truth, the clear separation between the categories of civilized and uncivilized was something imagined by the missionaries and did not match the lived experience of anyone at the various posts served by the ABCFM. Mixed-race families and their Native relatives lived together seamlessly. In fact, their livelihoods depended on this coexistence. The missionaries, in spite of their habit of distinguishing between the civilized and uncivilized, would find it necessary to accommodate themselves within a social world that was essentially Indigenous. Edmund Ely, for example, left divinity school to join the ABCFM mission in the Lake Superior country in 1833. Like Boutwell before him, Ely stayed with Aitkin at his Sandy Lake post when he arrived that fall. He, too, opened a school and began to teach the children of the post, which he identified as the "families of the clerks . . . and Indian children." Ely found that his school could operate only according to the seasonal calendar of the fur trade; his pupils would leave the post "as Mr. A's clerks will leave for their respective posts, and the Indians on their hunts."[43]

The clerks did not winter alone but with their families, who would depart from villages such as Leech Lake, Sandy Lake, Yellow Lake, and La Pointe for smaller posts associated with the winter hunting grounds of the different doodemag. Men like François Brunet would follow them. All of the men associated with the fur trade, clerks like Brunet and proprietors like Aitkin, depended upon the domestic labor of their wives and daughters. William Aitkin would pass most of the winter at his house in Sandy Lake with his wife and children, who returned from the Mackinac Island mission school with their father in 1833. They would attend Ely's school held in their father's buildings. William's oldest son, Alfred,

42. Boutwell Diary, Oct. 1, 2, 1833, Boutwell Papers. Lucy Eldersveld Murphy argues that, although U.S. officials could have racialized people like Beshibiiaanakwad as nonwhite, "newly and uncertainly dominant, the young United States needed these Creoles, people on the margins between Indian and white worlds, to help them achieve the critical mass of population that would allow them to dominate and control the other peoples of the Midwest." See Murphy, *Great Lakes Creoles*, 63. See also Saler, *The Settlers' Empire*, 211–248.

43. Edmund Ely to Greene, Sept. 25, 1833, ABCFM, box 1.

entered the trade and began to manage the American Fur Company post at Red Cedar Lake.[44]

Women were central to the complex networks that allowed non-Native and mixed-race peoples like the voyageurs, clerks, and traders to occupy posts embedded in Native village communities. From the beginning of the French fur trade in the seventeenth century and the establishment of the Hudson's Bay Company in the eighteenth century, Native women had helped to integrate male European traders into the extended kinship networks of Native village communities. This integration made the fur trade possible. Hunting, trapping, and processing furs were part of the social relations of production for most Native peoples in North America. The fur trade was easily incorporated into the seasonal patterns of harvesting resources that sustained Indigenous communities. In places like the Great Lakes and upper Mississippi Valley, trade also relied on kinship, which facilitated the peaceful exchange of goods. Relatives were obligated to take care of one another. The prosperous and the powerful provided for the people of their extended families, their doodem. Being connected to a trader through intermarriage could benefit a village or an individual leader. By the nineteenth century, the fur trade had become more commercial, but Native hunters and their extended families, such as Zhaazhaawanibiisens in the Red River Valley, still considered themselves attached to individual traders and their companies. Often, as was the case with Aitkin, a trader lived at and operated a post associated with the village of his Native wife.[45]

The kinship ties that had earlier facilitated the fur trade played an equally important role in the daily life of traders and their clerks in the nineteenth century. Men like Aitkin and Brunet depended on their families to do their work. When Boutwell lodged with Brunet on his first night

44. For the departure of the Aitkins' children from the Mackinac mission school, see Widder, *Battle for the Soul*, 137–143.

45. For the history of Native women acting as cultural brokers and intermediaries between their communities and traders, see Sylvia Van Kirk, *Many Tender Ties: Women in Fur-Trade Society*, 1st American ed. (Norman, Okla., 1983); Jennifer S.H. Brown, *Strangers in Blood: Fur Trade Company Families in Indian Country* (Vancouver, 1980); Susan Sleeper-Smith, *Indian Women and French Men: Rethinking Cultural Encounter in the Western Great Lakes* (Amherst, Mass., 2001). For the mixed-race communities that emerged within the trade in the United States and Canadian Northwest, see Nicole St-Onge, Carolyn Podruchny, and Brenda Macdougall, eds., *Contours of a People: Metis Family, Mobility, and History* (Norman, Okla., 2012); Murphy, *Great Lakes Creoles*.

at Leech Lake, he wrote in his journal, "Our board was served with bears meat and potatoes, tea, and short-cake (called in French galette)." The next morning, he noted: "Breakfasted this morning with Mr. Brunet, the half-breed clerk of whom I have spoken above. Our table was served as last night, with the addition only of butter, which came from Mackinac or the Sault." Brunet did not live off the supplies of Aitkin or the American Fur Company. And although he managed to purchase Euro-American-produced commodities such as butter and tea, the rest of the fare he shared with Boutwell was produced from the family larder maintained by his Native wife.[46]

The importance of the domestic arrangements required to sustain anybody—trader, clerk, or missionary—was not lost on Boutwell. He wrote the board explaining that a mission family "should be three persons—at all events there should be two." He thought a man and two women ideal, which was the situation at Yellow Lake with the Ayers and Hester Crooks. He worried, however, that this arrangement would seem like polygamy. Many prominent Ojibwe men practiced polygamy, and Boutwell did not want to seem to validate this choice in making his living arrangements. "Much as I have been wont to deprecate the idea of a missionary to these Inds. being married," he wrote, "I must frankly admit its propriety if a mission is to be located here." Eight months later, Boutwell wrote in his diary: "Left Le Pointe this morning in company with Bro. Ayer for Yellow Lake. The object of my going to Yellow Lake is to take my friend, Miss Hester Crooks with me to Leech Lake." He had waited patiently for the board to send him "a person to accompany me hither." When they failed to produce such an individual, Boutwell mused, "The idea of attempting to keep house alone, to do my own cooking, washing, mending, to sustain a school," was too demanding. The answer, he informed the ABCFM, "seemed to demand that I should have a wife." Accordingly, he married Hester Crooks at Fond du Lac on September 11, 1834.[47]

"Her Manners and Dress Being That of an American Woman"

William Boutwell married a Native woman, like the American Fur Company employees he derided, because he realized that to maintain his independence he needed a family, or at least a spouse. Hester Crooks was a

46. Boutwell Diary, Oct. 1, 2, 1833, Boutwell Papers.

47. Boutwell to Greene, Dec. 18, 1833, ABCFM, box 1; Boutwell Diary, Aug. 27, 1834, Boutwell Papers. Historian Catherine J. Denial argues that women's labor was critical

fellow ABCFM missionary, so their union made sense on that level. She was also the daughter of an Ojibwe woman, from Drummond Island, and Ramsay Crooks, a Scott who immigrated to British Canada in 1803 and became one of four partners to purchase the Northern Department of the American Fur Company in 1834. Boutwell's choice of a "helpmate" was extremely strategic. The couple returned to Leech Lake, where Boutwell observed: "My wife, I find, is no small curiosity to this people, though one of their kindred, according to the flesh. Her manners and dress being that of an American woman, which most of the number never saw." Being identified as an American was the ultimate marker of civilization and signifier of whiteness, which Boutwell, his fellow missionaries, and American Fur Company employees applied to the mixed-race daughters and wives of the men engaged in the fur trade. This same signifier of whiteness was also attributed to the mixed-race sons who joined their fathers in the trade. Increasingly, however, their whiteness would be tied to their identity as Americans and their ability to speak English. Both Alfred Aitkin and Hester Crooks attended the mission school at Mackinac and spoke English. It was this skill rather than any desire to bring Protestant Christianity or civilization to Native peoples that spurred fur-trade proprietors like William Aitkin and the Cadottes to ask the ABCFM to send missionaries to their communities.[48]

Boutwell, again like the traders, understood his marriage as a necessary condition for the success of his mission. He made this explicit in a letter to

---

to the success of the ABCFM missions. "For both the Christian missionaries of the American Board of Commissioners for Foreign Missions (ABCFM) and the Dakota and Ojibwe communities that they sought to convert," she writes, "marriage was a spiritual matter, a labor agreement, an indicator of social status, and—hopefully—a means to assure companionship." See Denial, *Making Marriage: Husbands, Wives, and the American State in Dakota and Ojibwe Country* (Saint Paul, Minn., 2013), 56.

48. Boutwell Diary, Oct. 9, 1834, Boutwell Papers; Tanis C. Thorne, "Crooks, Ramsay," *Dictionary of Canadian Biography*, VIII, University of Toronto / Université Laval, 2002–, http://www.biographi.ca/en/bio/crooks_ramsay_8E.html; Hester Crooks Boutwell, Life Memoranda, ABCFM Archives, ABC: 6.5.3, I, 183. As Lucy Eldersveld Murphy notes: "Indian peoples in the Midwest had approved of—and even encouraged—intermarriage. During the fur-trade era, traders learned that their Native customers expected them to marry local daughters, creating bonds of obligations to their in-laws and their communities. Native wives became interpreters who learned and taught both their own Native families and their husbands about each other's expectations and cultures" (Murphy, *Great Lakes Creoles*, 33). Boutwell liked to assert that his marriage was different from that of the many fur traders attached to the Anishinaabeg, but it was not.

the ABCFM. "I was willing to return alone," he wrote, "but experience had taught me, that to reside in a trader's family, however I might be called a missionary, yet it was impossible to remove the impression from the Inds. mind, that I was interested in the trade." Boutwell insisted that he felt duty bound to resolve this situation. "Instead of going into the first lodge I should chance to fall upon and throwing down my blanket," he wrote, "providence directed me to send a dispatch three days march across the wilderness to Yellow Lake with proposals to Miss Hester Crooks." After the marriage, the clerk at Leech Lake offered to let the couple live in his house. "I thought it best to decline his offer," Boutwell noted, "and on the 13th inst. removed my effects and commenced housekeeping in a bark lodge."[49]

In an effort to secure more permanent housing and to demonstrate that he intended to reside permanently at Leech Lake, Boutwell began construction of a log cabin. He miscalculated, however, in that when he arrived most of the families were away at their fall hunting grounds, and he made a "present" to the sister of Gichiaya'aa nisayehn for a piece of land. From Boutwell's perspective, he had purchased this plot of land, where he quickly erected his cabin. In a letter to the board, Boutwell wrote, "Elder Brother, the second chief, who expressed satisfaction, that I had returned and regretted that he was not present at my arrival, while there remained a few men with whom he would have smoked and spoken on the occasion." This was a generous interpretation of the missionary's encounter with the number two ogimaa of Leech Lake. In his diary, Boutwell offered a more candid account of this exchange. He told the ogimaa, "I was sorry he was not present when I arrived, and before I made his sister the present for the point of land which she has occupied." Gichiaya'aa nisayehn replied that he would have "assisted me in obtaining land by speaking to the older men, and smoking with them, on the occasion, which would have been better." Boutwell responded that when the families returned from their hunts, he would "give him some tobacco and he might make a smoking party." The ogimaa replied, "He said he could do nothing alone, but must act in concert with the other chiefs. I know those whose ancestors first found this lake. Those are the ones I would have called." The difference between Boutwell's letter to the ABCFM and his diary suggests that he knew he had over reached, taking advantage of his status as an American official to acquire Indigenous land. Even with his Ojibwe wife, Boutwell struggled to understand how to live as part of

49. Boutwell to Greene, Jan. 23, 1835, ABCFM, box 1.

the community at Leech Lake. Rather than reflecting Ojibwe customs, his purchase of land for his cabin underscored the ideological logic behind the political economy of plunder that would become intertwined with the civilizing mission of the United States.[50]

While William and Hester Boutwell established their home and mission among the Ojibweg of Leech Lake, Edmund Ely moved his mission to Fond du Lac, following William Aitkin, who had shifted his principal trading post to this village in 1834. Ely boarded with the Aitkin family, who offered him multiple forms of support. Aitkin's head clerk, Pierre Cotte, began to build a schoolhouse for the missionary to use. While he constructed the building, Cotte offered his home for Ely's school. Cotte, Ely remarked in his journal, "was himself as much interested as any scholar." Only two Native scholars attended, but "Madame Cotte has commenced the English with much zeal." Similarly, he reported that Pierre Cotte "reads only French but has learned the Eng[lish] alphabet and spends hours in teaching it to others." Ely also wrote that "Mr. Aitkins two eldest daughters are able to read the Scriptures, and have commenced Geography." In effect, the ABCFM school at Fond du Lac primarily served the mixed-race population associated with the trading post, much like the mission schools at La Pointe and Yellow Lake. One of the reasons for the low rate of Native attendance can be gleaned from another of Ely's journal entries. A band of Ojibweg came to the post for ammunition and expressed dismay on learning of the mission. "One of them," he wrote, "an old man, was very urgent that none become praying Indians."[51]

A month later, on October 24, 1834, Ely moved out on his own, living and teaching in the house built for his mission by Cotte, but he faced numerous obstacles. Native attendance at the school remained low not only because many people from the village at Fond du Lac were not interested in becoming "praying Indians" but also because of the seasonal migration of the Ojibweg. Ely wrote, for example, that the youngest son of Ininini, the brother-in-law of Beshibiiaanakwad, had become a proficient reader. "He remained in the school until his father called him to embark, and anxious to be taught all the time, read his lesson twice over, and when I could not teach him, he was teaching those less forward than himself." Moreover, Ely fell into a querulous relationship with Cotte over sectarian differences. Cotte agitated among the sizable Native and mixed-race Catholic community at Fond du Lac, telling them that Ely was prejudiced

50. Ibid.; Boutwell Diary, Oct. 15, 1834, Boutwell Papers.

51. Theresa M. Schenck, ed., *The Ojibwe Journals of Edmund F. Ely, 1833–1849* (Lincoln, Nebr., 2012), Sept. 29, 1834, 116, Oct. 2, 1834, 117.

against Catholicism. This accusation was true enough, at least in private. But publicly Ely strived to include Catholic Natives and mixed-blood children in his school if only to open them to what he believed was the truer form of Christianity.[52]

The following summer, Ely traveled with the Boutwells to La Pointe, the headquarters for the Ojibwe missions in the Northern Department, a trip that would prove momentous. They arrived at the mission on June 30, 1835, and found the Ayers already there visiting with the Halls. In his journal, Ely also noted: "Henry Blatchford and Catharine Bissell from the Mackinaw Mission School had recently arrived to labour as assistants at such places as most expedient. They were hopefully converted the last winter. Speak Chippeway." Henry was a young, mixed-race Ojibwe man from the Lake Superior country originally named François Descharrault. Catherine was the mixed-race Ojibwe daughter of Joseph Goulais and Josette Grant, and she was also born in the Lake Superior country, at Fort William in Thunder Bay. The missionaries at Mackinac changed their names to honor American benefactors of the mission school. The renaming of Native converts was an old practice among the French, English, and, later, American settlers, usually meant to provide European names to Native people to signify their conversion and embrace of civilization. François and Catherine were renamed seemingly with the intent of making their names sound more American, or at least less French. Shortly after the new assistants arrived, Elizabeth Campbell, who served as the interpreter for the La Pointe mission, returned to Mackinac with her family.[53]

Ely remained at La Pointe for five weeks before returning to Fond du Lac with William Aitkin to resume his school. "I have been somewhat oppressed in spirits last evening and to-day," he recorded in his journal. "After such a friendly interview as I have enjoyed at Lapointe, to find myself *alone* (for those around me are little better to me as companions than if they were not) is somewhat heart-sickening." In this same passage, he wrote, "By the help of Isabella [Cotte] I endeavoured to preach the truth to the children and others who came in at the usual meeting of the school." Isabella was the mixed-race wife of Henry Cotte and the daughter-in-law of Ely's Catholic nemesis Pierre Cotte. She not only helped Ely in the school but also served as his interpreter, speaking Anishinaabemowin,

52. Ibid., Nov. 4, 1834, 122 (quotation), Nov. 20, 1834, 123–124.

53. Ibid., June 30, 1835, 162; Widder, *Battle for the Soul*, 138, 141; Catherine Bissell Ely, Life Memorandum, ABCFM Archives, ABC 6.5.3, I, 451. For Henry Blatchford and Catherine Bissell, see Widder, *Battle for the Soul*, 130, 141.

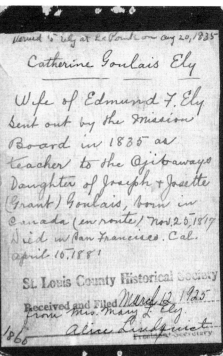

Married to Ely at La Pointe on Aug 20, 1835

Catherine Goulais Ely

Wife of Edmund F. Ely
Sent out by the mission
Board in 1835 as
teacher to the Ojibaways
Daughter of Joseph & Josette
(Grant) Goulais, born in
Canada (en route) Nov. 25, 1817
Died in San Francisco, Cal.
april 16, 1881

St. Louis County Historical Society

Received and Filed March 12, 1925
from Mrs. Mary L. Ely
                Alice Lindquist
1866

Figure 10. *Catherine Goulais Ely.* Biographical information was provided
by Catherine Goulais as a student at the Mackinac mission school of
the American Board of Commissioners for Foreign Missions.
St. Louis County Historical Society, Duluth, Minn.

English, and French as needed. He concluded his journal entry, "God sees
my want of a mouth to speak to this people and in his own time he will
doubtless send me an interpreter." In the midst of this spiritual crisis, Ely
returned to La Pointe when it became clear that the store of provisions at
the Aitkin's household would be insufficient to feed him through the summer. Approximately six weeks later, Ely wrote in his journal for August 30,
1835, "This P.M. I was married to Miss Catharine Bissell of the Mackinaw
Mission. Ceremonies in Church, by Br. Boutwell." In the six weeks spent
at La Pointe before his marriage, Ely never mentioned interacting with,
speaking to, or thinking about Catherine in his journal.[54]

Ely's marriage to Catherine Bissell, like Boutwell's marriage to Hester

54. Schenck, ed., *Journals of Edmund F. Ely,* July 12, 1835, 163, Aug. 30, 1835, 166;
Catherine Bissell Ely, "Life Memoranda," ABCFM Archives, ABC 6.5.3, I, 451 ("married").

Crooks, revealed the extent to which the missions, like the fur trade, re-lied on the domestic and linguistic labor of Native women to function. The missionaries depended on the domestic labor of Native women, but what they really needed to perform their work was the bilingual skills of their Native spouses. Although less frequently, the missions also used young mixed-race Native men. Henry Blatchford took on Hester Crooks's role at Yellow Lake after her departure with Boutwell. And when Hester assumed the role of interpreter for Boutwell, the Leech Lake mission hired Josette Pyant, a mixed-race Ojibwe woman and former scholar at the Mackinac mission school, as a domestic laborer and additional in-terpreter. Catherine Ely served as an interpreter at La Pointe until the arrival of additional missionaries Joseph and Hannah Town, Grenville Sproat, and Susan Bennett. Ely identified Bennett, a mixed-race Cree woman, as "a Mackinaw scholar. She was the confidential school mate of my dear Catharine." Cree was closely related to Anishinaabemowin, and some doodemag north of Lake Superior spoke a mixed Cree-Ojibwe dialect. Ely saw Bennett as domestic help for the mission, but her real value, like his wife, derived from her linguistic skills. Bennett likely began to act as an interpreter because shortly after she arrived at Leech Lake, Ely departed for Fond du Lac with his wife Catherine and Hester's father Ramsay Crooks on an American Fur Company boat, leaving the mission without an interpreter. Returning to Fond du Lac, Ely resumed his mis-sion school, relying on his wife as a translator / interpreter. In a note to the ABCFM about his school, he wrote, "An interesting half breed woman—the sister of Henry Blatchford (Br. Ayer's interpreter) attends school daily, with her children and is making good progress." The ABCFM missions had become entirely dependent on the work of mixed-race Native women laboring as translators. Without the labor of these women, the mission schools could not operate.[55]

"The Whites . . . Have Never Given Me Anything for Nothing"

Although the ABCFM missions and schools continued to serve the mixed-race children of American Fur Company employees, their relations with the larger Native community at Leech Lake and Fond du Lac grew in-creasingly strained as William Boutwell and Edmund Ely attempted to

55. Hall, Boutwell, Ayer, and Ely to Greene, Sept. 12, 1835, Hall to Greene, Sept. 24, 1835, Ely to Greene, Oct. 15, Dec. 21, 1835 ("interesting"), all in ABCFM, box 1; Schenck, ed., *Journals of Edmund F. Ely*, Oct. 11, 1835, 168 ("Mackinaw scholar"); Widder,

settle in with their wives. In late May 1835, Boutwell asked the ogimaag to call a council so that he could address the people of Leech Lake. They suggested he join them at their Midewiwin ceremony, a time when all the people would be gathered together. Boutwell arrived at the ceremony with George Bonga, the half-black and half-Ojibwe clerk employed by William Aitkin, who would act as interpreter. In his diary, Boutwell noted that he explained the goals of the mission, the assimilation or Americanization of the Ojibweg. In answer to Boutwell, Maajigaabaw rose and said that he once heard an Odawa ogimaa say "that ministers and missionaries are bad, and evil designing men, and therefore to be avoided." He had heard traders say the same thing, but he made it clear that these were not his words but rather the sentiments of others.[56]

Maajigaabaw then rejected the assimilationist message offered by the missionary directly and proceeded to question the motives of the Americans in coming to his country. "My brethren," he asserted, "I speak my mind. Others may speak for themselves, but when you think of me, you will think of what I say." He stated plainly: "I can not take your advice. The whites, as yet have never given me anything for nothing, and if I am to live but two years longer I wish to live as I now am." Another man told Boutwell that, in his opinion, "not one Indian would, within the space of two years, send his children to be instructed." Eshkibagikoonzh told the missionary that he had nothing to say—even though days before the ceremony the Leech Lake ogimaa had reassured Boutwell that he was welcome and told him not to mind those who were unhappy about where he built his house. When Eshkibagikoonzh declined to speak at this council, Maajigaabaw addressed Boutwell a second time, asking him "how long I expected to stay, how large I should make my garden, and whether other white people would come and make houses." Finally, he asked Boutwell what he would do "should we all tell you to go on." The missionary replied that they could not send him away. In his diary, Boutwell wrote, "And thus concluded the interview, which was more civil than some of my friends had feared." Boutwell believed he represented the United States and consequently that the Leech Lake ogimaag wielded no authority over his person or his mission. On the contrary, his mission was charged with

---

Battle for the Soul, 141. As Catherine J. Denial argues, "For all Americans vested in the 'civilizing' of the Upper Midwest, the maintenance of Euro-American family life was of singular importance, an active component of the social and cultural world they hoped to make." See Denial, *Making Marriage*, 81.

56. Boutwell Diary, May 29, 1835, Boutwell Papers.

helping the Ojibweg prepare for a future without Native peoples living as part of distinct and autonomous Indigenous nations because this was the goal of the civilizing mission.[57]

Edmund Ely believed in the same future as William Boutwell, and he imagined himself to be endowed with a similar authority. Accordingly, after his marriage to Catherine, he hired an employee of the American Fur Company to build a bigger house for his new family. He and his wife would not live in the mission's schoolhouse. On February 23, 1836, five days after work began on his cabin, a young Ojibwe man named Nindipens visited Ely, and the missionary recorded the encounter in his diary: "The Indian said he was not pleased because I did not first give him notice that I wanted to build yonder. He said his father (Shing up) told him, before he died, that if anyone wanted to build here, they must speak to him about it." Zhingobiins (The Little Balsam Fir), the father of Nindipens, had been the principal ogimaa of Fond du Lac. "I felt very strongly tempted to scold the fellow for this *show* of authority," Ely wrote, "but curbed myself, and said that this place where I now was, was a very unsuitable spot." Ely understood that Zhingobiins had been an ogimaa, but when confronted by Nindipens, he wrote in his diary, "This man has no more authority in the band than any other man." Perhaps more telling, Ely also informed Nindipens that he had consulted with William Aitkin about where he should build his home rather than seeking out the ogimaag of Fond du Lac.[58]

The confrontation between Nindipens and Ely triggered a political crisis at Fond du Lac. The death of Zhingobiins had created a political vacuum in the village. Civil leadership was hereditary among the Ojibweg, but Nindipens was a very young man and had not assumed or asserted political authority since the death of his father. Maangozid, who had acted as the *giigidowinini*, or orator, for Zhingobiins, was recognized as a leader by U.S. authorities, and both he and the ogimaa had been given medals by Henry Schoolcraft in 1820. Maangozid was married to the daughter of Zhingobiins, but he was also the second son of the ogimaa of Sandy Lake. Although the medal and his service to Zhingobiins enhanced his standing at Fond du Lac, he was an outsider and could not claim the authority of an ogimaa in this village. Three days after his

57. Ibid.
58. Schenck, ed., *Journals of Edmund F. Ely*, Feb. 23, 1836, 190. For the role played by ogimaag in exercising authority over village territory and usufruct rights, see Miller, *Ogimaag*, 99–100.

initial confrontation with Ely, Nindipens returned with several senior men. With Isabella Cotte acting as translator, Nindipens said to Ely, "You ought to have asked permission of me before you began to build—this land is mine." He then addressed his status: "It is true I am not the chief. The governor did not make me so. I have not a medal, as you see, but my father was a chief, and gave me his medal before he died." Nindipens concluded, "My Father was a chief, and I own this land. I know of no one who owned this land but my Grandfather, and my father gave it to me. If I do not own this land, let these Indians who sit here speak." Moreover, he informed Ely that Maangozid was not an ogimaa but a person who spoke on their behalf. None of the men who accompanied Nindipens disputed his statements about his status or that of Maangozid.[59]

Nindipens used his confrontation with Ely to assert an authority that the community of Fond du Lac had yet to confer upon him. The process played out over the course of several weeks, with senior men periodically visiting Ely while they debated among themselves if he should build and where and whether he had a right to cut timber. On May 20, 1836, Ely sent tobacco to Nindipens, asking him "to call together the Indians and ask them for a building spot." Thirteen men came to Ely's schoolhouse. "They were dressed for council—some painted—others besmeared with white clay, face and hair, and zigzag lines drawn across their faces, giving them a most hideous appearance." The men informed Ely that they could not answer him, as too many families remained away from the village harvesting sugar bush. One man, however, did address Ely. "They wondered much to what end I came here and was so anxious to stay," Ely wrote in his journal; "I was not like the traders." "They had been told that the Americans wished to do with them as they had done to other Indian nations"—namely: "They would get possession of a little land, then claim much and finally drive the Indians away entirely. They (the Indians) believed me to be a forerunner of the Americans." In response, Ely concluded, "It is apparent that there is a strong prejudice against the American government, and it is increasing rather than diminishing."[60]

In spite of these strong reservations about Ely and the government he represented, the Gichi-Ansihinaabeg, or elders, of Fond du Lac granted

59. Schenck, ed., *Journals of Edmund F. Ely*, Feb. 26, 1836, 191. For the political status of Maangozid and Nindipens, see Miller, *Ogimaag*, 196–200; and Rebecca Kugel, *To Be the Main Leaders of Our People: A History of Minnesota Ojibwe Politics, 1825–1898* (East Lansing, Mich., 1998), 39–41.

60. Schenck, ed., *Journals of Edmund F. Ely*, May 20, 1836, 211–212.

him permission to stay and build a house. On May 31, 1836, they called Ely to a council and told him that "what Nindibans should say would be so." Ely wrote that Nindipens "would give [lend] me a spot which my house would cover." Nindipens then informed the missionary: "You can use the land 4 years. If you treat the Indians well and wish to stay longer I will tell you how many years longer you may stay." With this gesture, Nindipens signaled a provisional acceptance of the missionary and his family at Fond du Lac. Ely secured permission to build his house, and Nindipens secured the recognition of his authority as ogimaa at Fond du Lac. A few days later, Nindipens called on Ely with three Native people who had just arrived at Fond du Lac. "N. gave me the names of each, then said they were hungry. I replied nothing," Ely wrote in his journal. Eventually, the strangers left. "I then asked N. if he expected I would give them provisions. He said yes. I told him the river was full of fish." The missionary interpreted the visit of Nindipens and his guests as a power play by the ogimaa. The point, however, had been to prod Ely into conforming to an Ojibwe sense of social obligation. If a fellow Anishinaabe arrived in your village for a visit, you treated that person as family. If they were hungry, you fed them. Nindipens, in effect, made his own attempt at a civilizing mission, pushing the American missionary to act like an Anishinaabe, like a real human being.[61]

"To Submit Ourselves to the Laws of That Country"

During the months that Ely negotiated with the ogimaag about whether he could build a house at Fond du Lac, at least three separate parties of Odawa and Ojibwe men made their way to Washington, D.C. Their journey was the mirror image of Tocqueville's visit to Saginaw, or of the ABCFM missionaries' voyage west into the Lake Superior and the Mississippi country. They traveled east to the seat of American political power in order to find civilization, at least as the United States understood it, and to discuss the fate of Native peoples in an expanding republic. In effect, they came to ask U.S. officials the same sorts of questions that Tocqueville asked of the Natives of Saginaw and that the ogimaag of Leech Lake and Fond du Lac asked of their missionaries. One of these parties, Odawa men from L'Arbre Croche, included Augustin Hamelin, Jr., a mixed-race Odawa, and an ogimaa named Apokisigan (Smoking Mixture). The intention of these two men was to sell some of their lands for an annuity and to reject categorically the idea of relocating to country west of the

61. Ibid., May 31, 1836, 218–219, June 11, 1836, 221.

Mississippi. Their trip prompted the Grand River Odawaag from villages on the northern shore of the Lower Peninsula of Michigan to send their own delegation to the capital. They also came to reject the Indian removal policy of the United States and to prevent their lands from being sold out from under them by the Odawaag of L'Arbre Croche. This group was composed of young men and only one ogimaa, named Muckatosha (Blackskin)—men explicitly not empowered to negotiate treaties. They were accompanied by Leonard Slater and Isaac McCoy, Baptist missionaries from the Grand River, who sought to safeguard the interests of the Odawaag. A delegation of Ojibweg from Sault Sainte Marie led by the ogimaa Waishkee, uncle of Jane Schoolcraft, the Ojibwe wife of Indian agent Henry Schoolcraft, also journeyed to Washington, D.C., to negotiate a treaty with the United States and to debate land cessions, annuities, and removal.[62]

Henry Schoolcraft joined these delegations in Washington, D.C., and, after securing permission to negotiate a treaty from Lewis Cass, then secretary of war (and former governor of the Michigan Territory), he called the Ojibweg and Odawaag together at the capital's Masonic Hall on March 15, 1836. In addition to the Baptist missionaries, the Ojibwe and Odawa delegations were accompanied by a number of men associated with the fur trade. Rix Robinson, the head trader for the American Fur Company at Mackinac, wrote to Schoolcraft in January to assure him he would "use every effort to get them Indians on their way to Washington," and he promised to accompany them. He also warned Schoolcraft that "there is already some little clamours raised by the half bloods and some others objecting to the treaty being held at Washington."[63]

Holding a treaty council in a distant city removed the negotiators from the influence of community members and made them more likely to self-deal or succumb to pressure from traders or government officials. Indeed, for the traders, the treaty negotiation represented an opportunity to recover debt allegedly owed to them and to make money by providing provisions as part of any settlement. Robinson was married to the sister of Nabunagiizhig, one of the young men representing the Grand River Odawaag. The Odawaag, according to the American Fur Company,

62. Charles E. Cleland, *Rites of Conquest: The History and Culture of Michigan's Native Americans* (Ann Arbor, Mich., 1992), 225–226.

63. Rix Robinson to Schoolcraft, Jan. 13, 1836, Records of the Michigan Superintendency of Indian Affairs, Mackinac Agency Records, Letters Received, film X3296, reel 59, Harlan Hatcher Graduate Library, University of Michigan, Ann Arbor.

owed thirty thousand dollars, and Robinson aimed to recover this money through the treaty process. John Drew, an independent trader operating out of Mackinac and married to an Odawa woman, also joined the negotiations at the Masonic Hall, as did William Brewster, the New York–based business partner of Ramsay Crooks, part owner and manager of the Northern Department of the American Fur Company. Following the departure of Robinson and Drew for Washington, D.C., the American Fur Company trader Gabriel Franchère wrote to Lyman Warren at La Pointe, "The Indians of Mackinac are gone to Washington where a treaty is to be held next month for the purchase of their lands by the general government, and those of La grand riviere and Sault Saint Marie are invited to do the same." He continued, "It is the general impression here that the treaty is to be held at this place, if so, it will enable us to collect our old Indian debts, as I have no new ones not having trusted an Indian since last spring." Franchère concluded optimistically, "I hope it will give us a good business besides." By the winter of 1836, the fur trade, and the American Fur Company, still extant in the northern Lower Peninsula of Michigan and in the Lake Superior country, had become fully integrated into the political economy of plunder that defined U.S treaty making in the Northwest Territory.[64]

It was, however, the civilizing mission of the United States that set in motion the events that drew the Ojibweg and Odawaag from Sault Sainte Marie, L'Arbre Croche, and Grand River to Washington, D.C., in 1836. In the aftermath of the passage of the Indian Removal Act (1830), the Ansishinaabeg in the Michigan Territory feared they would be pressed to sell their lands and move west of the Mississippi. A year earlier, in 1835, seeking to pay off their trade debts, the Odawaag and Ojibweg had approached Schoolcraft about selling their land on the Manitou Islands in Lake Michigan, Drummond Island in Lake Huron, and some land in the Upper Peninsula of the Michigan Territory. Cass informed Schoolcraft that the United States might consider such a purchase if the cost was reasonable and instructed Schoolcraft to ask the Anishinaabeg living north of the Grand River if they would also sell their lands in the Lower Peninsula. Schoolcraft responded that they would sell, even though he was aware of strong opposition to such a cession. Schoolcraft obfuscated the attempt of the Anishinaabeg to sell limited and less desirable land on islands and in the Upper Peninsula while openly pushing for removal and

64. Gabriel Franchère to Lyman Warren, Mar. 1, 1836, box 1, folder 10, Gabriel Franchère Papers, 1834–1851, Bentley Library, University of Michigan.

the sale of more valuable land on the Lower Peninsula. Feeling ill-served by their Indian agent, a delegation of L'Arbre Croche Odawaag, led by the ogimaa Apokisigan, traveled to the capital in the fall of 1835 without seeking Schoolcraft's permission. Accompanying the Odawa delegation was Augustin Hamelin, who spoke Anishinaabemowin, French, and English and who had been authorized to speak for the Odawa and Ojibwe ogimaag in the northern Lower Peninsula.[65]

The ogimaag of the L'Arbre Croche Odawaag met with Michigan senator John Norvell and then with Secretary of War Cass to explain their position. Cass asked that Hamelin put their requests in writing. Hamelin began his memorial with a complaint about Schoolcraft, noting, "We have endeavored to reach the seat of government (so far at our own expense) in order that we might have the satisfaction of knowing its true sentiments. . . . Truth and falsehood blended together, has so often been represented to us in our country, that we scarcely know the difference between the two." Hamelin then made it clear that the Odawaag wished to remain in their homeland and proposed only a limited sale of land. "The principal objects of our visit here are these," he wrote; "We would make some arrangements with government for remaining in the Territory of Michigan in the quiet possession of our lands, and to transmit the same safely to our posterity." "We do not wish to sell all the lands claimed by us, and consequently not to remove to the west of the Mississippi," he asserted; "It is a heart-rending thought to our simple feelings to think of leaving our native country forever; the land where the bones of our forefathers lay thick in the earth; the land which has drank, and which has been bought with the price of, their native blood, and which has been thus safely transmitted to us." Hamelin wrote bluntly, "We are aware of this plain fact, that we Indians cannot long remain peaceably and happy in the place where the tribe is at present if we persist in pursuing that way and manner of life, which we have hitherto loved, although now in a less degree." He continued, "We now deem the life of a savage incompatible with that of a civilized man; and therefore we would wish to exchange the former for the latter," and noted, "We have already made some progress in this pleasing path, and tasted some of its comforts; and it is our desire and will to advance

65. For Schoolcraft's deceptive dealings regarding land cessions in 1835, see James Michael McClurken, "We Wish to Be Civilized: Ottawa-American Political Contests on the Michigan Frontier" (Ph.D. diss., Michigan State University, 1988), 168–170. See also Matthew L. M. Fletcher, *The Eagle Returns: The Legal History of the Grand Traverse Band of Ottawa and Chippewa Indians* (East Lansing, Mich., 2012), 17–22.

more and more in it." Whereas Maajigaabaw and the Leech Lake Ojibweg rejected the idea of becoming "civilized," Hamelin and the Odawaag accepted this path as the key to remaining in their homeland.[66]

Although the Odawaag were not U.S. citizens, they might become civilized and, in this way, claim the right to remain in Michigan. "With these things in view," Hamelin concluded his memorial to Cass, "we propose to submit ourselves to the Laws of that country within whose limits we reside." But he pleaded for a gradual transition: "Perhaps, a few years hence, our people could not very well submit themselves to the laws of that State, we are confident, however, that when the benefits of civilization would be more generally diffused amongst them, they would embrace those salutary regulations with cheerfulness." The Odawaag, through Hamelin, asked the federal government for time and assistance to make the transition to a civilized life. "It is also the object of our visit here," he wrote, "to obtain some assistance from government," specifically, with "our Agricultural pursuits"; "We would be happy to obtain implements of husbandry." Moreover, "We would wish to represent to government the need of assistance we have, in the education of our young people and children in the necessary and useful branches of arts and sciences." In a separate letter, Bishop Rese of Detroit, benefactor and confidant of Hamelin, informed Norvell that the Odawaag "are unwilling to cede all their lands, and remove; but prefer to remain and become subject to the laws."[67]

If this was not quite Thomas Jefferson's vision of Indigenous nations disbanding and individual Native peoples becoming citizens of the United States, it was an outright rejection of the future offered by Lewis Cass, who insisted Native peoples be removed to the west because they were incapable of embracing the ways of civilization. Hamelin and the Odawaag suggested that they continue to live on their homeland, as a distinct people but subject to the laws of the United States. They asked that the social contract that the United States extended to white settlers in Michigan be expanded to include the original inhabitants of the territory. Rejecting removal, they offered the United States an Indigenous version of the social contract, one that recognized the political authority of the Republic but maintained a Native identity. They would embrace the

66. "Memorial of the Ottawa Delegation by A. Hamlin, Jr.," Dec. 5, 1835, Michigan Superintendency, RG 75, M234, roll 421, 722–725.

67. Ibid.; [Bishop Rese] to John Norvell, [Dec. 5, 1835], Michigan Superintendency, RG 75, M234, roll 421, 771 ("unwilling").

American definition of civilization, and all—Natives and newcomers—would be equal before the laws of the United States.

The requests of the L'Arbre Croche Odawaag reflected the influence and agenda of the various Christian missionaries working among the Ojibwe and Odawa villagers in the Lower Peninsula of Michigan. However, they also reflected the experience of men like Augustin Hamelin as well as of traders such as William Aitkin, Lyman Warren, Michel Cadotte, Rix Robinson, and John Drew. Mixed-race men with mixed-race families were prepared to make a bargain with the American state. The missionaries sent to live among them would educate their children. They would embrace the civilizing mission, and, in exchange, they and their families would be included within the social contract that the United States was extending across the Northwest Territory. Hamelin, the author of the memorial, was the child of a mixed-race trader working out of Saint Ignace on the Upper Peninsula, and his mother was the daughter of a prominent L'Arbre Croche ogimaa. He had been educated at a Catholic academy in Cincinnati and a seminary in Rome. It was because of this combination of education and lineage that the ogimaag empowered the young man to speak for the L'Arbre Croche Odawaag.[68] Like the post commanders of the American Fur Company with mixed-race families, Hamelin realized that Anishinaabe children must learn to speak, read, and write in English if they hoped to claim a place in U.S. civil society. Even more important, Hamelin spoke for the L'Arbre Croche Odawaag. They, too, wanted to become civilized Indians—that is, like their mixed-race relatives, they wanted to maintain both their Indigenous identity and their national homeland while claiming a place in the civil society of the United States. They wanted access to the same social contract that the American government extended to settlers moving to the Michigan Territory, which at least tacitly included the mixed-race families of fur traders.[69]

"The Question of the Sale of Your Possessions in Michigan"

Lewis Cass, however, was not concerned about the civilization of the Odawaag. He wanted to convert their homeland into the public domain of the United States, and he wanted to sell that land to white settlers. Cass

68. For the education of Hamlin and his appointment as a spokesperson for the L'Arbre Croche Odawaag, see Theodore J. Karamanski, *Blackbird's Song: Andrew J. Blackbird and the Odawa People* (East Lansing, Mich., 2012), 48–49, 70–72.

69. This desire to establish a dual identity as both Anishinaabeg and as civilized Natives willing to live under the rule of law represented by the institutions of the U.S.

realized that Hamelin essentially spoke for only one Odawa village and could not grant him the extensive land cession that he wanted. He therefore declined to negotiate with the delegation from L'Arbre Croche and instead tasked Henry Schoolcraft to bring an Anishinaabe delegation to Washington, D.C., that could negotiate for the extinction of Native title to all of the lands north of the Grand River. Acting on Cass's instructions, Schoolcraft, who had followed the Odawaag to the capital, returned to Michigan and in the summer and fall of 1835 and 1836 held a series of councils with the Odawaag and Ojibweg in the northern Lower Peninsula.[70]

The Anishinaabeg in the Michigan Territory had witnessed the dispossession and eventual removal of their kin in Ohio and Indiana following significant land cessions resulting from treaty negotiations. And the Odawaag and Ojibweg who lived in the Lower Peninsula of Michigan were acutely aware of the rapid growth of the settler population in the southeast part of the territory following the opening of the Erie Canal in 1825. In 1820, fewer than 9,000 white settlers lived in the Michigan Territory. By 1830, that number had grown to 31,369. By 1834, however, nine years after the opening of the Erie Canal, the settler population in the Lower Peninsula east of Lake Michigan had reached 85,856, and Michigan was in the process of negotiating its contemporary boundaries and nearing the time when the territory would seek admission to the union as a state.[71]

Republic differed slightly but in significant ways from Indigenous nations of the Old Southwest. As with the Cherokee, it was mixed-race Natives and men with mixed-race Anishinaabe families who negotiated with the state for some form of inclusion. Mixed-race leaders, for example, dominated the Cherokee National Committee, the governing body established in 1817. These leaders, Tiya Miles has argued, "believed that the best way to protect Cherokee peoplehood and land was to demonstrate Cherokee progress to American federal and state powers by proving that the Cherokees were a sovereign, civilized nation with rights to be respected and a government to be reckoned with." The creation of the National Committee as a singular governing body that later drafted and adapted a constitution reflected this assertion of Cherokee sovereignty. The Anishinaabeg, in contrast, maintained a diffuse, nonhierarchical political organization centered on doodem and village authority. As a result, the Anishinaabeg were both more difficult for the federal government to deal with politically and less of a direct threat to fledgling state governments. See Miles, *Ties That Bind: The Story of an Afro-Cherokee Family in Slavery and Freedom* (Berkeley, Calif., 2005), 104–105.

70. Cleland, *Rites of Conquest*, 225–226; Karamanski, *Blackbird's Song*, 74–76.

71. For removal of Native peoples from the Ohio country, see John P. Bowes, *A Land Too Good for Indians: Northern Indian Removal* (Norman, Okla., 2016); and Mary Stockwell, *The Other Trail of Tears: The Removal of the Ohio Indians* (Yardley,

This rapid demographic change also threatened the end of the fur trade, at least in the Lower Peninsula of Michigan, and the treaty sought by Cass represented the opportunity for traders to begin to cash out of a declining business. In January 1836, following the return of the L'Arbre Croche delegation, Ramsay Crooks wrote to Gabriel Franchère, his principal agent at Sault Sainte Marie. "The government will hold a treaty at Washington the beginning of next March with the Ottawas for the cession of the entire Michigan peninsula north of the Grand River," he noted, and "the Secretary of War has sent some Indians, who accompanied young Hamlin to the Metropolis, back to their own country in order to bring a full deputation, and perhaps they may also invite the Chippewas of the Sault." Crooks instructed Franchère to send a record of "what they owe your outfit by the Chippewas . . . so that I may try to secure the payment of them at the treaty." Franchère replied the following month, "Our Indians have not as yet received an invitation to attend the treaty, but I nevertheless enclose a duly authenticated claim against them." Proprietors like Crooks and post commanders like Franchère increasingly saw treaties as the driving engine of their business. They represented a chance to claim and clear debt, to make money by providing provisions and trade goods for council, and to deliver commodities as part of the settlement. Finally, they saw the treaty process as a way to secure title to homesteads carved out of the homelands of their relatives and clients, which were about to be converted into the public domain and sold to settlers.[72]

With statehood looming, the settler population booming, and Schoolcraft pressuring the Anishinaabeg to sell their lands and accept new

---

Pa., 2014). On the population of the Michigan Territory, see Willis Frederick Dunbar, *Michigan: A History of the Wolverine State* (Grand Rapids, Mich., 1965), 272, 303, 322–324.

72. Ramsay Crooks to Franchère, Jan. 2, 1836, Franchère to Crooks, Feb. 13, 1836, box 1, folder 10, Franchère Papers. The relative wealth of the Indigenous peoples in the Southeast resulted in a significant difference in the plunder economy / strategy used by white settlers / expansionists. People such as the Creeks and Cherokees had made the transition to commercial farming. In many cases, they had made what white settlers would recognize as significant improvements on their land, and they owned livestock. This wealth made Native peoples the targets of white settlers who not only wanted their land, more valuable than land in northern Michigan, but also their accumulated property. White settlers confiscated property, goods, and livestock, claiming unpaid debt. For the plunder of Creek lands and property, see Christopher D. Haveman, *Rivers of Sand: Creek Indian Emigration, Relocation, and Ethnic Cleansing in the American South* (Lincoln, Nebr., 2016), 106, 208, 238.

territory west of the Mississippi River, the Odawaag decided to communicate directly with the president of the United States. Enlisting the help of the missionary Leonard Slater, the Grand River Odawaag composed a letter to Andrew Jackson on January 27, 1836. "We are afraid," they wrote, "and the reason is, because you already would take our land." They rejected this course of action outright. "We hear that you would make a treaty for our land," and they countered succinctly: "We refuse to go, it is too hard for us. We think to remain on our land here and not sell it." They pointed out the hypocrisy behind Schoolcraft's push to encourage them to give up the rights to their homeland. "Were we desirous to make a treaty for your land you would refuse us, you would say I cannot sell the graves of my relation." The Odawaag concluded by telling the president, "We have not a mind to remove to a distant land our children would suffer."[73]

The message to Jackson was signed by ogimaag from eight of the nine Grand River Odawa villages and by a cross-section of the religious and political factions living in these communities. Signers included Cobmoosa, the mixed-race son of Antoine Campau, the brother of Louis Campau, the trader instrumental in helping Cass coerce land cessions from the Ojibweg in the 1819 Treaty of Saginaw. Cobmoosa identified and lived as an Odawa and was tied to the mixed-race Francophone community among the Michigan Anishinaabeg. He was also connected to the Nativist community among the Odawaag and Ojibweg that had been associated with the pan-Indian movement lead by Tecumseh. The signers also included Nabunagiizhig, Megiss Ininee, and Muckatosha, ogimaag opposed to further land cessions who nevertheless found themselves at the Masonic Hall in Washington, D.C., on March 15, 1836, as part of a six-man delegation representing the Grand River Odawaag.[74]

On March 14, when all twenty-four of the Odawa and Ojibwe delegates arrived in the capital accompanied by the various traders, missionaries, and interpreters who traveled with them, they visited Andrew Jackson at the White House, hoping to negotiate with the president directly. Their meeting, however, was a mere formality. The delegates shook hands with the president, and one of them, most likely Hamelin, addressed the

73. Ottawa Chiefs of Grand River to President Andrew Jackson, Jan. 27, 1836, Michigan Superintendency, RG 75, M234, roll 422, 146–148.

74. The Nativist factions among the Anishinaabeg advocated for traditional spiritual practices and resisted cooperation with the leaders tied to the U.S. government. See Gregory Evans Dowd, *A Spirited Resistance: The North American Indian Struggle for Unity, 1745–1815* (Baltimore, 1992), xvii–xviii, 17, 19. See also McClurken, "We Wish to Be Civilized," 176–177.

president in English, and then their meeting came to an end. They would gather the next day, not at the White House, but at the Masonic Hall to treat directly with Henry Schoolcraft, the man pushing them to sell their land and relocate to country west of the Mississippi River. When the council opened on March 15, Schoolcraft greeted the delegates, "My Children, You have heard the voice of your great father the President, and shaken hands with him." He then informed them: "He has by the Secretary of War, furnished me with written instructions by which to act. You will, therefore, consider my words, as his words and listen attentively while I proceed to lay before you, the object of your being called together."[75]

A reporter provided an account of the council, which was open to the public. "The Hall was enveloped in smoke," he wrote, "most of the Indians smoking the calumet." Shortly after eleven in the morning, when the council was scheduled to start, "two Chippewa chiefs entered, dressed in Indian Character, leading in the interpreter, who was blind. A young and noble chief, who spoke good English, led him to a chair by the side of another interpreter and by the commissioners." The reporter continued: "At one end of the table the catholic priest was placed, taking notes of what was passing between the commissioners and the chiefs. The priest was a young man, apparently not more than twenty-five years of age." The blind interpreter was John Holiday, the subagent from Keweenaw, who was accompanied by his mixed-race daughter Mary. The young man taking careful notes, who had been mistaken for a priest, was Augustin Hamelin. The reporter subsequently described Hamelin as "the full blood Indian Catholic Priest, born in America, christened in America, and educated in Rome." The commissioners sat with the two Ojibwe ogimaag at a table covered with maps of the Michigan Territory. Members of the public, including a classroom of young students, entered the hall to watch the proceedings.[76]

Schoolcraft opened the council by acknowledging the visit of the Odawa delegation in December 1835 and their wish at that time to sell land and pay their debts to the traders. He then intimated that this offer had been improper. "The President's desire," he stated, "on all occasions, to know that the persons who offer to sell lands are the proper authorized

75. Records of the Treaty Concluded with the Ottawa and Chippewa Nations at Washington, D.C., Mar. 28, 1836, Henry Rowe Schoolcraft Papers, Library of Congress, Washington, D.C.

76. "Correspondence of the New-York Daily Advertiser," *Democratic Free Press* (Detroit), Apr. 20, 1836, [1].

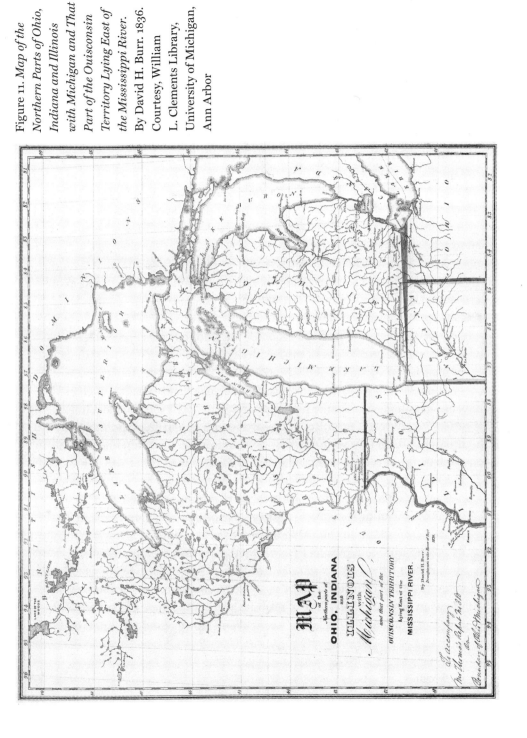

Figure 11. *Map of the Northern Parts of Ohio, Indiana and Illinois with Michigan and That Part of the Ouisconsin Territory Lying East of the Mississippi River. By David H. Burr. 1836. Courtesy, William L. Clements Library, University of Michigan, Ann Arbor*

chiefs or delegates, and that whatever is doing should be done with the consent of all." The president, he informed the delegation, decided "to send for you all that you might act together." He noted the presence of the Ojibweg "from the north shore of the Straits" as well as from Sault Sainte Marie. "The President," he told the delegation, "is informed that you are brother tribes, have always lived in peace together, and are each inter- mixed in blood and location, he has authorized me to treaty with them, as with you, and I asked you together." He then asserted that both the Ojibweg and Odawaag had recently offered to sell land to the federal gov- ernment. Schoolcraft had made certain that this delegation included the Ojibweg as well as the Odawaag, thus giving him added influence because he was related by marriage to Waishkee, the Ojibwe ogimaa from Sault Sainte Marie. Moreover, treating with both Ojibwe and Odawa doodemag inhabiting both sides of the straits of Mackinac enabled the government to ask for a more-extensive land cession.[77]

Accordingly, Schoolcraft proposed a significant cession, what would amount to more than thirteen million acres of land and the extinction of Native title on the last unincorporated portion of the Anishinaabe land base in the Lower Peninsula of the Michigan Territory. This land would be transferred to the public domain of the United States and sold to set- tlers under the provisions of the Northwest Ordinance. The government's proposal, Schoolcraft stated succinctly, "opens the question of the sale of your possessions in Michigan." He told the delegates that "for such ces- sions as you agree to make I am authorized to make you the most liberal offers," including a promise on the president's behalf "to appoint a com- missioner to go into your country next summer to ascertain and pay the amount of every just debt and claim against you so that everyone may receive simple justice." Schoolcraft also indicated that the United States was prepared to allow the Anishinaabeg to remain in Michigan. He con- cluded his opening remarks by stating, "No objection will be made, if you deem it important, to you fixing on proposed and limited reservations to be held *in common;* but the President judged it best, that no reservations should be made to *individuals.*" He then stated: "Your relations, who could be entitled to such conditions will be compensated for their value in money. The usual privilege of residing and hunting on the lands sold till they are wanted, will be guaranteed." The Ojibwe ogimaa Ogimagigido

77. Records of the Treaty Concluded with the Ottawa and Chippewa Nations at Washington, D.C., Mar. 28, 1836, Schoolcraft Papers.

rose to speak and asked Schoolcraft to allow the delegation three days to consider the proposal.[78]

There are no records of any meetings held by the Anishinaabe delegation before returning to the council at the Masonic Hall, only the intimation in subsequent councils that during this period they were lobbied extensively by the traders who joined them in Washington, D.C. When the council reconvened, Muckatosha was the first to speak. He addressed the commissioner as "Father," and "requested him to listen to the few words he had to say." He noted that they had been called to Washington to talk about their lands: "Your children were pleased to hear your proposition at the first council, to purchase their lands . . . but when we look at the map of our country it appears very small and we conclude not to part with any of our lands." He also remarked that they were confused about their father's statement regarding "our half breeds" and "white friends," that they would be denied reservations and given money as the ogimaag thought best. "This course we do not fully understand," Muckatosha informed Schoolcraft, "and we object to it, same reason why we do not wish to dispose of our lands, is this, we fear that the whites who will not be our friends, will come into our country and trouble us, and that we shall not be able to know where our possessions are." "If we do sell our land," he concluded, "it will be our wish that some of our white friends have lands among us and be associated with us." Muckatosha also questioned Schoolcraft about the intentions of the ogimaag from L'Arbre Croche who had visited Washington earlier without permission from the government. Megiss Ininee, also a delegate from Grand River, "made objections to the course which the chief and party from L'Arbre Croache Apakosigan had taken," and he questioned the validity of including the Ojibweg, "who

78. Ibid. This decision to grant reservations to hold in common reflected the more limited value and demand for land in northern Michigan. In contrast, the 1832 Treaty of Washington that the United States negotiated with the Creeks allotted land to individual Creek heads of household, one full section of 640 acres for chiefs, and half a section for non-council members. Christopher D. Haveman argues that "the War Department saw the treaty as a way to ethnically cleanse Alabama of Creek Indians, and in an attempt to hurry the process along, the administration tried to enter into negotiations with the Creeks for the wholesale purchase of their allotted reserves." Traders and territorial officials in Michigan, in contrast, saw the presence of Anishinaabeg on small reservations of land as a source of income that was more lucrative than taking their land outright. For the ethnic cleansing of the Creeks, see Haveman, *Rivers of Sand*, 95.

occupy a different section of the country." He also expressed displeasure at the exclusion of "Half breeds" and "white friends" from any new reservation.[79]

These accusations did not sit well with Apokisigan, the L'Arbre Croche ogimaa who had been the leader of the 1835 delegation. In the council record kept by Schoolcraft, Apokisigan responded to the suggestion of double-dealing: "I wish to say that some chiefs present have sold lands and have benefited, but as for myself and my people, we have not received so much as one pipe of tobacco, that he [Apokisigan] was satisfied with propositions respecting reservations made to them [the Grand River ogimaag] at the first council." This statement was a rebuke to the Grand River ogimaag, who had ceded a large tract of land in the 1821 Treaty of Chicago. If Apokisigan consented to the sale of land now, however, the reporter covering the council also suggested that he demanded to remain in his homeland. According to this account, Apokisigan "presented a most savage appearance." "He was a noble looking fellow, dressed in full Indian costume, with his face painted, and his hair queerly arranged." He stood and grasped both commissioners by the hand. Then, according to the reporter, he began an impressive oratory through an interpreter, "'We ask our father,' said he naming the President of the United States, 'that he would reserve some lands for us and our posterity.' The surrounding chiefs nodded in assent." The Grand River Odawaag, wary that their Ojibwe kin from the Upper Peninsula might sell their land out from under them, believed they had negotiated a right to remain in their homeland on the northern Lower Peninsula of the Michigan Territory.[80]

"The Words of White Men
Who Wanted Reservations"

Following the speech of Apokisigan, the council became tumultuous as the various factions debated the merits of selling land. Mackadepenessy (Blackbird), the prominent Odawa ogimaa and usually an ally of Apokisigan, stated that, although at other times his voice had been with the Odawaag, now "he was opposed to the sale of lands." At this point, Schoolcraft used the Ojibweg to leverage the Odawaag. He told the Odawa negotiators that "the Great father now had a wish to do them good, but as

79. Records of the Treaty Concluded with the Ottawa and Chippewa Nations at Washington, D.C., Mar. 28, 1836, Schoolcraft Papers.

80. Ibid.; "Correspondence of the New-York Daily Advertiser," *Democratic Free Press*, Apr. 20, 1836, [1]. For the interpretation that Apokisigan's remarks were a rebuke to the Grand River ogimaag, see Karamanski, *Blackbird's Song*, 83.

they had given no for an answer it was uncertain when he would listen to them again." Instead, "he would now call the minds of the Chippewa chiefs north of the straits." He informed the Ojibwe leaders that their father knew their lands were of poor quality, but, "notwithstanding your country is of little value, yet feeling a desire to benefit you, he thinks your lands may be of some value to him, and on this account a proposition will be made to the Chippewas." He then suggested that the Odawaag should take advice from their Ojibwe kin and sell their land "so to act that when they went home they should not feel ashamed of many goods and much money, and themselves entirely destitute and very poor."[81]

With the Ojibweg seeming to accept the proposed land sale and the Odawaag poised to return home empty-handed, Augustin Hamelin asked to address the commissioner. Speaking in English, he informed School-craft "that the words the Commissioner had just heard from the chiefs, was not their words was not the feelings of their hearts but the words of white men who wanted reservations." Had they been left to reach their own conclusions, Hamelin asserted, they would have spoken differently to the commissioners, "but they were constantly beset by individuals, and disturbed in their private councils . . . their minds were disturbed on purpose and they did not know how to act, in answer to the proposition respecting the treaty." In effect, Hamelin claimed the traders instructed the delegates to reject the treaty in order to drive up the amount of their annuity. "If the Indians were left alone they would sell, with some reservations for themselves . . . to dispose of their lands and derive present benefit." As most of the delegation did not speak English, Schoolcraft requested the translator convey the substance of Hamelin's speech to the delegation and then adjourned the council for three additional days.[82]

The council reconvened at the Masonic Hall on March 22, 1836, and continued the proceedings for the next six days until a treaty was signed by all twenty-four of the Odawa and Ojibwe delegates that ceded a little more than thirteen million acres of land within the boundaries of what was about to become the state of Michigan. The treaty signed by the delegation created reservations "to be held in common," amounting to approximately 142,000 acres in the Lower Peninsula, including 50,000 acres in Little Traverse Bay, the core of the territory of the L'Arbre Croche Odawaag. It also created reservations on the northern side of the Straits of Mackinac and on islands in Lake Michigan and Lake Huron.

81. Records of the Treaty Concluded with the Ottawa and Chippewa Nations at Washington, D.C., Mar. 28, 1836, Schoolcraft Papers.
82. Ibid.

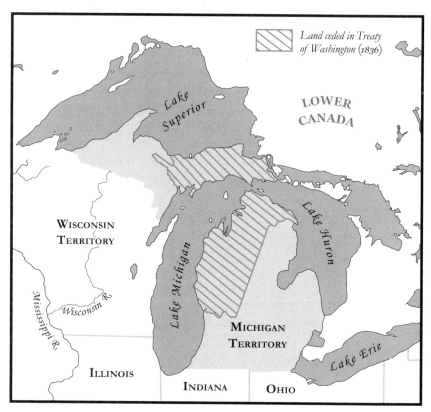

Map 5. Treaty of Washington, 1836. Drawn by Rebecca Wrenn

In exchange for the approximately 13,000,000 acres ceded, the Odawa and Ojibwe delegation secured annuity payments of $30,000 over twenty years. Article 5 of the treaty stipulated, "The sum of three hundred thousand dollars shall be paid to said Indians to enable them, with the aid and assistance of their agent, to adjust and pay such debts as they may justly owe." This was, in effect, a direct payment to the various independent traders and the American Fur Company. In addition to the cash payments for the land cession, the Ojibweg and Odawaag would receive $150,000 in "goods and provisions" to be dispensed at Mackinac Island. These goods would, of course, be purchased by the federal government from the same traders who received payment for debt claims, assuring them an additional payout. Article 6 established that "the sum of one hundred and fifty thousand dollars shall be set apart as a fund for said half breeds." This provision stipulated that recipients must be "of Indian descent and actually resident within the boundaries described in the first article of this treaty." Another article set aside cash payments in lieu of land grants to Rix Robinson, John Drew, John Holiday and his daughter Mary, and several other people, traders married to Native women or the mixed-race children of such families. The final article gave the Odawaag and Ojibweg "the right of hunting on the lands ceded, with other usual privileges of occupancy until the land is required for settlement."[83]

The Baptist missionaries Leonard Slater and Isaac McCoy who traveled to Washington with the Grand River delegation were dismayed that the treaty had been signed. "To my extreme grief and mortification," McCoy wrote, "the treaty was concluded, and signed by the very delegation that was sent to Washington *to prevent it.*" He subsequently wrote a book about the history of the Baptist Indian mission, noting, "These treaties were looked to by many hangers-on about the Indians as times when large sums of money could be obtained under the title of *claims,* or something else." McCoy worried that as a result of this land sale, the Odawaag and Ojibweg of Michigan would be "more crowded and injured by a white population than they had been previously; their deterioration would daily become more rapid, and then another treaty would be demanded, for the extinguishment of their claims to these reservations." This concern reflected the trope of the vanishing Indian, a central ideological construction that appeared in various forms of cultural production, such as the James Fenimore Cooper's novel *The Last of the Mohicans* (1826) and Tocqueville's essay *Two Weeks in the Wilderness.* Native peoples who lived among white settlers became a degraded version of themselves until, eventually, they literally died off as a people.[84]

Unfortunately, the vanishing Indian was not only a literary motif but also central to the expansionist republican ideology of politicians like Lewis Cass. The Odawaag and Ojibweg of the pre-statehood Michigan Territory had been able to resist removal, rejecting the policy advocated by the Republic when pressed by Cass at treaty negotiations in 1817, 1818, and 1819. The treaty signed at Washington in 1836 contained no provision regarding removal, but in a letter to Secretary Cass sent along with the

83. "Treaty with the Ottawa, etc., 1836," Mar. 28, 1836, in Kappler, comp. and ed., *Indian Affairs,* II, 450–455 (quotations on 452, 454). Payment of debts was limited to debts paid during the sixteen years before the treaty; for this stipulation, see Schoolcraft to Cass, Apr. 1, 1836, 24th Congress of the United States, Records of the Senate, Foreign Affairs and Indian Treaties, NARA.

84. Isaac McCoy, *History of the Baptist Indian Missions: Embracing Remarks on the Former and Present Condition of the Aboriginal Tribes; Their Settlement within the Indian Territory, and Their Future Prospects* (Washington, D.C., 1840), 494–495.

treaty, Schoolcraft wrote, "Their removal to the west of the Mississippi, or the region north of St. Anthony's falls, is contemplated, and under the present impulse of emigration, the incipient steps for this measure may be anticipated within a few years." Schoolcraft, like Cass when he negotiated treaties as governor, usually included such statements in documents pertaining to treaties made with the Anishinaabeg in the Michigan Territory. They are reflected in the provisions of article 8, which stipulate that "as soon as the said Indians desire it," a deputation will be sent west "to select a suitable place for the final settlement of said Indians." In this instance, however, the Senate changed the language regarding the reservations in article 3 when they ratified the treaty. The ratified treaty granted the communities of the treaty signers their reserved land "for the term of five years from the date of the ratification of this treaty and no longer, unless the United States shall grant them permission to remain on said lands for a longer period."[85]

In effect, by creating temporary reservations, the 1836 Treaty of Washington amounted to an attempt to remove the Anishinaabeg from what would become the state of Michigan in 1841. In response to this change, the missionary Leonard Slater began to buy land for the Odawaag. He had been appointed a guardian for the mixed-race Odawa Chiminoquat, who was not a citizen of the United States but as an Anishinaabe was granted sixty-four hundred dollars instead of a tract of land in article 9. Slater used this money to purchase land for the people of his ministry. "Mr. Slater's plan," McCoy wrote, "now appeared to be to take as many Ottawas as would follow him, and purchase land with his money, and their annuities, within the white settlements, and there form a settlement of Indians." This band of the Grand River Odawaag, like Hamelin and the L'Arbre Croche Odawaag, wanted to signal that they were embracing civilized life. With Slater's help, they sought to secure their land as property rather than as a reservation because any Indigenous land base not configured as private property would be vulnerable to attempts by U.S. officials to extinguish Native title.[86]

85. Schoolcraft to Cass, Mar. 30, 1836, 24th Congress of the United States, Records of the Senate, Foreign Affairs and Indian Treaties; "Treaty with the Ottawa, etc., 1836," Mar. 28, 1836, in Kappler, comp. and ed., Indian Affairs, II, 451 ("five years"), 453 ("suitable place"). For a narrative account of the treaty negotiation and analysis of the treaty, see Fletcher, The Eagle Returns, 22–28.

86. McCoy, History of the Baptist Indian Missions, 495–496. For the argument that the Anishinaabeg partnered with missionaries to avoid removal, see Fletcher, The Eagle Returns, 30–33.

The Anishinaabeg who traveled to Washington in March 1836 sought annuities to pay their debts and permission to remain in their homelands. The delegation, which never intended to sign a treaty, ended up signing one anyway, thinking that they had secured these goals. In the summer of that same year, they learned that the American Senate had arbitrarily revised their agreement, setting a five-year limit to their reservations and leaving them vulnerable to removal, the thing they feared most. Shortly after the return of the delegation to their homelands, Schoolcraft called the Anishinaabeg from both sides of the straits to a council at Mackinac Island to sign the ratified treaty. Over four thousand Ansihinaabeg encamped on the island from July 12 to July 22 while the ogimaag debated with Michigan's Indian agent whether to accept the revised treaty. Schoolcraft used the promise of goods and provisions to coax the gathered Anishinaabeg into accepting the treaty. These provisions were desperately needed after a disastrous winter hunt in 1836.

The American Fur Company posts reported that the Anishinaabeg suffered illness, most likely smallpox, that largely prevented them from hunting during the winter months of 1836. The posts from Sault Sainte Marie to the Keweenaw Peninsula also complained about severe cold that reduced the game populations. In mid-January, Gabriel Franchère, post commander at Sault Sainte Marie, informed Ramsay Crooks, "There is nothing doing in the fur trade, Indians in our vicinity do not hunt." He noted that "there is not more than one pack of all kind of peltries" in his department. In February, Franchère wrote Lyman Warren at La Pointe, "I also received a letter from Mr. Roussain, who states that sickness has prevented the Indians of Ance Quiouinon to pursue their hunts"—that is, from the Keweenaw Peninsula. He noted that "the sudden appearance of winter at a much earlier period than usual in these climes, has affected us all materially in our fishing concerns." That same month, Franchère informed Crooks, "Indians sick, and some three deaths occurred, has prevented them from hunting." Compounding the poor hunting, which meant limited peltry to trade, and poor fishing, which deprived all of the Anishinaabeg of a vital food source, late frosts destroyed the crops planted at L'Arbre Croch.[87]

When Schoolcraft called the council to discuss the ratified treaty, he counted on the fact that widespread illness and a harsh winter left all of

---

87. Franchère to Crooks, Jan. 15, 1836, Franchère to Warren, Feb. 2, 1836, Franchère to Crooks, Feb. 13, 1836, box 1, folder 10, Franchère Papers; McClurken, "We Wish to Be Civilized," 190.

the Anishinaabeg in rough shape. They arrived hungry and with virtu-ally no peltry to pay debts or secure provisions for a fall hunt. He also soothed fears about the imminent removal implied by the revised treaty terms that would limit their right to reservations in the Lower Peninsula of Michigan to five years. Schoolcraft assured the Anishinaabe ogimaag that article 13 of the treaty guaranteed them "indefinitely, the right of hunting on the lands ceded, with the other usual privileges of occupancy, until the land is required for settlement." Over the course of ten days, all of the Odawa and Ojibwe ogimaag from L'Arbre Croche, Grand River, and Sault Sainte Marie signed the ratified treaty. The need for provisions and cash, along with Schoolcraft's assurance that article 13 would allow them to circumvent the sunset clause on their reservations, persuaded the Anishinaabeg living in what would soon be the state of Michigan to accept the treaty.[88]

The American Republic as a Colonial Power

The first post-Revolutionary generation of American politicians, men like Henry Schoolcraft, Lewis Cass, and Andrew Jackson, aspired to establish a perfect settler sovereignty in the Trans-Appalachian West of the United States—that is, they imagined the expansion of American sovereignty as the complete eradication of Indigenous territory and social formations. There could be no autonomous Native nations within a sovereign state in the Republic of the United States. Michigan Territory, imagined ex-pansively as a vast territory that stretched from the Great Lakes to the Mississippi River valley, challenged this conception of American sover-eignty. In the Michigan Territory, sovereignty and jurisdiction remained fluid, and Native peoples struggled to preserve their place in this rapidly changing social and political landscape after a long period of Indigenous domination.[89]

The Northwest Territory was not like either New England or the Ches-apeake Bay, where European colonies existed for one and a half centuries before being reorganized as settler states in the U.S. Republic. The demo-graphic transition from a Native majority to a Native minority population

---

88. McClurken, "We Wish to Be Civilized," 191. The 1832 Treaty of Washington with the Creeks allowed some Creeks to remain on their allotment in a "life estate" until they died, and then the land would be converted into public domain. See Haveman, *Rivers of Sand*, 266.

89. For the idea of perfect territorial sovereignty, see Lisa Ford, *Settler Sovereignty: Jurisdiction and Indigenous People in America and Australia, 1788–1836* (Cam-bridge, Mass., 2010), 25–29.

within these spaces occurred during this long period of colonization. This transformation was punctuated by extreme periods of intercultural violence but generally proceeded gradually as a result of conflict with settler communities and between Indigenous nations who fought over resources, found themselves exposed to new diseases, and were pushed into the Trans-Appalachian West by white settlers. During this same period, the relatively slow but steady advance of the European population changed the environment and infrastructure of the human population along the Eastern Seaboard. In the face of this historical transformation, it was easier to adapt the self-serving ideology of the vanishing Indian than to reckon the deadly cost of settler colonialism.[90]

In contrast, when the Northwest Territory was organized by the United States in 1787, the entire region was recognized as Indian country by the very same politicians who sought to incorporate that land into the Republic. As a result of this organization, however, the majority Native population in what would become Ohio, Indiana, and Illinois became a small minority population within these states when they were incorporated into the union in 1803, 1816, and 1818, respectively. This transformation took less than thirty-five years, not a century and a half. During this period, there were constant low-level conflicts between Native peoples and settlers, but only three major military confrontations. Of these, only one, the Battle of Fallen Timbers (1794), was a victory for the United States. In the other two conflicts, the United States suffered significant casualties while Native forces suffered practically none.

To attribute this compressed transformation to some mythological phenomenon in which Native peoples confronting the modern world simply vanished would be ridiculous. In fact, the United States actively sought to replace the Native population with American settlers. The construct of the vanishing Indian was a central trope of the ideology that imagined North America as the New World and was meant to rationalize what U.S. citizens would now recognize as ethnic cleansing. The Northwest Ordinance facilitated the rapid, systematic dispossession of Native peoples in the service of expanding the territorial boundaries of the United States. In spite of this rapid transformation, however, most of the Northwest Territory remained an Indigenous space in terms of demography, economy, and politics. This was true of the Michigan Territory,

90. For an example of this phenomenon, see Jean M. O'Brien, *Firsting and Lasting: Writing Indians out of Existence in New England* (Saint Paul, Minn., 2010). See also Christine M. DeLucia, *Memory Lands: King Philip's War and the Place of Violence in the Northeast* (New Haven, Conn., 2018).

approximately two-thirds of the original Northwest Territory, organized by the U.S. government in 1805. Although the Michigan Territory was claimed by the United States as a federal territory, U.S. officials with experience in the Trans-Appalachian West, men such as Schoolcraft, Cass, and Jackson, knew that it was, in the parlance of the nineteenth century, Indian country.

In effect, the Michigan Territory remained a part of the Native New World even as the southern Great Lakes region was rapidly absorbed into the union following the creation of the Northwest Ordinance. When Zhaazhaawanibiisens arrived at the village of L'Arbre Croche at the end of the eighteenth century, the Odawaag and Ojibweg living in villages on both shores of the straits of Mackinac routinely traveled deep into the West. They ranged from Red Lake in the upper Mississippi Valley to the prairie parklands of the Red River valley and further west onto the Great Plains surrounding Turtle Mountain to hunt for beaver and bison for extended periods. Most would return to their home villages after a lengthy stay in the far West. Some remained in the region permanently but stayed connected through trade and kinship to those who chose to make a sojourn to the Great Plains as part of an occasional seasonal round. Yet, when transformation came at long last to the Michigan Territory, it came rapidly.

In 1825, the Erie Canal opened for business, connecting the northern Great Lakes directly to markets in the cities and states of the United States east of the Appalachian Mountains for the first time. Within a decade of the opening of the canal, the demography of Michigan's Lower Peninsula flipped. Native peoples went from the majority population to a minority population, and most settlers were interested in farming and logging Indian lands as opposed to trading with Indians. The dramatic increase of settlers and new settlements drastically circumscribed the hunting territories of the L'Arbre Croche Odawaag and the Ojibweg from the straits of Mackinac. The collapse of the fur trade in this region contributed to the collapse of the economic network connecting the villages of the Great Lakes to the northern Great Plains and brought an end to the long-distance seasonal round that integrated these two regions economically and politically as part of a Native New World that emerged during the first wave of European colonization in the early seventeenth century.

Despite this rapid economic and demographic change at their doorstep, the Ojibweg in the Lake Superior country and the upper Mississippi Valley did not yet feel the pressure of a settler population like their relatives in the Lower Peninsula of Michigan. In fact, they seldom saw any

Americans other than the traders and voyageurs who were integrated into their village communities. The missionaries who began to arrive in the 1830s represented the first outsiders to attempt to settle among them while remaining apart from their villages, customs, and economy. More significantly, they were the first Euro-American people, in spite of their small numbers, to insist that the Ojibweg conform to the social, political, and spiritual norms and the property regime of the U.S. Republic. Even when confronted with this harbinger of the future, ogimaag such as Nindipens and Maajigaabaw rejected the civilizing mission with a surety that the ogimaag of L'Arbee Croche, Grand River, and Sault Sainte Marie could no longer muster. Nindipens and Maajigaabaw told the American missionaries that the land was their land and that their way of life, their civilization, suited them just fine. These ogimaag spurned the American idea of civilization, whereas the ogimaag who signed the ratified 1836 Treaty of Washington promised to acquiesce to this idea. They assured American officials that their communities would enter into a social compact with the United States. They would become civilized while remaining Indigenous, living under the legal and political regime of the United States while maintaining their collective identity as Anishinaabe peoples. Their condition for embarking on this transformation was that the United States would allow them to remain in their homeland—a compromise that was, at best, rendered ambivalent by the U.S Senate's placing a time limit on the reservations established by the treaty.

Embracing the Civilizing Mission

During this time of rapid change in Anishinaabewaki, some Anishinaabe women pursued a parallel strategy. They sought to secure a future for their people by attaching their families to the civilizing mission of the United States. For two centuries, the path to economic and political security for the Anishinaabeg involved embracing trade with Europeans and with their North American settlements in the East. This embrace required the creation of kinship ties between Native communities and European traders. Native women formed partnerships with individual traders, which created obligations that bound the individual trader and his business associates with the communities of their wives. As a result of these relationships, a community of mixed-race and bicultural people emerged in conjunction with the fur trade. The Aitkin, the Cadotte, and the Cotte families were examples of the extended mixed-race families who became important proprietors and managers in the fur trade. They also served as a bridge to the political leadership of the Anishinaabe villages where they lived and traded. When Henry Schoolcraft led a diplomatic mission to the Ojibwe villages of the upper Mississippi to promote peace with the Dakota and to introduce Edmund Ely and the civilizing mission, he relied on the traders of the American Fur Company. It was the traders, not the Indian agent, who called the people to council at each village they visited.[91]

Now, as American settlements began to encroach upon their homeland, women like Beshibiiaanakwad, Hester Crooks, and Catherine Goulais became partners in the civilizing mission of the United States. This partnership promised to secure an education for their children and the inclusion of their families within the racial hierarchy of American civil society. Participation in the fur trade by the mid-nineteenth century ensured inclusion within a rapidly diminishing political economy that existed largely outside the civil society of North America's settler states. Embracing the civilizing mission represented a means of entering into the social contract that the Republic offered to settlers moving into the Northwest Territory. Fur traders required Native partners to embed themselves in the kinship networks that facilitated the circulation of goods and people throughout Anishinaabewaki. Missionaries such as William Boutwell and Edmund Ely and even married couples such as the Halls and the Ayers relied on the linguistic and domestic labor of Indigenous women to fulfill their mission. That mission was not widely adapted by the so-called uncivilized Anishinaabeg who lived in the village communities surrounding their missions. The civilizing mission was, however, accepted by the mixed-race families attached to both the fur trade and the village life of the Anishinaabeg. This embrace was part of an unspoken political bargain that identified this mixed-race subset of the Anishinaabeg as civilized, and therefore citizens of the expanding United States.

The political reconfiguration of Michigan underscored the necessity of supporting the civilizing mission. Organized under the provisions of the Northwest Ordinance, Michigan entered the union as a free state in January 1837, thus preserving the Missouri Compromise, but with a fugitive slave law written into the state's constitution. On June 15, 1836, Arkansas was admitted to the union as a slave state. The formation of Arkansas as a state followed the enforcement of the Indian Removal Act by territorial officials, resulting in a forced exodus of Indigenous peoples

91. For a description of this bicultural community and world, see Child, *Holding Our World Together*, 1–63; Murphy, *Great Lakes Creoles*, 148–186; Susan Sleeper-Smith, *Indigenous Prosperity and American Conquest: Indian Women of the Ohio River Valley, 1690–1792* (Williamsburg, Va., and Chapel Hill, N.C., 2018).

into the Indian Territory. In the Old Southwest, Indian removal and the expansion of "King Cotton" and a slave-labor regime followed the extinction of Native title.[92]

In the Old Northwest, in contrast, power and money flowed to territorial officials and businessmen in the Michigan Territory from the presence of Native peoples who remained on the land. With the extinction of Native title came land sales, timber rights, the purchase and dispensing of trade goods and cash payments, and the recovery of claims against these various forms of compensation—supposedly to pay debts and settle accounts—creating a political economy of plunder that benefited government officials, white settlers, and traders with kinship and business ties to Native peoples or jurisdiction over them. At the time of their first $30,000 annuity payment for the 1836 Treaty of Washington, traders would again claim unpaid debt, leaving a mere $2,274 of the first annuity payment to be dispersed to the Anishinaabeg. This pattern would repeat throughout the terms of the treaty. This political economy of plunder in Michigan required the continued presence of Native peoples in their homeland as politically subordinated noncitizen subjects. At stake in this treaty negotiation was not only the fate of Native homelands but also the place of Native peoples in an expanding Republic. What political and legal rights could they claim? An important part of this political struggle would be the fate of mixed-race Native people and the question of whether they could claim U.S. citizenship.[93]

The Anishinaabeg fought to preserve their homeland in some form, to find a place in the United States where they could continue to be Indigenous. In doing so, they forced the United States to negotiate place and belonging with the Indigenous inhabitants of a land they wanted to imagine as an empty wilderness. This struggle underscored the colonial nature of the American state. The United States was a colonial power expanding into the West through a political economy of plunder that sought to subordinate Native peoples while stripping them of their land and resources. In the northern tier of the Northwest Territory, this process proved to be

92. Adam Rothman, *Slave Country; American Expansion and the Origins of the Deep South* (Cambridge, Mass., 2005), 1–72; Walter Johnson, *River of Dark Dreams: Slavery and Empire in the Cotton Kingdom* (Cambridge, Mass., 2013), 1–72; Tiya Miles, *The House on Diamond Hill: A Cherokee Plantation Story* (Chapel Hill, N.C., 2010).

93. "List of Claims for 'Debt' Allowed . . . under the 6th Clause of the 4th Art of the Treaty with the Chippewas of Saginaw of 14th Jany 1837," 1836, Saginaw Agency, 1824–1850, RG 75, roll M234, 180–181.

most lucrative, not when Native peoples were eliminated, but when they remained in place as part of an ongoing colonial project that existed in conjunction with the settler colonial project of the U.S. Republic. In the decades following the American Revolution, the democratic experiment in an expanding United States relied on Indigenous dispossession, but it also, in places, hinged on and profited from the permanent colonization and exploitation of Indigenous peoples.

CHAPTER 4

Justice Weighed in Two Scales

On New Year's Day in 1837, one American Indian man killed another in the western region of the newly organized Wisconsin Territory. This, at least, was the ruling of the circuit court at Prairie du Chien. The facts of the case were not in dispute. An Anishinaabe man named Chigawaasking (The Big Birch) shot and killed a mixed-race man named Alfred Aitkin, the son of an American fur trader and an Anishinaabe woman. The crime occurred at Red Cedar Lake in the headwaters region of the upper Mississippi Valley where both men resided. In a ruling that shocked and angered the Aitkin family, the American judge presiding over Chigawaasking's trial set the accused free on the grounds that "our laws did not recognize Indian murder." For the court, the issue at stake was, not murder, but race. To adjudicate Alfred's murder as a crime, at least one man involved in the incident needed to be white or a citizen of the United States. Yet when the jury examined the case presented to them, all they could see was red. That is, the jurors decided that both men were Natives. Accordingly, they determined that neither Alfred nor Chigawaasking were U.S. citizens and therefore had no legal standing in an American court of law.[1]

The court's ruling threatened to unravel the fragile political infrastructure of the Northwest Territory, where U.S. sovereignty operated conditionally and only with the cooperation of men such as Alfred and his father, William Aitkin. Following the incorporation of this territory into the Republic, federal and state governments in the region consistently recognized the mixed-race children of fur traders and Native women as citizens, even granting men the right to vote and hold public office. They relied on men like William and Alfred Aitkin to facilitate the negotiation of treaties that extinguished Native title to Indigenous homelands, making this land base available for public consumption through the

---

1. "The Murder of Alfred Aitkin," William T. Boutwell Papers, 1832–1881, Gale Family Library, Minnesota Historical Society (MHS), Saint Paul.

Northwest Ordinance. Ominously, the murder trial of Chigawaasking pointed toward a darker future, one in which the United States no longer felt the need to incorporate Native peoples within the settler state. In truth, however, the murder of Alfred Aitkin and the trial of Chigawaasking represented a history of colonization, racial identity formation, and an evolving American national identity that was far more complicated than the binary simplicity of the court's ruling.[2]

The story of Alfred Aitkin is the story of the fur trade in the Northwest Territory. Men such as William Aitkin, or trader Michel Cadotte and clerk François Brunet, migrated to the Lake Superior country from British Canada and married Anishinaabe women to facilitate their work with the American Fur Company. Their mixed-race and multiracial families not only provided the kinship connections that made the regional economy function but also connected the Indigenous leadership of Anishinaabe-waki with the incoming political leadership of the advancing Republic. Without the cooperation of these men and their Indigenous, multiracial families, the expansion of the United States into Indian country would have been violent and costly, a lesson the Republic learned the hard way in the Ohio country during the late eighteenth century.[3]

Alfred, like his father, worked for the American Fur Company, but he was born and educated in the country of his Anishinaabe mother, an area claimed by the United States, first as part of the Michigan Territory and then as part of the Wisconsin Territory. Alfred spent the winter of

2. For recognition of citizenship rights for mixed-race Native peoples in the Northwest, see Chippewa Halfbreeds to Daniel P. Bushnell, July 24, 1839, in Clarence Edwin Carter et al., eds., *The Territorial Papers of the United States*, 28 vols. (Washington, D.C. and New York, 1934–), XXVIII, 16–18; Lucius Lyon to [Thomas Hartley] Crawford, July 16, 1839, ibid., 12–13.

3. Jack P. Greene has argued that the colonial process did not end with the formation of national states in North America. "In the United States and Canada," he argues, "it actually intensified with the colonization of vast new areas of the continent as swarms of settlers brought new areas under their hegemony, pushing out or confining to unwanted catchment areas thousands of indigenous peoples and in the United States, wherever it was legally possible and profitable, making extensive use of enslaved African Americans in doing so." See Greene, "Colonial History and National History: Reflections on a Continuing Problem," *William and Mary Quarterly*, 3d Ser., LXIV (2007), 240. Bethel Saler has made a similar argument, describing American expansion in the Old Northwest as an attempt to create "an expansive, settler republic and domestic empire." Like Greene, she argues that the United States was at once a republic and an aspiring colonial power. See Saler, *The Settlers' Empire: Colonialism and State Formation in America's Old Northwest* (Philadelphia, 2015), 13–15.

1836 in an Ojibwe village at Red Cedar Lake at the northern edge of his father's trading territory in the Fond du Lac Department of the American Fur Company. In the last days of December, he directed an *engagé*, or employee, to retrieve supplies he had cached for the winter at Lake Winnipeg. The employee embarked on his assignment in the company of his wife, a Native woman from the village at Red Cedar Lake. Chigawaasking intercepted the couple en route and sought to physically detain the woman while he tried to persuade her to abandon her husband. The engagé told Chigawaasking, "Let go of that woman, she is not your wife, you could not feed or clothe her," implying that it was the fur trade that sustained the Ojibweg economically and socially. The clerks, engagés, and traders of the American Fur Company married into villages throughout the region providing the lifeblood of the Ojibwe political economy. Responding to this assertion of self-importance, Chigawaasking countered, "I will kill your Bushem [clerk]." Although the engagé dismissed the threat and pressed on with his task in the company of his wife, the encounter hints at something more significant than a fight over a woman's affections. Confronted with the insinuation that he was a poor provider, Chigawaasking responded with a threat to kill, not the engagé, but his employer, an action that would have brought a halt to the fur trade at Red Cedar Lake if not to the entire region. In other words, these men were fighting over the ability to make a living in the upper Mississippi Valley and Lake Superior country and how that living would be made.[4]

The day after this encounter, Chigawaasking broke into the American Fur Company storehouse at Red Cedar Lake. When Alfred entered the storehouse to confront the intruder, Chigawaasking, waving a tomahawk, demanded ammunition and tobacco. Alfred disarmed the man and hauled him out of the storehouse, but Chigawaasking promptly retrieved a gun hidden alongside the building and shot Alfred in the chest, killing him instantly. Word of the murder spread quickly throughout the region.[5]

The American Fur Company clerk from Leech Lake learned of the crime that afternoon from the villagers at Red Cedar Lake when he arrived for a New Year's visit. William Aitkin heard of Alfred's death as he was making his way home from a business trip to Prairie du Chien. Determined to avenge his eldest son's murder, Aitkin recruited clerks and engagés from company posts as he traveled west. He would eventually arrive at the Ojibwe village at Leech Lake—a key post in the American Fur

4. "The Murder of Alfred Aitkin," Boutwell Papers.
5. Ibid.

Company trading operation in the upper Mississippi Valley and where company officials had taken Alfred's body—at the head of a posse of twenty-five armed men intent on capturing Chigawaasking.[6]

In the meantime, as William Aitkin journeyed toward Leech Lake, the news of Alfred's murder reached his mother, Beshibiiaanakwad, at Fond du Lac, the Ojibwe village at the bottom of Lake Superior where Aitkin made his base of operations. Beshibiiaanakwad resided at the village with her five younger children so they could attend the school recently established by Edmund Ely, a missionary for the American Board of Commissioners for Foreign Missions (ABCFM). Ely recorded in his journal the moment when Beshibiiaanakwad became aware of the death of her oldest son. Ely sat visiting with Delia Cook, who served as a domestic for the "mission family," when he heard "many voices crying out." According to Ely: "I stept to the door and the air resounded with the most dreadful wail. I immediately went over, and found Mrs. Aitkins and her whole family in the snow by the side of the fence near the stable, surrounded by Indian women, in an agony of wailing. Mr. Scott was near, and told me Alfred had been killed (shot) by an Indian at [Upper] Red Cedar Lake." Ely begged the family to go into their house. "They went, *wailing*"; "I proposed prayer—the wailing ceased, and we knelt before God."[7]

The keening of Native women and the chaos of the scene disturbed Ely. After prayer, he instructed the mixed-race fur-company employee Peter Crebassa to tell Beshibiiaanakwad "that such excessive grief was improper and injurious, that it was not consistent with Christian submission." Although he had lived among the Anishinaabeg for approximately two and a half years, Ely still could not speak directly to Beshibiiaanakwad, for he had yet to learn Anishinaabemowin. Instead, Ely relied on the mixed-race, bilingual men and women associated with the American Fur Company at Fond du Lac and his mixed-race wife to communicate.[8]

Ely's concern for the tenor of Beshibiiaanakwad's mourning reflected his pastoral and political roles as an ABCFM missionary. From Ely's perspective, the civilizing mission of the United States entailed a rejection of Native ritual and spiritual practices and the embrace of Protestant Christianity, which included an emphasis on emotional restraint.

6. Ibid.; William T. Boutwell to David Greene, Jan. 18, 1837, American Board of Commissioners for Foreign Missions, Correspondence, 1827–1878, box 1, Gale Family Library, MHS (hereafter cited as ABCFM).

7. Theresa M. Schenck, ed., *The Ojibwe Journals of Edmund F. Ely, 1833–1849* (Lincoln, Nebr., 2012), Mar. 30, 1836, 200, Jan. 7, 1837, 239.

8. Ibid., Jan. 7, 1837, 239.

The belief that Native peoples were ruled by their emotions derived from the ideology that categorized Native people as uncivilized beings. Such overt emotional expression was a manifestation of the primitive nature of Indigenous peoples. Accordingly, as part of his mission, Ely pushed the residents of Fond du Lac to conform to American social norms as he understood them. In this case, he demanded a quiet piety in the face of devastating personal loss.[9]

Although Alfred's murderer had been an uncivilized Indian in their view, Ely and the other ABCFM missionaries soon found themselves entangled in a morality play that focused almost exclusively on the mixed-race Anishinaabeg affected by the tragedy. Ely failed to understand the extent to which this violence revealed a power struggle between mixed-race traders and their Indigenous kin and trading partners.

The Capture of Chigawaasking

Like Edmund Ely, William Boutwell, the ABCFM missionary at Leech Lake, also saw Alfred Aitkin's murder as an opportunity to extend the civilizing mission to the mixed-race communities within the Anishinaabe villages in the newly formed Wisconsin Territory. The response to this murder would enable those who would claim U.S. citizenship to impose the norms of civilization onto a space that still followed the norms and practices of its Indigenous population. When William Aitkin arrived at Leech Lake to claim Alfred's body, the missionary urged restraint and offered to accompany him and his men as they set out to capture Chigawaasking, a gesture that the grieving father accepted, admitting, "I would like your company, for I don't know what I may do if I get my hands on that wretch." It was not entirely clear, however, what sort of outcome Aitkin expected in seeking to apprehend Chigawaasking. The fur trade operated within the Indigenous social world of the Northwest Territory, and Alfred and William, as the respective child and husband of an Anishinaabe woman, were integrated into that world. The trade functioned as part of the seasonal round that required Native peoples to move across

9. For a more detailed exploration of Edmund Ely, the ABCFM, and America's civilizing mission, see Rebecca Kugel, *To Be the Main Leaders of Our People: A History of Minnesota Ojibwe Politics, 1825–1898* (East Lansing, Mich., 1998), 27–29. Lewis Cass wrote, "The Indians are impelled to war by passions, which acknowledge no control." He also argued that Native peoples "had no principles of religion or morality to repress their passions." See [Cass], *Remarks on the Policy and Practice of the United States and Great Britain in Their Treatment of the Indians, from the North American Review, No. LV, for April, 1827* (Boston, 1827), 10.

extensive jointly occupied territories to hunt, trap, fish, and harvest rice and maple sugar. Kinship ties facilitated the migration associated with these practices, defining use rights and establishing the social obligations that governed harvesting, gift giving, and exchange. These obligations structured social relations between Native peoples and between Native peoples and fur-trade employees, most of whom married into the communities where they worked.[10]

These same kinship ties and obligations determined how conflict and disputes were resolved. If, for example, a Dakota man had killed Alfred Aitkin, the most likely outcome would have been warfare at some level. The Anishinaabeg and Dakota endured alternating cycles of alliance and warfare as their communities fought for the most advantageous position within the evolving fur-trade economy that developed after European colonization in North America. Had Alfred died at the hands of a Dakota warrior, his Indigenous relatives and the people of his village would have been expected to raise a war party. They might even have appealed to other surrounding Anishinaabe villages to aid in their quest for revenge. The relatives of the deceased as well as the civil and war leaders among the Anishinaabeg would have met to determine the appropriate level of response—considering the social status of the deceased as well as the political and economic consequences of large-scale or limited retaliation. And American Fur Company traders, regional Indian agents, and territorial officials would have likely tried to intervene, arguing for a peaceful resolution through a negotiated compensation in gifts and trade goods.[11]

Because Alfred was murdered by one of his own people, however, circumstances dictated a different course. An internal resolution would have to be negotiated, which could include a retaliatory death, though it more likely meant compensation, or a covering of the dead. Native nations did not raise war parties to punish or resolve conflicts among their own

10. "The Murder of Alfred Aitken," Boutwell Papers. For an analysis of the fur trade and Native territoriality in the Great Lakes, see Patricia Albers and Jeanne Kay, "Sharing the Land: A Study in American Indian Territoriality," in Thomas E. Ross and Tyrel G. Moore, eds., *A Cultural Geography of North American Indians* (Boulder, Colo., 1987), 47–91.

11. For Anishinaabe practices to punish murderers and for the relation between such violence and the Anishinaabe relationship with the Dakota, see Michael Witgen, *An Infinity of Nations: How the Native New World Shaped Early North America* (Philadelphia, 2012), 200–211. For Anishinaabe political decision making in response to murders, see Cary Miller, *Ogimaag: Anishinaabeg Leadership, 1760–1845* (Lincoln, Nebr., 2010), 85–97.

people. But then again, Alfred occupied what was becoming an increasingly liminal space in the Northwest Territory as a mixed-race individual. Was he a Native, a settler, or something in between? If he was, in fact, a settler and therefore a U.S. citizen, how could Native custom and not the rule of law determine the fate of his murderer? Many of the men who came to William Aitkin's aid were themselves mixed-race, some married to Native women and all of them intimately acquainted with Native custom. Boutwell was aware of the complications that could ensue from these connections to Native peoples. It soon became apparent that he offered to join the posse to uphold the authority of the United States, which for the missionary meant upholding the rule of law.

The capture of Chigawaasking played out in dramatic fashion and in the process revealed the ambiguous nature of political power and authority in the Northwest Territory. William Aitkin's posse quickly apprehended the killer at an encampment where he had taken refuge with his brother, mother, and other relatives. Before turning him over to American authorities, Aitkin sought an audience with Chigawaasking's uncle Gichiaya'aa nisayehn (Elder Brother), an important *ogimaa*, or civil leader, from Leech Lake. While they waited for Gichiaya'aa nisayehn to make his way to their camp, Chigawaasking escaped. Furious at this turn of events, Aitkin shouted at the missionary, "Mr. Boutwell, if it had not been for your advice, I should have hung the wretch!" Boutwell responded: "We did not go for a dead dog, but to apprehend and bring to justice a living one, had you taken his life it would have been private revenge in the mind of every Indian and no white man's life would have been safe or sacred in the country. I believe in the justice of our cause and that we shall apprehend him and bring him to justice." If Aitkin's angry declaration made it clear that he expected a Native version of justice rooted in blood revenge, Boutwell's response made it equally clear that he sought the kind of justice dispensed by the American state.[12]

On Gichiaya'aa nisayehn's arrival at Aitkin's camp, he reassured the traders that he would return the killer to their custody. Chigawaasking was on the run in a world that revolved around kinship ties and their attendant obligations. Warriors acting on behalf of the ogimaa found Chigawaasking in a camp with relatives who had aided in his escape but who also acquiesced to his surrender. On delivering Chigawaasking to William Aitkin, Gichiaya'aa nisayehn admonished the trader to secure his nephew, otherwise he would escape again and find refuge among his

12. "The Murder of Alfred Aitkin," Boutwell Papers.

Figure 12. *Que-we-ya (Ke-che-o-sun-ya or Elder Brother)*. Circa 1860.
Minnestoa Historical Society, Saint Paul

relatives. The ogimaa also chastised his nephew, telling him, "You have been serving the devil and to the devil you ought to go, but if you were my own son I would knock you in the head with this tomahawk." Thus, while some of Chigawaasking's extended family sought to shelter him, his uncle appeared willing to turn him over to American authorities. With the consent of the ogimaa, Aitkin's posse delivered their prisoner to Lawrence Taliaferro, the Indian agent for the upper Mississippi at Fort Snelling in Saint Peters.[13]

All social relationships, responsibilities, and obligations among the Anishinaabeg were structured by kinship connections. If kinship connections to his Anishinaabe wife benefited William Aitkin the fur trader, they also put him at a disadvantage when seeking redress for the murder of his son. The Anishinaabeg are patrilineal. Children lived with their father and his male relatives, learning to hunt and trap within territories associated with their lineage. Alfred Aitkin thus lived and worked with his father as a trader year round in the territory of his Anishinaabe mother rather than staying with his Native relatives and participating in their seasonal migration. Kinship connections to his mother's people served him well in the trade, but without a Native father he had no clear advocate when this community sought a resolution to his murder. This could explain William's decision to follow Boutwell's lead in asking the state to punish Chigawaasking. It could also indicate why many Ojibweg in the territory wanted the crime to be settled according to Indigenous custom, even after Gichiaya'aa nisayehn seemed to yield to the father's demand for state intervention.

The Decision to Prosecute Chigawaasking and the Limits of American Sovereignty

Lawrence Taliaferro, like the Reverend William Boutwell, worried about the preservation of U.S. authority in the wake of Alfred's murder. In his report to Wisconsin governor Henry Dodge, however, Taliaferro described the victim as "a half breed" and argued that "the circumstances under which the act was committed does not in my opinion call for official action in this particular case." For Taliaferro, the response to the crime was not about the rule of law, or even about the need for justice. Instead, his chief concern centered on how this incident would impact relations between the United States and the Anishinaabeg. "From recent statements," he informed Governor Dodge, "it would seem that the Chippeway

13. Ibid.

Indians are extremely hostile to Mr. William Aitkins and may do him harm." He concluded that he was not prepared to act "until you have had an interview personally with those of the nation who may desire him removed from their country."[14]

Taliaferro, it seemed, was willing to remove William Aitkin from Indian country to maintain good relations with the Anishinaabeg. Moreover, while he even went so far as to characterize the murder as "premeditated on the part of the Indians" in a subsequent letter, he still did not believe U.S. government intervention to be appropriate. By choosing to identify Alfred as a "half breed," and thus as a Native man and not an American citizen, Taliaferro opened the door for Alfred's murder to be handled in the context of Indian affairs, among the Anishinaabeg, rather than through a court of law. This calculation also suggests that Taliaferro saw mixed-race Natives as non-citizens and therefore not as white or civilized people. It is also significant, in terms of the relative power of the United States, that Taliaferro thought of the territory administered by the governor as the "country," or national territory, of the Ojibweg.[15]

William Aitkin evidently anticipated this hesitation on the part of American officials because he immediately began to restrict trade to his post at Sandy Lake in the eastern part of the territory. In doing so, he placed all of the Anishinaabeg living in the watersheds of the upper Mississippi Valley in economic distress. On February 11, 1837, Edmund Ely received word from Boutwell at Leech Lake:

> "The Inds. are just beginning to come in from their hunts. Some of them are as full of wrath as they can contain, not so much because we arrested the murderer, as because Mr. A. prohibits ammunition and tobacco from being given out." (Mr. A. has so ordered and told the Indians that none will be given until the accomplice in the murder, *Green Feather*, be given up.) "One or two have threatened to kill another white man if the murderer should be arrested."

In addition to withholding provisions, Aitkin publicly promised to avenge his son. Arriving at Fond du Lac with Alfred's body, he told Ely, "My heart is broke." Ely noted in his journal, "He seems determined to revenge on the Indians." The missionary presided over Alfred's funeral service, at the conclusion of which he wrote, "Mr. A. with a voice almost stifled with

14. Lawrence Taliaferro to Henry Dodge, Jan. 30, 1837, Letters Received, Saint Peters, 1837, U.S. Office of Indian Affairs, Microfilm M105, MHS.

15. Ibid., Feb. 15, 1837.

anguish, addressing the body of his departed boy, said, '*I will not cast earth on you. I will revenge your blood if God almighty gives me strength.*'"[16]

Yet even as he sought to punish the people related to Chigawaasking by severing trade ties, Aitkin also worked unofficial political channels to obtain a resolution for his son's murder. Before handing Chigawaasking over to U.S. authorities, he had conferred with Gichiaya'aa nisayehn, who had not only admitted his nephew's guilt but also had seemed to signal that he deserved punishment. And afterward he forced the hands of territorial officials, who, in spite of Taliaferro's reservations, eventually sent Chigawaasking to stand trial in the U.S. circuit court at Prairie du Chien in the spring of 1838. Aitkin managed to apprehend Green Feather and escort him to Prairie Du Chien as well, though he was not charged and there is no record of his incarceration.[17]

Taliaferro continued to express serious concern about the instability created by the prosecution of Chigawaasking and the behavior of Aitkin. Even once the trial was under way, Aitkin persisted in restricting trade to Sandy Lake, and the Indian agent warned Governor Dodge: "I fear the course which Mr. A is about to pursue since this melancholy event will be likely to change the feelings as well as the political conditions of the Chippeways of Leech Lake and render them not only hostile to him but alas to the United States by eventually causing these peoples to seek protection and supplies from the British Trading posts." Taliaferro's letter to the governor spoke to the political power and autonomy of the Anishinaabeg. It also addressed the relative weakness of the American government in the Great Lakes and the upper Mississippi Valley. Taliaferro openly worried about the Anishinaabeg shifting their political allegiance to British traders operating in the region. With the War of 1812 and the American surrender at Mackinac and Detroit a fresh memory, the prospect of hostile Indians aligned with the British Empire in a contested border region seemed a genuine threat to U.S. security. This sort of instability would impede the already slow pace of American settlement in the northern region of the Northwest Territory.[18]

16. Schenck, ed., *Ojibwe Journals of Edmund F. Ely*, Feb. 11, 1837, 246, Feb. 24–25, 1837, 254.

17. Taliaferro to Dodge, May 12, 1837, Letters Received by the Office of Indian Affairs, 1824–1880, Microfilm M175, MHS; Schenck, ed., *Ojibwe Journals of Edmund F. Ely*, May 6, 1837, 263.

18. Taliaferro to Dodge, May 12, 1837, Letters Received by the Office of Indian Affairs, Microfilm M175.

The missionaries operating in Anishinaabe territory echoed Talia-ferro's fears about the growing hostility of the Anishinaabeg toward the United States. Writing to ABCFM officials shortly after Chigawaasking's arrest, Boutwell warned that Aitkin's actions "will disaffect the Inds. To-wards the whites, I fear. To say nothing of the barbarous murder at Red Cedar Lake, all the clerks throughout this section of the country, concur in the fact that they have never known the Inds. so troublesome and over-bearing as they were last fall." Frederick Ayer, the ABCFM missionary at Yellow Lake in the country south of Lake Superior, expressed anxiety that with the withdrawal of the traders from the western territory, "Brother B [Boutwell] will therefore be left alone amidst a band of the most law-less savages who fear no power above or beneath." George Bonga, a half-Ojibwe, half-Black trader working for William Aitkin, confirmed these concerns. He informed Boutwell in a letter that the Indians of Leech Lake "say if Chi ga waa sking is hung they will set fire to my store and break my canoes." Alfred's murder and the confusion about how to punish Chigawaasking created significant political volatility and the potential for racialized violence, revealing the limits of American sovereignty in the Northwest Territory.[19]

The Trial of Chigawaasking and the Question of Jurisdiction

Whether Chigawaasking would be convicted or let go hinged on whether the jury would recognize Alfred Aitkin as a mixed-race man or as a Na-tive, or Indian, man. Missionaries, traders, and territorial officials usu-ally made a distinction between the Anishinaabeg and their mixed-race kin. They categorized Native peoples as "uncivilized" and identified their mixed-race kin as "civilized," with these markers of identity serving as signifiers of race. To be civilized was to be white and, at least potentially, a citizen, accorded political and legal rights. The jury in Chigawaasking's trial, however, rejected this distinction, regarding both the defendant and the victim, Alfred Aitkin, as Native.

Thomas Burnett, the district attorney who prosecuted the case, wrote to Alfred's father after the proceedings were over, "The trial of the Chip-pewa Indian at this place ended and you will be disappointed in learn-ing that he was acquitted." Despite that "the facts of his guilt were all

19. Boutwell to Greene, Jan. 18, 1837, Fredrick Ayer to Greene, June 12, 1837, both in ABCFM, box 1; George Bonga to Boutwell, June 7, 1838, Henry H. Sibley Papers, 1815–1932, MHS.

satisfactorily established," he told Aitkin, "the point upon which the verdict of the jury was given, was as I understand, whether the deceased was an Indian or a white man and they decided that he was not a white man. The law of Congress extending the laws of the United States in criminal cases over the Indian country excepts offenses committed by one Indian against the person or property of another Indian." According to Burnett, although the judge, Charles Dunn, acknowledged "that the first rule of law was that the character and name of children followed that of the mother," he informed the jury that this law was "superseded" by the legitimate marriage of William and Beshibiiaanakwad, as well as by the fact that Alfred "was brought up and educated as a white man." In other words, Judge Dunn instructed the jury to regard Alfred Aitkin as a white man. Yet, Burnett wrote, "the jury decided that he was not such." The attorney concluded that "both the law and the evidence were against the decision, but as the decision has been given it must be abided by and the case considered at an end."[20]

The jury's ruling reflected the logic of Agent Taliaferro. Alfred Aitkin, as a "half breed," was an Indian. As such, he resided outside the legal and civil boundaries of the social contract that the Republic extended to its citizens. Ignoring the judge's instructions, the jury imposed a ruling that linked the rule of law to white racial privilege. Burnett, in his letter to Aitkin, noted, "We were unable to introduce the black halfbreed as a witness on account of his ignorance of the obligation of an oath." This was a reference to Bonga, the half-Ojibwe and half-Black man who managed William Aitkin's trading operation at Leech Lake and who also led the posse that originally apprehended Chigawaasking. An astute businessman with an eastern education, Bonga understood the meaning of an oath. Yet, from the perspective of the jury, the combination of his Blackness and his Indianness made him unfit to serve as a witness in a criminal trial.[21]

Bonga's exclusion from the trial foreshadowed the jury's decision. Indeed, the composition of the jury itself suggested the political and institutional shift that would deliver an acquittal. Ira Brunson, a Crawford County judge who witnessed the trial, later observed that "the parties agreed to have none on the jury except those who could understand the

20. Thomas Pendelton Burnett to William A. Aitkin, May 28, 1838, Henry H. Sibley Papers.

21. Ibid. For Bonga and the issue of mixed-race or "halfbreed" identity, see Bruce M. White, "The Power of Whiteness; or, The Life and Times of Joe Rolette Jr.," in *Making Minnesota Territory, 1849–1858*, special issue of *Minnesota History*, LVI (1998–1999), 178–197.

Figure 13. *George Bonga*. Photograph by Charles A. Zimmerman. Circa 1870.
Minnesota Historical Society, Saint Paul

English language." This decision was an attempt by the court to exclude the Francophone residents of Prairie du Chien from the jury pool. This population included many mixed-race people with Native heritage as well as people involved in the fur trade. Their omission represented a political and demographic shift in favor of American settlers who equated whiteness with citizenship. Nevertheless, in the end, it is difficult to know whether this ruling signaled a hardening of the race line and the codification of white supremacy or a desire to secure the compliance and cooperation of the Anishinaabe bands embroiled in a contentious treaty negotiation. The case was decided while Congress was deliberating over the provisions of the 1837 Treaty of Saint Peters, which Taliaferro and Henry Schoolcraft had negotiated with the Lake Superior and Mississippi Valley Anishinaabe *doodemag* in the months following Chigawaasking's arrest. On the ground in Prairie du Chien, the decision of the jury seemed to indicate a desire to place all Native people on the nonwhite or uncivilized side of the race line, even as territorial officials wanted to blur this distinction to preserve their influence with traders and their families.[22]

Not long after Chigawaasking's trial, Henry Schoolcraft, acting as Michigan's Indian agent, was also confronted with charges of murder in his jurisdiction involving two Native men. On October 2, 1837, Schoolcraft received a message from the Anishinaabe ogimaa Joseph Wakazo informing him that a member of Wakazo's band had killed a Native companion during a dispute. Wakazo, also known as Ogemainini, was the civil leader of an Odawa doodem from Little Traverse in the northern Lower Peninsula of Michigan. Schoolcraft took a position similar to Taliaferro and the circuit court at Prairie du Chien. He told Wakazo: "An Indian killing an Indian on a reserve, where the case occurred, which is still 'Indian Country,' did not call for the interposition of our law. Our criminal Indian code, which is defective, applies only to the murder of white men in the Indian country. So that justice for a white man and

22. Judicial History of Prairie du Chien, Wis., 1823–1841, Compiled from Court Records at Prairie du Chien, Crawford County, by Judge Ira B. Brunson, and Survey Notes (Jan. 4, 1837) of Prairie du Chien, Manuscript 11, n.p., Wisconsin Historical Society Library, Madison. Lucy Eldersveld Murphy has argued that the exclusion of Francophone or Creole residents from juries empaneled in Crawford County signaled that settlers and territorial officials increasingly believed that they did not need the mixed-race and Francophone fur traders to assert their authority over Native peoples. See Murphy, *Great Lakes Creoles: A French-Indian Community on the Northern Borderlands, Prairie du Chien, 1750–1860* (New York, 2014), 142–144.

an Indian is weighed in two scales." Like the court ruling in Prairie du Chien, Schoolcraft adhered to the idea that the U.S. government could not punish Native peoples for committing crimes against one another in "Indian country," even when those lands existed as part of a federal territory or when they had been incorporated into the boundaries of a state, like Michigan, organized through the Northwest Ordinance.[23]

The law was not ambiguous when it came to the murder of white men in Indian country, but the sovereignty of the settler state was less than perfect when Native people retained political and demographic power. In these circumstances, Indigenous jurisdiction could supersede the authority claimed by the government. In 1802, Giishkako, the son of Manidoogiizhig (Little Cedar Spirit-Tree) and adopted brother of Zhaazhaawanibiisens, or John Tanner, killed a French-Canadian trader named Antoine Lauzon. The Lower Peninsula of Michigan, where the murder took place, was part of the Indiana Territory but commonly regarded as Indian country. Consequently, Giishkako would not be indicted for Lauzon's murder until September 1805, in the Supreme Court of the newly organized Michigan Territory. According to the indictment, "Kiskakon, a Chippeway Indian man, commonly called the Chippeway Rogue, late of Saguinan in the Indian Country, in the Territory of Michigan, . . . willfully and of his malice aforethought," assaulted and killed Lauzon. Giishkako nevertheless managed to escape justice. Although he was arrested by the U.S. marshal for the Michigan Territory, the marshal reported to the court shortly thereafter that "in bringing him to prison he was rescued from me by an Indian called Little Cedar, his son and other Indians unknown." Giishkako's escape from a Detroit jail with the help of his father, Manidoogiizhig, a Saginaw ogimaa, would not have occurred without the consent of the jailers.[24]

23. Henry R. Schoolcraft, *Personal Memoirs of a Residence of Thirty Years with the Indian Tribes on the American Frontiers: With Brief Notices of Passing Events, Facts, and Opinions, A.D. 1812 to A.D. 1842* (Philadelphia, 1900), 610.

24. "Indictm[en]t for Murder: The United States vs KisKacon a Chipaway Indian Man etc," Case 8, Paper 1, Sept. 19, 1805, in William Wirt Blume, ed., *Transactions of the Supreme Court of the Territory of Michigan, 1805–1814*, 2 vols. (Ann Arbor, Mich., 1935), II, 17–18; "The United States vs Kiskacon, an Indian Man, of the Chipaway Nation Late of Saguina," Case 8, Paper 2, ibid., 18; "The United States vs Kiscacon, an Indian," Case 8, Paper 3, ibid., 19. "The fluidity of sovereignty," writes Lisa Ford, "is nowhere more apparent than in jurisdictional practice—the responses of governors, law officers, and courts to indigenous violence against settlers." See Ford, *Settler Sovereignty: Jurisdiction and Indigenous People in America and Australia, 1788–1836* (Cambridge, Mass., 2010), 30.

The willingness of territorial authorities to allow a Native prisoner to be "rescued" reveals the limitations of U.S. sovereignty and the power of the Anishinaabeg to assert an Indigenous jurisdiction in the Michigan Territory. At the time of the murder, William Hull, the governor of the Michigan Territory, informed the secretary of war that "Little Cedar, is an influential chief" and noted that, "until very lately, he and all his tribe have been unfriendly to the U. States." Manidoogiizhig visited the governor at Detroit in 1807 and pledged "to be my friend, and the friend of the U. States" in exchange for a pardon for his son. "I have promised him to use my influence with the President," Hull wrote to the secretary of war; "I believe it would be attended with useful consequence." Whether or not Hull secured an official pardon from the president, Giishkako remained a free man. The diplomatic cost of enforcing U.S. jurisdiction in the Michigan Territory, a place dominated by the Anishinaabeg, was too high in 1805.[25]

Sixteen years after the governor pardoned Giishkako, however, the authorities of the Michigan Territory felt more confident in asserting their jurisdiction over Indians who murdered white men in Indian country. In 1821, the Supreme Court of the Michigan Territory tried two Native men for murder: a Menominee man named Kewabishkim and an Ojibwe man named Ketawkah. Kewabishkim and Ketawkah lived in the upper Mississippi Valley on lands claimed as federal territory by the United States but where Native title had yet to be extinguished. Both men were accused of killing white men who were U.S. citizens. Kewabishkim, witnessed by several men, had stabbed Charles Ulrick, a settler in the Green Bay region after a dispute over the theft of a hat. Ketawkah, also observed by witnesses, had shot and killed William Madison, a doctor serving in the U.S. army, though testimony at trial failed to reveal the motivation behind this act of violence. Both men were removed from the Indian country west of Lake Michigan and brought to trial in Detroit.[26]

At Kewabishkim's and Ketawkah's subsequent arraignments, the

25. William Hull to Henry Dearborn, Dec. 28, 1807, in *Michigan Historical Collections*, XL, *Documents relating to Detroit and Vicinity, 1805–1813* (Lansing, Mich., 1929), 240–241.

26. "The United States of America vs Ke-wa-bish-kim," Case 706, Paper 5, Sept. 19, 1821, in William Wirt Blume, ed., *Transactions of the Supreme Court of the Territory of Michigan, 1814–1824*, 2 vols. (Ann Arbor, Mich., 1938), I, 631–632; Ketaukah Verdict, Michigan Territory Court, Sept. 12, 1821, Solomon Sibley Papers, 1750–1918, LMS: Miscellaneous Papers, folder 12, 1820–1830, Burton Historical Collection, Detroit Public Library.

lawyers for both the state and the accused raised questions about U.S. jurisdiction. At Kewabishkim's arraignment, Solomon Sibley, lawyer for the plaintiff (the Territory of Michigan) argued for U.S. jurisdiction based on the Treaty of Greenville, the first American treaty negotiated with the Anishinaabeg in 1795 at the conclusion of the Northwest Indian war. He informed the grand jury that "the treaty of Grenville provides for punishing Indians who come upon our lands and commit murder." At Ketawkah's arraignment, however, James Duane Doty, Ketawkah's attorney, challenged this claim. Although Sibley, once again the attorney for the Territory of Michigan, noted that the crime had been committed "within the U.S. and territory of Michigan, and within a district of county to which the Indian title has not been extinguished," Doty submitted a plea signed by the defendant with an *X* disputing the court's jurisdiction on the basis that the "Winnebago and Chippewa nations were sovereign and independent, exercising exclusive jurisdiction over all offences committed within their respective territorial limits." Sibley, in turn, countered

> that inasmuch as that country was within the *limits* of the United States the government must have jurisdiction over it; that these nations were *conquered,* or if not, their permitting the French, English, and Americans to take possession of their country, was a relinquishment of their sovereignty—that as they are mere barbarians, and do not cultivate the earth, the first civilized nation who obtained possession of it acquired thereby a right to the soil and dominion over the whole.

Ultimately, the judge sided with the plaintiff, Doty's plea was overruled, and both men were found to have committed assault with "malice aforethought" resulting in the deaths of their victims and establishing criminal intent. This was justice "weighed in two scales." On December 27, 1821, Kewabishkim and Ketawkah were escorted from their jail cells in Detroit to the public gallows and hanged.[27]

The logic behind Sibley's argument for U.S. jurisdiction in these cases echoed the indictment and verdict finding the defendants guilty. Specifically, the court found that Kewabishkim and Ketawkah were savages living in an unsettled land that had been colonized by civilized men. In

27. "Notes of Trials, Arguments, Decisions, and Proceedings, in the Supreme Court of the Territory of Michigan—September Term, 1821," in Blume, ed., *Transactions, 1814–1824,* I, Sept. 18, 1821, 485, Sept. 27, 1821, 494–495; "Miscellaneous Items: Supreme Court," *Illinois Gazette* (Shawneetown), Dec. 1, 1821, [3]; "Execution," *Maryland Gazette and Political Intelligencer* (Annapolis), Jan. 24, 1822, [2].

each case, the court ruled that the defendant, "not having the fear of God before his eyes, but being moved and seduced by the instigations of the Devil . . . feloniously, and in the fury of his mind, did make an assault" resulting in the death of his victim. These men were not seeking revenge or caught up in a violent dispute with other savages. Rather, they were savages caught committing acts of a barbarous nature against civilized men. Similarly, the United States exercised legal jurisdiction within the homelands of Kewabishkim and Ketawkah because Native peoples failed to properly cultivate this territory, allowing the United States to take possession of it as unsettled land. In both instances, the court's decision made the distinction between the uncivilized world of Native peoples and the civilized world of the settler colonial state. When these two worlds overlapped, the sovereignty of the settler state superseded any claims of Indigenous autonomy or sovereignty.[28]

Yet if the courts allowed that Native peoples were excluded from American civil society, they also established that this did not make them alien residents living within U.S. territory. When the lawyers began empaneling a jury, Doty, Ketawkah's lawyer, moved for a jury de medietate linguae, a practice in English common law that allowed for a mixed-language jury when one of the parties was an alien who did not speak English. Since Ketawkah spoke Anishinaabemowin, not English, Doty asked the court to recognize his client as an alien or foreigner and requested the judge to empanel a jury that included an equal number of English jurors and resident aliens, or Native people, to reflect the status of the defendant. The prosecutor, however, argued in response that "an Indian cannot be sworn, as he has no ideas of future rewards and punishments. On this and other accounts they are not competent jurors." This was the same reasoning that prevented George Bonga from testifying at the trial of Chigawaasking, namely that Native peoples could not understand the "obligation of an oath." Yet, in Ketawkah's case, the prosecutor also argued that Ketawkah was "not an alien. He and his country are at least under the protection of the U.S." The judge agreed with the prosecutor and ruled against Doty's motion. Ketawkah, as an Indian, was excluded from American civil society; nonetheless, his person and his homeland fell under the jurisdiction of the United States. Following this line of argument, if the jury in Prairie du Chien had concluded that Alfred

28. "The United States of America vs. Ke-wa-bish-kim," Case 706, Paper 5, Sept. 19, 1821, in Blume, ed., *Transactions, 1814–1824,* I, 632; Ketaukah Verdict, Sept. 12, 1821, Michigan Territory Court, Solomon Sibley Papers.

Aitkin was a white man, then Chigawaasking should have been tried and convicted of murder.[29]

Indian Murders and U.S. Jurisdiction

In 1826, five years after the public execution of Kewabishkim and Ketawkah, the Michigan Territory also confronted the issue of jurisdiction in multiple cases of Native peoples caught murdering other Native peoples. Even when not adjudicated in U.S. courts, this violence was reported in territorial newspapers. In January 1826, Giishkako was arrested for murder a second time, along with his son Chi-Amik. Records of the arrest no longer exist, but, as the *Daily National Journal* reported the case on the night of January 10, "an Indian of the Saginaw tribe" was found dead from a tomahawk blow to the back of the head in downtown Detroit.

> Suspicion immediately rested upon *Kishkauko*, the notorious war-chief, long known for his many and atrocious murders. He was pursued by the deputy sheriff, Mr. Hunt, with a posse, and overtaken about midnight, at the house of the agent, Col. Beufait. He and his son, with two other Indians, were found asleep, the young man with his father's tomahawk under his head. On being awakened, and finding the tomahawk and other weapons secured, he observed that the same might have blood on it as he had used it to cut meat the day before.—On being told that it was the governor's wish that they should immediately appear before him, they quietly suffered themselves to be taken to prison.

Following the arrest of Giishkako and Chi-Amik, the Wayne County coroner empaneled a jury, which "after a strict investigation, which occupied nearly the entire day, unanimously found a verdict of *murder* against *Kishkauko* and his son the 'Big Beaver;' the latter as principal, and the former as accessory before the fact." This same article also reported the discovery of the bodies of three other Native people, found dead near Swan Creek in Monroe, Michigan. Aside from offering that the bodies of the deceased had been "mangled in a most shocking manner," the paper provided no other details about the crime.[30]

29. "Notes of Trials, Arguments, Decisions, and Proceedings, in the Supreme Court of the Territory of Michigan—September Term, 1821," Sept. 28, 1821, in Blume, ed., *Transactions, 1814–1824*, I, 496. For jury de medietate linguae, see Austin Sarat, ed., *The Blackwell Companion to Law and Society* (Malden, Mass., 2004), 196.

30. "Detroit, Jan 10—Indian Murder," *Daily National Journal* (Washington, D.C.), Jan. 30, 1826, [3].

On February 21, 1826, a little more than a month after Giishkako and Chi-Amik were taken into custody, the *Detroit Gazette* recounted an additional series of murders committed by Native peoples against other Native peoples. "Six Indians have been slaughtered by their own countrymen, within our settlements, since the first week in January," the paper observed. "Our courts and juries have a heavy responsibility upon them in this matter," the paper continued, arguing that "it would seem to be a severe, if not tyrannical, exercise of power, to deprive these miserable beings of the poor boon of life, for executing their own laws in their own way, in a country so recently theirs." This assertion amounted to a tacit recognition of Native sovereignty and suggested how the rapid dispossession of Native peoples in the Lower Peninsula of Michigan made it difficult to distinguish between Indigenous and U.S. jurisdictions. Nevertheless, the paper called for the government to intervene, stating, "Blood must not be illegally shed on our soil." This same article announced that a sixteen-year-old Saginaw Ojibwe boy named Shabagajick mortally wounded two drinking companions in Oakland County, north of Detroit. He was subsequently "apprehended, a coroner's jury were summoned, and after due inquiry, they found a verdict of *willful murder* against Sha ba gajick." The paper reported the young man to be confined in the Pontiac jail but did not state the length of his incarceration. A subsequent article also noted that an Odawa man named Jacques Crow had been tried in the circuit court of Monroe County, south of Detroit, for the murder of a Boodewaadami woman named Ambequaw. Jacques Crow "was found guilty of manslaughter, and sentenced to one year of hard labour in the county prison." A final article in the same column concluded the subject of Indian murders by relating that Giishkako and his son remained in jail in Detroit "and probably will continue there un[til] the next regular session of the circuit court," when, in addition to the recent murder, old charges related to the murder of Antoine Lauzon would be revived. In stark contrast to the murder of Alfred Aitkin by Chigawaasking, the lower courts in the Michigan Territory asserted jurisdiction over Native peoples for committing crimes, even when they involved other Native peoples and not U.S. citizens.[31]

31. "More Indian Murders," *Detroit Gazette*, Feb. 21, 1826, [2], "Trial for Murder," [2], "Kishkauko and His Son," [2]. In the Old Southwest, Indian Agent Benjamin Hawkins routinely exempted Native people from state jurisdiction. As Lisa Ford writes: "Hawkins uniformly ignored state demands for the surrender of indigenous criminals. He argued that, so long as the Creek Nation punished Creek offenders for crimes against settlers, they honored the spirit, if not the letter, of Creek–United States treaties." See Ford, *Settler Sovereignty*, 114.

A key distinction between these murders and the murder of Alfred Aitkin or the murder reported by Joseph Wakazo was that they occurred in American settlements. Therefore, even though they involved Native people killing other Native people, these acts were committed in spaces where U.S. sovereignty and jurisdiction were clearly established. These murders also occurred at a time when the demography in the southeast of the Michigan Territory had changed significantly. By 1826, a year after the opening of the Erie Canal, the Anishinaabeg living in Michigan's Lower Peninsula had become a minority population in their homeland for the first time. This demographic change severely disrupted the seasonal round of Native peoples living in the Detroit area, the most densely populated part of the Michigan Territory. Violence, frequently associated with the consumption of alcohol, was a painful consequence of the economic hardship as well as waning political power experienced by the Anishinaabeg.

The diminished political influence of the Anishinaabeg exposed men like Shabagajick and Jacques Crow to U.S. sovereignty and placed them under the jurisdiction of territorial officials. Asserting jurisdiction over a person such as Giishkako, a prominent ogimaa who enjoyed significant political status, was far more problematic. The jury empaneled by the coroner found Giishkako and Chi-Amik guilty. Yet they were not sentenced and were being held until they could be tried in the supreme court. They would not be imprisoned on the basis of a coroner's inquest. This political dilemma was compounded when Giishkako died in jail while awaiting trial. On May 25, 1826, after being incarcerated for three and a half months, the ogimaa apparently committed suicide. The coroner determined that Giishkako died from poison. The *Daily National Intelligencer* reported that the "celebrated chief of the Chippewas" had been visited by one of his wives "who handed him a small cup, and then left the cell." Later that same day, members of his family and doodem visited Giishkako, "held a long conference, and took leave with a solemnity, earnestness, and affection, never observed in their previous visits." The following morning, the family members returned to the jail and asked to see the ogimaa. When the jailer escorted the visitors to his cell, they found his lifeless body. They "expressed exultation rather than surprise" at this discovery, according to the newspaper, and they returned to Saginaw after burying the deceased ogimaa at a nearby farm. "Thus has perished one of the most despotic and influential savage monarchs of modern times. . . . His history, like that of other warriors, is marked with many atrocious murders; but he had the virtues also of the savage." Apparently, the *Daily National Intelligencer* concluded that Giishkako, as a fearsome but noble savage, accepted his own death rather than continue to suffer the indignity of prison. Vanishing Indians were going to vanish one way or another.[32]

It is impossible to know why Giishkako chose to take his own life rather than demanding release by asserting that he had simply exercised a customary right of revenge. His death, however, elevated his son as ogimaa, a hereditary position among the Anishinaabeg. After the death of Giishkako, the civil leaders of the Saginaw Ojibweg led a party of eighty men to Detroit to call on the governor of the Michigan Territory, Lewis Cass. They demanded Chi-Amik's release. Governor Cass was preparing to travel to La Pointe to negotiate a treaty with the Ojibwe doodemag from Lake Superior, and he declined to meet with the men from Saginaw. Instead, he asked the larger party to return to their village, and he directed the ogimaag to meet with William Woodbridge, the secretary of the Michigan Territory. At council with the secretary, the ogimaag stated "that none had just right to interfere in their private difficulties but themselves—that the charge against the prisoner was in reality a matter of their own; that his father had already died in consequence of his close confinement, that they believed no sufficient proof could be advanced against him to establish his guilt; but whether so or not, their desire was that he should be set at liberty." The ogimaag added that the relatives of the man killed by Giishkako, who according to their custom could claim a right of revenge, instead wanted the young chief to be set free.[33]

In response, Woodbridge asserted that the issue at stake was jurisdiction. He advised the ogimaag

> that it could not be without pain, that this [the U.S.] government would ever interfere in any matter of private difficulty which might unhappily occur among them: but that such difficulties, if they existed, should be settled on their own land—away from white people. . . . But that the offence alluded to, was not a mere private difficulty;

32. "Death of Kishauko," *Daily National Intelligencer* (Washington, D.C.), June 14, 1826, [3].

33. William Woodbridge to James Barbour, June 30, 1826, Saginaw Agency, 1824–1850, Letters Received, 1824–1880, Record Group (RG) 75: Records of the Bureau of Indian Affairs, 1793–1999, M234, roll 745, 15, National Archives and Records Administration (NARA), Washington, D.C.

it was committed here too; and that our Laws which applied to *all* and were intended to protect all alike, of whatsoever colour; expressly forbade violence and quarrels in the street.

The officers of the law, he asserted, could not ignore a violent crime that took place within the city limits of Detroit. Woodbridge told the Saginaw ogimaag, however, that "as their whole nation asked for it, it was possible, that the President might listen to their prayer and pardon the prisoner." They could wait until the circuit court convened in September, or they could petition the president of the United States. The ogimaag met in council at the home of the Indian subagent Joseph Godfroy, who translated a letter on their behalf asking the president to pardon Chi-Amik. "I am inclined to the opinion," Woodbridge wrote to Secretary of War James Barbour, "that the homicide was in fact committed by the prisoner; but nevertheless believe, that the public good would be best promoted by his liberation."[34]

After insisting that Giizhkako and Chi-Amik committed a crime in the city of Detroit, thus falling under the jurisdiction of the territorial government meant to protect people of all races, Woodbridge made the case for a public pardon. He informed the secretary of war that there would be no direct testimony, only circumstantial evidence. "The effect upon the Tribe, of a pardon by the President," he wrote, "will be more salutary than that of a discharge after a fruitless attempt to convict." Equally important, he argued, "The feelings of the Indians will have been soothed and flattered by such an act of grace on the part of the President." Woodbridge warned the secretary of war: "The proposition 'that because the homicide was committed, by an Indian upon the body of an Indian of the said Tribe, the judicial authorities here, have therefore no jurisdiction'" was "in itself untenable." Furthermore, this misperception about the law was widely believed among Native peoples. In his estimation, this "sufficiently prove[d] there was no consciousness in the mind of the aggressor of offending against the Laws of this government."[35]

According to Woodbridge, there was no malice aforethought or criminal intent in the commission of the violent act. To imprison a man for breaking a law he was unaware of and would not understand would be perceived as an injustice by the Saginaw Ojibweg. Woodbridge also reminded the secretary, "The power to pardon offences committed against our local laws has been expressly conferred upon the executive of this

34. Ibid., 15–16, 17 ("homicide").
35. Ibid., 17–18.

Territory." He lamented that Governor Cass was not only absent from the seat of government but was "removed beyond the verge of the settlements; He is in the Indian Country—on public business—yet he continues within the Geographical limits of the Territory." Cass was, in effect, beyond reach of communication but still within the Michigan Territory. Therefore, at least one supreme court judge insisted it would be illegal for Secretary Woodbridge to exercise any contingent power to act as chief executive. Given this confusion, Woodbridge declined to act without the consent of "general government" and asked instead that the president pardon Chi-Amik, or direct him to do so.[36]

Neither the president nor the secretary of war responded to Woodbridge. The problem of Chi-Amik, however, resolved itself. According to the Detroit jailer, the unarmed young warrior tricked and overpowered his guard one morning, walked out of the prison complex undetected, and returned to Saginaw without any interference from territorial officials. Another interpretation of events might be that Secretary Woodbridge doubted the right or ability of the territory of Michigan to exercise jurisdiction over a politically important Native leader and therefore chose to release him. In any case, Chi-Amik, like his father in 1805, conveniently escaped from the Detroit jail.[37]

Customary Practice and the Right of Revenge

Related to the question of U.S. jurisdiction over Native subjects was the issue of Native customary rights or practices. This was both a matter of Indigenous jurisdiction and the diplomacy required to manage relationships between the Republic and Native nations. In 1830, four years after Chi-Amik escaped jail and murder charges, a jury in Green Bay acting

36. Ibid., 18 ("power to pardon"), 19 ("on public business"), 20 ("general government").

37. B. P. H. Witherell, "Reminiscences of the Northwest: XIII.—Kish-kaw-ko and Big Beaver," in *Third Annual Report and Collections of the State Historical Society of Wisconsin, for the Year 1856* (Madison, Wis., 1857), III, 332–334. It could be argued that in allowing Chi-Amik to escape, Woodward recognized the existence of multiple jurisdictions in the Michigan Territory. As Lisa Ford writes: "Neither policy makers nor settlers understood settler sovereignty to imply unfettered territorial jurisdiction in the early nineteenth century. Instead, together with indigenous people, they crafted and practiced plural jurisdiction, the boundaries of which were policed by governments, settlers, and indigenous people in the centers and peripheries of settlement." See Ford, *Settler Sovereignty*, 54. See also Sydney L. Harring, "Indian Law, Sovereignty, and State Law: Native People and the Law," in Philip J. Deloria and Neal Salisbury, eds., *A Companion to American Indian History* (Malden, Mass., 2002), 441–459.

as the U.S. circuit court for Brown County, which was then part of the Michigan Territory, exonerated Oshkosh, a Menominee war chief charged with murder, on the basis of lex talionis (the law of retaliation)—that is, the court ruled that Oshkosh acted according to an accepted custom respecting a right of revenge. Oshkosh admitted to killing a Pawnee Indian named Okewa, who had accidently shot and killed a Menominee while hunting. Oshkosh killed the man in retaliation, on lands within the jurisdiction of the Brown County circuit court and on territory where Native title had been extinguished. In his defense, Oshkosh testified that "the laws of the White People, meaning the laws of this Territory, were of no validity in regard to the matter and not binding upon any Indian." The Brown County jury of Michigan Territory agreed with Oshkosh. Citing "the law and custom of the said [Menominee] tribe," they found "that the said AshKosh did kill and slay the said OKewa in pursuance of the said Indian Law and usage." They concluded that if Oshkosh committed the murder with "malice aforethought," then he would indeed be guilty of murder as charged. "But if upon the facts aforesaid, . . . the law of the land does not presume malice aforethought, that then said AshKosh is guilty of Manslaughter."[38]

The jury determined that Oshkosh acted according to Menominee law and custom, which included the right of revenge, or lex talionis. He was acquitted of the charge of murder and discharged. Legal scholars identify recognition of customary law exercised by colonial subjects as a "cultural defense"—that is, if a person acts without a "guilty mind," or mens rea, then that person's actions are not criminal. If Oshkosh believed he acted within his rights in taking revenge on Okewa, then he did not act with "malice aforethought." Malice in criminal law signified intent, meaning that the accused acted maliciously to kill or grievously harm his victim without any mitigating factors. In *U.S. v. Oshkosh*, the jury reached the same conclusion as the jury that tried Chigawaasking. They refused to impose the law of the settler state in a dispute between Indians. Like the circuit court in 1837, they ruled "that American laws did not recognize Indian murder."[39]

38. Horrace Kent Tenney, "A Case of Lex Talionis," *American Bar Association Journal*, XIX (1933), 146, 148.

39. "The Murder of Alfred Aitkin," Boutwell Papers; Tenney, "A Case of Lex Talionis," *American Bar Association Journal*, XIX, no. 3 (March 1933), 146; Henry Campbell Black, *A Dictionary of Law: Containing Definitions of the Terms and Phrases of American and English Jurisprudence Ancient and Modern* . . . (Saint Paul, Minn., 1891), 31. For the significance of the "cultural defense" in North American law, see

This interpretation of the law recognized the homelands of Native peoples as a distinct kind of space where, at least with regard to internal affairs, Native peoples maintained some measure of sovereignty or political autonomy. This idea, that there were jurisdictional limits to American authority in Indian country, was stipulated by Congress in 1817 when it passed An Act to Provide for the Punishment of Crimes and Offences Committed within the Indian Boundaries. Section 1 granted the United States the right to punish crimes committed by "any Indian, or other person . . . if committed in any place or district of country under the sole and exclusive jurisdiction of the United States." Yet section 2 stipulated that the legislation did not "extend to any offence committed by one Indian against another, within any Indian boundary." It authorized the Territorial Superior Circuit Court to try offenses against this act. At the same time, it also invested the governors and the president with "the same powers, for the punishment of offences against this act." This distinction between the courts and the governor and president would prove important, providing the chief executive with flexibility in the management of Indian affairs in western territories where American authority remained weak and without significant coercive power. This was, in effect, the power to pardon that William Woodbridge had sought from the president and then imposed himself under the guise of allowing Chi-Amik to escape.[40]

Yet whereas the Brown County circuit courts in Green Bay and Prairie du Chien consistently recognized Indigenous customary rights or jurisdiction, the circuit courts in Detroit and Mackinac at times asserted an exclusive jurisdiction over Native defendants. The jury empaneled by the Detroit coroner found Shabagajick and Jacques Crow guilty of murder and manslaughter respectively and incarcerated them even though their crimes were committed against other Native people because the incidents occurred within U.S. settlements. In July 1833, the Michilimackinac County circuit court charged Waabenemickee (White Thunder) with the murder of Jean Baptiste Brunet. Both men were Ojibwe, and the court

---

Catherine L. Evans, "Crime, Punishment, and the Indigenous Subject in Colonial Canada," paper presented at the annual meeting of the American Society for Legal History, Oct. 29, 2016, Toronto, Ontario, Canada; and Oliver Wendell Holmes, Jr., "Privilege, Malice, and Intent," *Harvard Law Review*, VIII, no. 1 (Apr. 25, 1894), 1–14.

40. An Act to Provide for the Punishment of Crimes and Offences Committed within the Indian Boundaries, Mar. 3, 1817, *The Public Statutes at Large of the United States of America, from the Organization of the Government in 1789, to March 3, 1845 . . .*, III (Boston, 1846), Fourteenth Congress, Sess. 2, Chap. 92, 383.

stipulated that the murder occurred "beyond the Indian boundary line, within the territorial limits of the United States, and within the jurisdiction of this court, which said county is in the possession of the Chippewa Nation or tribe of Indians and to which Indian title has not been extinguished." The indictment stated that Waabenemickee "with malice aforethought did strike and prostrate . . . the said Jean Baptiste Brunet." After hearing evidence, the jury retired, deliberated, and returned to court. On being asked for the verdict, they "found the prisoner, White Thunder, guilty of willful murder of Jean Bt. Brunet." In this case, the court asserted its jurisdiction over Native subjects residing in Indian country specifically defined as territory in the "possession of the Chippewa nation," where Indian title had not been extinguished.[41]

The Mackinac County court in *U.S. v. Wa Ben e Mickee (White Thunder)* maintained the right to prosecute Native peoples for breaking U.S. laws in Indian country in contradiction to the Brown County court in *U.S. v. Oshkosh* and the 1817 Act of Congress providing for the punishment of crimes within Indian boundaries. The council for Waabenemickee filed for an arrest of judgment, arguing: "First the said person is an Indian of the Chippeway tribe residing in the Indian country. Secondly the said Jean Bt. Brunet the person alleged to have been killed by the prisoner was an Indian and the offence was committed upon land which the Indian title had not been extinguished in a country occupied by the Chippewa nation of Indians." But the motion to arrest judgment was rejected, and Waabenemickee was ordered to be "taken to the place of public execution and there hanged by the neck until dead." The foreman of the jury that delivered this sentence was George Johnston, the mixed-race Ojibwe brother-in-law of Henry Schoolcraft, Indian agent of the Michigan Territory. It is reasonable to suspect that the victim, Jean Baptiste Brunet, might have been mixed-race given his French name. If so, the court considered him, like Alfred Aitkin, to be an Indian, yet the court allowed Johnston, also a mixed-race Native, to serve on a jury, thereby categorizing Johnston as civilized and therefore white, capable of understanding the obligation of an oath, and a citizen of the United States.[42]

41. Judgment Record, July 18, 1833, County Court of Michilimackinac, Supreme Court, Michigan Territory Records, box 30, Archives of Michigan, Lansing; United States v. Wawben e mickee (White Thunder), July 18, 1833, Minutes of the Mackinac County Archives Circuit Court, 1825–1848, Burton Historical Collection.

42. United States v. Wawben e mickee (White Thunder), July 18, 1833, Minutes of the Mackinac County Archives Circuit Court, 1825–1848, Burton Historical Collection.

The tremendous discrepancy in these court cases suggests that although the law establishing newly organized U.S. territories and states presumed the sovereignty of the settler state, the reality on the ground was that such exclusive settler sovereignty rarely existed. More often than not, U.S. authorities were forced to act like the agents of a colonizing power, which in fact they were. Colonial powers ruled subordinated subjects, but they often engaged with subjects over whom they exercised only limited power. This was especially true when the colonial officials and the settler population were in the minority demographically. In such cases, colonial officials were forced to co-opt the politically powerful among the subject population in an effort to sustain the project of extracting wealth from the colonized.

Frequently forced to act on behalf of a colonial power rather than a settler state, U.S. territorial officials and Indian agents often demanded that Native leaders follow customary practices to restore peace and to resolve violent conflict. In 1839, nine years after the *U.S. v. Oshkosh* decision, the Wisconsin territorial governor, James Doty, Ketawkah's lawyer from 1825, wrote to the Indian agent in the Green Bay region about another murder indirectly involving a Menominee leader: "It would appear that the Menominee had murdered a Winnebago Indian. If this last report be true, you will please notify Oshkosh from me that I expect and require him to go at once to the Portage, and offer the customary presents in order to restore peace and harmony, whatever price shall be agreed upon—will be faithfully paid to the Winnebagos at the approaching payment of annuities to the Menominees." Rather than adjudicate a mens rea cultural defense within the legal system, Doty acted according to the power granted him by the congressional act of 1817. He demanded that the Menominee follow customary practice and provide compensation to the victim's community. The governor did not seek to impose American sovereignty in a space with so many Indians, so few settlers, and so much unsettled territory. Instead, he worked to forge a colonial relationship with the Indigenous subjects of the Old Northwest where the goal was to mitigate violence among Natives peoples and between Natives and settlers while the state worked to transfer this land base from the Indigenous population to citizen settlers of the Republic. This was justice weighed in two scales. U.S. officials tolerated and even encouraged jurisdictional pluralism to safeguard the process of extinguishing Native title

---

For the complicated and changing relationship of mixed-race jurors and U.S. courts in the Northwest, see Murphy, *Great Lakes Creoles*, 108–147.

and transforming Native homelands into public domain that could then be purchased as private property at a subsidized rate by white settlers.[43]

Henry Dodge, who was governor of the Wisconsin Territory when Chigawaasking was arrested for murder in 1837, could have made a similar intervention and pardoned the accused. He did not because the father of the victim, William Aitkin, was a white man and a prominent trader who demanded that his son's killer be tried for murder. Territorial officials complied with this demand. During the summer of 1837 when Chigawaasking awaited trial in Prairie du Chien, however, Governor Dodge was also engaged in treaty negotiations with the Ojibweg from the Wisconsin Territory, which included the doodemag from the Lake Superior country and the upper Mississippi Valley. As Lawrence Taliaferro, the Indian agent for the Mississippi region, recommended to the governor, a pardon would have been the smart move politically. George Bonga similarly reported that the Ojibweg of Leech Lake remained angry about the prospect of Chigawaasking's punishment by U.S. authorities. But Aitkin, influenced by the missionaries of the ABCFM, demanded that the rule of law and the sovereignty of the state be applied to his son's killer. And, as Dodge negotiated a treaty demanding a large cession of Ojibwe land, he needed the good will of men like Aitkin as much as he needed the good will of the Ojibwe ogimaag.

The need to resolve murder in Indian country, particularly murder that involved Native people killing white or mixed-race Native peoples, revealed the extent to which shifting ideas about race became entangled with questions of sovereignty. Were Indigenous people sovereign in their homelands? Did this sovereignty hold up when the Republic expanded its authority onto Indian territory? Was the social contract of the Republic extended to mixed-race Natives? These questions bled over into questions of political economy, specifically the viability of the fur trade and the transfer of Native wealth (in the form of land and annuities) into the hands of white settlers and traders. The answers to these questions changed over time, particularly when the white population increased dramatically. Mixed-race Native men, and men with mixed-race Native families, would emerge as central political figures in the negotiation of this transformation.

43. James Duane Doty to Crawford, June 8, 1839, Wisconsin Superintendency, 1836–1848, Letters Received, 1824–1880, RG 75, M234, NARA.

The 1837 Treaty of Saint Peters

In 1837, there was not a significant demand for the transformation of the Ojibwe homeland into American homesteads, but there was a demand for timber. Alexis Bailly, a fur trader and merchant, wrote to the Michigan Territory's congressional delegate George Wallace Jones in April 1836, advising the government to purchase Ojibwe lands "on account of its immense Pineries, north of the Ouisconsin running parallel with the Missisipi." With the rapid development of the lower Mississippi Valley, he wrote, "Thick settlements, beside the Mississipi above Saint Louis are as mad for Lumber of that description and would gladly give high prices for it." Later that same year, Governor Henry Dodge wrote to the secretary of Indian Affairs about the creation of a company "formed for the erection of saw-mills in the Chippewa Country" by Hercules Dousman, Joseph Roulette, and Henry Sibley, three traders with the American Fur Company. He complained that the compensation paid to the Ojibweg for these rights was too little. According to Dodge, "It is true that for the mill privileges heretofore granted by the Indians, but little advantage has been derived to them, while those who have enjoyed them have made it a productive business." The Ojibwe country "abounds in pine, is barren of game and unfit for cultivation, and valuable alone for its lumber materials." "That being the case," Dodge concluded, "it would not be difficult to effect a purchase of the whole pine region of country. The Chippewa Indians are poor and in want . . . the sooner the pine country can be purchased the better, both for the Indians and the citizens of this Territory."[44]

Dodge called the Ojibwe ogimaag to attend treaty negotiations at Fort Snelling in July 1837. In a letter to the commissioner of Indian Affairs, Dodge wrote that he "deemed it a subject of the first importance, that as many of the different Bands should be present at the treaty ground, as could be collected, for the purpose of fully meeting the views of the government, as well as to produce harmony and concert among the Indians themselves." When negotiations opened at the council house on July 20, ogimaag from Leech Lake, Gull Lake, Swan River, Mille Lac, Sandy Lake, Snake River, Fond du Lac, and Saint Croix, all Mississippi Valley villages, were recognized by the governor. "Your Great Father The President of the United States," he apprised the assembled leaders, "has

44. Alexis Bailly to G. W. Jones, Apr. 15, 1836, in Carter et al., eds., *Territorial Papers of the United States*, XXVII, 40; Henry Dodge to C. A. Harris, Nov. 23, 1836, ibid., 673–674.

sent me to see you in Council, to propose to you the purchase of a small part of your country East of the Mississippi River." Dodge estimated the cession requested by the U.S. government to be between nine and ten million acres. "This country, as I am informed," he told the council, "is not valuable to you for its game, and not suited to the culture of corn, and other Agricultural purposes." The United States, Dodge declared, "wishes to purchase your country on the Chippewa and St. Croix Rivers, for the advantage of its Pine Timber." Frederick Ayer, the missionary at Yellow Lake, a village within the boundaries of the proposed cession, reported to the board of the ABCFM: "There is some excitement here on the subject of the sale of Indian territory laying south of Lake Superior . . . . I fear these poor Indians will not very much longer be left undisturbed in possession of their country."[45]

Perhaps reflecting the missionary's trepidation, the ogimaag from the villages of Lac du Flambeau, Lac Courte Oreilles, and La Pointe, located in the territory earmarked for cession by Governor Dodge, were not in attendance when the council opened. Eshkibagikoonzh, the Leech Lake ogimaa, was the first to speak on behalf of the gathered ogimaag. "Living in a different part of the country from that which you propose to buy from us," he stated, "I will be among the last of those who will speak to you upon that subject." The four additional ogimaag who rose to be heard at the opening council repeated this sentiment. They must wait for the people who lived in the proposed cession to arrive before negotiations could proceed. After two days passed, however, Dodge convened the council again, even though the ogimaag they waited for had not arrived. Dodge asked the assembled leaders "what they might have to say about their absent friends." Eshkibagikoonzh, once again, spoke first in response. "My Father," he began, "I am called a chief. I am not the Chief of the whole nation, but only of my people or tribe. I speak to you now only because I see nobody else ready to do so. I do not wish to take any further steps about what you have proposed to us, until the other people arrive, who have been expected here." Dodge had pressed the leadership of the Mississippi

45. Dodge to Carey Allen Harris, Aug. 7, 1837, Documents Relating to the Negotiations of Ratified and Unratified Treaties with Various Indian Tribes, 1801–1869, RG 75, T494, roll 3, NARA; "Secretary Verplank Van Antwerp's Journal of the Proceedings of the Council Held by Governor Henry Dodge in 1837," in Ronald N. Satz, *Chippewa Treaty Rights: The Reserved Rights of Wisconsin's Chippewa Indians in Historical Perspective*, Wisconsin Academy of Sciences, Arts, and Letters, *Transactions*, LXXIX, no. 1 (Madison, Wis., 1991), Appendix 1, 131; Ayer to Greene, June 12, 1837, ABCFM, box 1.

Valley doodemag to agree to the cession, only to be reminded by Esh-kibagikoonzh that the Ojibweg did not have a single, paramount leader.[46]

Finally, on July 25, the subagent for La Pointe, Daniel Bushnell, and the resident trader, Lyman Warren, arrived with the delegation from his agency and ogimaag from the Ojibwe villages in the Wisconsin interior. The following day, Governor Dodge called the council to order, presented a map of the territory he hoped to purchase on behalf of the U.S. government, and pressed the new arrivals to consider his offer. Gichi-Bizhiki (The Great Buffalo), the principal ogimaa from La Pointe, pushed back. "My Father," he observed, "we have come from a distance, and but lately arrive here." "What you have proposed to us, we want more time to think about." In reply to this request, Dodge suggested they "examine the map now and have it explained to them." He then offered to remain at the council ground until sundown to answer any questions the ogimaag might have. Nonetheless, he stipulated once again that "he wished them to be prepared tomorrow morning, to tell him not only, whether or not they would sell him the land, but their price for it." Dodge asked that they "unite and act together, as one people." Accordingly, he directed that they select "two Chiefs in whom they had confidence to speak for them." He concluded the council, telling them their "Great Father" would be just and fair toward them and admonishing them "that in their consultations he did not wish them to *forget* their Half breed relatives and their traders." His statement served as a reminder to the traders, agents, and translators that they, too, stood to benefit from any sale of Ojibwe land.[47]

The council resumed on the morning of July 27, 1837, and Dodge once again presented the map and explained the proposed cession. Maajigaa-baw and Bagonegiizhig (Hole in the Day), from Leech Lake and Gull Lake respectively, both villages in the upper Mississippi Valley, arose to speak for the assembled Ojibwe ogimaag. Maajigaabaw, wearing only leggings and a breechcloth with a headdress of bald eagle feathers and the peace medals of several ogimaag around his neck, advanced to the table where the governor sat in front of the map. He planted his war flag. "I stand here to represent the Chiefs of the different bands of my nation assembled here, and to tell you of their determination, to sell you the lands that you want of them," he declared. But then he said, *"Of all the country that we grant*

46. "Secretary Verplank Van Antwerp's Journal of the Proceedings of the Council Held by Governor Henry Dodge in 1837," in Satz, *Chippewa Treaty Rights*, App. 1, 131–133.
47. Ibid., 140–141.

you we wish to hold on to a tree where we get our living, and to reserve the streams where we drink the waters that give us life." With this turn of phrase, the Indian agent recording the council speeches made a note describing the statement as "nonsense . . . rendered by the Interpreters" to which he concluded, "I presume it to mean that the Indians wish to reserve the privilege of hunting and fishing on the lands and making sugar from the Maple." Maajigaabaw then placed a sprig with an oak leaf on the table, telling the governor this was the tree they wished to preserve for themselves. Dodge asked Maajigaabaw what price the ogimaag wanted for their land. In response, he counted six fingers, saying each represented ten, "for so many years we wish you to secure to us the payment of an annuity." At the end of this time, he declared, their grandchildren "will have grown up, and can speak to you for themselves." In effect, the Ojibweg proposed to lease their timber lands to the U.S. government.[48]

Maajigaabaw proceeded to raise the issue of the Ojibwe mixed-race relatives that the governor had asked them to consider as part of their negotiation. He stated, "We wish you to select a place for them on this River, where they may live and raise their children." "If I have rightly understood you," Maajigaabaw clarified, "we can remain on the lands and hunt here." Given that they would remain on the land living in their accustomed manner, they required their mixed-race relatives to live among them. "We have heretofore got our living on them," he explained, meaning that the fur trade and the fur traders were an essential part of their political economy. Maajigaabaw also corrected the governor regarding the quality of their land declaring, "There is no better soil to cultivate than it, until you get up, to where the Pine region commences." In other words, they recognized that their land was more valuable than the governor represented it to be.[49]

Governor Dodge inquired of Maajigaabaw whether the ogimaag wanted to hear his answer, and they deferred, asking that he speak to them the following morning. He agreed, but before closing the council, the governor informed the delegates, "It is proper for me to explain to you that your Great Father, never buys land for a term of years." Rejecting the idea of a lease, he nevertheless conceded, "I will agree on the part of the President, that you shall have the free use of the rivers, and the privilege of hunting upon the lands you are to sell to the United States, during his pleasure." Dodge then went on to address the subject of their mixed-race

48. Ibid., 142n, 143
49. Ibid., 143.

relatives. "You have spoken frequently of your half breed relations," he observed; "It is a good principle in you, to wish to provide for them." But he stipulated, "You must do so in money, and can not give them land." As with the 1836 treaty negotiated with the Anishinaabe doodemag from Michigan, the United States refused to provide reservations to the mixed-race relatives of the treaty signers. In effect, they were Indian enough to be compensated for the extinction of Native title to their ancestral lands but not Indian enough to be granted a reserved homeland.[50]

When the council convened the following day, Eshkibagikoonzh once again spoke for the assembled ogimaag. "My Father,"

> Your children are willing to let you have their lands, but they wish to reserve the privilege of making sugar from the trees, and getting their living from the Lakes and Rivers, as they have done heretofore, and of remaining in this Country. It is hard to give up the lands. They will remain, and can not be destroyed—but you may cut down the Trees, and others will grow up. You know we can not live deprived of our Lakes and Rivers.

In response, Governor Dodge offered reassurances, affirming: "You will be allowed, during his pleasure, to hunt and fish on them. It will probably be many years, before your Great Father will want all these lands for the use of his white Children." With this treaty, the Ojibweg agreed to a land cession that would amount to more than half of what would become the state of Wisconsin. Nevertheless, unlike the Anishinaabe doodemag from Michigan who treated with the U.S. government in 1836, they also made it clear that they intended to remain in their homeland. They did not promise to consider relocation west of the Mississippi, and there was no fixed time when they would lose title to their reserved territory. They expected Americans to harvest their timber, specifically white pine, for the price of an annuity for a fixed number of years, but they did not expect permanent settlers. From their perspective, the use rights conceded by the Americans signaled an acceptance of their desire to remain on the land. That is, the 1837 Saint Peters Treaty ensured their right to maintain themselves in their homelands, harvesting resources necessary for their survival as their ancestors had done for generations.[51]

50. Ibid., 144.

51. Ibid., 145–146. For a detailed analysis of Ojibwe expectations regarding this treaty, see Erik M. Redix, *The Murder of Joe White: Ojibwe Leadership and Colonialism in Wisconsin* (East Lansing, Mich., 2014), 32–39. See also Satz, *Chippewa Treaty Rights*, 23–27. This outcome, allowing Native peoples to remain in their homelands to

Although the Lake Superior Ojibweg were allowed to remain in their homeland, the negotiations over the annuity payments were contentious and required an additional day of negotiation. The governor offered an annuity of twenty thousand dollars for twenty years, half of this amount to be delivered in trade goods. Ultimately, he agreed to a payment of ninety-five hundred dollars in cash and nineteen thousand dollars in goods with another two thousand dollars in provisions. The government, of course, would purchase these goods and provisions from the traders, thus guaranteeing them profits annually for the next twenty years. Dodge also proposed that this annuity should provide one hundred thousand dollars to the "half breed" relatives of the treaty signers and seventy thousand dollars to pay for debts owed to the fur traders. Eshkibagikoonzh complained about the diversion of annuity money to pay the traders. "My Father," he declared, "if I had thought that these old accounts were to be brought up against us, I would have stayed away." He noted that the traders sustained themselves by living off of their land: "Where have they got the Fish that they have eaten, and the wood that they have burned? They were caught from our Lakes, and Rivers, and taken from our Land." In the end, the treaty awarded seventy thousand dollars to the traders for their claims on past debts. William Aitkin received twenty-eight thousand dollars, and Lyman Warren twenty-five thousand from this cash

---

hunt and harvest on ceded territory, was a marked contrast to American expansion in the Old Southwest, where treaty making with peoples like the Creeks, Cherokees, and Seminoles was explicitly tied to removal. Immediately before passage of the Indian Removal Act, and with mounting aggression afterward, Native peoples in the South were besieged by squatters moving onto their lands. They also faced state governments intent on imposing state law on Native people and Indigenous homelands to facilitate the legal transfer of this land to white settlers. As historian Christopher D. Haveman argues, in the years leading up to their forced relocation, the Creeks made multiple trips to Washington, D.C., to complain about "the intrusions on their land by white squatters and the assertion of state jurisdiction over the Creek Nation." Each time they confronted federal officials, they were told the remedy to their problems was removal west of the Mississippi. The government then linked annuity payments to a Creek commitment to move west and countenanced settler violence against Creek holdouts. Similarly, in Florida, treaty making with the Seminoles linked territorial confiscation with removal. Refusal to acquiesce to the removal clauses of treaties that the Seminoles regarded as illegitimate resulted in a war of extermination. For the Creeks, see Haveman, *Rivers of Sand: Creek Indian Emigration, Relocation, and Ethnic Cleansing in the American South* (Lincoln, Nebr., 2016), 92–93, 148. For the Seminoles, see C. S. Monaco, *The Second Seminole War and the Limits of American Aggression* (Baltimore, 2018), 24–25.

payout. Indian agents would also continue to allow traders to claim large portions of subsequent annuity payments as compensation for debts owed to them by the Ojibweg.[52]

The treaty process signaled an economic shift aligning the Wisconsin Territory with the state of Michigan. It represented the adaptation of a political economy of plunder that depended on the creation of an ongoing colonial relationship between the state, federal government, and Native peoples. This relationship would become the source of wealth for American citizens involved in the business of treating and trading with the Indigenous nations of the Northwest Territory. This political economy of plunder also facilitated the transfer of Indigenous homelands into the public domain of the Republic, subsidizing white property ownership in the free states of the upper Midwest. This was the promise offered by the Northwest Ordinance, what Salmon P. Chase described as "the true theory of American liberty." This was the social contract embodied in the ideology of the free-soil movement that linked freedom, in the form of economic independence, to an accessible land base, or "free soil." The terms of this social contract were clearly articulated at the 1848 Free Territory Convention in Ohio, where delegates "*Resolved* That we recognize as valid that interpretation of the doctrine of free soil which assures to actual settlers, under suitable limitations, the free grant of reasonable por-[t]ions of the Public Domain, as permanent homes for themselves and their children." This land transfer also came with the stipulation, required by the Northwest Ordinance, that newly formed territories like Wisconsin enact fugitive slave laws to protect the property of the slaveholding citizens of the Old Southwest. Of course, the ultimate beneficiaries of both the land transfer and the creation of a political economy of plunder were the traders who profited from the dispossession of their Indigenous trading partners while also being able to claim U.S. citizenship as settlers in these newly created states and territories.[53]

52. "Secretary Verplank Van Antwerp's Journal of the Proceedings of the Council Held by Governor Henry Dodge in 1837," in Satz, *Chippewa Treaty Rights*, App. 1, 146–147; "Treaty with the Chippewa," July 29, 1837, in Charles J. Kappler, comp. and ed., *Indian Affairs: Laws and Treaties*, II, *Treaties* (Washington, D.C., 1904), 491–493. See also Satz, *Chippewa Treaty Rights*, 30.

53. Salmon P. Chase, ed., *The Statutes of Ohio and of the Northwestern Territory, Adopted or Enacted from 1788 to 1833 Inclusive . . .* , I (Cincinnati, Ohio, 1833), 18; Eric Foner, *Free Soil, Free Labor, Free Men: The Ideology of the Republican Party before the Civil War* (New York, 1995), xxv, 87; "Resolutions Adopted by the Independent State Free Territory Convention of Ohio, at Columbus, June 20th and 21st,

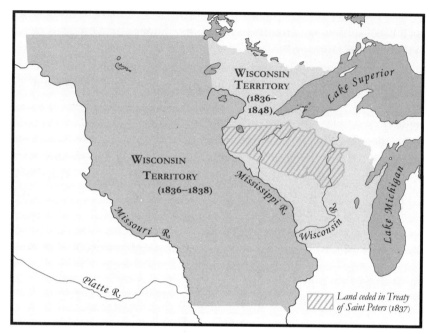

Map 6. Wisconsin Territory, 1836–1848. Drawn by Rebecca Wrenn

Preventing Consensus and Creating a False Political Hierarchy

Preserving the fur trade in some form, however, also represented the only possibility of avoiding a complete dependence on government annuities as a source of economic and political power. Many of the warriors from the upper Mississippi Valley pushed for the cash payout with the hope of

---

1848," in *Addresses and Proceedings of the State Independent Free Territory Convention of the People of Ohio, Held at Columbus, June 20 and 21, 1848* (Cincinnati, Ohio, 1848), 6. Jonathan H. Earle describes the free-soil ideology of Chase "as a particularly *Jacksonian* brand of antislavery"; however, he fails to make any connection to Indian removal or Indigenous dispossession. See Earle, *Jacksonian Antislavery and the Politics of Free Soil, 1824–1854* (Williamsburg, Va., and Chapel Hill, N.C., 2004), 160. Similarly Eric Foner argues, "As the nation's political system began to dissolve under the impact of the question of the expansion of slavery, the idea of free labor was yoked ever more tightly to free soil, as access to Western land came to be seen as the necessary condition for avoiding the further growth of wage slavery in the North." Yet, he, too, fails to discuss or even mention Indian removal, Indian territory, or the treaty process that dispossessed Native nations and created the U.S. public domain. See Foner, *Free Soil, Free Labor, Free Men*, xxv.

restoring relations with the traders of the American Fur Company damaged by the murder of Alfred Aitkin. Zhaagobe (The Little Six) informed Governor Dodge that although the warriors attending the council did not want to undo the negotiations of the ogimaag, "they are afraid to return home, if the traders are not paid. They fear they should not survive during the winter without their aid." Zhaagobe also told the governor that he hoped this payment eased the "bad feelings" of the traders. "I came here this morning with my Braves," he stated, "and asked a favor for the Traders, which has been granted. Let them now give us, our friend who they have in jail." This was a request to free Chigawaasking. In response, the governor asked the interpreter to tell the warriors: "Their friend is in the hands of our Laws, and of their Great Father The President of the United States--That neither I or the Traders have any power over him—That he will be judged by the Laws, and his case submitted to the President, who will do him justice." Zhaagobe accepted the governor's answer but nonetheless pushed him to help repair their relationship with the traders. He was from the Ojibwe village at Snake River in the upper Mississippi Valley where William Aitkin had closed trading outposts. "We do not know whether you have a control over all the Traders," he observed, "but we wish you to aid us, by speaking to them in our favor, as you have done to us, in theirs." He concluded, "There are some of them who have dealt severely with us." Governor Dodge replied that it was his duty to serve their interests. Then he advised both the traders and the Ojibweg attending the council to respect one another's rights.[54]

Following this exchange, Governor Dodge had the terms of the treaty written and read to the assembled council. He then signed the document and waited for the ogimaag to step forward and sign, or, more accurately, to touch the pen poised on an X next to a phonetic approximation of their name. No one stepped forward, the "older Chiefs, evincing a reluctance, and hesitating," according to the secretary recording the proceedings. At last, Bagonegiizhig, the Gull Lake ogimaa, stepped to the table and signed the treaty. This was the second time he intervened when the council seemed at an impasse. The previous day, when Eshkibagikoonzh had complained about the traders' debt being paid from the proposed annuity, Bagonegiizhig spoke out in favor of making the payment. He admonished the ogimaag not to "undo" the agreement they had reached

54. "Secretary Verplank Van Antwerp's Journal of the Proceedings of the Council Held by Governor Henry Dodge in 1837," in Satz, *Chippewa Treaty Rights*, App. 1, 148–150.

with the governor. "Chiefs what we agreed and determined upon yesterday; shall consent to undo," he declared, "when my head is severed from my body and my life no more—We must abide by it, firmly." Stepping up and signing the treaty when everyone else hesitated, he once again pushed the ogimaag to agree to the terms offered by Dodge.[55]

Bagonegiizhig asserted his leadership in council in part because Governor Dodge had pushed the ogimaag to speak with one voice, as a singular nation, with an identifiable and hierarchical leadership. When he asked them to pick two men to speak on behalf of all those assembled at council, he indicated "that this was done merely to save time." It is more likely that he wanted to circumvent the deliberative process where each ogimaa spoke until they reached a consensus that reflected the collective will of their various communities. Instead, he wanted the Ojibweg to consolidate their leadership, telling the ogimaag "that altho' they were of different bands, they belonged to the same great nation." Once the treaty was signed, Dodge asked the Ojibwe ogimaag to select one leader to hold on to their copy of the document. When they declined to designate such a person, the governor complained: "It becomes necessary and proper, for me to name one. I will hand it to the man who was the first among you to give it his signature." With this gesture, the governor once again elevated Bagonegiizhig. Throughout the treaty negotiations, in fact, U.S. officials had also allowed the ogimaag from the upper Mississippi Valley to play an outsized role in ceding territory where they did not reside, hunt, or harvest resources.[56]

Privileging the ogimaag from the upper Mississippi Valley villages undermined the political influence of the leaders who lived in the ceded territory. Two of the three ogimaag from Lac Courte Oreilles, a village community within the ceded lands, refused to sign the treaty. Their names were written and then scratched off the original text. Other prominent ogimaag from this community refused to even attend the council. A year after the treaty, Michigan's Indian agent, Henry Schoolcraft, learned from Lyman Warren, then American Fur Company trader, that Mississippi Valley Indian agent Lawrence Taliaferro "flattered" two of the Leech

55. Ibid., 149, 152. For Bagonegiizhig and the attempt by warriors to wrest control of annuities from the civil chiefs, see Kugel, *To Be the Main Leaders of Our People*, 76–77.

56. "Secretary Verplank Van Antwerp's Journal of the Proceedings of the Council Held by Governor Henry Dodge in 1837," in Satz, *Chippewa Treaty Rights*, App. 1, 141, 152.

Lake ogimaag in advance of the July council meeting. Taliaferro summoned these men to Fort Snelling in June "and loaded them with new clothes and presents." Warren identified Bagonegiizhig, who was actually from Gull Lake, as one of the Leech Lake leaders singled out by Taliaferro. He also told Schoolcraft: "The bands of the St. Croix and Chippewa Rivers, who really lived on the land and owned it, had, in effect, no voice. So with respect to the La Pointe Indians." Schoolcraft wrote that, according to Warren, "the *Lac Courtorielle* band had not united in the sale, and would not attend the payment of the annuities; nor would the St. Croix and Lac du Flambeau Indians." Schoolcraft also observed that the provisions promised by Article 2 of the treaty were inadequate compensation. According to Warren, a licensed trader, "the present of $19,000 would not exceed a breech-cloth and a pair of leggins apiece."[57]

The 1837 Treaty of Saint Peters signed at Fort Snelling led to an immediate windfall for the American settlers in the Wisconsin Territory, most of whom were associated with the fur trade. The annuity payments, cash, and provisions were initially dispensed at Fort Snelling, a benefit to merchants and traders in the western part of the territory. It also opened the pinery ceded by the Ojibweg. "The day after the Inds gave up their country," wrote ABCFM missionary William Boutwell one month later, "some dozens of speculators rushed into the country and as I came through to this place I found one here who had taken possession of a mill seat and another who had selected a pinery." Boutwell predicted, "Should the treaty be ratified another season will bring not less than 1000 speculators into the St. Croix." The missionary communicated with the ABCFM that "they are to receive their annuities for twenty years, but can remain on their lands only during the pleasure of the Pres." Familiar with U.S. treaty practices, Boutwell assumed the Ojibweg would be removed. "I am much mistaken if our Govt. are not involved in trouble with the Chip. Ys before five years should they attempt to remove them," he speculated.[58]

ABCFM missionary Frederick Ayer echoed Boutwell's fears that the 1837 Saint Peters Treaty would result in the dispossession and removal of the Wisconsin Ojibweg. In September, two months after the council

57. Schoolcraft, *Personal Memoirs*, 611. For analysis of Lac Courte Oreilles and Lac du Flambeau leadership regarding the 1837 treaty, see Redix, *Murder of Joe White*, 33–34. See also Satz, *Chippewa Treaty Rights*, 13–31.
58. Boutwell to Greene, Aug. 17, 1837, ABCFM, box 1.

that produced the agreement, he forwarded a petition from the Snake River Ojibweg to the president of the United States. According to Ayer, the Snake River Ojibweg "as a body regretted the sale of their land by the recent treaty." The Snake River ogimaa Noodin (The Wind) touched the pen to the X next to his name on the treaty but questioned the legitimacy of the process. "I am an Indian and I do not know how to sign my name," he told Ayer. He also complained about the role played by Bagonegiizhig in the treaty: "But only one, however, sold the land (The hole in the day). He does not own the land where I dwell he is a mere child." Around this same time, the La Pointe ogimaa Gichi-Bizhiki provided a similar statement to Indian agent Daniel Bushnell. "I have nothing to say about the Treaty good, or bad, because the country was not mine," he declared. "But when it comes my turn I shall know how to act. If the Americans want my land, I shall know what to say. I did not like to stand in the road of the Indians at St. Peters [Fort Snelling]. . . . The Indians acted like children; they tried to cheat each other and got cheated themselves; When it comes my turn to sell my land, I do not think I shall give it up as they did."[59]

The leadership of the Wisconsin Ojibweg emerged from the 1837 Treaty of Saint Peters divided and unhappy about the cession of their land. Yet, according to the subagent at La Pointe, Bushnell, they remained attached to the U.S. government in spite of the discord. "No case of intermeddling by any foreign government, on the officers, or subjects thereof with the Indians under my charge or any others, directly, or indirectly, has come to my knowledge," he wrote to Governor Dodge. In the past, he reported, "the Indians from this region" made an annual visit to Drummond Island in Lake Huron to receive presents and renew their alliance with the British in Canada. "But the Treaty made last summer between them and the United States and the small distribution of presents that has been made within the last year, under the direction of our government," he assured the governor in August 1838, "have had the effect to prevent any of them from visiting the english Territory this year, These Indians have generally manifested a desire to live upon terms of friendship with the American people." U.S. officials feared military cooperation between the British and the Anishinaabeg in the Northwest from the moment they organized the

59. Ayer to Martin Van Buren, Sept. 30, 1837, La Pointe Agency, 1831–1880, Letters Received, 1824–1880, RG 75, M234, roll 387, 161 ("regretted"), 163 ("sign"), 164 ("mere child"), NARA; "Speech of the Buffalo Principal Chief at Lapointe" to Daniel P. Bushnell, Dec. 10, 1837, enclosed in Dodge to Harris, Feb. 19, 1838, ibid., 266.

territory, a fear that had been borne out in the Michigan Territory during the War of 1812.[60]

The ability of the United States to project power, particularly military power, in the Northwest Territory, remained minimal even in 1837. The U.S. army during this period consisted of approximately five thousand troops scattered across a few posts such as Fort Snelling. Moreover, during the mid-1830s, most of these forces were deployed against the Seminoles, who waged a successful armed resistance to U.S. expansion into their territory in Florida. In 1836, Governor Dodge had called on the legislative assembly of the Wisconsin Territory to organize a militia to protect "our exposed and defenceless frontiers," warning the representatives that "experience should teach us, and the existing war in the South, with the Seminole Indians admonishes us, of the necessity of being prepared." In November 1838, a little more than a year after the Treaty with the Ojibweg, he made a similar statement to the assembly regarding the possibility of conflict with Native peoples in the Wisconsin Territory: "The amount now paid by the U. States in annuities to the Chippeway, Sioux, and Winebago Indians will have the salutary effect in restraining them from Committing acts of hostility on our border settlements, Knowing that a violation of their treaty stipulations would be the means of forfeiting their annuities, upon which they place great reliance." In spite of Agent Bushnell's assurances of friendship in the months before Dodge delivered this speech, the governor appeared to fear the potential for violence between Native peoples and settlers. He also gave voice to the significance of annuities in asserting political control over Native peoples who were, in effect, colonial subjects of the United States.[61]

60. Bushnell to Dodge, Aug. 14, 1838, enclosed in Dodge to Harris, Oct. 15, 1838, La Pointe Agency, RG 75, M234, roll 387, 306–307.

61. "Message of His Excellency Henry Dodge, Delivered at Belmont," Oct. 26, 1836, in Carter et al., eds., *Territorial Papers of the United States*, XXVII, 93; Henry Dodge, "Message to the Legislative Assembly," Nov. 27, 1838, ibid., 176. For the number and deployment of U.S. armed forces during the 1830s, see Satz, *Chippewa Treaty Rights*, 17. For the U.S. army in the Seminole War, see Monaco, *Second Seminole War*, 64–80. Historian Laurel Clark Shire documents the wide-scale circulation of stories about Florida Natives attacking white settlers, a genre of narrative she identifies as "depredation narratives." "Resonant with the long-standing genre of Indian Captivity narratives," she writes, "Indian depredation narratives from Florida framed stories about Native American violence on white settlers in the sensationalist language of early nineteenth-century print culture, using a term drawn from federal frontier policy." See Shire, *The Threshold of Manifest Destiny: Gender and National Expansion in Florida* (Philadelphia, 2016), 60.

Half-Breed Indians and the Battle to
Control the Plunder Economy

In creating the Wisconsin Territory, the United States began colonizing what remained of Anishinaabewaki, the homeland of the Anishinaabe peoples—specifically, the territory of the Lake Superior and Mississippi Valley Ojibweg. The United States, via the Northwest Ordinance, aspired to be a settler colonial state, re-creating itself in the West by supplanting an Indigenous population with a population of white settlers. In the process, the Indigenous population, it was thought, would be eliminated through warfare, removal, or assimilation. Ostensibly, the United States sought the peaceful assimilation of Native peoples through the civilizing mission. In truth, for much of the history of the Northwest Territory, and certainly before its creation, Americans in the region wanted Native peoples to continue living as Native peoples. That was how the fur trade worked. By the 1830s, however, the fur trade began to play out, and land and timber, especially after the opening of the Erie Canal, became more valuable resources than processed furs. The decline of the fur trade, in turn, led to the political economy of plunder—the extraction of wealth from colonized Indigenous subject nations through the treaty process. This, then, was the ongoing economic association between traders (both white and mixed-race), the colonized Native population, and government officials presiding over the transformation of Indigenous homelands into American homesteads.

The colonial relationship between the United States and the Ojibweg—particularly the desire to preserve this political economy of plunder combined with the potential for violent conflict between Native peoples and white settlers—informed the relationship between federal and territorial officials and the mixed-race relatives of the Anishinaabeg. U.S. officials relied on mixed-race traders, or traders and interpreters with mixed-race families, to negotiate the treaties that made the massive land cessions of the political economy of plunder possible. In August 1837, immediately following the treaty negotiations at Saint Peters, the mixed-race Natives living at La Pointe who did not attend the council at Fort Snelling sent a petition to the congressional delegate for the Wisconsin Territory. The petitioners, led by Michel Cadotte, identified themselves as the "Chippewa Half-Breeds citizens of the United States." They apprised the president of the United States:

> Having lately heard that a Treaty had been concluded between the
> Government of the United States and the Chippewa Indians at St.

Peters, for the cession of certain lands belonging to that tribe: That, The said Chippewa Indians, having a just regard to the interest and welfare of their Half-Breed brethren, did there and then stipulate; that, a certain sum of money should be paid once and for all unto the said Half-Breeds, to satisfy all claim they might have on the lands so ceded to the United States.

The petition also sought to redirect the political focus of the settlement from the Mississippi agency to the agency at La Pointe. The document noted that "the great majority of the Half-Breeds entitled to a distribution of said sum of money, are either residing at La Pointe on Lake Superior, or being for the most part earning their livelihood from the Traders, are consequently congregated during the summer months at the aforesaid place." Accordingly, they requested the money be dispensed at La Pointe by Agent Daniel Bushnell and resident trader Lyman Warren. The petition, which simultaneously asserted an Ojibwe identity and claimed U.S. citizenship, was signed by twenty-five men—including Michel, Joseph, and Antoine Cadotte, prominent La Pointe traders, and Jean Baptiste DuBay, who had signed the Saint Peters Treaty as a witness. The signatories also included nine white men, employed by the American Fur Company and married to Ojibwe women, who signed "for wife and children." This was, in effect, a struggle between the traders, merchants, and Indian agents at Fort Snelling and La Pointe to control the venue where treaties were made and annuities settled. All of these men—both white and mixed-race—were married into the Indigenous communities that were subject to U.S. jurisdiction and the treaty process.[62]

All of the traders benefited financially from the 1837 Saint Peters

62. Michel Cadotte et al., "To the President of the United States of America," Aug. 31, 1837, enclosed in George W. Jones to Harris, Jan. 9, 1838, La Pointe Agency, RG 75, M234, roll 387, 252. Carole Pateman argues that "modern patriarchy is fraternal in form and the original contract is a fraternal pact." Men, she argues, enter the social contract on behalf of their families, women and children, who are deemed unfit for civil business—specifically, entering into contracts. These male heads of household "are acting as brothers; . . . and by contracting together they constitute themselves as a civil fraternity." At this particular moment in the history of Anishinaabewaki and the Northwest Territory, we see a compact of men related through marriage asserting their authority to negotiate the sale of property, in the form of land, for their Native wives and by extension all of their Native relatives, all of whom are deemed domestic dependents under U.S. law. See Pateman, *The Sexual Contract* (Stanford, Calif., 1988), 77–78.

Treaty, but their mixed-race family members and trading partners remained politically vulnerable within the Republic. The cause of this vulnerability was the botched trial of Chigawaasking for the murder of Alfred Aitkin. In August 1838, Jean Baptiste DuBay delivered a speech to Agent Bushnell at La Pointe on behalf of the mixed-race, or "half Breed," population identified by article 3 of the treaty. The audience for the speech was the commissioner of Indian Affairs. As DuBay outlined the situation:

> We have come to you for the purpose of speaking on the subject of the murder that was committed two years ago by an Indian on one of our Brothers. I allude to Alfred Aitken. We have always considered ourselves Subject to the Laws of the United States and have consequently relied upon their protection. But it appears by the decision of the United States court in this case *"That it was an Indian Killed an Indian, on Indian ground, and did not therefore come under its jurisdiction."*

The mixed-race Anishinaabeg, DuBay declared, felt abandoned by the federal government. Left to seek justice on their own terms, he stated, "We here solemnly pledge ourselves in your presence, to each other, that we will enforce in the Indian country, the Indian Law, Blood for Blood." This was exactly the sort of jurisdictional pluralism that multiple officials in the Michigan and Wisconsin Territories consistently relied on to avoid confrontation between a weak state and autonomous Indigenous nations. The mixed-race Anishinaabeg, however, recognized that in this case, insisting that they follow Native custom undermined their claims to whiteness and U.S. citizenship. "We pay taxes," DuBay declared, making the point that Native peoples—as members of sovereign Indigenous nations—were not citizens of the United States, and therefore paid no taxes.[63]

DuBay then made the case that Alfred Aitkin and other mixed-race Native peoples were civilized persons, or citizens, and therefore distinct from colonized Native subjects. He stated that "our brother was a gentlemanly young man. He was educated." If he did not use the term "civilized," DuBay nonetheless described Alfred in a way that signaled his civilized identity. DuBay then extended this civilized or white identity

63. "Speech of John B DuBay a Half Breed Chippewa, on Behalf of the Half Breeds Assembled in a Numerous Body at the United States Sub Indian Agency Office at La Pointe on the 15 Day of August 1838," Aug. 15, 1838, enclosed in Dodge to Harris, Oct. 15, 1838, La Pointe Agency, RG 75, M234, roll 387, 309.

onto all mixed-race Natives: "For injuries committed upon the persons or property of whites, although within the Indian country we are still willing to be held responsible to the Laws of the United States, notwithstanding the decision of a United States court that we are Indians. And for like injuries committed upon us by whites we will appeal to the same tribunal." DuBay's speech was an appeal to the rule of law and an expression of the desire of traders and their mixed-race families to live under U.S. jurisdiction. More important, Dubay signaled the expectation on behalf of mixed-race people that the federal government would punish Native peoples who committed crimes against any mixed-race Native, just as they would those who committed crimes against any white man. Mixed-race persons should not be left to resolve disputes or address violence according to Native custom. They did not want justice weighed in two scales. They claimed their identity as Native people, as Anishinaabeg, but they also asserted their identity as U.S. citizens.[64]

DuBay next suggested the military value of his people and called on the government to recognize their place within the Republic's civil society. "The half breeds matter strong on the northern frontier," he declared. "We can fight the Indians or white man, in his own manner," he asserted, "and would pledge ourselves to keep peace among the different Indians and tribes." He asked Agent Bushnell to request the president to intervene on their behalf and promised to wait patiently for one year for him to fulfill his promise. "Let the government extend its protection to us and we will be found its staunchest friends," he concluded. In response, Agent Bushnell offered an affirmation to this call for inclusion:

> I have lived several years on the frontier and have known many half breeds, They have to my knowledge paid taxes, and held offices under State, Territorial, and United States authorities and been treated in every respect by the Laws as American citizens; and I have hitherto supposed they were entitled to the protection of the Laws. The decision of the court in this case, if correct is a virtual acknowledgement of your title to the Indians land, in common with the Indians.

Although Bushnell recognized mixed-race Natives as both Indigenous people and U.S. citizens, he suggested that their rightful claim of Native title to their homelands unfairly influenced the court. In acknowledging their Indianness, the court unfortunately placed them outside the civil society of the Republic. He then lamented, "I see no other way for you

64. Ibid., 310.

to obtain satisfaction then to enforce the Indian Law." He promised to forward their request to Washington, D.C., and asked that if compelled to seek revenge, "You will not wage an indiscriminate warfare."[65]

The exchange between DuBay and Bushnell illustrates the political vulnerability created by the Aitkin ruling. This vulnerability threatened to alienate mixed-race Natives from the civil society of the United States and from all of the rights and privileges that came with that inclusion. Indeed, that political and legal threat portended an economic one: the alienation of mixed-race Natives could cause the collapse of the political economy of plunder that benefited both the traders and the government officials of the Northwest Territory. The ambiguity of their status as both Native and civilized U.S. citizens allowed mixed-race traders and white traders with Native families to claim part of the treaty annuity while simultaneously profiting from the diversion of these funds to cover their claimed debt and to pay for their supply of provisions. The court ruling classifying Alfred Aitkin as Native, even though he was mixed-race, removed him and others like him from the legal and civil protections that the Republic offered white settler citizens. Native people, the people U.S. settlers and officials identified as Indians, living under the treaty process that made up the political economy of plunder, lacked political leverage. Indians as a category of people existed outside the social and political boundaries of the Republic.

Governor Dodge likewise acknowledged that the Aitkin case threatened the political economy of plunder, which he saw as the driving force behind the development of the Wisconsin Territory. Shortly after the exchange between DuBay and Agent Bushnell, he wrote to the commissioner of Indian Affairs, Thomas Crawford, informing him that "the Chippewa Indians are friendly disposed towards the United States, at present." But he advised that this relationship must be cultivated: "They are poor, and their annuities will be of great service to them; and, if properly distributed, are calculated to make them friendly to the Settlers who are building mills and making extensive improvements within the limits of the pine region." He then referenced DuBay's speech, which had been forwarded to the commissioner. "On that occasion," he recalled,

> they complained that the Indian who murdered young Aitken, a half-breed Chippewa, had been acquitted by the U.S. District Court, upon the ground that his mother was an Indian woman, and that

65. Ibid., 310; "Reply of the Subagent [Daniel P. Bushnell]," Aug. 15, 1838, ibid., 311.

the half breeds, in a legal point of view, were placed upon the same footing that one Indian would be for killing another. Satisfactory explanations should be made them on that subject. The half-breeds always exercise a great degree of influence over the minds of the Indians, and I consider them as a connecting link between the whites and the Indians.

He concluded by predicting that should the mixed-race Ojibwe people "instigate the Indians to mischief . . . it might be attended with the most fatal consequences to our settlements on that remote border." There was always a threat of violence, Dodge warned, on a "exposed frontier" with a large population of autonomous Native peoples. The United States needed to cultivate the mixed-race people attached to these Indigenous nations to preserve the peace in a region where the United States struggled to assert its sovereignty. That is, the Republic depended on the cooperation of these particular mixed-race people to effectively colonize their Indigenous relatives, members of autonomous Native nations living on homelands in the Wisconsin Territory. The price of this political strategy was the inclusion of mixed-race people in the Republic as citizens. The U.S. government needed to recognize their full humanity, or, in the terminology of the early Republic, it needed to acknowledge them as civilized people.[66]

Crawford, however, insisted on treating the "Half Breeds" as Natives whose behavior could be influenced through U.S. Indian policy—he wanted to treat them as colonial subjects rather than Indigenous citizens. Crawford understood the point of contention, "whether the determination of the court was correct" would "depend upon the fact of a half breed being, or not, an Indian." He himself declined to answer this question. Instead, he wrote: "The decision of the court, right or wrong, must stand for the law in this particular case. The person charged with the murder has been acquitted, and his life cannot be again legally jeopardized for the same offense." The government was bound to obey the law. The secretary then instructed the governor and Agent Bushnell to seek a peaceful resolution. "In pressing upon them the necessity of abstaining from the destruction of the life of the Indian who took that of Aitkin," he wrote, "you will urge the Indians to 'cover the dead' and inform them that if they do not, the govt will withhold from them their annuity money due this year—at the same time say to the half breeds that if they resort to violence, the $100,000, which it is intended this season, and as early

66. Dodge to Crawford, Feb. 8, 1839, in Carter et al., eds., *Territorial Papers of the United States*, XXVII, 1185–1186.

as practicable, to distribute among them under the last treaty, will not be paid." The commissioner of Indian Affairs sought to intervene in the Aitkin affair by asking territorial officials to insist on customary Native diplomatic practice while threatening to withhold the "Half Breed" annuity payments to prevent any act of retaliation.[67]

Lucius Lyon, the Michigan senator charged with dispersing these payments, argued against this course of action. He informed Commissioner Crawford, "They are a proud, sensitive people who are anxious to be recognized by the Government of the United States and to receive protection from its laws." They proved this, he noted, "by delivering up the murderer of Alfred Aitken to the civil authorities instead of punishing him according to Indian customs by taking his life themselves." Lyon concluded by reminding the commissioner, "It is a matter of deep interest with the Government to retain the good feelings of these Indians." The importance of those "good feelings" was evident both nationally and locally. When Lyon wrote, the United States was engaged in a devastating war with the Seminole Indians as well as a bloody conflict with the Creek over removal. Those conflicts made for an ominous backdrop for these negotiations. Moreover, Lyon, like Governor Dodge, lived in the Northwest Territory and recognized that both the economy and political stability of the region required the co-opting of mixed-race Native peoples so that weak state and territorial institutions could maintain influence among the Anishinaabeg while their land was peaceably transferred into the public domain.[68]

Half-Breed Citizens of the Chippewa Nation

The mixed-race community concentrated around La Pointe was very much aware of the key role they played in U.S. political schemes. They were every bit as aware of their own political vulnerability in a Republic that reserved the franchise for white men. A "Council of the Half Breeds, . . . with the approbation of all the Half-Breeds of the Chippewa Nation" submitted a letter to Agent Daniel Bushnell at La Pointe on July 24, 1839,

67. Crawford to Dodge, Apr. 12, 1839, box 12, Lucius Lyon Papers, 1770–1934, William L. Clements Library, University of Michigan, Ann Arbor.

68. Lyon to Crawford, July 16, 1839, in Carter et al., eds., *Territorial Papers of the United States*, XXVIII, 12–13. As Laurel Clark Shire writes, "White Americans and Seminole people terrorized each other between 1835 and 1842"; see Shire, *Threshold of Manifest Destiny*, 58. Similarly, the Second Creek War was the result of Andrew Jackson's coercive implementation of Creek removal; see Haveman, *Rivers of Sand*, 200–233.

seeking to resolve the issues attached to the Aitkin murder. In this letter, they chastised U.S. officials and U.S. courts:

> We are regarded as Indians or white men, to suit the Exigencies of the Case. These being the facts, then, can it be a matter of wonder that we have taken the course, and asked the redress we have in a matter which at once involves our liberty our property and our lives? That our situation is one of doubt and anxiety will not be denied— At one time we have the decision of a *"Competent Tribunal"* giving to us the privileges and immunities of free White Citizens of the United States—the right of Suffrage.

The "Council of the Half Breeds" of the Chippewa Nation, asked for nothing less than life, liberty, and the pursuit of happiness. These rights they claimed by asserting their equality as free U.S. citizens. Also, notably, in the 1839 petition they made a racial distinction, claiming white privilege. In 1837, they identified themselves as "Half Breeds citizens of the United States." In the 1839 petition, they claimed "the privileges and immunities of free White Citizens of the United States."[69]

To assert this claim to whiteness, or to a civilized identity, the 1839 letter made specific reference to the right of suffrage granted to the mixed-race Native peoples of the Michigan Territory by the Nineteenth Congress of the United States. The letter to Agent Bushnell noted that they had been given the right to vote in the election for the congressional delegate for the Michigan Territory in 1826, "which right has never been Extended to the Indian tribes." The outcome of the election was contested because mixed-race Native peoples voted at Mackinac. The Whig delegate appointed to the two-person board of canvassers empaneled to resolve the issue asserted that "it is peurile to suppose that Congress could have intended to confer upon a Wyandot or Chippewa Indian a right to vote at our elections." The Democrat board member countered, arguing "the half breeds (so called,) . . . are not in their habits like wandering Indians, . . . but on the contrary many of them are the owners of comfortable houses, speak English or French, and dress like white men." The Committee of Elections for the Nineteenth Congress sided with the Democrat and determined that any person in the Michigan Territory who "by his manner

---

69. Chippewa Halfbreeds to Bushnell, July 24, 1839, in Carter et al., eds., *Territorial Papers of the United States*, XXVIII, 16–18; Michel Cadotte et al., "To the President of the United States of America," Aug. 31, 1837, enclosed in Jones to Harris, Jan. 9, 1838, La Pointe Agency, RG 75, M234, roll 387, 252.

of living and place of abode, . . . was assimilated to. *[sic]* and associated with, the great body of the civilized community; had never belonged to any tribe of Indians, as a member of their community: . . . no good reason is perceived against such a person being considered as a qualified elector."[70]

Congress sanctioned the inclusion of mixed-race Native peoples in the body politic of the Michigan Territory. Of course, the stipulation that these individuals had never "belonged to any tribe of Indians" was problematic. In the Northwest Territory, the business of virtually all mixed-race Native people was the fur trade, and the trade required a close connection with their Anishinaabe relatives. Maajigaabaw attested to this fact at the 1837 treaty negotiations when he declared, "We have heretofore got our living on them," after requesting that their "half breed" relatives receive a land grant from ceded Ojibwe ancestral lands. In spite of this obvious association, the ABCFM missionaries recognized these mixed-race families as civilized, and so, too, had most territorial officials in the Northwest. This was why the "Council of the Half Breeds" wrote with consternation in reference to the trial of Chigawaasking:

> At another time we have the decision of a *"Competent Tribunal"* *"[sic]* That Half Breeds are Indians and Consequently come within the perview of the Act of Congress, which declares that the Jurisdiction of the United States shall not extend to crimes committed by one Indian against the person or property of an other Indian in the Indian Country, as instanced in the decision of Judge Dunn in the case which has given rise to our dissatisfaction.

The "Half Breed" council pointed out the inconsistency. "It is told us that the decision of Judge Dunn must be considered as the Law," they complained; "Is not the decision of the House of Representatives alluded to Equally the Law?" Nevertheless, the letter concluded by promising "to give you the pledge you require, and we do accordingly promise to bury the hatchet." And they were true to their word. Senator Lyon noted that

70. Chippewa Halfbreeds to Bushnell, July 24, 1839, in Carter et al., eds., *Territorial Papers of the United States*, XXVIII, 17; "A Report on the Proceedings in Relation to the Contested Election for Delegate to the Nineteenth Congress, from the Territory of Michigan . . . ," XI, ibid., 731, 742, 748; Michigan Election, Feb. 13, 1826, House Committee on Elections, Report no. 69, Nineteenth Congress, 1st Sess., 7. As Lucy Murphy has argued, to disenfranchise mixed-race Natives "would have alienated a group that the Anglos needed as allies to rule the territory and control the Indians"; see Murphy, *Great Lakes Creoles*, 92.

this conflict had been settled six months after the submission of this petition to Agent Bushnell. In December 1839, he wrote, "On my arrival at La Pointe, I found that the difficulty between the Half breeds, and Indians, occasioned by the murder of Alfred Aitkin, had been settled, and disposed of, as far as it was possible to settle it."[71]

To kill a white man was a capital offense for a Native person. For one Indigenous person to kill another Indigenous person could be excused as savage custom. As Michigan's Indian agent Henry Schoolcraft had noted, "Justice for a white man and an Indian is weighed in two scales." There was, however, a singular logic that produced these two seemingly divergent outcomes. This logic began with the ontology that understood North America as the New World. The symbolic order conjured by this division of the planet into an Old World and a New World created a political imaginary that divided humanity between the savage and the civilized. This political imaginary was fundamental, indeed it was foundational, to the colonial project in North America.[72]

North America, from the first days of encounter to the creation of the current American and Canadian settler states, was conceptualized as an uninhabited wilderness, an ideological conceit that allowed the U.S. government to imagine that Indian country existed in a state of nature. This is the political logic behind the Louisiana Purchase, the Northwest Ordinance, and the Indian Removal Act, all of which were predicated on Indigenous dispossession. Native peoples in North America, citizens of sovereign Indigenous nations, could accept their dispossession as evidence of human progress and seek assimilation in the civilized society of the United States. If Native peoples failed to make this choice, they would be forced into a doomed fight against the advance of civilization into the untamed wilderness of their homelands (think Alexis de Tocqueville in the Michigan woods). Or they could retreat, fading in power and numbers west of the Mississippi River as the American and Canadian settler states

71. "Secretary Verplank Van Antwerp's Journal of the Proceedings of the Council Held by Governor Henry Dodge in 1837," in Satz, *Chippewa Treaty Rights*, App. 1, 143; Chippewa Halfbreeds to Bushnell, July 24, 1839, in Carter et al., eds., *Territorial Papers of the United States*, XXVIII, 17–18; Lucius Lyon to Crawford, Dec. 16, 1839, ibid., 92.

72. Modern colonialism, Jürgen Osterhammel argues, "is not just any relationship between masters and servants, but one in which an entire society is robbed of its historical line of development, *externally manipulated* and transformed according to the needs and interests of the colonial rulers." See Osterhammel, *Colonialism: A Theoretical Overview*, trans. Shelley L. Frisch (Princeton, N.J., 1997), 15.

advanced across the continent, claiming their territory as their own and settling their citizens on stolen land.

This was the political calculation that the Aitkin family believed they had made with the hybrid colonial/settler colonial United States. The civilizing mission, central to U.S. Indian policy, required the elimination of Native peoples through assimilation or their removal with the promise of eventual assimilation and inclusion within civil society. For men such as William Aitkin who married Native women, this bargain paid off handsomely. A Scottish immigrant (via Canada), he easily entered into the social contract that the Republic offered its white male citizens. U.S. land law and Indian policy depended on the cooperation of men like Aitkin to negotiate the treaties that transferred Native homelands into the public domain. Territorial officials also recognized Aitkin's wife, Beshibiiaanakwad, and her mixed-race children as civilized settler citizens. As such, they claimed a dual identity, nominally white but also Native. They were Anishinaabe enough to be compensated for the land cessions made by their Indigenous relatives, but white enough to be denied a reserved portion of the ancestral homeland. Recognition of this dual citizenship had been the practice of federal and territorial officials who relied on the families of the fur trade to negotiate treaties in the sparsely settled northern tier of the Northwest Territory.

This claim to whiteness and white privilege came at a political and social cost. When Beshibiiaanakwad accepted her status as a civilized American citizen, she sublimated her identity as a Native woman and became a domestic dependent of her husband in exchange for the promise of a political and social future for her children. Her children, like their father, could claim both whiteness and the mantle of U.S. citizenship. Alfred, like his father, would enter into a social contract with the Republic and be counted as a citizen of the newly formed Wisconsin Territory. He could claim the right to vote, exercise legal rights in a court of law, or even hold elective office. Such assurances of U.S. citizenship, at least, were used by American missionaries, Indian agents, and territorial administrators to explain the expansion of the United States to the families of elite and mid-level fur traders who were deeply connected to the Native peoples of the Great Lakes.[73]

The circuit court at Prairie du Chien, however, denied Alfred Aitkin

73. The choice made by Native women such as Beshibiiaanakwad was an integral part of the expansion of the Republic into the Northwest Territory. As Laurel Clark Shire has argued, "the reproductive work at the center of families and households is

his status as a citizen of the United States. Instead, it identified Alfred as an Indian—that is, as a colonized Indigenous subject rather than as a settler citizen. For the jury, dominated by recent immigrants from the original thirteen states of the union, to imagine Alfred as a white man was simply unthinkable. Presented with the story of his life, they could only see red. His mother, her history, and the history of her people (and therefore Alfred's people) marked him as Indigenous and therefore un-civilized. In the Republic, from its creation into the nineteenth century, Native peoples, along with free and enslaved Blacks, represented a class of people that could never be fully enfranchised but must always exist as subordinated colonial subjects.

The jury's ruling turned the murder of Alfred Aitkin by Chigawaask-ing into a conflict between Indians—something that occurred outside American law even if it occurred within American territory. American Indians could not become part of the settler state if they continued to live as Indigenous people, and therefore they could not become citizens of the United States. In this version of the Republic, American Indians were destined to disappear—the ideological goal of settler colonialism. Yet the murder of Alfred Aitkin and the trial of Chigawaasking serve as stark reminders of Indigenous survivance, that active presence of Native peoples in the history of the Republic refusing to be dominated, elimi-nated, or vanished.

This story of Indigenous survivance in the Old Northwest runs counter to the national narrative centered on the conquest and removal of Na-tive peoples from the territory east of the Mississippi. A history of the Northwest Territory that must account for the ongoing presence of Native people, for their active subjugation as colonized subjects of the American state, reveals that the freedom struggle embodied in the free-soil move-ment among white settler citizens in the North was predicated on Native dispossession. The free land that facilitated America's western expansion was stolen Indian land. The American project, the experiment in self-governance based on the equality of all human beings, required the sub-jugation and dispossession of the Indigenous people of North America.

---

not apolitical or inevitable." See Shire, "Sentimental Racism and Sympathetic Pater-nalism: Feeling Like a Jacksonian," *Journal of the Early Republic*, XXXIX (2019), 122.

CHAPTER 5

Indigenous Land and Black Lives

The Politics of Exclusion and Privilege in the Old Northwest

 In 1842, the trustees of Xenia Township in Greene County, Ohio, refused to count the vote of Parker Jeffries, believing him to be "a person of color." Court records indicate that Jeffries was "the off-spring of a white man and half-breed Indian woman." The trustees of the township asserted that this fact—Jeffries's racial identity as a mixed-race Native person—marked him as a person of color. As such, he was not qualified as a lawful voter in the state of Ohio. Jeffries appealed, and his case made it to the Ohio Supreme Court, where attorneys, referring to article 4, section 1, of the Ohio Constitution, argued on behalf of the township trustees that "the right of suffrage is conferred upon white persons, and them alone." The issue at stake was how to classify the racial identity of mixed-race Native peoples and whether Native peoples could claim the rights of U.S. citizenship, including the right to vote.[1]

Jeffries's case implicitly challenged the logic behind the civilizing mission. Could Native peoples transcend their racial identity, transforming from Indians to civilized human beings? Could they make the transition

---

1. Parker Jeffries v. John Ankeny et al., 11 Ohio 372, 1, 2 (1842). See also Ohio Const., art. 4, sec. 1, in Salmon P. Chase, ed., *The Statutes of Ohio and of the Northwestern Territory, Adopted or Enacted from 1788 to 1833 Inclusive . . .* , I (Cincinnati, Ohio, 1833), 79. According to historian Martha S. Jones, "This process of making rights was linked, for black Americans, to a broad claim to the 'privileges and immunities of citizenship.'" She argues that the connection between rights and citizenship was not self-evident during the antebellum period, and free African Americans laid claim to U.S. citizenship "by acting like rights-bearing people." This included exercising the right to vote and the right to testify in a court of law. In the Old Northwest, mixed-race Native peoples laid claim to citizenship in similar fashion. See Jones, *Birthright Citizens: A History of Race and Rights in Antebellum America* (New York, 2018), 10–11.

from savage or uncivilized others into persons capable of entering into the civil society of the U.S. Republic? What about mixed-race Native people—were they savage or civilized, could they be both Indians and U.S. citizens? Did the social contract of the United States extend to people of color, and did this socially constructed category include Indigenous people? The importance of the case was amplified by the changing demography of the Northwest Territory and by the region's emerging geopolitical power. Multiple states in the Old Northwest included significant numbers of Native people as well as autonomous Native communities that engaged in nation-to-nation negotiations with the U.S. federal government. The Northwest Ordinance had imagined the region as an unsettled wilderness, and yet it was not. Indian removal policy set out to correct this problem, and yet it did not. Because removal was not fully implemented, many Indigenous nations in the Old Northwest remained intact and claimed their sovereignty on dramatically reduced versions of their homelands.

The answers to the kinds of questions that emerged from Jeffries's challenge to the trustees of Xenia, Ohio, would be determined by the complex and shifting ideology surrounding racial identity in the United States. Was "Indian" a racial category that marked one as an outsider in a white republic, or was it a sociopolitical identity that could evolve, as suggested by proponents of the civilizing mission ideology? As the Ohio Supreme Court wrestled with the details and implications of Jeffries's case, the justices invoked jurisprudence that stretched back to the Northwest Ordinance. They also struggled to establish whether and to what extent the rights of Ohio's mixed-race Natives resembled the rights of free Black settlers.

In the judgment of the Ohio Supreme Court, finding for the plaintiff Jeffries, the majority asserted that the question of his right to vote depended on how the state constitution defined "free white citizens." Were persons of mixed racial heritage meant to be excluded from this category? The majority wrote that "there have been, even in this state, since its organization, many persons of the precise breed of this plaintiff." The opinion concluded that "half-breed Indians" had always exercised political privileges in Ohio, and to exclude them now "will be equally unexpected and startling." In other words, the court asserted that mixed-race Native peoples had been included within the state of Ohio's civil society and social contract "since its organization."[2]

The court regarded this matter as settled law, and cited *Polly Gray v.*

2. *Jeffries v. Ankeny*, 11 Ohio 372, at 4.

State of Ohio (1831) as precedent. In that case, Polly Gray, identified by the court as a "quarteroon," or person of one-fourth African American ancestry, was indicted for robbery in Hamilton County in 1829. The prosecution relied on the testimony of a Black individual to convict Gray. She objected, on the basis that as a mulatto she had the same rights as a white person, making the testimony of a Black witness inadmissible. The Ohio Supreme Court ruled, "We believe a man, of a race nearer white than mulatto, is admissible as a witness, and should partake in the privileges of whites." Following this logic, the court found that "the witness was improperly admitted," meaning for all practical purposes the "quarteroon" Gray enjoyed the privileges of whiteness and the Black witness who testified against her did not. Based on this 1831 decision, the majority, arguing for Jeffries, stated that Ohio's constitution and laws "enumerated three descriptions of persons—whites, blacks, and mulattoes" and that "disabilities" were applied to the latter two "descriptions." To forestall confusion, the majority further stipulated that "mulatto" was a middle category, "between the extremes" of Black and white, and concluded "that all nearer white than black, or of the grade between the mulattoes and the whites, were entitled to enjoy every political and social privilege of the white citizen."[3]

The dissenting opinion in the Jeffries voting rights case took issue both with this definition of whiteness and with the precedent established by *Gray v. Ohio*. The dissenting opinion asserted that "Indians are a distinct people, governed by their own laws and customs." Accordingly, "Indians are not designated as white men." "To hold that all persons less than half Indian, are white," the dissenting judge further added, "would establish a principle that would make all persons less than half black, or negro, *white*." He concluded that this interpretation of the law would require the admission of mixed-race Black children into the public schools, something he believed the people of Ohio would not tolerate. The dissenting judge spelled out what he regarded as the real issue at the heart of the Jeffries case. It was not so much the definition of whiteness, and whether it could be applied to mixed-race Native peoples, but rather the identity and status of Black people residing in the state of Ohio. Creating a category that allowed mixed-race Natives to access the privileges of whiteness opened up the possibility for Black individuals of mixed race to do the same. The specific threat identified by the dissent was, not voting rights,

3. Polly Gray v. the State of Ohio, 4 Ohio 353, 1, 2–3 (1831); *Jeffries v. Ankeny*, 11 Ohio 372, at 5.

but integration, specifically the prospect of integrating citizens of African descent into institutions such as the public schools. The dissenting judge found this prospect unacceptable.[4]

To further elaborate his argument pertaining to race and citizenship, the dissenting judge cited another Ohio Supreme Court case decided earlier the same year, *Edwill Thacker v. John Hawk et al.* When Edwill Thacker attempted to vote for justice of the peace for Wilkesville Township in Vinton County, Ohio, he was denied this right on account of his racial identity. Like Jeffries, Thacker was a mixed-race individual, or, as the court noted, "the plaintiff in this case had some negro blood in him." The majority opinion in the Thacker case found for the plaintiff and affirmed Thacker's right to vote. They reached their decision based on *Gray v. Ohio* as well as another case, *Williamson v. School Directors* (1832), in which the court ruled that the children of a white mother and a father identified as one-quarter Black should be allowed to attend public school. The precedent established in both *Gray v. Ohio* and *Williamson v. School Directors*, the majority concurred, was that light-skinned mixed-race African Americans "have been considered white." The court in the Thacker case concluded that "this case presents the same question as in *Jeffries v. Ankeny et al.*, and must be decided by the same principles." Thus, Thacker, the court ruled, was a lawful elector.[5]

Despite this outcome, the dissenting judge in *Jeffries v. Ankeny* cited *Thacker v. Hawk* because of the dissenting opinion's explanation in that case for denying the vote to mixed-race individuals. This opinion linked the decision to exclude African Americans from the franchise to the initial political organization of the state and the desire to prevent free Blacks from settling in Ohio. In this dissent, the judge reiterated the argument that "color is a constitutional qualifier of an elector in Ohio," citing the state constitution. This statute, he argued, necessarily excluded any non-white persons from exercising the right to vote: "It has always been admitted that our political institutions embrace the white population only. Persons of color were not recognized as having any political existence. They had no agency in our political organization, and possess no political rights under it." This exclusion was a deliberate political act, according to the dissenting opinion. When the territory was organized, the Northwest Ordinance defined electors as "free male inhabitants," a phrase he noted

4. *Jeffries v. Ankeny*, 11 Ohio 372, at 6.
5. Edwill Thacker v. John Hawk et al., 11 Ohio 376, 1, 5 (1842); Williamson v. School Directors, 11 Ohio 178, 1 (1833).

the framers of the Ohio state constitution later changed to limit the franchise to *"white* male' inhabitants."[6]

Finally, the dissenting opinion in *Thacker v. Hawk* linked the status of free Blacks with Native peoples, designating both as temporary residents of the state of Ohio. The opinion referenced the account of Judge Jacob Burnet, who wrote a history of the settlement of the Northwest Territory, including a history of the Ohio state constitutional convention. In his account of the writing of Ohio's constitution, Burnet asserted:

> Every person who reads the Constitution must discover, that colored people cannot be represented in the Legislature; and that they have not, and cannot have, any agency in conducting the government, or in making, or administering the laws. In these respects they stand on the ground of the aborigines, who remain in the State, after they have ceded their lands to the government. While they are suffered to continue, they have a right to claim the protection of the laws of the State, and to be treated with justice and humanity, but beyond that, no claims are secured to them.

Following this logic, Burnet claimed that Black persons, like Native people, "cannot be citizens." The dissent then linked this political exclusion of Black settlers to laws passed in 1804 and 1807, "statutes discouraging the immigration of blacks into our state, and imposing upon those among us such conditions and restrictions as would induce a vast majority of them to quit the state." The political intention of the 1804 and 1807 statutes, in other words, was to remove free Blacks from Ohio in much the same manner that the 1817 and 1818 treaties negotiated with various Wyandott, Anishinaabe, and Algonquian peoples aimed to induce their removal from the state. The reasoning behind the laws and the treaties was that if Black and Native peoples were excluded from the process of self-government, they would be compelled to leave Ohio to avoid political subjugation.[7]

6. *Thacker v. Hawk,* 11 Ohio 376, at 6, 10–12. See also "An Ordinance for the Government of the Territory of the United States, North-West of the River Ohio," July 13, 1787, Miscellaneous Papers of the Continental Congress, 1774–1789, Record Group (RG) 360: Records of the Continental and Confederation Congresses and the Constitutional Convention, 1765–1821, M332, roll 9, National Archives and Records Administration (NARA), Washington, D.C.

7. Jacob Burnet, *Notes on the Early Settlement of the North-Western Territory* (New York, 1847), 355–356; *Thacker v. Hawk,* 11 Ohio 376, at 14. These Ohio jurists found that they could not think about the rights of Native peoples, particularly mixed-race

The Black Codes of the Old Northwest

The Ohio Constitution and Judge Burnet's historical narrative explaining its origins underscore what are often described as the twin original sins of the U.S. Republic—the theft of Native land and slavery and its legacy. The state of Ohio, like the Republic, was founded on a settler colonial ideology that established the property rights of white settlers through the dispossession of Native peoples and incorporated Black people (enslaved and free) as a fungible source of labor and largely denied them the privileges of legal personhood. This denial was resisted and its imposition incomplete, yet the state, through its Black laws, continued the attempt to refuse Black people the rights due other settlers. A fugitive slave law was part of the state constitution that also implicitly blocked the agency of Native peoples who remained in the state. The legal apparatus of the state thus linked Native elimination and Black exclusion.[8]

Ohio lawmakers feared a connection between the sovereign Indigenous nations and fugitive slaves, and they worried their state might be overrun with indigent free Blacks. The 1804 statute, in fact, explicitly

---

Native peoples, without thinking about the rights and political status of Blacks. Jan Ellen Lewis makes a similar argument with respect to women and enslaved Blacks, stating, "Any discussion of the Three-Fifths Clause sooner or later leads to a discussion of women, but—once again—never in or of themselves, but always in relationship to slaves." In debating the disabilities of mixed-race Natives, the courts inevitably turned to the disabilities of free Blacks. See Lewis, "What Happened to the Three-Fifths Clause: The Relationship between Women and Slaves in Constitutional Thought, 1787–1866," *Journal of the Early Republic*, XXXVII (2017), 2. See also Lewis, "'Of Every Sex and Condition': The Representation of Women in the Constitution," ibid., XV (1995), 359–387. For the linkage of rights and citizenship for free Blacks as related to the exercise of privileges and immunities, see Jones, *Birthright Citizenship*. For the legal idiosyncrasy of rights exercised in court by persons categorized as mulatto, see Anne Twitty, *Before Dred Scott: Slavery and Legal Culture in the American Confluence, 1787–1857* (New York, 2016), 67–69. For mixed-race or mulatto identities as performative in terms of rights, privileges, and claims to whiteness, see Ariela J. Gross, *What Blood Won't Tell: A History of Race on Trial in America* (Cambridge, Mass., 2008), 48–72; and Gross, "Litigating Whiteness: Trials of Racial Determination in the Nineteenth-Century South," *Yale Law Journal*, CVIII (1998), 109–188. For the rights of Blacks, free and enslaved, in the Northwest Territory, see Lea VanderVelde and Sandhya Subramanian, "Mrs. Dred Scott," ibid., CVI (1997), 1033.

8. Ethnic Studies scholar K. Wayne Yang describes this phenomenon as "the settler-native-slave triad." See la paperson [Yang], *A Third University Is Possible* (Minneapolis, Minn., 2017), 8. For resistance to Ohio's Black laws, see Nikki M. Taylor, *Frontiers of Freedom: Cincinnati's Black Community, 1802–1868* (Athens, Ohio, 2005), 34, 44.

linked the political status of escaped enslaved Blacks and politically autonomous Native communities. In December 1803, Philemon Beecher, a
representative of the Ohio state legislature, tabled a resolution that stated,
"Sundry black and mulatto persons, supposed to be the property of citizens in neighboring states, have made a settlement within this state, on
the lands on which Indian title is not yet extinguished, and are of course
measurably under Indian protection." The resolution vested the governor
with the power "to require of the chiefs of the Indian tribes a delivery
of all such black or mulatto persons, or so many of them as do not possess proper credentials of their being free." On January 5, 1804, the Ohio
legislature then passed An Act to Regulate Black and Mulatto Persons,
demanding that free Black immigrants acquire proper credentials from
state authorities. Any Black or mulatto person who desired to settle in the
state of Ohio had to "produce a fair certificate from some court within the
United States, of his or her actual freedom." No Black or mulatto person
could be hired without such a certificate; to do so would result in a fine of
fifty dollars. Similarly, harboring a Black or mulatto without a certificate
who was the property of another person would result in the imposition
of a fine. The law also stipulated that Black and mulatto persons already
resident in the state must register their name and the names of any children with the clerk in the county where they resided.[9]

The 1804 law sought to enforce removal of escaped enslaved Blacks
seeking safe haven on Native-held lands and to restrict the immigration
of free Black persons by imposing a legal burden on this population that
would make it difficult to find work. But requiring Black people in Ohio
to prove their status as free people, and linking this certification to their
employment, did not stop their immigration into the state. Between 1800
and 1810, the population of free Blacks increased from 337 to 1,899. Responding to this demographic change, the Ohio state legislature passed
an amendment to the Act to Regulate Black and Mulatto Persons in 1807
that stipulated that any "negro or mulatto person" must post a bond of
five hundred dollars with the clerk of the county where they wished to
reside. Failure to post such a bond would result in removal from the state.
The amendment also prohibited any "black or mulatto person or persons"
from testifying "in any court of record, . . . where either party to the same

9. "Ohio Legislature, Extract of the Journal of the House of Representatives," *Scioto
Gazette* (Chillicothe, Ohio), Jan. 9, 1804, [1]; An Act to Regulate Black and Mulatto
Persons, Jan. 5, 1804, in Chase, ed., *Statutes of Ohio and of the Northwestern Terri-
tory*, I, 393–394; Taylor, *Frontiers of Freedom*, 33–35.

is a white person." On the ground, these laws were unevenly enforced; in *Gray v. Ohio, Thacker v. Hawk*, and several other cases, the Ohio Supreme Court made exceptions for light-skinned mixed-race Black and Native peoples. The intent of the legislature, however, was to pass laws that explicitly discouraged the immigration of either fugitive or free Black settlers.[10]

The anti-Black racism of the Ohio legislature was adapted by Indiana and Illinois, the next two states organized in the Northwest Territory. Indiana, established as a territory in 1800 and as a state in 1816, restricted the vote to "every free white male" over the age of twenty-one and required free Black and mulatto persons immigrating to the new state to register a certificate of freedom and post a five-hundred-dollar bond. The Indiana legislature passed these restrictive Black laws despite that article 1 of the Indiana Constitution read, "We declare that all men are born equally free and independent, and have certain natural, inherent, and unalienable rights, among which are the enjoying and defending life and liberty, and of acquiring, possessing and protecting property and pursuing and obtaining happiness and safety." Illinois, established as a territory in 1809 and as a state in 1818, similarly limited the vote to "white male inhabitants" over the age of twenty-one and required Black and "mulatto" settlers to register a certificate of freedom and post a one-thousand-dollar bond. These laws, like the laws first crafted in Ohio, imposed financial and legal burdens on Black settlers with the goal of discouraging their immigration to the free states of the Northwest Territory.[11]

10. An Act to Amend the Act, Entitled, "An Act Regulating Black and Mulatto Persons," Jan. 25, 1807, in Chase, ed., *Statutes of Ohio and of the Northwestern Territory*, I, 555–556. For the Black population in Ohio and the laws of 1804 and 1807, see Eugene H. Berwanger, *The Frontier against Slavery: Western Anti-Negro Prejudice and the Slavery Extension Controversy* (1967; rpt. Chicago, 2002), 22–23. As historian Nikki M. Taylor writes regarding Ohio's Black laws, "Enforcement was impractical; only with great difficulty and diligence could local officials regulate black settlement. African Americans—fugitive and legitimately free—settled in the state without registering with the court or finding sureties, in some cases avoiding these requirements for decades." See Taylor, *Frontiers of Freedom*, 34.

11. An Act Regulating the General Elections of the Indiana Territory, Dec. 17, 1811, in Louis B. Ewbank and Dorothy L. Riker, eds., *The Laws of Indiana Territory, 1809–1816* (Indianapolis, Ind., 1934), 225–226; *Constitutions of 1816 and 1851 of the State of Indiana and Amendments* (Indianapolis, Ind., 1895), 5; Illinois Const. (1818), art. II, sec. 27; An Act respecting Free Negroes, Mulattoes, Servants, and Slaves, Mar. 30, 1819, in *The Revised Laws of Illinois, Containing All Laws of a General and Public Nature Passed by the Eighth General Assembly, at Their Session Held at Vandalia,*

When Ohio entered the union as a state, slaveholders in the Indiana Territory, which at that time included the Illinois country, sought to protect their enslaved property and legally preserve an indenture system that perpetuated slavery. Following the creation of the Northwest Territory, slaveholders in the region began petitioning the federal government to repeal or modify article 6, which stipulated that all new states in the territory be free. Neither Congress nor the executive branch acted to effect a repeal, but the territorial governor, Arthur St. Clair, publicly affirmed that article 6 represented a prohibition against the introduction of new enslaved laborers into the region, not a call for the emancipation of those already residing in the territory. As the historian Paul Finkelman has argued, the political leadership of the Northwest Territory "creatively developed *de facto* slavery through a system of long-term indentures, rental contracts, enforcement statutes, and the recognition of the status of slaves who had been brought to the territory before 1787."[12]

As a result of these restrictive laws and the perpetuation of various forms of indenture, the Black population in the states of the Old Northwest remained low while the white population continued to expand dramatically, with white settlers taking advantage of easy access to a subsidized land base. By 1830, the state of Ohio, for example, had slightly fewer than 10,000 Black residents living alongside a population of 937,903 white settlers, with comparable ratios of Black and white settlers in Indiana and Illinois. Yet in 1832, the Ohio state legislature's Committee on the Colored Population in Ohio issued a report declaring: "The existence in any community of a people forming a distinct and degraded caste, who are forever excluded by the fiat of society and the laws of the land, from all hopes of equality in social intercourse and political privileges, must, from the nature of things, be fraught with unmixed evil." Chief among these evils, the committee identified "the exclusion of a large amount of the labor of white men, who will not degrade themselves in society by adopting the

---

Commencing on the Third Day of December, 1832, and Ending the Second Day of March, 1833, Together with All Laws Required to Be Re-published by the Said General Assembly (Vandalia, Ill., 1833), 457–463. For the need to secure a bond in Indiana, see An Act Concerning Free Negroes and Mulattoes, Servants and Slaves, Feb. 10, 1831, in *The Revised Laws of Indiana* . . . (Indianapolis, Ind., 1831), 375–376, and An Act Regulating the Practice in Suits at Law, Jan. 29, 1831, 407. For the legal logic of the Black codes of Illinois, see M. Scott Heerman, *The Alchemy of Slavery: Human Bondage and Emancipation in the Illinois Country, 1730–1865* (Philadelphia, 2018), 100–101.

12. Paul Finkelman, "Evading the Ordinance: The Persistence of Bondage in Indiana and Illinois," *JER*, IX (1989), 22. See also Heerman, *Alchemy of Slavery*, 60–61.

employments, and coming into competition with blacks." In other words, from the committee's perspective, the labor of free Blacks represented a threat parallel to that of enslaved labor in the South because both degraded the value of white workers.[13]

For white settlers moving into the Northwest Territory, it was simply unthinkable to imagine living on an equal footing with free Black settlers, just as it was impossible to imagine Natives as people with rights equal to their own. Laws such as Ohio's Act to Regulate Black and Mulatto Persons and similar regulations in Indiana and Illinois were an attempt to deny free Black settlers access to the subsidized land base and social contract promised by the Northwest Ordinance. The Ohio legislature's Committee on the Colored Population, for example, asserted: "For the purposes of legislation, it is sufficient to know, that the blacks in Ohio must always exist as a separate and degraded race; that when the Leopard shall change his spots and the Ethiopian his skin, then, but not 'till then, may we expect that the descendants of Africans will be admitted into society, on terms of social and political equality." The committee concluded that the laws of 1804 and 1807 "have in practice proved almost entirely inefficient" but nevertheless declared these laws a necessity; "their continuance on the statute book proves that the succeeding Legislatures of Ohio, have considered the immigration of blacks as a great evil, and have sought to remedy that evil."[14]

Race and the Right to Vote

The U.S. government, imagining the Old Northwest as an unsettled wilderness, a territory that had yet to be politically organized, saw the creation of new states such as Ohio, Indiana, and Illinois as both the advance of civilization and a broadening of the Republic's social contract to the settlements of these new states. This social contract was not extended to Native peoples in these newly organized territories, however, who, viewed as savages, existed outside the civil society established by the Republic. The ideals and policies of the civilizing mission had offered the prospect that one day Native peoples might transcend their status, become civilized, and be incorporated into the Republic as citizens. But the Indian Removal Act and the countless attempts to insert removal provisions

13. "Legislative Report of the Committee on the Colored Population of Ohio," *Ohio State Journal, and Columbus Gazette*, Feb. 1, 1832, [1]; Berwanger, *Frontier against Slavery*, 31.

14. "Legislative Report of the Committee on the Colored Population of Ohio," *Ohio State Journal, and Columbus Gazette*, Feb. 1, 1832, [1].

into treaties negotiated with the Native nations of the Northwest Territory indicated that, from the perspective of the federal government, Native peoples remained unfit for inclusion within the social and political boundaries of the Republic.[15]

Similarly, the Black laws enacted by the legislatures in Ohio, Indiana, and Illinois signaled a desire to exclude free Blacks from the social contract promised by the Northwest Ordinance to settlers willing to expand the settled territory of the Republic in the West. Describing African Americans "as a separate and degraded race" was comparable to imagining Native peoples as savage or uncivilized. Like Native peoples, they were a race apart. If they were, as the Ohio legislature reported, "excluded . . . from all hopes of equality in social intercourse and political privileges," they could never participate in the democratic self-government offered by the Northwest Ordinance. White legislatures in these new states would restrict the access of free Blacks to the rights and privileges of U.S. citizenship, including property in the form of a subsidized land base created by the dispossession of Native peoples, who, from the perspective of U.S. authorities, had failed to improve the land.

The Michigan Territory likewise sought to exclude Black settlers and to limit the rights of those who did take up residence. Although low migration delayed statehood, the legislature nevertheless passed An Act to Regulate Blacks and Mulattoes, and to Punish the Kidnapping of Such Persons in 1827, which—like the Black laws of other states organized in the Old Northwest—required African American settlers to register a certificate "of his or her actual freedom" and to post a five-hundred-dollar bond with the clerk in the county of their residence. The state constitution limited the franchise to "white male inhabitants," but at the constitutional convention held in 1835, this provision was debated. The delegate from Lenawee County proposed that the word "white" be replaced with the word "freeman." The proposal was challenged by the delegate from Wayne County, who stated that such a change represented an attempt "to allow the admission of Indians and negroes to the polls." This was a reasonable objection given that the territory had allowed mixed-race Natives to vote in the election for the congressional delegate in 1826. When this practice was challenged then, it had been upheld by the Committee on Elections in the U.S. Congress with the stipulation that if the mixed-race Native elector lived among and identified with the civilized population

15. For a history of northern Indian removal, see John P. Bowes, *Land Too Good for Indians: Northern Indian Removal* (Norman, Okla., 2016).

of Michigan, he had the right to vote, the franchise being restricted to white men.[16]

The delegate from Lenawee, in response to the contention that he wanted to expand the franchise to include Blacks and Indians, invoked the U.S. Constitution, the Declaration of Independence, and the natural law formulation of inalienable rights expressed in these texts. "If then all men are free and equal," he stated on the convention floor, "and we want to confine ourselves to the principles of the Declaration of Independence, where is the propriety of confining the right of voting exclusively to white male inhabitants." The right to vote was not entirely a natural right," countered the Wayne County delegate. "Why, then, should we invite within our limits; why hold out inducements to the migration hither, of a description of population confessedly injurious, confessedly a nuisance, to the community? It would not be denied that the negro belonged to a degraded caste of mankind." The delegate from Wayne County was echoing the bigoted sentiment advanced by the Ohio state legislature's Committee on the Colored Population of Ohio—both refused to recognize the full humanity of African Americans. Like Native peoples, they existed apart from the civilized world and therefore outside the civil society of the United States.[17]

The delegate from Calhoun County expanded on this sentiment, objecting to the interpretation of natural law that recognized the equality of Black and white settlers, specifically, the idea that the right to vote was a natural right. "We are, it is true, born equal in a state of nature—but not so, of necessity, in a state of society," he argued. Then invoking the idea of the social contract, he asserted: "When we enter into a state of society, we give up a portion of our natural rights. In a state of nature, all have an equal liberty to do as they think proper—the will of the strongest being the only law that commands obedience, but is far otherwise in a state of society. In the later case such laws are to be passed as will conduce to the greatest happiness of the greatest number." Voting rights, he concluded,

16. An Act to Regulate Blacks and Mulattoes, and to Punish the Kidnapping of Such Persons, Apr. 13, 1827, in *Laws of the Territory of Michigan*, II (Lansing, Mich., 1874), 634–636; "The Convention of 1835," Debates and Minutes, May 22, 1835, in Harold M. Dorr, ed., *The Michigan Constitutional Conventions of 1835-36: Debates and Proceedings* (Ann Arbor, Mich., 1940), 155.

17. "The Convention of 1835," Debates and Minutes, May 22, 1835, in Dorr, ed., *Michigan Constitutional Conventions*, 155, 157.

were a matter of expediency, "and in his opinion it was expedient to exclude the colored population from the privilege of the elective franchise."[18]

The debates over suffrage at Michigan's constitutional convention
never returned to the status of Natives as people of color and whether
they had the right to vote. In the end, though, the convention refused to
strike the word "white" as a qualifier for the right to vote. Michigan, like
the states of Ohio, Indiana, and Illinois, chose to restrict suffrage to white
men and actively sought to exclude African Americans from settling in
the free states created on the homelands of the dispossessed Native peoples of the Old Northwest.[19]

For all of these new states, the case for exclusion, ironically, drew on
the natural law formulation of inalienable rights that formed the basis of
British and, later, American political society. The Indiana state constitution, for example, had echoed the Declaration of Independence, proclaim-
ing "that all men are born equally free and independent, and have certain
natural, inherent, and unalienable rights, among which are the enjoying
and defending life and liberty, and of acquiring, possessing and protecting
property and pursuing and obtaining happiness and safety." This statement of inalienable rights, in turn, derived from late-seventeenth-century
English philosopher John Locke, who wrote in the second treatise of his
Two Treatises of Government that all men were free and equal in the state
of nature. The only reason to leave the state of nature, divesting one's self
of this natural liberty, Locke contended, was to accept the bonds of civil
society "by agreeing with other Men to joyn and unite into a Community,
for their comfortable, safe, and peaceable living one amongst another, in
a secure Enjoyment of their Properties, and a greater Security against any
that are not of it."[20]

Those who failed to enter into society remained in a state of nature.
According to the delegates from Wayne and Calhoun Counties, the exclusion of Blacks from the franchise did not deny them their inalienable
rights to life, liberty, and the pursuit of happiness. Rather, it left them
with these rights intact but excluded them from the social compact of
the U.S. Republic. This certainly was how U.S. officials and citizens understood the political status of Native peoples. They existed in a state of

18. Ibid., 162.

19. "Detroit, Friday May 29, 1835: The Convention," *Democratic Free Press* (Detroit),
June 3, 1835, [1].

20. *Constitutions of 1816 and 1851 of the State of Indiana and Amendments*, 5; John
Locke, *Two Treatises of Government: A Critical Edition with an Introduction and
Apparatus Criticus*, ed. Peter Laslett (Cambridge, 1960), 349.

nature, where they, too, exercised rights but where they also lived in a wilderness that was shared by all of mankind in common. From the perspective of the United States and the British Empire, Native peoples lived on homelands that they did not fashion into private property, to which they retained an imperfect title, and, as a consequence, that they had failed to establish dominion over.[21]

The Michigan delegates imagined that free Blacks could be granted a political and legal status similar to that of wives and children. In effect, free Black citizens, from a natural law perspective, could be categorized as domestic dependents. African Americans were like Native peoples; they constituted a racialized category with either severely restricted rights and privileges or none of the rights and privileges of a white citizen. As the Ohio jurist Jacob Burnet asserted, free Blacks "stand on the ground of the aborigines"—that is, they were not included within civil society, but as long as they trespassed on free soil and could prove they were not an escaped slave, "they have a right to claim the protection of the laws of the State." Before the passage of the Fourteenth Amendment establishing birthright citizenship, the political rights and status of free Black settlers remained precarious even in free states. They could be, like Native peoples, excluded from the American experiment in self-government. Negotiating their way around this exclusion often meant negotiating the meaning of race and racial identity as a social category in a political world organized around the idea of white supremacy.[22]

The Treaty of Saint Peters and the Half-Breed Annuity

For African Americans, but especially free Blacks, political negotiations about the meaning and consequences of their racial identity most often manifested as a negotiation about the privileges and disabilities of citizenship. Could they vote or testify in court? Could their children attend a public school? These negotiations determined the social boundaries that

21. This formulation refers to the settler contract described by Carole Pateman in "The Settler Contract," in Pateman and Charles W. Mills, eds., *Contract and Domination* (Cambridge, 2007), 35–78. For the U.S. Supreme Court's understanding of Native land tenure and dominion, see Robert A. Williams, Jr., *The American Indian in Western Legal Thought: The Discourses of Conquest* (New York, 1990), 305–317.

22. Burnet, *Notes on the Early Settlement of the North-Western Territory*, 356; Locke, *Two Treatises of Government*, ed. Laslett, 337, 340–341. For the argument linking the status of free Black persons and women, see Lewis, "What Happened to the Three-Fifths Clause," *JER*, XXXVII (2017), 1–46.

defined their existence, their right to be and live in a particular place. For the Anishinaabeg, negotiations about race also centered on place and belonging but focused particularly on land and land rights. Because of this connection, the Anishinaabeg were coerced into forfeiting enormous swaths of their homeland, which, from the perspective of the Republic, they had no right to possess permanently as they had not organized this territory as private property.

Mixed-race Native peoples asserting a dual citizenship, as Indian and American, struggled to claim both land rights and the privileges of citizenship. The mixed-race Native peoples associated with the Anishinaabeg who negotiated the 1837 Treaty of Saint Peters could claim a portion of the annuity set aside for them as compensation for the millions of acres of land they ceded in the Wisconsin Territory. To receive this compensation, ironically, they needed to prove their Indianness to U.S. officials. Thus, after struggling to assert their whiteness and citizenship in courts and at the ballot box, the mixed-race Anishinaabeg of the Lake Superior country found it necessary to prove that they belonged on the ceded territory now claimed by the United States. Unlike free Black people, they did not have to demonstrate that they had a legal right to live in the Northwest Territory, but they did have to prove that they had a legal right to be compensated for their dispossession by the United States.

In the summer of 1839, the secretary of Indian affairs, Thomas Hartley Crawford, appointed Michigan senator Lucius Lyon to serve as commissioner for the dispensation of the 1837 Treaty of Saint Peters "Halfbreed" annuity. The instructions stated that "no distinction should be made among the halfbreeds" and noted that "this term identifies Indians of mixed-blood, of whatever degree." Unlike in the cases before the Ohio Supreme Court adjudicating the political privileges and disabilities afforded to Blacks, "quarteroons," and mulattoes, all mixed-race Native peoples were to be treated as equally "entitled" to the one-hundred-thousand-dollar annuity. The instructions signaled that, unlike the Black laws or voting rights cases, which hinged on white citizens' assessments of race, the United States intended to allow the Anishinaabeg to determine who counted as Native and who could make a claim to the ceded territory. They at least tacitly recognized a limited Indigenous sovereignty and land rights and that Native peoples understood identity in terms of kinship as opposed to race or phenotype.[23]

23. Thomas Hartley Crawford to Lucius Lyon, June 5, 1839, box 12, Lucius Lyon Papers, William L. Clements Library, University of Michigan, Ann Arbor; Jones, *Birthright Citizenship*.

Senator Lyon responded to his appointment with a statement that acknowledged the problematic nature of the land cession associated with the Treaty of Saint Peters. He was aware that "the Leech Lake Indians . . . who took an active part in the treaty had no interest or right whatever in the country ceded" and that they signed the treaty "disposing of lands which they never occupied." He also informed Secretary Crawford that "most of the Indians residing in the country, sold, refused to sign it, or to assent to it in any manner whatever." Given these circumstances, Lyon asked whether "the half breeds of the Leech Lake Indians (or the half breeds of other similar Indians, who have signed a treaty for the cession of lands to which they had no just claim)" should receive money from the promised half-breed annuity. Crawford advised the senator that Indians Lyon believed had no right to participate in the 1837 treaty should be excluded from the half-breed fund. Lyon could, however, "resort to other evidence to ascertain the facts," seemingly leaving the determination of who could claim a right to the ceded land to the senator's discretion. He called on Lyon to proceed "as you deem most expedient," but, the secretary concluded, "it is important that the half breeds should be pacified."[24]

This confusion about who belonged to the ceded territory stemmed at least in part from a misperception on the part of U.S. officials, who wanted to negotiate with a singular "Chippewa Nation." The diffuse nature of political power among the myriad Anishinaabe communities throughout the Great Lakes frustrated a federal government that wanted Native peoples from the region to negotiate with a single voice. Adding to the confusion, the mixed-race Anishinaabeg from Lake Superior, many of whom did not speak English, grasped the political significance of nationalism and national identity in the post-Revolutionary United States and sought to establish a sense of political parity with the American polity by identifying themselves as the "Half-Breeds of the Chippewa Nation" when addressing U.S. officials. In effect, they asserted their sovereignty as members of an Indigenous nation at the same time as they claimed their citizenship in the United States.[25]

In an attempt to clarify matters, Secretary Crawford sent an additional letter of instruction to Senator Lyon cautioning him to restrict the half-breed annuity to people from the territory ceded in 1837. He noted that

24. Lyon to Crawford, July 15, 1839, Crawford to Lyon, July 25, 1839, box 12, Lyon Papers.

25. Chippewa Halfbreeds to Daniel P. Bushnell, July 24, 1839, in Clarence Edwin Carter et al., eds., *The Territorial Papers of the United States*, 28 vols. (Washington, D.C., and New York, 1934–), XXVIII, 16.

the 1836 treaty "with the Ottawa and Chippewa nations of Indians" also contained an article that provided an annuity for half-breeds, but it restricted these funds for people "actually resident within the boundaries described in the first article of the treaty," which were within the state of Michigan. In contrast, "that of 1837 is general for the 'half breeds of the Chippewa nation.'" The problem was that "the Indian party to each treaty is called in both 'The Chippewa nations of Indians,' although it is certain that they were severally executed by the chiefs and head men of separate communities." The secretary admonished Lyon to make the distinction between the *doodemag*, or bands, that signed these two distinct treaties and to allocate the annuity funds accordingly. "From the chiefs and headmen parties to the treaty of 29th July 1837, under which you act," he wrote, "you can readily learn who are *their* half breeds, and they only will be entitled to an interest in the $100,000."[26]

Lyon promised to defer to the Anishinaabe *ogimaag* but informed Crawford that he doubted they would be able to agree about who belonged to the ceded territory and thus who should receive the annuity. Both the secretary and the senator recognized that at least a portion of the mixed-race Anishinaabe population was more likely to be mobile or to have moved away from the ceded territory as a function of their participation in the fur trade. In fact, Lyon reported to Crawford that "as some of the half breeds and most of the claimants, under the 4th article of the treaty under which I am now acting, reside in this state, I have thought proper to publish a notice to them in the newspapers of this city." On July 13, 1839, the *Detroit Free Press* printed: "Notice—To such of the half breeds of the Chippewa nation of Indians as are entitled to share the hundred thousand dollars provided them by the 3d article of the treaty concluded at St. Peters on the 29th day, of July 1837," Lyon, acting as treaty commissioner, would review claims in September at La Pointe. "Persons having claims, under either of said articles," he instructed, "will please present them to him, at that place as early as practicable, accompanied by all the evidence relied upon for their support."[27]

Even when the government attempted to compensate Indigenous people for their land loss, however, it created ways for non-Native settlers to make money. A significant portion of any given annuity stipulated by the multitude of treaties negotiated throughout the Northwest Territory

26. Crawford to Lyon, July 11, 1839, box 12, Lyon Papers.

27. Lyon to Crawford, July 15, 1839, box 12, Lyon Papers; *Detroit Free Press*, July 13, 1839.

always included the dispensation of provisions to Native parties in addition to cash payments, which enabled non-Native settlers to profit in two ways. Natives had cash in hand for purchases from white merchants, and the government provided white settlers with the opportunity to supply the treaty provisions that the government would distribute. For example, on the day that Senator Lyon published his notice that he would accept and review claims by any "half breed" believed to be entitled to the annuity established by the 1837 treaty, the *Detroit Free Press* also printed a notification from Michigan's Indian agent Henry Schoolcraft that, as acting superintendent of Indian affairs, he would accept sealed proposals "for furnishing provisions for the Indians assembled to receive their annuities at the several agencies and subagencies, attached to this superintendancy, in the following amounts, namely: At Michilimackinac, 1st August to the value of $1000; At Green Bay, 15th August $100; At La Pointe, Lake Superior, 1st September $500; At Saginaw, 1st September $225; At Detroit, 20th July $50." The advertisement specified that "the provisions required are prime pork, superfine flour, and corn, in proportions equal to their cash value, to be delivered in store, at the places and times stated, and to be inspected at the contractor's expense." Treaty annuities thus provided the circumstances for white settlers to profit considerably from the extinction of Native title to land through treaty negotiations. They were part of the political economy of plunder, the ongoing colonial relationship between U.S. officials and settlers and the subordinated subject populations of Native peoples who lived on reservations, the last remnants of their homelands in the Old Northwest.[28]

Essential to the political economy of plunder was the transfer of wealth to white settlers through the sale of Native land that had been converted, through the treaty process, into the public domain of the United States. In fact, that same issue of the *Detroit Free Press* provides further evidence of this systematic transfer of wealth with a public notice, "on behalf of the president of the United States, of the sale of land '[heretofore reserved to the Indians]' available through the land offices of the cities of Gennessee, Monroe, and Macon, ceded to the United States by treaty." These land sales not only provided an important source of revenue to the federal government but also a publicly subsidized land base for white settlers willing to move to the Northwest.[29]

28. *Detroit Free Press*, July 13, 1839.
29. Ibid.

Claiming the Status and Rights of Half-Breeds

In September 1839, mixed-race Native peoples, "half breeds" in the language of the nineteenth-century United States, from throughout the Great Lakes region converged on the village of La Pointe, in the Wisconsin Territory, hoping for some measure of compensation for these massive transfers of wealth to white citizens of the United States. They traveled to the west end of Lake Superior to claim their share of the one hundred thousand dollars promised to the mixed-race Anishinaabeg with roots in the territory ceded at Saint Peters in 1837. In seeking this redress, however, they needed to prove their Indian identity while simultaneously maintaining their rights and status as U.S. citizens. Of course, there was also a significant mixed-race population already living in the Lake Superior country. The schools established by the missionaries of the American Board of Commissioners for Foreign Missions (ABCFM), for example, continued to serve mixed-race Native students almost exclusively. As the missionary at Fond du Lac noted, "The school since its establishment has been made up principally of half breed Catholic children connected with the trading house." He also recorded that "prejudices against us as Americans have very much increased and strengthened since the treaty." In addition to the coerced land cessions, the Anishinaabeg were aware of the U.S. removal policy. "The affairs of the Govt with the southern tribes," the missionary informed the council of the ABCFM, "has reached their ears and excited new jealousies."[30]

The mixed-race Anishinaabeg posed a conceptual and a political problem for the United States. Officials like Daniel Bushnell, the Indian agent at La Pointe, and Senator Lucius Lyon identified them as civilized, but the missionaries believed they were hardly distinguishable from their savage relatives. Sherman Hall, the missionary at La Pointe, informed the board that "the Canadians and half-breeds of Canadian descent are of course Roman Catholic." Even worse, they were "mixing with the Indians and following the same business with them, have many opportunities for exerting an influence over them. They are very little elevated in point of moral or intellectual character, above the Indians." This intermixed community, he concluded, "are generally attached to their heathen ways."[31]

In the face of this prejudice, the mixed-race Anishinaabe citizens who

30. Frederic Ayer to David Greene, Oct. 31, 1838, American Board of Commissioners for Foreign Missions, Correspondence, 1827–1878, box 1, Gale Family Library, Minnesota Historical Society (MHS), Saint Paul (hereafter cited as ABCFM).

31. Sherman Hall to Greene, Oct. 24, 1838, ABCFM, box 1.

traveled to La Pointe in September 1839 had to demonstrate their indigeneity and their connection to the Wisconsin Territory to claim their share of the 1837 annuity. Yet, in a type of balancing act, they also needed to assert their civilized status to fight for their political rights as U.S. citizens. For example, three of the men who signed the half-breed petition sent to La Pointe's Indian agent demanding justice for Alfred Aitkin in July 1839, Michel Cadotte, George Bonga, and François Brunet, were now requesting a share of the half-breed annuity. Their earlier petition had reminded the agent, "At one time we have the decision of a *'Competent Tribunal'* giving to us the privileges and immunities of free White Citizens of the United States." And, in spite of Sherman Hall's complaint about the "heathen ways" of Canadian half-breeds, the missionaries frequently described Michel Cadotte, Jr., and his extended family as civilized. They also recognized that the Cadotte family was among the most influential of the mixed-race traders in the Lake Superior country.[32]

Indeed, as noted previously, this multigenerational family of fur traders was deeply connected to the political infrastructure of Anishinaabewaki. Cadotte was the eldest child of Michel Cadotte, Sr., and his wife, Esther, the daughter of a Lac du Flambeau ogimaa. Michel, Sr., was the son of Jean-Baptiste Cadotte and his Ojibwe wife, originally from Sault Sainte Marie. Michel, Sr., was also the first cousin of Noodin, the ogimaa of Snake River, and Gichi-Bizhiki (The Great Buffalo), the ogimaa of La Pointe. Michel, Jr., applied for a share of the 1837 annuity for himself and his seven children. On his claim, Senator Lyon wrote, "Michel Cadotte jun a ¾ Chippewa is the son of the late Michel Cadotte and Magdalen his wife, was born on Chippeway River within the ceded country age 52 years." Lyon also noted that Cadotte had resided at La Pointe since 1812. He concluded: "History correct, but it is stated that the children claimed for have rec'd goods and portion of the annuity as Indians, this year. This report is correct. But claimant states without his consent. Mr. Bushnell agent of the government, confirms the above statement but says the goods and annuities drawn Cadottes children have been returned to him. The claim is therefore allowed." The Cadotte children claimed a portion of the annuity as Native people because their family was so thoroughly integrated into the Ojibwe community at La Pointe. Among the Anishinaabeg, kinship, not phenotype or race, determined belonging. Mixed-race Anishinaabeg considered themselves Anishinaabe, or, in the case of the

32. Chippewa Halfbreeds to Bushnell, July 24, 1839, in Carter et al., eds., *Territorial Papers of the United States*, XXVIII, 16.

Cadottes, Chippewa, the Anglicized version of Ojibwe. U.S. treaties that created territories like Wisconsin and carved out small reservations for the resident Indian population made the idea of race or racial identity increasingly important politically. Half-breeds could claim whiteness, and thus U.S. citizenship and political rights, which their Indian relatives could not access. In the 1850 U.S. census, all of the Cadottes resident at La Pointe were enumerated as white. The children of Michel, Jr., claimed their annuities as Indians, but they returned these benefits and sought an annuity as half-breeds because they recognized that in the United States, unlike Anishinaabewaki, whiteness brought political and social privileges denied to Native peoples.[33]

François Brunet made a similar calculation. He, too, signed the half-breed petition asserting his status as a U.S. citizen, and he filed a half-breed claim for the 1837 treaty. On his claim, Senator Lyon wrote: "Francis Brunet ½ breed 40 years born at the Grand Portage on the north side of Lake Superior, on a voyage with the family. Has always resided in the St. Croix, Sandy Lake, Leech Lake and Mississippi countries. His mother was a full Chippewa woman from Lac Court Oreille. He claims for himself and 4 children ¾ breeds." "History of the above is correct," Lyon determined. Although he admitted Brunet for his own claims, however, he rejected those filed on behalf of his children. Brunet was from the Saint Croix River country in the ceded territory. The ABCFM missionary Edmund Ely stated in his diary that Brunet was the brother of Kabamappa, the ogimaa of the Saint Croix Ojibweg. In the late 1830s, he worked as a clerk for the American Fur Company at Leech Lake, where he invited William Boutwell into his home for dinner when the ABCFM missionary arrived to establish a school and mission. Lyon's rejection of the claims of the children suggest they were born at Leech Lake to a Leech Lake Ojibwe mother, a residence and kinship connection that placed them outside the ceded territory.[34]

33. Michel Cadotte, for Himself and Seven Children, Chippewa Claims, Half Breed Claims (HBC) no. 163, box 21, Lyon Papers; "Wisconsin," *The Seventh Census of the United States, 1850: Embracing a Statistical View of Each of the States and Territories . . .* (Washington, D.C., 1853), 914. See also Theresa M. Schenck, *All Our Relations: Chippewa Mixed-Bloods and the Treaty of 1837; Compiled with Notes and Introduction* (Madison, Wis., 2010). For the Cadotte family and mixed-race fur-trade families, see Brenda J. Child, *Holding Our World Together: Ojibwe Women and the Survival of Community* (New York, 2012), 31–62.

34. François Brunet, Chippewa Claims, HBC no. 123, box 21, Lyon Papers; Theresa M. Schenck, ed., *The Ojibwe Journals of Edmund F. Ely, 1833–1849* (Lincoln, Nebr., 2012), Feb. 9, 1834, 74.

Other white men working for the American Fur Company at their Wisconsin Territory posts married to Ojibwe women also filed claims for their families. They did so even though their wives and children benefited from the privileges of whiteness; their families were enumerated as white in the census and were regarded as "Americans" by fellow traders, missionaries, and territorial officials. Charles Oakes, an American Fur Company trader based at La Pointe, filed a claim for his wife and children. "Charles Oakes," Lyon wrote,

> claims for his wife Julia Oakes ½ breed. 26 years of age born at Lac du Flambeau where she remained (except while at school) until wither the last 4 years when she removed to Ground River in Michigan & from there to La Pointe in the spring of 1839 where she at present resides. He also claims for his son Geo. Henry ¼ breed aged 6 years born at Lac du Flambeau and residing at present with his parents at La Pointe.

He also noted that Julia was related to prominent political figures at Lac du Flambeau and that she filed a claim under the 1836 Treaty of Washington "but was rejected in consequence of being an inhabitant of the country ceded by the treaty of July 29, 1837." Julia was the daughter of the French-Canadian trader Bazil Beaulieu and Ogenaw-gizzhigokwe (Respected Sky Woman), the daughter of a Lac du Flambeau ogimaa. Bazil had been a trader with the North West Company and had worked as a clerk for the American Fur Company, and his daughter Julia attended the mission school at Mackinac. Julia's residence on the island for five years is likely why she tried to claim a portion of the annuity for the 1836 Treaty of Washington with the Michigan Anishinaabeg. Her sister Elizabeth, who also attended the AFCBM mission school at Mackinac, married American Fur Company trader Charles Borup, who filed a claim on her behalf as well as for his three children. The claim designated the wife and children as "half breeds" from the ceded territory, but otherwise they were regarded as white citizens of the United States. In the United States, the legal system of coverture allowed these white traders to claim the annuities owed their wives, as they could all other property of their spouses.[35]

35. Charles Oakes for His Wife and Child, Chippewa Claims, HBC no. 53, Charles M. Borup for His Wife and Family, Chippewa Claims, HBC no. 54, both in box 21, Lyon Papers. See also Keith R. Widder, *Battle for the Soul: Métis Children Encounter Evangelical Protestants at Mackinaw Mission, 1823–1837* (East Lansing, Mich., 1999), 6, 129; and Schenck, *All Our Relations*. For coverture, see Carole Pateman, *The Sexual Contract* (Stanford, Calif., 1988), 90–100; and Laurel A. Clark, "The Rights of a

Lyman Warren, the American Fur Company trader who lived at La Pointe and was instrumental in helping the ABCFM missionaries establish their school in this important village, filed multiple successful claims. He filed for his three wards George, Edward, and Nancy, the children of his deceased brother Truman who was married to Charlotte Cadotte, the daughter of Michel, Sr. Lyon listed the children as "3/8 Chippewa blood" and noted "their father was principal trader in the Lac du Flambeau Wisconsin and Chippeway Rivers district within the ceded country. Their mother was sent or left at La Pointe where assistance could be obtained in childbed." Warren also claimed for his wife, Mary, who Lyon recorded as "¾ Chippewa blood" and "the daughter of the late Michel Cadotte and his wife Magdalen born at La Pointe Lake Superior." He also filed claims for his six children, claims that were accepted by the senator.[36]

Pierre Cotte, the French-speaking Catholic American Fur Company trader at Fond du Lac who frequently sparred with the missionary Edmund Ely over spiritual matters, also filed a successful claim. Lyon recorded: "Pierre Cotte claims for his wife Margaret halfbreed daughter of an Indian woman from Folle Avoine. She has always resided in the Chippewa country with her husband who is at present engaged in the trade at Grand Portage in Folle Avoine country. She is born in Folle Avoine 40 years age." The senator judged this "history correct." Similarly, William Aitkin, who profited handsomely from the 1837 treaty by claiming a large portion of the annuity as compensation for debt, also cashed in on the half-breed annuity. William and the mixed-race Ojibwe community of the Mississippi and Lake Superior country had been outraged when the Prairie du Chien jury identified his murdered son Alfred as an Indian in 1837. The verdict meant that Alfred was a noncitizen with no standing in a U.S. court of law. In 1839, however, Lyon recorded, "William A Aitkin claims for his children halfbreeds by an Indian woman from Lac du Flambeau who had removed to St. Croix at the time he married her, she has since resided at Sandy Lake and Fond du Lac until last summer when she removed to La Pointe her present residence." Aitkin's claim, according to the senator, was "corroborated by testimony." William's oldest surviving son, John, also filed a successful claim for himself and his son, both of whom Lyon described as "1/2 breed." John's claim was accepted,

Florida Wife: Slavery, U.S. Expansion, and Married Women's Property Law," *Journal of Women's History*, XXII, no. 4 (Winter 2010), 39–63.

36. L. Warren for His Three Wards, Chippewa Claims, HBC no. 156, box 21, Lyon Papers.

even though he had been born at Leech Lake, because his mother, Beshi-biiaanakwad, "was a full Chippewa woman of Lac du Flambeau where she married his father Wm A Aitkin." Beshibiiaanakwad was actually a mixed-race Anishinaabe woman, also named Magdalene, but she did not attend the Mackinac mission school and did not speak English, resulting in her identification by the senator as a "full Chippewa woman." The Aitkin family, which had asserted their whiteness in 1837, claimed their identity as mixed-race Anishinaabeg in 1839.[37]

George Bonga, another American Fur Company clerk and the third "half-breed" petitioner to file a claim for the mixed-blood annuity for the 1837 treaty, was judged to have a valid claim to the ceded territory by Senator Lyon. "George Bonga halfbreed 34 years born in Folle Avoine his mother an Indian woman from Folle Avoine," Lyon wrote. He also noted: George "has always resided in the Chippeway country ceded until 1832 since when he has been in Leech Lake, claims for himself and child John 19 months old, ¾ Chippewa. The mother is a full Chippewa of Leech Lake." George filed claims for his twenty-two-year-old brother, Jack, and three teenaged sisters as well. The female siblings shared Bonga's Black father but had a different mother who lived at Lake Winnipeg, outside the ceded territory. Their claims were denied, but George's and his brother Jack's were accepted. Another brother, Stephen Bonga, also described by Lyon as a "half-breed," filed a claim. "His mother was a full Chippewa from the St. Croix river," Lyon noted; "His father (Peter Bongo a black man) was forty years in the country in the employ of the Indian traders." Stephen filed for his daughter Angelique, who lived with the family of her deceased mother at Fond du Lac. Lyon accepted both claims.[38]

Officials associated with the expansion of the Republic into the North-west married to mixed-race Native women also filed claims for the half-breed annuity. Like the fur traders, these men relied on an infrastructure dependent on the labor and linguistic and cultural expertise of mixed-race Anishinaabe women. Edmund Ely, the ABCFM missionary who ran the mission school at Fond du Lac, filed a claim for his wife. "Edmund F. Ely," Lyon recorded, "claims for Catherine Ely ½ breed aged 23 born at St. Marie where she remained for five or six years, then removed to Mackinac where she stayed until she was 18 yrs of age when she came to Fond du

37. Pierre Cotte for Wife, Chippewa Claims, HBC no. 168, Wm A Aitkin for Children, Chippewa Claims, HBC no. 74, Jno Aitkin and Children, Chippewa Claims, HBC no. 116, all in box 21, Lyon Papers.

38. The Bonga Family, Chippewa Claims, HBC no. 103 and HBC no. 110, both in box 21, Lyon Papers.

Figure 14. *Stephen Bonga*. Photograph by William D. Baldwin. Circa 1880. Minnesota Historical Society, Saint Paul

Lac and left there in 1839 for Snake River where she is now residing. He also claims for two children ¼ breeds." Lyon noted that "the mother of Mrs. Ely was a full Chippewa from the north shore of the lake," but, he concluded, "no connexion with the Indians of the ceded country by the showing of the applicant. (Rejected)."[39]

Helena Maria Evelyn Schoolcraft, the niece of Michigan's Indian agent Henry Schoolcraft, also filed a claim for the half-breed annuity of the 1837 treaty, even though she had very little connection to the Wisconsin Territory. Evelyn was the daughter of James Schoolcraft, brother of Henry, and Anna Maria Johnston, sister of Henry's wife, Jane. "Mrs. Johnston of Sault Ste. Marie," Senator Lyon wrote, "is the daughter of Waub Ojeeg, and grandmother of Evelyn and Pizhikee [Gichi-Bizhiki] of La Pointe, Lake Superior, one of the chiefs who signed the treaty under which you act, is the uncle of Mrs. Johnston, and consequently the G. G. uncle of Miss Evelyn." Although she was a resident of Mackinac Island in Michigan, according to Lyon, "Miss Evelyn rests *her* claim on the fact of her being allied to the 'blood royal' in a direct line of the chieftains, from her mother back, through Pizhikee, one of the chiefs who signed the treaty, etc. La Pointe being the center of Evelyn's ancestry, her blood relatives are numerous throughout the region of La Pointe and the interior portions of Lake Superior." Lyon also alleged that "Mrs Johnston is still consulted by Pizhikee," a dubious assertion but one that recognized the importance of both the Johnston and Schoolcraft families in the political affairs involving the United States and the Anishinaabeg. The Schoolcraft and Johnston families had received a little less than two thousand dollars from the half-breed annuity of the 1836 Treaty of Washington. Evelyn, however, had not been born when that treaty was signed, and her claim represented the family's attempt to seek compensation through the 1837 Treaty of Saint Peters. Their effort proved unsuccessful, suggesting that there were limits for mixed-race children of public officials seeking to benefit from the plunder economy of the Old Northwest.[40]

Evelyn Schoolcraft was not the only mixed-race Anishinaabe with ties to Michigan to be rejected. Margaret White Thunder was also denied. Lyon listed White Thunder with the notation "Alias Tanner." According to

39. Edmund F. Ely for Wife and Children, Chippewa Claims, HBC no. 177, box 21, Lyon Papers; Catherine Bissell Ely, Life Memoranda, American Board of Commissioners for Foreign Missions Archives, ABC 6.5.3, I, 451, Houghton Library, Harvard University, Cambridge, Mass.; Widder, *Battle for the Soul*, 141.

40. Helena Schoolcraft, Chippewa Claims, HBC no. 19, box 21, Lyon Papers; Schenck, *All Our Relations*.

Lyon: "Margaret White Thunder ¾ breed 20 yrs of age born at Leech Lake where she always resided until about 1 yr since when she removed to Lac du Flambeau with her husband James Tanner a ½ breed of the Ottawa nation whom she married about 2 yrs since at La Pointe. Her husband has been for the last 6 or 7 yrs in the employ of the Indian traders and the American Fur Company." She claimed for herself and her child John, who Lyon listed as "3/8 ths Chippewa born at Lac du Flambeau." Margaret White Thunder's husband, James, was the son of Zhaazhaawanibiisens, or John Tanner, for whom her son was named. Jean Baptiste DuBay, the mixed-race Anishinaaebe from La Pointe who led the demand for redress for Alfred Aitkin's murder, presented White Thunder's case to Senator Lyon. "History is correct," Lyon recorded, but he added that "Margaret Tanner is in no way connected with the Indians of the ceded country," and her claim was rejected. Her child, however, was admitted because he had been born at Lac du Flambeau to an Anishinaabe woman.[41]

The half-breed claims compiled and adjudicated by Senator Lyon represented a strange amalgamation of Anishinaabe notions of kinship, identity, and belonging with the evolving ideas about race in the early Republic. These treaty claims recognized Indigenous land rights, even for mixed-race Natives, while they also implemented the natural law ideology that justified Indigenous dispossession. Mixed-race Anishinaabe families negotiated their way through this amalgamation. They insisted on their right to partake in the social contract created by the expansion of the Republic into the Old Northwest. And, at times, men such as Aitkin, Warren, and Schoolcraft profited from the plunder economy that stripped their Indigenous families of their land. For many of the traders of the American Fur Company with Native families, claiming a portion of the treaty annuities designated for their Native kin represented a means of cashing out of the fur-trade economy, which could only come to an end with the advance of U.S. settlements. To a lesser extent, men such as the Cadottes and DuBay also participated in this political economy of plunder because they, like their Anishinaabe relatives, had no other choice. They could facilitate the treaties and take the money while asserting their U.S. citizenship or they could face dispossession, destitution, and removal from their homelands.

Claiming these so-called half-breed annuities compelled mixed-race traders and white traders married to Native or mixed-race women to

---

41. Margaret White Thunder and Child, Chippewa Claims, HBC no. 142, box 21, Lyon Papers; Schenck, *All Our Relations*.

conform to U.S. marriage and property laws, which had the effect of including Native-descended women and their children within the civil society of the Republic. As historian Lucy Eldersveld Murphy has argued, though, inclusion came at a price, potentially disengaging these women and their children legally and politically from Native nations, which were not subject to U.S. marriage and property laws. U.S. courts enforced the subordination of Native-descended wives married to white and mixed-race men through the system of coverture, which prevented wives from owning property or making contracts on their own. According to Murphy, "The new American territorial laws, instead of facilitating assimilation of Euro-Americans into Native communities did the opposite: they drew Native wives into the U.S. body politic, subjecting them, their children, and their property to the control of their husbands and to the new government and its courts." The price of this inclusion for Native women and their children was thus economic and legal subordination. Their Native relatives faced a similar subordination but remained outside the U.S. body politic.[42]

Indigenous Nations, Native People, and the U.S. Body Politic

By 1840, the treaty process extended the laws and political regime of the United States to all of the land first organized as the Northwest Territory. Places like northern Michigan and Wisconsin that had seemed remote and unfavorable for U.S. settlement now appeared as hospitable places for resource extraction. That year, the congressional Committee on Roads and Canals reported, "The Territory of Wiskonsan has as many lakes within her borders as the Empire State, and bids fair, from her fine forests, her copper, her lead, her iron, her zinc, her incomparable fish, her fertile soil and, above all, her proverbially salubrious climate." To facilitate the harvest of these resources, the committee called for "improving this section of the country, by construction of roads for military purposes." With the construction of these roads, "the unsold lands would soon be disposed of to industrious and hardy settlers." The report concluded with

42. Lucy Eldersveld Murphy, *Great Lakes Creoles: A French-Indian Community on the Northern Borderlands, Prairie du Chien, 1750–1860* (New York, 2014), 155–157 (quotation on 157). Bethel Saler makes a similar argument about marriage customs and the law as it relates to the conveyance of property to husbands and the establishment of patriarchal family organization modeling the customs of the Republic. See Saler, *The Settlers' Empire: Colonialism and State Formation in America's Old Northwest* (Philadelphia, 2015), 214.

a dire warning: "If Florida had been properly settled, the Indians would long since either have hushed their war whoop, or, it is more probable, would never have raised it."[43]

The committee's reference to Florida was timely. In 1835, the territory of Florida erupted in a devastating war with the Seminole Indians, who refused the attempt by U.S. authorities to force their removal to Indian Territory. Contrary to the statement issued by the congressional Committee on Roads and Canals, Florida was populated by American settlers when the war broke out. It was, in fact, demand for Native land that led the U.S. government under President Andrew Jackson to seek to negotiate a treaty with the Seminoles whereby they would cede their land in Florida and relocate west of the Mississippi. Secretary of War Lewis Cass appointed a treaty commissioner who threatened to use U.S. military force against the Seminoles if they refused to sign a treaty consenting to removal. The principal leaders of the Seminoles, including the war leader Osceola, refused to sign. The commissioner responded that he no longer recognized these individuals as part of "'the council of the nation,'" resulting in a treaty, signed by secondary leaders with questionable authority, that was widely regarded as fraudulent by the Seminoles. It also provoked the Seminoles to embark on a devastating war against the United States that captured the nation's attention owing to the loss of life and property. Aside from significant property damage and serious military losses, many American settlers, including the treaty commissioner, lost their lives. The Seminole War dispelled the idea of a perfect settler sovereignty. It exploded the mythology of the vanishing Indian and the idea of the inevitable advancement of the Republic into the unsettled territories of North America.[44]

Like the Seminoles in Florida, the Anishinaabeg constituted a large community of Native peoples who had managed to resist removal west of the Mississippi. Like Congress, Thomas Hartley Crawford, the secretary of Indian affairs, worried about the presence of a semi-autonomous Native population living on territory that the United States hoped to settle. Writing to James Doty, the governor of the Wisconsin Territory, Crawford stated, "It is the primary object to lead the Indians from their present

43. "Navigation of Rivers in Wiskonsan," H.R. Rep. No. 96, 26th Cong., 2d Sess. (1841), 1–2, 5.

44. C. S. Monaco, *The Second Seminole War and the Limits of American Aggression* (Baltimore, 2018), 49–51 (quotation on 49). Monaco described the Seminoles' war strategy as "a scorched-earth approach that would cause massive economic loses [*sic*] and destroy virtually every homestead and plantation in East Florida" (50–51).

wild lives to habits of agriculture." And, he noted, "There are Indians yet in the northwestern parts of Michigan and the northern portions of Wiskonsan . . . who ought if possible, to be induced to make a part of the projected settlement." If lands ceded in Michigan and Wisconsin became a flourishing agricultural settlement, "perhaps Indians north and north-west . . . might wisely determine to better their condition, by becoming members of the new community."[45]

In effect, Crawford thought it might be less expensive and more advantageous to the United States to grant one hundred acres of its own land to the estimated thirty-six thousand Native people who remained in the Northwest Territory. "The opinion is entertained by the head of the War Department," he wrote, "that large annuities cannot be considered a blessing to the Indians, or even an advantage." Such a thing, he asserted, would promote "the corrosion of idleness." Better they should become a part of the U.S. settlements in the Northwest, an idea that at least in theory fit with the United States' civilizing mission. In reality, this transition would require the Anishinaabeg and other Indigenous peoples to no longer exist as sovereign nations, a political dissolution they were not willing to undertake. The Seminoles were successful cattle ranchers and a vital part of the market economy in the Florida Panhandle, yet in the end they would not forfeit their sovereignty, and the United States refused to grant them a place in civil society. From a U.S. political and legal perspective, an independent Seminole nation was uncivilized or savage and could not be incorporated into the Republic.[46]

Similarly, the presence of the Anishinaabeg as a sovereign people within the territory claimed by the Republic posed a dilemma for U.S. lawmakers. Michigan's Indian agent Robert Stuart was aware that the Anishinaabeg in the state of Michigan had no intention of removing to the west. "These Indians," he informed the secretary of war, "it would seem, do not contemplate a removal before the extirpation of the five years in which they are secured in the possession of the reservations provided for them in the treaty of Michigan." He also warned the secretary, "The Ottawas and the different bands of Chippewas in Michigan and on the borders of Ohio and Indiana . . . are determined never to be removed to the west of the Missouri." As an alternative to forced migration west

45. Crawford to James D. Doty, May 10, 1841, Committee Reports and Papers of the Committee on Indian Affairs from the 27th Congress, Committee Papers, 1820–1946, RG 46: Records of the U.S. Senate, 1789–2015, NARA.

46. Ibid.; Monaco, *Second Seminole War*, 29–32.

of the Missouri, Stuart proposed that the Anishinaabeg in Michigan be removed to the territory ceded by the Dakota in the upper Mississippi Valley in 1837, "where these tribes would be abundantly clear of all foreign intercourse and influence, whereas in the present position this cannot be prevented." Stuart advised that the British post on Manitoulin Island annually attracted visits from Anishinaabeg resident in the United States, where they received gifts and affirmed their relationship with the British government of Canada. They could not remain in their home country because of the increasing settler demand for their land, and it was only a matter of time before they sought out British protection; "a strong savage force will thus be assembled close to our line, ready and willing at any moment to ravage our sparse and unprotected settlements." Indeed, the Seminoles' relationship with the Spanish in Cuba allowed them access to weapons that fueled their conflict with the United States. The secretary of Indian affairs would have been keenly aware of this fact and its parallel to the Anishinaabe relationship with British Canada.[47]

Secretary of War John Spencer sought the advice of the American Fur Company about the idea of removing the Anishinaabeg from the Michigan Territory. He wrote to Hercules Dousman and Henry Sibley, both Michigan-born partners of the company who resided at posts in Prairie Du Chien and Saint Peters, respectively. He asked if the Anishinaabeg could be removed west of the Missouri. The traders responded, "These tribes have expressed, one and all, a firm determination not to remove West of the Missouri, and we verily believe that they would run the hazard of utter extermination rather than consent to any proposition of this kind." The secretary also raised the possibility of removal to the country ceded by the Dakota and whether that would leave the Anishinaabeg susceptible to influence from the British at Red River. Dousman and Sibley indicated that at the time of the 1836 treaty the Anishinaabeg had been willing to contemplate a removal to land on the Mississippi above the Rum River at the center of present-day Minnesota. "The British power in the North," they wrote, "is exceedingly circumscribed, if we except the great influence they maintain over their Indians." The "Half-breeds," on the other hand, are "exceedingly turbulent, dissatisfied with the Hudson's Bay Company, and much more to be dreaded by that association than by

47. Robert Stuart to John Spencer, Feb. 14, 1842, Committee Reports and Papers of the Committee on Indian Affairs from the 27th Congress, RG 46. For the significance of the Seminole relationship with Cuba, see Monaco, *Second Seminole War,* 52, 126–127.

us." The traders also asserted, "We do not believe that these men have any particular attachment to the British or any other government." The accuracy of these sentiments was reflected in the fear that the government of British Canada expressed in response to the Indian Liberating Army, which marched to Red River in 1837. When this army of mixed-race Native soldiers disbanded en route to Red River, the Hudson's Bay Company nevertheless made trading positions available to its officers. British authorities feared dissent and even rebellion among the growing mixed-race community at Hudson's Bay's Red River colony.[48]

U.S. officials thus worried that the Anishinaabeg in Michigan's Upper Peninsula might defect to British Canada and impede the ability of the United States to extract resources from the region. Accordingly, in 1842, Congress appointed Michigan's Indian agent Robert Stuart as a treaty commissioner to negotiate with the Anishinaabeg "for the extinguishment of their titles to their lands." Secretary of Indian Affairs Crawford informed Stuart, "There are valuable minerals on the land that the Chippewas are possessed of, (and they are the only Indians that hold any land in Michigan), which extend westward, however, of that state." "It is important, it strikes me, that we should have the uninterrupted control of the whole southern shore of Lake Superior for commercial and other purposes, as well as farming."[49]

Crawford foresaw two impediments to the proposed treaty negotiation. "It is probable," he wrote, "some provision will be sought to be made for the payment of the debts due by the Chippewas." He objected to this practice, a hallmark of the plunder economy in the Old Northwest, and informed Stuart, "If you find that you cannot make a treaty without providing for their debts, you are instructed to investigate them before the treaty is concluded." Regarding the issue of using treaties to pay "Indian debts," he noted, "the Indians will be less likely to admit claims for when a certain sum is set apart for debts they regard it as gone from them." The other worry was the inability of the government to forcibly remove the Anishinaabeg from land not coveted by settlers. "There must be a stipulation," he wrote, "that they will remove from the land ceded to that which will remain to the Chippewas west of the cession, which will entitle the whole band to participate in the annuity etc, that shall be raised by the treaty." However, "it is not likely that it will be necessary for them to

48. Hercules Dousman and Henry Sibley to Spencer, Feb. 18, 1842, Committee Reports and Papers of the Committee on Indian Affairs from the 27 Congress, RG 46.
49. Crawford to Stuart, Aug. 1, 1842, ibid.

remove for a considerable time." Since it was impossible to know when demand for their land would require their removal, "their removal and obligation to go, it should be stipulated, shall be at the pleasure of the President." He concluded that "the mines that are the object of the cession will be opened probably very soon, under such laws as it shall be the pleasure of the congress to pass on the subject."[50]

Crawford's instructions represented an attempt to consolidate and circumscribe the political authority of the Anishinaabeg. He linked the promise of annuity payments to doodemag in the east, in Michigan's Upper Peninsula, to their future removal to unceded Native territory southwest of Lake Superior. This removal, he argued, "would be making the land west of the cession common property." In other words, moving onto land ceded by the Dakota southwest of Lake Superior or onto the unceded land of the western Anishinaabeg in Wisconsin would unite the doodemag into a single political entity for the purpose of treaty negotiations and annuity payments. This consolidation fit with the political desire of the federal government to force the Anishinaabeg to treat with the United States as a single nation, as opposed to allied but autonomous bands.[51]

"Your Commissioner Came and Took
Our Lands Away with Him"

Treaty commissioner Robert Stuart called together the Anishinaabe doodemag from the Lake Superior country and the Mississippi Valley late in the fall of 1842 to negotiate what would become known as the Treaty of La Pointe. He did not provide Secretary Crawford with a narrative account of the council, but Leonard Wheeler, the ABCFM missionary stationed at La Pointe, had his translator, Henry Blatchford, keep a journal of the proceedings. Blatchford estimated attendance at approximately four thousand Anishinaabeg. When all the expected doodemag arrived, their respective ogimaag assembled as a council to hear Stuart speak. Stuart presented them with a large keg of tobacco and informed them he had met the previous year with their "great father" in Washington, D.C. "He knows you are poor and have but very little to support your women and children," and "has sent me to see what can be done for your benefit." Following this statement, however, Stuart told the ogimaag, "By the treaty you made with Gov Cass, several years ago, you gave permission to your great father to carry away all the minerals that were on your lands they

50. Ibid.
51. Ibid.

therefore do not belong to you." White settlers now wanted these minerals, "but your father wishes to pay you something for your lands." Stuart promised the ogimaag goods, provisions, farmers to teach them to "cultivate the soil," and money for schools. "Some of you think you may live as formerly," he asserted, "but do you not see that the great spirit is changing all things about you? Once the whole country was owned and inhabited by Indians, but now white men have almost the whole country." White settlers, he declared, were everywhere, like pigeons. "But if you educate your children they will become as rich and wise as the whites. They will learn to worship the great spirit aright."[52]

Stuart thus offered the standard combination of cash annuities, goods, and provisions, but he also emphasized the social contract embedded within the policy of the civilizing mission. Protestant Christianity and education, he instructed the Anishinaabe ogimaag, represented the key to the future for their children. He also informed the leaders that they had forfeited their mineral rights when they signed the 1826 treaty at Fond du Lac with Lewis Cass. Like the 1836 Michigan treaty, however, Stuart promised the Lake Superior Ojibweg they could remain on ceded lands until the United States and the mining companies required it. "The great benefit your father expects to derive from these lands is from the minerals that are on them," Stuart declared. Their father did not wish for them "to be without a home," however, and therefore, as a gift, reserved lands for them around Fond du Lac and Sandy Lake. The terms of the treaty were that the whites would take their land and their minerals, and, Stuart explicitly stated, "This will be done whether you sell your lands or not." The Lake Superior ogimaag responded to Stuart with silence. As they would tell the commissioner of Indian affairs a little more than two decades after the treaty was ratified, "The Chiefs along the Lake Shore did not say a word, not being willing to sell or make any agreement."[53]

Wisconsin governor James Doty had been confronted with a similar nonresponse at Saint Peters in 1837. Neither Doty nor Stuart, however, recognized the significance of this response in terms of the diplomatic protocols of the Anishinaabeg. In fact, Stuart ended the council with a

52. Henry Blatchford's journal, 3–4, enclosed with Leonard Wheeler to Greene, May 3, 1843, ABCFM, box 1. The journal was sent to the ABCFM along with this letter one year after the treaty council.

53. Ibid., 5–6; "Statement of the Treaties between the Chippewas and the United States, from 1825 to 1864, from the Chippewa Standpoint, as Presented to the Commissioner of Indian Affairs," 1864, Small Collections, Oversize, file 40, Archives Division, State Historical Society of Wisconsin, Madison.

threat: "I desire to see you and benefit you if you wish me to, but if you refuse now it will be a long time before your great Father will make you another offer." In other words, Stuart made it clear that the Anishinaabeg had already forfeited their mineral rights and that this treaty represented their only chance for compensation for this loss. He then called on the ogimaag to divide up his gift of tobacco and asked them to return to council tomorrow with an answer.[54]

When the council reconvened the following day, the ogimaag voiced their skepticism, disappointment, and anger. Zhingobiins (The Little Balsam Fir), the hereditary civil leader of Fond du Lac, was the first to speak. After shaking hands with Commissioner Stuart, he stated, "We now understand the purpose you have come for and we don't want to displease you." He commented on the large number of people gathered at council to hear his words and then continued, "I want to know what our great Father will give us for our lands." He admonished Stuart not to "tell a lie"; "I want to see the writing and who it is that gave our great father permission to take our minerals." Stuart responded by reading article 3 of the 1826 Treaty of Fond du Lac, which gave the United States permission to "carry away any minerals from any part of the country." He also read the names of the ogimaag who signed the document. According to Blatchford's journal, "The chiefs answered that the Indians had been deceived." Following this exchange, Gichi-Bizhiki, the principal ogimaa from La Pointe, rose to speak. He remarked affirmatively on the promise to provide teachers, missionaries, and a blacksmith. He said he would not repeat the words spoken by Zhingobiins but rather that "he thought the commissioner was urging them forward a little too fast in their deliberations." Of this second council, Blatchford wrote in his journal, "Their speeches today were rather indefinite." Stuart then dismissed the ogimaag and pledged that when they reconvened he "would tell them what gov would give for their lands."[55]

The ogimaag returned to council two days later. Before hearing Stuart's terms, they raised the issue of their debt with the traders and

54. Blatchford's journal, 4–5, enclosed with Wheeler to Greene, May 3, 1843, ABCFM, box 1.

55. Ibid., 6–8. Article 3 of the 1826 "Treaty with the Chippewas" signed at Fond du Lac stated, "The Chippewa tribe grant to the government of the United States, the right to search for, and carry away any metals or minerals, from any part of their country. But this grant is not to affect the title of the land, nor existing jurisdiction over it." See "Treaty with the Chippewa, 1826," in Charles J. Kappler, comp. and ed., *Indian Affairs: Laws and Treaties*, II, *Treaties* (Washington, D.C., 1904), 269.

Figure 15. *Chief Buffalo* [Gichi-Bizhiki]. N.d. Over-painted enlargement,
possibly from a double portrait (possibly an ambrotype).
Wisconsin Historical Society, WHS-3957

compensation for their mixed-race relatives. Gichi-Bizhiki told Stuart,
"Father, our traders are such a class of people we cannot live one winter
without them." And "our children the half breeds also, we want to have
provided for." White Crow, the Lac du Flambeau ogimaa, took a more
contentious position. He stated that he would now speak to the president
of the United States and to the traders and half-breeds. "We want nothing wrong on paper," he declared; "You may think I am troublesome but
the way the treaty was made at St. Peters, we think was wrong, we want
nothing of the kind again." White Crow then proclaimed, "I have raised
the half breeds, and I want you to provide for them, we all eat out of
one dish, we are like one family." The traders, he complained, had over-
charged them for years, and he did not wish to provide for them, "but of
late years, they have had losses, and I wish those debts to be paid."[56]

56. Blatchford's journal, 9–10, enclosed with Wheeler to Greene, May 3, 1843,
ABCFM, box 1.

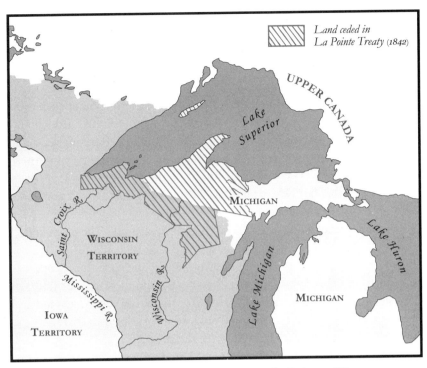

Map 7. Treaty of La Pointe, 1842. Drawn by Rebecca Wrenn

In the end, Stuart agreed to compensation for both the traders and the "half breeds" as part of the treaty. He informed Crawford that he paid out "ultimately $75,000 for debts only, and the Indian annuities were somewhat increased so as to enable them annually to aid their half breed relatives." He thus increased the annual cash payment with the expectation that the ogimaag would divert some of this money to their mixed-race relatives if they so desired. The treaty ceded all of the land on the southern shore of Lake Superior from Fond du Lac through the Keweenaw Peninsula to the territory ceded by the Michigan Anishinaabeg, with all the land west of Fond du Lac "to belong to the Indians in common." Stuart concluded the council by restating, "You are to have the privilege of living on your lands to hunt and fish, till your great father requires you to remove, you understand he does not want the land now, it is only the minerals he wants." Stuart wrote to Crawford that "these Indians are through our late efforts, entirely reconciled among themselves, and highly delighted with the kind and generous dealings of the government toward them." Yet Blatchford's journal reported that "White Crow approached the business of signing the treaty with a good deal of reluctance." He also noted that Gichi-Bizhiki "came up and thinking the commissioner too much in haste to have him sign his name, said 'My Father what is the reason you wish to stop my mouth.'"[57]

Shortly after Stuart departed with the signed treaty, the ogimaag Gichi-Bizhiki, White Crow, and Martin sent or dictated letters, or speeches, to Alfred Brunson, the subagent at La Pointe, to protest the coercive and hurried nature of the negotiation. In a letter dictated to the American Fur Company trader Lyman Warren, who acted as a translator and witness at the treaty council, Gichi-Bizhiki stated, "I am very sorry for that treaty we made here this fall." He explained, "I thought to make a very good one, and spoke always to that purpose, but my fellow chiefs did not agree with me, and the commissioner would not listen to us at all." The ogimaa had requested that Warren write to Brunson so that he could ask the president of the United States "whether it was his will and wish thus to oppress his children in this remote country." Gichi-Bizhiki dictated this letter in October, approximately three months after the treaty was concluded and a few weeks before Stuart wrote to Crawford informing him that the Lake Superior Ojibweg were "delighted" with the proceedings.[58]

White Crow, the principal ogimaa of Lac du Flambeau, made a similar appeal to Brunson on December 18, 1842, at a council at Chippewa Falls. He, too, addressed the president through the agent, and he accused the chief executive of the United States of neglect. "My father," he began, "we have been orphans for a while, having no father." Not only were the Ojibwe children without a father, but they were also ignored. "I know that what we say to our father is thrown away," he said; "it never reaches the ear of our grand father." Then White Crow stated bluntly:

> I did not want to sell any more of my land, but I was told that it made no difference whether I did or not, if the majority of the chiefs signed the treaty our grand father would take the land. But I did not agree to remove, nor to sell unless my *relations* of Indian blood were

57. Stuart to Crawford, Nov. 19, 1842, Committee Reports and Papers of the Committee on Indian Affairs from the 27th Congress, RG 46; Blatchford's journal, 14–16, enclosed with Wheeler to Greene, May 3, 1843, ABCFM, box 1.

58. "From Buffalo, Head Chief at La Pointe," Oct. 29, 1842, enclosed in Alfred Brunson to Doty, Jan. 6, 1843 (which is enclosed in Brunson to Spencer, Jan. 8, 1843), La Pointe Agency, 1831–1880, Letters Received, 1824–1880, RG 75: Records of the Bureau of Indian Affairs, 1793–1999, M234, roll 388, 573, NARA.

provided for. But I am told since the treaty that I *must* remove when *my grand* father wants me to, and yet that no provision is made for my relations. (raising his voice) I speak louder to my grand father, that I do not consider my land sold unless something is put into the hands of my relations. And what I say is the voice of all my people.

Martin, the ogimaa at Lac Courte Oreilles, also dictated a letter for sub-agent Brunson to forward to the president. He affirmed the words of White Crow, and he reported that two of the ogimaag from his doodem had "refused to touch the pen" because they felt their "half breed relations" had not been properly provided for under the terms of the treaty. Martin asserted that he had signed the treaty with the understanding that all his relations would be provided for, including his mixed-race relatives. He concluded, "We have no objection to the white mans working the mines, and the timber and making farms, But we reserve the Birch bark and ceder, for canoes." He also claimed "the Rice and the Sugar tree and the priviledge of hunting without being disturbed by the whites," and he called for the half-breeds to be paid, not from their annuity, but from the president, who "can better afford to pay them than we can."[59]

Gichi-Bizhiki dictated a second letter to the president through sub-agent Brunson on January 5, 1843, that registered his growing distress at the outcome of the treaty negotiated by Stuart. He began, "I want you to open your ears and listen to me attentively." He then spoke of the importance of the village of La Pointe and of Shagwaamikong, the small peninsula that stretched across the top of a bay on the southwestern shore of Lake Superior. "I have always had great hopes for my tribe," Gichi-Bizhiki declared, "for this place, which you are old enough to know is the place from which all the Indians that sit by my side (meaning all the Chippewas on this side of the Lake) sprang." This was the place, he asserted, where the Ojibweg became a people and it was the resting place for the bones of their ancestors. Then Gichi-Bizhiki suggested he was losing the hope he once felt. "*Father:* it is now midnight. It is as yesterday that your commissioner set his foot on my land." The commissioner spoke of the copper "strewn along the shore of this Lake. He told us that we had given it away." He then stated bluntly, "Of that transaction I know nothing." With this speech, Gichi-Bizhiki declared, he had spoken more than he had at

59. "White Crow, Head Chief of the Lac Flambeau Bands," Dec. 18, 1842, ibid., 573–574; "Martin, Head Chief of the Ottawa or Lac Courte Oreille Bands Said," n.d., ibid., 574.

council, where the commissioner, he complained, prevented him from speaking his mind. The ogimaa then addressed the president in writing as if he were seated at council: "I shall now say a few words to you in regard to my half breeds. They grow from my side. My blood flows in their veins. I pity them, for in this treaty nothing is given them. My grand father gives them nothing—my heart aches on their account." He intimated that he suspected the traders failed to properly convey his words and in this manner deprived his mixed-race relations of the compensation they deserved. Gichi-Bizhiki concluded, *"Father,* Your commissioner came and took our lands away with him, and we could not say, no."[60]

"The Original Lords ... of the Soil"
Alfred Brunson sent these extraordinary letters to the U.S. secretary of war, John Spencer. He also sent copies to the governor of the Wisconsin Territory, James Doty, the man who had once served as a lawyer in the murder trial of Ketawkah at Detroit in 1826. In addition to forwarding the speeches, Brunson wrote an extensive letter to Doty detailing his interactions with the ogimaag and the "half breeds" following the conclusion of the treaty. He described Indigenous peoples as "the original Lords as well as occupants of the soil," and he included mixed-race Natives in this category. "The claim of half breeds to indemnity for their lands, he argued, "is based upon identically the same ground as that of the Indians or whole bloods: that is, of blood, birth upon, and occupancy of the soil." He noted that "by the laws of Nations, *civilized* governments claim a right to govern and control the lands and countries of discovered or conquered un civilized tribes." But in such cases, "these un civilized tribes are admitted to have the right of occupancy, and when they become *civi*lized, their right to the soil and to self government is acknowledged."[61]

Echoing the language of the Northwest Ordinance, if not the actual history of the United States, Brunson claimed that the Republic had always respected Native title and right of occupation to their homelands. "From the commencement of the operations of our gov't," he wrote, "the right of the Indians to the *occupancy* and *control* of the soil has been admitted, and in no instance has it been reverted from them without remuneration." Brunson it appears, imagined North America as something other than unsettled wilderness. He imagined something unthinkable

60. "In Council at La Pointe, Jany 5th, 1843, Buffalo, Head Chief of This Band Spoke as Follows," ibid., 574–575.
61. Brunson to Doty, Jan. 6, 1843, ibid., 556–557.

for most settlers. Brunson understood North America to be the domain of Native peoples, and although the agent believed civilized governments possessed the right to govern uncivilized Indigenous nations, they could not dispossess them without fair compensation. Subagent Brunson recognized the Wisconsin Territory as the homeland of the Lake Superior Ojibweg.[62]

Brunson then offered a critique of the political economy of plunder that accompanied the treaty process. He acknowledged to the governor that the argument against making payments to the "half breeds" was that "it does them little or no good, but falls into the hands of speculation"—the result, he complained, of providing the mixed-race Aniashinaabeg with a single cash payment instead of an annuity. They were left vulnerable to greedy white settlers. "The fault, in part, tho' unintentional," he wrote, "lay with the Govt. in appointing the commissioner; who, it is known, connived at the schemes of the speculators, if they did not abet and share with them in the profits of the enterprise." Brunson thus accused Stuart, a one-time employee of the American Fur Company, of conspiring with the traders to profit from the treaty. To sidestep this problem, Brunson proposed an amendment be added to the treaty granting the mixed-race relatives of the treaty signers a ten-thousand-dollar cash annuity for twenty years. "By this mode of distribution," he wrote, "the payments can be made by the proper agent without the intervention and expense of a commissioner, and the speculator will have no inducement to gnash at their pittance." Neither the governor nor the Office of Indian Affairs responded to this request.[63]

In addition to the scheming and speculation of the traders and treaty commissioner, Brunson objected to the meager annuities offered to the Anishinaabeg. He noted first that in 1837 the Dakota ceded four million acres, which with the cost of their annuity, provisions, goods, agricultural implements, and cash payouts to "half and quarter breeds" and traders amounted to twenty-five cents per acre. By the terms of the treaty with the Ojibweg signed at Saint Peters in 1837, in contrast, "the Chippewas will have received *$870,000* for 11,000,000, acres of land, which is *less* than 8 cents per acre." The treaty negotiated with the Ojibweg at La Pointe in 1842 ceded twelve million acres. The cash payout, including goods, provisions, money for schools and agriculture as well as debt payments to traders and added compensation for mixed-race relatives over

62. Ibid., 557.
63. Ibid., 558.

the twenty-five years of the annuity, amounted to "a little over 7. cts per acre." Brunson argued that such a low payment was unjust. "The Chippewa lands are less broken, even including the margin of Lake Superior," he wrote. "The soil is of equal quality, and in addition, they contain most of the Pine timber and all the copper. They also border upon the greatest lake in the world, which has a fishery second only to that of New England." This sentiment was echoed by William Boutwell, the missionary residing in the ceded territory. He informed the ABCFM that the Saint Croix lumber company "is doing an immense business." "They have about 12,000 logs on the ice at this place, which according to their estimate will make more than 8,000,000 feet of lumber." The timber boom, he concluded, brought "men from almost every state in the union." In other words, everyone except the Ojibweg was making money from the ceded territory. Moreover, Brunson argued that, in addition to being rich in resources, Wisconsin possessed natural advantages in transportation and communication afforded by the Great Lakes, which meant that the ceded land would increase in value as it was developed and integrated into the U.S. economy.[64]

Furthermore, given that the goal of U.S. policy was to civilize the Indians, they required the assistance and cooperation of their mixed-race relatives. Brunson asserted that "those who contribute to accomplish this object do a public service," and "the half breeds have done this." He informed Governor Doty, "The half breeds have done much to promote the civilization of the natives, by encouraging, sustaining, and in some instances introducing missionaries into the country, whose benevolent efforts are doing much to advance this desirable object." "Every half breed who lives in habits of civilization, is half an Indian civilized," Brunson concluded. Missionary Sherman Hall, writing to the ABCFM in 1842 from La Pointe, where Brunson was stationed, made a similar observation. "The fur trade," he wrote, "has been the occasion of introducing a considerable large number of French Cannadians into this country in years past." The Canadians "are invariably Catholics" and "have intermarried extensively with the Indians, and the consequence is, that there is getting to be a pretty population of mixed blood." Like Brunson, Hall argued that working with the mixed-race Anishinaabeg was the key to advancing the cause of civilization among their relatives who identified exclusively as Natives. "Perhaps you think we devote more of our attention

64. Ibid., 559 ("half and quarter breeds"), 561 ("$870,000"), 562 ("less broken"); William Boutwell to Greene, Mar. 6, 1842, ABCFM, box 1.

to the half breed population than we ought," he wrote, "but I would say in reply that I regard them as much the objects of missionary effort, as the Indians." He conceded that, being Catholic, they were nominally Christian, but their character was no better than their Native relatives. "They are virtually one with the Indians. They are one in language and feeling, and in many habits of life. They will always live among them and mix with them."[65]

Hall echoed the language of Gichi-Bizhiki, who declared that the "half-breeds" "grow from my side" and his blood flowed through their veins. The ogimaa, like the missionary, believed that the mixed-race Anishinaabeg and their Native kin were one and the same. They were all Anishinaabeg. Hall seemed to see the mixed-race population as fundamentally Native, however, and therefore appropriate subjects of his missionary work. Brunson, in contrast, viewed whiteness as opposed to Indianness as the thing that defined the "half breeds." He explained this quality to Governor Doty: "The very existance of white blood in a person seems to predispose him to civilization."[66]

Brunson saw intermarriage in gendered terms, as an institution that connected Native women to men of European descent. In his letter, he reminded the governor, "The history of Poccahontus and the effects of her attachments to and connections with the whites, is too well known to require a repetition." He then noted the long history of "French Settlers upon our Lakes and rivers, who mingled, mixed and intermarried with the natives till very little pure Eropeon blood flows in their veins." Similarly, the traders "who retained and instilled into their offspring the seeds of civilization, and its fruit is visible in wasting and wearing away their savage ferocity, and changing the aborigenes into something more like human beings." From this perspective, Indianness denied Native peoples their full humanity. The U.S. government, however, benefited from what he imagined as the civilizing influence of mixed-race Natives, who partly humanized their fully Indigenous relatives.[67]

The allusion to Pocahontas, like the designation of Evelyn Schoolcraft as an Indian of "blood royal," was a standard trope of the conquest narrative at the heart of the idea of the discovery of the New World. Marriage

65. Brunson to Doty, Jan. 6, 1843, La Pointe Agency, RG 75, M234, roll 388, 563–564; Hall to Greene, July 8, 1842, ABCFM, box 1.

66. Brunson to Doty, Jan. 6, 1843, La Pointe Agency, RG 75, M234, roll 388, 564.

67. Ibid., 565. For Pocahontas and the idea of Native women and the civilizing mission, see Rayna Green, "The Pocahontas Perplex: The Image of Indian Women in American Culture," *Massachusetts Review*, XVI (1975), 685–714.

to an Indian princess signified a union or merging of the nobility of the Old and New Worlds. It was a rhetorical device by which the European invader could claim or co-opt an Indigenous / New World identity. In this regard, men of European descent who married Native women advanced U.S. Indian policy by contributing to the civilization of the Indians. They also connected the peoples of the Republic to "the original Lords . . . of the soil," allowing American settlers to claim a New World identity that was not only Indigenous but also civilized—an identity that actual Native people could not claim from the perspective of settler colonial ideology.

Regardless of the interpretation of intermarriage and mixed-race identity advanced by Brunson, the Anishinaabeg did have a long history of using marriage to incorporate outsiders into their communities. Intermarriage was a typical feature of the fur trade throughout North America. As the missionary Sherman Hall suggested, this practice worked in a way that assimilated outsiders—in the Great Lakes, predominantly French-Canadian men—into the culture and communities of the Anishinaabeg. In the mid-nineteenth century, however, these marriages increasingly separated Native women from their Indigenous communities legally and economically and drew their mixed-race families into the body politic of the settler state. The missionary Edmund Ely, who frequently struggled to provide for himself before marriage, casually informed the ABCFM in the fall of 1843, "The goods payment will be made this week, and the cash on Monday or Tuesday next. . . . My family will probably share with the half breeds and Indians in the payment." He noted that the amount of goods and cash expected by the Anishinaabeg at La Pointe would be small. It is worth observing, however, that in the past Ely depended on the generosity of Natives and traders to supplement the money and supplies provided by the ABCFM. Access to treaty annuities through his Anishinaabe wife and children provided the missionary with greater economic stability and connected the mission to the Native community it served.[68]

The Rights of Half-Breeds

In spite of Edmund Ely's connection through marriage to the Anishinaabeg, however, he remained a cultural outsider. Of necessity, the fur traders engaged in exchanges of goods and services with their Native relatives and trading partners. They thus had to establish reciprocity or a mutual sense of obligation, providing food and tobacco as gifts regularly to

68. Edmund Ely to Greene, Sept. 21, 1843, ABCFM, box 1. For incorporating outsiders through marriage, see, for example, Susan Sleeper-Smith, *Indian Women and*

Native relatives but also to the families of the hunters on whom they depended for their livelihood. Ely, because he did not depend on trading, felt no compulsion to give gifts or even extend generosity by sharing his food. He believed in self-reliance and private property as Christian virtues and regarded Anishinaabe attempts to solicit gifts as a form of begging and as uncivilized behavior. As a result, Ely and his family never fully integrated socially into the Anishishinaabe community at Fond du Lac.[69]

That said, Ely's Native wife Catherine served as a mediator, connecting the social world of the mixed-race Anishinaabeg with the expanding civil society of the U.S. Republic. In the same letter that informed the ABCFM about the impending annuity payment, Ely advised the board that should they commit resources to establish another station inland from the post at La Pointe, "Mrs. Ely could also be more advantageously stationed as interpreter, in connexion with one of our better educated sisters from the east." He also noted that any missionary who replaced him "would find Mrs. Boutwell a valuable helper." Indeed, David Greene, the corresponding secretary for the ABCFM, in a letter to Boutwell wrote regarding his wife, "Let me say for her encouragement, that I do not know of a missionary female who has visited our vicinity for a long time who has left a better impression or is remembered with more interest." Esther Boutwell, like Catherine Ely, attended the mission school at Mackinac. Their missionary husbands found their work unsustainable without the domestic labor and interpreter skills of their mixed-race Anisahinaabe wives. As the United States sought to incorporate trading posts and mixed-race Native families into the body politic of the Republic, it, too, required the mediation of Native women.[70]

The failure to include this community in the ongoing relationship with

<hr />

French Men: Rethinking Cultural Encounter in the Western Great Lakes (Amherst, Mass., 2001); and Sylvia Van Kirk, *Many Tender Ties: Women in Fur-Trade Society, 1670–1870*, 1st American ed. (Norman, Okla., 1983). For marriage diminishing the standing of Indigenous women in the United States, see Murphy, *Great Lakes Creoles*, 157. As historian Catherine J. Denial has noted, "Women's labor added economic value to the supplies each mission received." See Denial, *Making Marriage: Husbands, Wives, and the American State in Dakota and Ojibwe Country* (Saint Paul, Minn., 2013), 65.

69. For example, Ely generally refused to feed visitors. See Schenck, ed., *Ojibwe Journals of Edmund F. Ely*, June 11, 1836, 221.

70. Ely to Greene, Sept. 21, 1843, ABCFM, box 1; Greene to W. T. Boutwell, Jan. 18, 1844, ibid. For the importance of mixed-race women as interpreters and cultural brokers, see Murphy, *Great Lakes Creoles*, 166.

the federal government established through the annuity process, Subagent Brunson argued, could be disastrous. "They at present hold the balance of power with the Indians on these Lakes," and, he warned Governor Doty in that same letter of Janury 6, "their influence is such that they can, in a great measure, controll them for war or peace, and in favour of ours or a foreign Gov't." Brunson then invoked the specter of the Seminole War. "The Florida Indians," he wrote, "did not intend to commence and continue a war, when they first refused to abide by the treaty with which they were dissatisfied." Just as the Seminoles went to war rather than submit to a treaty that called for their removal, the Lake Superior Ojibweg "as they have declared to me in council, refuse to remove when required so to do and if coerced into the measure will most likely breed another war." The 1842 treaty, concluded Brunson, was negotiated by the traders "interested in the *debts* to be paid, fearing no further attempt to treat and to pay them would be made for several years." The ogimaag signed the treaty, Brunson wrote; "They yielded. . . . It was all done on the spur of the moment. They were hurried into the measure without calm reflection, and the commissioner was not out of sight before they deeply regretted it, as Buffalos letter to Mr. Warren marked."[71]

When Stuart learned about Brunson's letter questioning the justness of the 1842 treaty and reporting the unhappiness of the ogimaag and their mixed-race relatives, he utterly rejected this interpretation of events. Stuart wrote to Secretary Crawford complaining that Brunson "is inexperienced, and for the time being, in danger of allowing himself to be imposed upon by a few *whining* half-breeds, who have got the Buffalo [Gichi-Bizhiki], a superannuated chief, and a few other Indians, some what under their influence." The subagent, he explained, was being manipulated. "When negotiating the treaty last fall," he explained, "I had some difficulty, (as I informed you.) in repressing the exactions of these half breeds; and had to read the old Buffalo a serious lecture on his conduct." He admonished him for corresponding with the British and even threatened to have the ogimaa "deposed." This threat, he reported, "suddenly transformed him into an excellent Republican, avowing unbounded love for the Long Knives (Americans) and so we parted." Stuart's account of the treaty negotiations contrasts dramatically with the council record kept by Henry Blatchford and the letter Gichi-Bizhiki dictated to Lyman Warren.[72]

71. Brunson to Doty, Jan. 6, 1843, La Pointe Agency, RG 75, M234, roll 388, 566–567 ("balance of power"), 570 (*"debts"*).

72. Stuart to Crawford, Feb. 28, 1843, La Pointe Agency, RG 75, M234, roll 388, 693.

Perhaps more significant than accusing Brunson of being gullible, Stuart challenged his understanding of the rights of "half breeds." In a letter sent directly to Brunson, Stuart wrote, "The half breeds have so long been accustomed to receive these *gratuities* that they look upon them now as a positive right; when in reality no such right exists." He then stated unequivocally, "The lands belong to the Indians, and when they sell, they have a right either to withhold, or give a portion to the half breeds." Shortly after writing to Brunson, Stuart wrote a second letter to Crawford indicating that he would not reply to Brunson's "disquisition on the Law of Nations"; "the rights he claims for half breeds, as well as the virtues and influence he attributes to them, are *superlatively magnified*." He asked the commissioner, "Should not Mr. Brunson be *strictly admonished* that he must never entertain nor yield to foolish complaints, or clamours of discontent against the policy of the Government, but on the contrary admonish all against such a course"?[73]

Brunson, however, continued to write to U.S. officials raising questions about the fairness of the 1842 treaty. On July 19, 1843, he sent another letter to Governor Doty, this time expressing his regret that Stuart felt compelled to complain about his behavior in office. He insisted, however, that "the uniform testimony of those who witnessed the whole transaction goes to show that the Indians *did not act free* and *voluntary,* but felt themselves pressed into the measure by a combination of circumstances which they could not controll." The Indians "wanted to sell, if they could get their price. But this was not offered, and they were compelled to take less." He also defended his assertion of half-breed rights, noting that "Mr. Stuart in his 'suggestion' admits their right to payment by suggesting that they be paid, in common with those of full blood."[74]

In a letter written the next day, Brunson asked Stuart to send U.S. soldiers to oversee the annuity payment at La Pointe. "You think there is no danger from the half breeds," he told Stuart, "but I do, and if you saw and heard what I do I can but think you would think so too." Brunson's interpreter had repeatedly warned him to expect trouble from the half-breeds. "A quarter breed, who married a half breed," he wrote, "told me, that if you came here you would be tarred and feathered, and the goods and money would be seized at any rate." He worried that to be "robbed of public funds" in such a manner would undermine his authority. "I think

73. Extract of a letter from Stuart to Brunson, Mar. 10, 1843, ibid., 701; Stuart to Crawford, Mar. 15, 1843, ibid., 696 *("magnified")*, 698–699 *("admonished")*.

74. Brunson to Doty, July 19, 1843, ibid., 581 ("uniform testimony"), 582 ("full blood").

it most prudent for myself and safe for the govt," he concluded, "to have troops on the ground." Stuart responded to Brunson by reminding him of his thirty years of "experience among these Indians and half-breeds." He then sternly admonished Brunson, "I beg of you for your own sake, and for the interests of both the gov't and the Indians, to discourage and frown upon the subtle whinings, or bombastic threats of either Indians or half breeds. If you too patiently listen, or *appear* anxious and inquisitive to find out their rumored designs, it will engender devious and wickedness they otherwise would never think of." Stuart then warned Brunson to be wary of his interpreter, who was himself a "half breed"; "they understand the power and energy of the govt, too well to hurt a hair of the head of even a citizen."[75]

Indigenous Land, Black Lives, and the Creation of White Wealth

These exchanges between Alfred Brunson and Robert Stuart, and between these agents and the governor of the Wisconsin Territory and the secretary of Indian affairs, underscored the precarious status of the mixed-race Anishinaabeg in the Northwest Territory. As the Republic advanced, establishing new territories and states, their status vacillated between U.S. citizens and racialized colonial subjects. Perhaps worse, men like Stuart refused to recognize their legal claims and land rights as Indigenous people, even when he excluded them from the category of citizen based on their perceived racial identity. Similarly, Stuart's assertion that Gichi-Bizhiki had been transformed into an "excellent Republican" signaled an alliance between Anishinaabe leadership and the U.S. settler state that belied the profound alienation from the ideology of the Republic felt by the ogimaa and his people as well as their political exclusion from the social contract of the United States.

In the first decades following the American Revolution, politicians and policymakers believed that Indigenous nations did not belong in the Republic, but they waivered on the inclusion and racial categorization of mixed-race Native peoples. This was particularly true in a region like the Northwest Territory, where the policy of Indian removal was not fully implemented and the federal government needed the cooperation of men engaged in the fur trade, many of whom married Native women, had mixed-race children, or were themselves mixed-race. The fur trade

75. Brunson to Stuart, July 20, 1843, ibid., 738–739; Stuart to Brunson, Aug. 30, 1843, ibid., 749–750.

had been built on the intercultural exchange between Natives and non-Natives. Fur traders, from company partners to clerks and voyageurs, embedded themselves in Native communities to operate their business. When the expansion of U.S. settlements into the Northwest resulted in the dismantling of this business model, the men and women of the fur trade became the most effective means of influencing Native communities and inducing them to cede land to the state. They were cultural insiders with connections to the market economies and governments of British Canada and the newly formed United States. More to the point, to make good on these connections and claim their place in the civil society of the U.S. Republic, the half-breeds of the Northwest would have to embrace their identity as a civilized people, denying or at least denigrating their Indigenous identities and selling out their Indigenous nations as part of the bargain.[76]

On the other hand, these connections also allowed mixed-race Natives to negotiate for the right of the Anishinaabeg to continue living in their homelands, even as the United States converted most of their territory into American homesteads. Initially, the treaty process established "half-breed," the designation of any mixed-race Native person, as a category of racialized colonial subject. Like the racialized category of "Indian," half-breeds received plots of land or reservations carved out from the ceded territory of their homelands. Over time, however, this compensation was transformed into a strictly monetary transaction, and they were denied their land in the form of reservations. Like Indians, the half-breeds were granted cash annuities, or portions of their Native relatives' cash annuities, as compensation for land ceded to the United States. With this change, "half-breed" increasingly functioned as a social status rather than as a racial identity—that is, half-breeds were evaluated according to the extent to which they acted and lived as civilized people. Did they conform to the norms and customs of white citizens of the Republic? Did they speak English, live in a house, and wear store-bought clothing as opposed to speaking Ojibwe or French, living in a wigwam, and wearing clothing fashioned from animal skins and trade cloth?

The answer to these subjective questions determined whether Indian agents, territorial officials, and American settlers identified a person as

76. As historian Jameson Sweet argues, the assertion of this identity "did not come from an internalized identity as white"; it was instead a conflation of three concepts: "whiteness, citizenship, and being civilized." See Sweet, "Native Suffrage: Race, Citizenship, and Dakota Indians in the Upper Midwest," *JER*, XXXIX (2019), 101.

an Indian, whether they were mixed-race or fully Native from a biological perspective. Of course, many people, settlers from the East Coast, agents like Stuart, and politicians such as the former Michigan governor Lewis Cass, regarded half-breeds as partly uncivilized, and therefore not as white people but as some degraded amalgamation of the two races. For the most part, however, Americans identified mixed-race Natives, particularly wives and children, as U.S. citizens, which coded them as white for political, legal, and social purposes. Their Indian relatives, on the other hand, shared a collective identity as savage or uncivilized, a racial status that denied them property rights as a nation and as individuals. The historian Bethel Saler has argued that the racial categories of "white" and "Indian" were crucial to the incorporation of Wisconsin and Michigan into the social fabric of the Republic because these categories were tied to the land. She argues that "territorial officers and their superiors in Washington used racial categories to distinguish Indian and U.S. territories along with the separate jurisdictions governing them." By imagining that Native people held title to their land but did not have property rights to this territory, the federal government could transfer Native homelands into the public domain of the Republic and sell that land to white citizens as private property.[77]

This sleight of hand linking Indians to a racial category devoid of either property rights or U.S. citizenship made it possible for the Republic to expand onto lands west of the original thirteen states in the union. A political imaginary that construed Native peoples as savages or uncivilized beings with no recognized form of private property or legitimate government allowed the United States to claim all of Native North America as unsettled wilderness. This process of expansion led to the formation of northern free states in the West that would become integral to the evolution of free-soil politics. The Northwest Ordinance represented a mechanism for creating value or wealth for nonslaveholding white settlers. Between 1820 and 1860, population growth in the North nearly doubled that of the South. This growth was linked to land values, which also doubled in the North during this same period. According to economic historian Gavin Wright, "The 'founding generation' of the early national era clearly had the best opportunity to capture these capital gains, by obtaining title to western lands early in the appreciation process." Wright characterized this appreciation process as the direct result of a policy designed "to

77. Saler, *Settlers' Empire*, 214.

create value from the wide-open spaces to the west." More accurately, increases in population and land values in the Northwest Territory resulted from the theft of Indian land and the political economy of plunder that facilitated this transfer of wealth.[78]

The Northwest Ordinance thus incentivized immigration and structured economic development in a way that prioritized growth in land values through the creation and improvement of individual homesteads and the development of the infrastructure to support them. This was an economic and political system that prioritized landownership. In some of the free states of the Northwest Territory, this system followed the pattern of settler colonialism and sought the elimination of the Native population through Indian removal. In the northern tier of the Northwest, territories like Michigan and Wisconsin with restricted access to navigable water routes to connect to East Coast and Gulf Coast markets, there was less pressure to remove Native peoples. In fact, their very presence as colonial subjects resulted in a political economy of plunder that generated wealth for American citizens.

The southern economy, in contrast, with the widespread adaptation of chattel slavery, structured economic growth around increasing the value of slave property. Northern free states surpassed the South in terms of population growth and land development. Nevertheless, slave labor allowed white slaveholding southerners to accumulate more wealth than northern settlers. Nonhuman wealth per capita for the free population in the South exceeded the North by 40 percent. Southern slaveholders accumulated wealth, not by deploying slave labor, but by possessing and increasing the value of their slave property. There was no economic or political incentive to allow Native peoples to remain on the land, and in the South the settler state removed Indians with brutal efficiency in the service of this slave economy—either through forced removal as experienced by the Cherokees and other southern Native Nations or grinding warfare as experienced by the Seminoles and the Creeks. An economy structured around chattel slavery easily converted this stolen land into wealth for white Americans, even as it discouraged immigration and limited the development of homesteads and their attendant infrastructure. Similarly, Black laws in the states fashioned out of the Northwest Territory inhibited and attempted to exclude free Black settlers from accumulating

78. Gavin Wright, *Slavery and American Economic Development* (Baton Rouge, La., 2006), 56, 60.

wealth and participating in the economy and civil society of the northern free-soil states.[79]

Slavery is generally characterized as the original sin of the U.S. Republic, and this is a truth. However, the sin of slavery and anti-Black racism must be paired with the legacy of land theft and Indigenous dispossession as the ugly foundation of the political and economic development of the United States. The triad of white settlers, Natives, and enslaved Blacks was foundational to the creation of the Republic. In the United States, these racial categories developed by virtue of their relationship to land. The settler identity became synonymous with whiteness, political rights, and property. The Native became the means through which land could be disaggregated from its original owners and recirculated to white settlers. And whenever possible settlers extracted wealth through an enslaved Black population, although where slavery was prohibited anti-Black racism could serve a similar function. It is in this sense that white immigrants are the normative settlers for whom the Northwest Ordinance was intended to work. This was the ideology and the power behind the Indian agent Robert Stuart, who could tell Gichi-Bizhiki that the United States would take Anishinaabe land, and its minerals, whether or not the ogimaa signed a treaty.[80]

79. According to economic historian Gavin Wright, "Slave labor made possible an accumulation of wealth for the free population of the South that put them considerably ahead of their northern counterparts." Moreover, "Southern slaveowners were justified in feeling that they were fully as successful as their northern counterparts in the game of wealth accumulation, if not more so; but they held their wealth mainly in the form of human property rather than land values." See Wright, *Slavery and American Economic Development,* 57, 61. See also Claudio Saunt, "Financing Dispossession: Stocks, Bonds, and the Deportation of Native Peoples in the Antebellum United States," *Journal of American History,* CVI (2019), 315–337; and Saunt, *Unworthy Republic: The Dispossession of Native Americans and the Road to Indian Territory* (New York, 2020). For the Cherokees, see Tiya Miles, *Ties That Bind: The Story of an Afro-Cherokee Family in Slavery and Freedom* (Berkeley, Calif., 2005). For the Creeks, see Saunt, *A New Order of Things: Property, Power, and the Transformation of the Creek Indians, 1733–1816* (New York, 1999); and Christopher D. Haveman, *Rivers of Sand: Creek Indian Emigration, Relocation, and Ethnic Cleansing in the American South* (Lincoln, Nebr., 2016).

80. "The settler-native-slave triad" of the settler state articulated by ethnic studies scholar K. Wayne Yang is, he argues, "a figurative shorthand." These categories created by the settler colonial state "are figurae to describe relations of power with respect to land." In this formulation (which echoes Bethel Saler's argument in *Settlers' Empire*), "the 'settler,' is a juridical space; the 'native' is a world to be disavowed and dismembered; the 'slave' is an ontological system." See la paperson [Yang], *Third University,* 9–10.

The Anishinaabeg, and all Native nations in North America, represented a social world meant to be "disavowed and dismembered." The world of the Anishinaabeg was disavowed when the United States obliterated Anishinaabewaki and created the Northwest Territory. It was dismembered by each treaty that forced an unwanted land cession and by the Northwest Ordinance that repurposed this ceded land and sold it to white settlers as individual homesteads. The Black body constituted by the settler colonial state was a fungible source of value. It was, not the labor of the enslaved, but the Black body itself that created wealth for the settler. The value of the Black body transformed the South into the property of white, slaveholding settlers. In the Northwest, the Black body was regulated and taxed for the benefit of white settlers. "Settler," "Native," and "slave" are the categories that defined the colonialism and settler colonialism that transformed North America from an Indigenous space into a country occupied by the settlers, Natives, and the enslaved that constituted the inhabitants of the United States in the era of the early Republic. These categories are explicitly tied to the land of North America, and we continue to live with the legacy of their creation to this day.[81]

81. See la paperson [Yang], *Third University*, 9–10. Tiffany King argues, "The space making practices of settler colonialism require the production of Black flesh as a fungible form of property, not just as a form of labor." See King, "Labor's Aphasia: Toward Antiblackness as Constitutive of Settler Colonialism," *Decolonization: Indigeneity, Education, and Society* (blog), June 10, 2014, https://decolonization.wordpress.com/2014/06/10/labors-aphasia-toward-antiblackness-as-constitutive-to-settler-colonialism.

CONCLUSION

Chief Buffalo Goes to Washington

On February 6, 1850, President Zachary Taylor issued an executive order revoking the right of the Anishinaabe people to continue living on lands ceded to the United States under the Treaty of Saint Peters in 1837 and the Treaty of La Pointe in 1842. The order specifically nullified "the right granted to the Chippewa Indians of the Mississippi and Lake Superior, by the Second Article of the treaty with them of October 4th, 1842 of hunting on the territory which they ceded by that treaty." The order also called for "all of the said Indians" to move onto lands not yet ceded to the federal government. The Office of Indian Affairs justified the removal order, like the congressional Indian Removal Act of 1830, as a necessary means of protecting Native peoples from encroaching white settlers and promoting their "civilization and prosperity." In fact, this removal order had nothing to do with the U.S. civilizing mission. It was instead a deadly manifestation of the political economy of plunder.[1]

Taylor's executive order ending the usufruct rights of the Anishinaabeg in Wisconsin and northern Michigan represented an effort to force the region's Native population to relocate to the newly created territory of Minnesota. Taylor appointed fellow Whig politician Alexander Ramsey as governor, and Ramsey passed a resolution through the territorial legislature calling for the removal of the Anishinaabeg in Wisconsin and the Upper Peninsula of Michigan to Minnesota. He explained this action as necessary to ensure "the security and tranquillity of the white

1. Zachary Taylor, Executive Order, Feb. 6, 1850, in Charles J. Kappler, comp. and ed., *Indian Affairs: Laws and Treaties*, V, *(Laws) Compiled from December 22, 1927, to June 29, 1938* (Washington, D.C., 1941), 663; "Report of the Commissioner of Indian Affairs," Nov. 27, 1850, in *The Congressional Globe: New Series: Containing Sketches of the Debates and Proceedings of the Second Session of the Thirty-First Congress*, XXIII (Washington, D.C., 1851), Appendix, 27, also cited in Ronald N. Satz, *Chippewa Treaty Rights: The Reserved Rights of Wisconsin's Chippewa Indians in Historical Perspective*, Wisconsin Academy of Sciences, Arts, and Letters, *Transactions*, LXXIX, no. 1 (Madison, Wis., 1991), 53–54.

settlements." Ramsey was not worried about an Indian war comparable to the Seminole conflict in Florida. Neither was he concerned about the welfare of the Anishinaabeg. Rather, he sought to enrich himself and his associates by enabling Minnesota traders to gain access to the annuities mandated for Native people in the 1837 and 1842 treaties. To expedite this relocation, Ramsey changed the venue of the 1850 annuity payment from La Pointe in Wisconsin to Sandy Lake in central Minnesota. Ramsey also delayed the payment, normally dispensed in the summer months, until the end of October. The consequence of these changes, the governor hoped, would be that the Anishinaabeg would be trapped in Minnesota for the winter, unable to return home across frozen waterways. This, he calculated, would result in the permanent relocation of Wisconsin and Michigan's Anishinaabe population, and their annuities, to the Minnesota Territory.[2]

Ramsey's machinations proved disastrous for the Anishinaabeg. Collecting their annuity payment at Sandy Lake required extensive travel, and many of the Anishinaabeg from Wisconsin and Michigan's Upper Peninsula, already destitute and lacking adequate supplies as a result of the delay in issuing their annuity payment, refused to make the trip. Most of those who did left their wives and children at home, foiling Ramsey's ill-conceived attempt at forcing their relocation. The stress of travel was magnified by the fact that Minnesota's Indian agent did not show up until six weeks after the Anishinaabeg began to arrive at Sandy Lake, where they waited without access to food. Stranded without provisions, the Anishinaabeg who made the trek to Sandy Lake immediately set out for home, traveling on foot for hundreds of miles in the dead of winter. As many as four hundred people died of starvation on what one scholar has called the "Wisconsin Death March." Ojibwe historian Erik Redix has described this event as "a deliberate act of ethnic cleansing" and noted that the death toll far surpassed the more infamous massacre at Sand Creek in 1864. The atrocity of the Wisconsin Death March, unlike the forced removal of the Cherokees or the Sand Creek Massacre, was not the result

2. "Joint Resolution relative to the Removal of the Chippewa Indians from the Ceded Lands within the Territory of Minnesota," Oct. 11, 1849, Minnesota Superintendency, 1849–1856, Letters Received, 1824–1880, Record Group (RG) 75: Records of the Bureau of Indian Affairs, 1793–1999, M234, roll 428, 129, National Archives and Records Administration (NARA), Washington, D.C., also cited in Erik M. Redix, *The Murder of Joe White: Ojibwe Leadership and Colonialism in Wisconsin* (East Lansing, Mich., 2014), 53. For Ramsey's role in effecting the removal order and changing the annuity venue, see ibid., 53–55. See also Satz, *Chippewa Treaty Rights*, 53–59.

of Indian hating, a common phenomenon in the United States. Rather, it was the tragic outcome of the avarice of American traders, most of whom were tied through marriage to the communities they sought to swindle out of their annuities. It also reflected a significant failure of the U.S. colonial regime to convert Anishinaabewaki into American homesteads. It is impossible to extract wealth from a subject population that has been exterminated. The traders benefited from the colonial relationship subordinating the Anishinaabeg to federal and state authorities. Yet their greed manifested itself in the concoction of a ridiculous scheme that brought about the death of the very populations they sought to exploit.[3]

This is not to say that there was no contemporaneous outrage. There was. And there was also a recognition that Native peoples were losing their lives as well as their livelihoods as a consequence of the plunder economy of the Old Northwest. In September 1851, the *New-York Daily Times* published an editorial from the *Cleveland Herald* describing the political economy of plunder and the cruelty of the 1850 annuity. An Ohio reporter, present at La Pointe during the 1848 annuity payment, which had also been delayed for weeks, used the history of the earlier payment as a jumping-off point. While waiting for their annuity payments, the paper reported, "the Indians gathered at La Pointe were without the necessaries of life, and the agents of the North American Fur Company, and a few old traders who were posted in the business, supplied them with provisions at exhorbitant rates." In the end, the "traders raked from the Paymasters table" a total of $26,000, and "the remaining $4,000 the Indians carried home; about one dollar each." Yet "the swindle in 1848 was not gross enough to suit certain grasping parties," the paper decried. The traders conspired to remove the Natives to a more isolated country so that they could take their money while facing less competition. "To effect this," the paper explained, "it was necessary to remove the Chippewa further West, and by some influence, not, perhaps, distinctly marked, but yet more than suspected, this order of removal was secured." Describing the removal as "abominable," the paper observed with relief that the new administration would not enforce the order. President Taylor had died in office, and as of 1850 President Millard Fillmore agreed to suspend his predecessor's executive order.[4]

3. James A. Clifton, "The Wisconsin Death March: Explaining the Extremes in Old Northwest Indian Removal," Wisconsin Academy of Sciences, Arts, and Letters, *Transactions*, LVII (1987), 1–39; Redix, *Murder of Joe White*, 55.

4. "Indian Moneys; from the *Cleveland Herald*," *New-York Daily Times*, Sept. 29, 1851, [4].

Fillmore's hesitation was in response to a petition organized by a prominent mining executive with ties to the Methodist missionary society active in the Lake Superior country. The petition signed by U.S. citizens living in towns along the southern shore of Lake Superior declared the removal of the Anishinaabeg, or the Chippewa, "uncalled for by any interest of the government or people of the United States." The ire of American citizens in Michigan and Wisconsin, however, seemed focused as much on the potential loss of money that the annuities brought to the region as it did on the cruel deaths inflicted on their Native neighbors. In May 1850, the *Lake Superior Journal* reported on the manipulation of the Minnesota Indian agent and the change of venue for the Anishinaabe annuity payment. "We believe we express the conviction of the entire population of the Lake Superior country," the paper asserted, "in regarding this removal as uncalled for by the best interests of the government, the whites or the Indians." At a national level, the policy of Indian removal had been justified because "the Indians have occupied rich agricultural districts, and they must be removed to new and wild regions, or be swallowed up by the tide of civilization sweeping in from the east." The situation concerning the Anishinaabeg, the paper argued, was different. They occupied a cold and remote country. "Until their little fields are needed for the accommodation of their white brethren, why should they be driven to strange places," the paper queried its readers. In other words, the paper accepted the logic of Indian removal: Native people must cede their land to the more productive population of white settlers, but not until there was a demand for that land. More to the point, the paper recognized that the region benefited from the presence of Native peoples, who received hard currency from the federal government that circulated among local merchants and businesses.[5]

By the middle of the nineteenth century, American citizens in the Lake Superior country, in particular white settlers, understood how the political economy of plunder worked. Even if they could not claim annuities as Indian debt, they benefited from the presence of Native peoples in or near their communities because they brought an annual infusion of cash into the local economy. Accordingly, the commissioner of Indian Affairs, Luke Lea, informed the secretary of the interior, Alexander H. H. Stuart, in June

5. *Lake Superior News and Mining Journal*, June 12, 1850, quoted in Satz, *Chippewa Treaty Rights*, 56; "Removal of the Indians; from the *Lake Superior Journal*," *New-York Daily Times*, Sept. 29, 1851, [4].

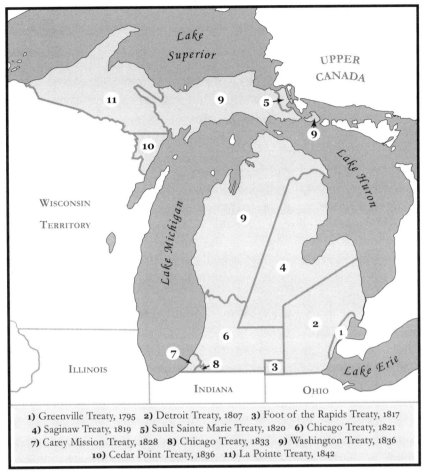

Map 8. Treaties between the United States and the Indigenous Nations in Michigan, 1795–1842. Drawn by Rebecca Wrenn

1851 that the citizens of Wisconsin and Michigan opposed the removal of the Anishinaabeg. "When the extent of this order became known," Lea wrote, "communications from sources of the highest consideration—embracing petitions from the Legislature of Wisconsin and the citizens resident in the ceded country; letters from the Authorities of missionary establishments, among the Chippewas of Lake Superior and other highly respected individuals were received at this office—remonstrating in strong terms against the application of the order to these Indians." In response to the petitions and the protest, the commissioner of Indian

affairs recommended that President Taylor's executive order "be so modified as to permit such portions of those bands as may desire it to remain
in the country they now occupy."[6]

During this same period, the *ogimaa* Gichi-Bizhiki (The Great Buffalo), the principal leader of the Lake Superior Ojibweg, began to organize
a response to government attempts to force the removal of his people
from their homeland. Benjamin Armstrong, the ogimaa's American son-
in-law who also served as a government interpreter, penned a narrative
account of Buffalo's resistance to the looming removal crisis. "Messengers
were sent out to all the different bands in every part of their country,"
he observed, "to get the understanding of all the people, and to inquire
if any depredations had been committed by any of their young men,
or what could be the reason for this sudden order to move." All of the
Gichigamiing-Anishinaabeg, or Lake Superior Ojibwe *doodemag*, sent
word to Buffalo that they had kept their word. There had been no instances of violence or disturbances with the small population of white settlers living in their country. "They now all realized," Armstrong remarked,
"that they had been induced to sign treaties that they did not understand,
and had been imposed upon."[7]

Gichi-Bizhiki, along with twenty-eight other ogimaag, dictated and
signed a letter of petition to Commissioner of Indian Affairs Lea complaining about the manipulation of Minnesota Indian agent John Watrous. The ogimaag contended: "We have ever been ready to listen to the
words of our Great Father whenever he has spoken to us, and to accede to
his wishes. But this time, in the matter of our removal, we are in the dark.
We are not satisfied that it is the President that requires us to remove.
We have asked to see the order, and the name of the President affixed
to it, but it has not been shewn us." In effect, the ogimaag accused Minnesota's Indian agent of attempting to orchestrate their removal. They
reminded the president that the commissioner present at the 1842 treaty
negotiations had promised them that the government did not want their
land to cultivate and settle but only to mine for copper. They then declared that "we have never shed the blood of the Whites; nor killed their
cattle; nor done them any injury; and we are not in their way." They called

6. Luke Lea to Alexander H. H. Stuart, June 3, 1851, Report Books of the Office of
Indian Affairs, 1838–1885, RG 75, M348, roll 6, NARA.

7. *Early Life among the Indians: Reminiscences from the Life of Benj. G. Armstrong;
Treaties of 1835, 1837, 1842, and 1854; Habits and Customs of the Red Men of the For-
est; Incidents, Biographical Sketches, Battles, etc.; Dictated to and Written by Thos. P.
Wentworth* (Ashland, Wis., 1892), 12, 15.

the decision to move the annuity payment to Sandy Lake in the Minnesota Territory an act of deception. "Believe these words, our father, which we have spoken about our Agent," they asserted, "that it is in consequence of what he has done that we are so poor." The letter concluded by admonishing the president of the United States, "You, our Father, are at the head of all authority, and you have it in your power to redress all our grievances."[8]

Gichi-Bizhiki and the ogimaag waited for a response to their petition. When it failed to materialize, they decided to embark on a journey to Washington, D.C., to seek an audience with President Fillmore. On April 5, 1852, Bizhiki and Oshoge, the ogimaa from the Saint Croix band of Ojibweg, accompanied by four warriors and their interpreter Armstrong, departed for the capital. Making their way east, they arrived in Ontonagon, Michigan, where they spent two days circulating a petition written by Armstrong, "asking that the Indians might be left and remain in their country; and the order for their removal be reconsidered." "I did not find a single man who refused to sign it," Armstrong recorded in his journal, "which showed the feelings of the people nearest the Indians upon the subject." As they continued east through the Upper Peninsula of Michigan, they stopped repeatedly at mining towns, adding signatures to their petition at each locale. When they reached Sault Sainte Marie, they met with the editor of the town newspaper, who not only signed the petition but also provided the party with letters of introduction to the president as well as "parties" in New York City. On their second day in town, they were approached by U.S. Army officers, who informed them they would not be allowed to proceed without permission from the government. Although Armstrong persuaded the officers to let them continue their journey, they warned the interpreter that he would surely be stopped at Detroit.[9]

They departed for Detroit by steamship the next day. They were met in the city by Michigan's Indian agent, who informed Armstrong, Bizhiki, Oshoge, and the warriors who accompanied them that they would not be allowed to proceed to Washington. Indian agents exerted control over their Native charges because they controlled the disbursement of annuity

8. Petition to the Hon. Luke Lea, Commissioner of Indian Affairs, Nov. 6, 1851, Indian Office Files, 1852, no. 70, Library-Archives Division, State Historical Society of Wisconsin, Madison, reprinted in Benjamin G. Armstrong, "Reminiscences of Life among the Chippewa (Part II)," *Wisconsin Magazine of History*, LV (1972), 290, 291.

9. *Early Life among the Indians*, 17, 18.

payments. Meeting with the agent and the U.S. marshal later that night, Armstrong "stated to them the facts as they existed in the northwest" and explained the delegation's "object in going to Washington." "If . . . turned back," he informed them, he "did not consider that a white man's life would long be safe in the Indian country, under the present state of excitement." Armstrong's statement about the potential for violence might have seemed an exaggeration to U.S. officials. As Bizhiki had pointed out in his 1851 petition, there had been no incidents of violence involving the Lake Superior Ojibweg and U.S. settlers, but their journey took place only eight years after the Second Seminole War, a conflict provoked by U.S. removal policy that resulted in traumatic loss of life and property for the U.S. army and American settlers. It had only been fourteen years since the violence of Cherokee removal, which, like the attempt to force Ojibwe people to relocate to Minnesota, caused the mass death of Native peoples legally regarded as wards of the United States. Apparently, the Indian agent and the U.S. marshal found Armstrong's dire warning credible because they allowed him and his party to proceed.[10]

Armstrong, Gichi-Bizhiki, Oshoge and the warriors ran out of funds in New York City. To resolve this problem, Armstrong determined, "I should exhibit my fellows and in this way raise the necessary funds to pay my bill and carry us to our destination." Working with the owner of the hotel, he charged New Yorkers for the spectacle of viewing Native warriors from the Northwest Territory. In a reversal of Alexis de Tocqueville's visit to the western frontier, Armstrong brought the frontier to New York City. The interpreter's scheme paid off, and the party raised sufficient funds to make their way to Washington, D.C. On arrival, Armstrong promptly met with the commissioner of Indian affairs, who not only refused to meet with the Anishinaabe delegation but also demanded they return immediately to the Northwest. He was similarly refused and ordered to return home by the secretary of the interior. Rejected, Armstrong returned to his hotel, where, by happenstance, he encountered New York senator George Briggs, who requested an interview with the Anishinaabe delegation after seeing Gichi-Bizhiki in the dining room. The senator arranged a meeting with President Fillmore the following day.[11]

Gichi-Bizhiki took charge of the Anishinaabe delegation's conference with the president by insisting they begin with the calumet ceremony. He then directed the president, the senator, the commissioner of Indian

10. Ibid., 19.
11. Ibid., 20.

affairs, and the secretary of the interior to smoke a pipe he had brought for the occasion. After the Americans took draughts from the pipe, the members of the Anishinaabe delegation did likewise. Then each man shook hands with the government officials. Gichi-Bizhiki next introduced Oshoge, who explained to the president how the Anishinaabeg understood the treaties of 1837 and 1842: "He did not understand that in either treaty they had ceded away the land and he further understood in both cases that the Indians were never to be asked to be removed from the lands included in those treaties, provided they were peaceable and behaved themselves and this they had done." Finally, the delegation presented their petition, signed by the citizens of the Lake Superior country, and Gichi-Bizhiki gave the president a memorial dictated to Armstrong the night before their visit. In the memorial, Gichi-Bizhiki requested an explanation of the removal order, and he complained about the 1850 annuity at Sandy Lake. "Is it not the obligation of white men to fulfill their contracts, and should they not fulfill them, their contracts become null and void consequently a misunderstanding exists, which can and ought to be adjusted to the mutual satisfaction of the parties concerned," Gichi-Bizhiki pressed the president. He then concluded his memorial, stating:

> It is generally the case with white men, when they have selected a spot to dwell at, that they begin to consider and look around them, to see what obstacles are in their way. They begin to cut away the under brush and bad trees, in order to make the land level and smoothe so that nothing will come in contact to hurt their feet, they see good trees and they are allowed to stand and live, and they are not cut down. We beseech you to do towards us as you do, allowing the good trees to stand and live in your domain. And furthermore, we pray, that in accordance to that, we so fully understood that our annuities should be paid to us at Lapointe.

Remarkably, Gichi-Bizhiki conceded that Anishinaabewaki was now within the domain of the United States.[12]

The combination of audacity and humility worked in Gichi-Bizhiki's favor. He and the delegation defied the Office of Indian Affairs in making

12. Ibid., 30; "To His Excellency Millard Fillmore President of the United States of America; the Memorial of the Buffalo, Head Chief at Lapointe and of His Chiefs, Head Men and Warriors . . . ," June 12, 1852, Chippewa Agency, 1851–1880, Letters Received, 1824–1880, RG 75, M234, roll 149, 318 ("did not understand"), 319–320 ("generally the case"), NARA.

their way to Washington and seeking an audience with President Fillmore. His memorial recognized U.S. dominion over the homeland of the Anishinaabeg but also demanded that the United States honor its contract established in the 1837 and 1842 treaties. The day after their meeting, the president requested another audience with the Anishinaabe delegation. "At this he handed Buffalo a written instrument," Armstrong wrote, "which he said would explain to his people when interpreted the promises he made as to the removal order and the payment of annuities at La Pointe." When Gichi-Bizhiki returned home, he was to call a council "and have all the statements therein contained explained fully to them as the words of their great father at Washington."[13]

Two years after Bizhiki made his clandestine journey to Washington to meet with the president and demand he fulfill his contract allowing the Anishinaabeg to remain in their homeland, the United States established permanent reservations for the "Lake Superior Chippewa" in the state of Wisconsin. That same year, the Wisconsin state legislature drafted a memorial to the president stating that "the Chippewa Indians in the region of Lake Superior are a peaceable, quiet, and inoffensive people rapidly improving in the arts and sciences." Moreover, "many of them have intermarried with the white inhabitants, and are generally anxious to become educated and adopt the habits of the 'white man.'" The legislature brought their memorial to a close by insisting that all future annuity payments to the "Lake Superior Chippewa" be made at La Pointe, Wisconsin. The legislature offered homage to the U.S. civilizing mission, acknowledging that their Native neighbors were improving and adopting the habits of the state's white settlers, but they simultaneously signaled the real reason they wished the Anishinaabeg to continue living as their neighbors— the annual payments they received from the federal government in compensation for the land stolen from them.[14]

In the last states to be forged out of the Northwest Territory, Native peoples as well as Native land had become a source of wealth creation for American settlers. Native peoples were no longer obstacles in the way of U.S. immigrants as they had been in Ohio, Illinois, and Indiana. Rather, the presence of Native peoples, stripped of virtually all their land, denied citizenship in the Republic, and legally deemed wards of the federal

13. *Early Life among the Indians*, 30–31.

14. "Memorial to the Pres[i]dent and Congress of the United States, relative to the Chippewa Indians of Lake Superior," Feb. 27, 1854, in *General Acts Passed by the Legislature of Wisconsin, in the Year Eighteen Hundred and Fifty-Four, Together with Memorials and Resolutions* (Madison, Wis., 1854), 156–157.

government, represented a source of cash income. Gichi-Bizhiki and Anishinaabe people throughout the Great Lakes region refused to vanish. Divested of their land base and receiving only meager compensation for this loss, the Anishinaabeg insisted that the United States allow them to remain in their homelands and continually negotiate the terms of their colonization. They forced the United States to see itself as a nation of settlers living on stolen land.

The More Things Change,
the More They Stay the Same
The Legacy of the Political Economy of Plunder

On July 24, 1920, Evelyn St. Onge was born in Iron Mountain, a town in the Upper Peninsula of Michigan on the Wisconsin state border. Evelyn was an enrolled member of the Red Cliff Band of Lake Superior Chippewa, and her extended family lived on the Red Cliff and Bad River reservations in northern Wisconsin. Evelyn was my grandmother, and she was the great-great-great-granddaughter of Amons Buffalo, the daughter of Gichi-Bizhiki. The fact of her birth meant that the calculation made by Bizhiki when he reluctantly signed the 1842 treaty with the United States at La Pointe, Wisconsin, paid off. His descendants remained in their homeland, some living on the Wisconsin reservations he forced the United States to create after his unauthorized trip to Washington, D.C., others living nearby on ceded territory. Of course, because Evelyn was an enrolled member of a federally recognized Indian tribe, she could not, technically, be a citizen of the United States. This legacy of politically excluding Native peoples from the social contract of the U.S. Republic, however, would come to an end legally in 1924, when Evelyn was four and Congress passed the Indian Citizenship Act, granting citizenship to Native peoples born in the United States.[1]

Although the United States decided to make Native people citizens of the Republic, the federal government continued to dispossess Native peoples of their land. In 1910, ten years before Evelyn was born but sixty-eight years after Bizhiki signed the La Pointe Treaty, the Department of

---

1. An Act to Authorize the Secretary of the Interior to Issue Certificates of Citizenship to Indians, June 2, 1924 (Pub. L. No. 68-175, 43 Stat. 253 [1924]), Enrolled Acts and Resolutions of Congress, 1789–1996, General Records of the U.S. Government, Record Group 11, National Archives and Records Administration (NARA), Washington, D.C.

the Interior advertised "INDIAN LAND FOR SALE" in Wisconsin. To sell this land, the department produced posters featuring a Native man in a buckskin shirt with two eagle feathers in his hair that read "GET A HOME OF YOUR OWN. EASY PAYMENTS. PERFECT TITLE. POSSESSION WITHIN THIRTY DAYS." The promise of "PERFECT TITLE" echoed the dream of the settler state to secure a perfect settler sovereignty, linked as always to the eradication of Indigenous rights. The poster advertised 1,069 acres in Wisconsin for the price of seventeen dollars per acre. This was surplus land culled from reservations like Red Cliff and Bad River that had been transferred to the public domain as a result of the Dawes Act.[2]

The Dawes Act, also known as the General Allotment Act, passed in 1887, was intended to advance the civilizing mission by forcing Native peoples to take individual ownership of their land, apportioned into 160-acre homesteads, thereby dismantling the tribe as a social unit. This policy did not result in the dissolution of Indian reservations or the destruction of semi-autonomous Indigenous nations within the borders of the United States. Rather, Native land not allotted to Native people was transferred to the public domain and made available for purchase, as advertised on the Department of the Interior's poster. In other words, long after the government stopped forcing Indigenous nations to cede land through treaties, the United States continued to appropriate Native land and sell it to American settlers at a subsidized price. The political economy of plunder continued into the twentieth century. This was the promise of the New World, which imagined North America as an unsettled wilderness waiting for white settlers to bring civilization to the continent. The New World offered the promise of landed wealth to white immigrants willing to "settle" the territory claimed by the United States.[3]

In his highly influential 2014 article "The Case for Reparations," Ta-Nehisi Coates writes that "America begins in black plunder and white democracy, two features that are not contradictory but complementary." He explains this phenomenon by asserting that slavery "originated in a simple fact of the New World—land was boundless but cheap labor was

2. For the idea of perfect settler sovereignty, see Lisa Ford, *Settler Sovereignty: Jurisdiction and Indigenous People in America and Australia, 1788-1836* (Cambridge, Mass., 2010), 25.

3. An Act to Provide for the Allotment of Lands in Severalty to Indians on the Various Reservations . . . (General Allotment Act, or Dawes Act), Feb. 8, 1887, Statutes at Large 24, 388-91, Document A 1887, NARA.

INDIAN LAND FOR SALE

GET A HOME

OF

YOUR OWN

✦

EASY PAYMENTS

PERFECT TITLE

✦

POSSESSION

WITHIN

THIRTY DAYS

FINE LANDS IN THE WEST

IRRIGATED
IRRIGABLE
GRAZING
AGRICULTURAL
DRY FARMING

IN 1910 THE DEPARTMENT OF THE INTERIOR SOLD UNDER SEALED BIDS ALLOTTED INDIAN LAND AS FOLLOWS:

Location.	Acres.	Average Price per Acre.	Location.	Acres.	Average Price per Acre.
Colorado	5,211.21	$7.27	Oklahoma	34,664.00	$19.14
Idaho	17,013.00	24.85	Oregon	1,020.00	15.43
Kansas	1,684.50	33.45	South Dakota	120,445.00	16.53
Montana	11,034.00	9.86	Washington	4,879.00	41.37
Nebraska	5,641.00	36.65	Wisconsin	1,069.00	17.00
North Dakota	22,610.70	9.93	Wyoming	865.00	20.64

FOR THE YEAR 1911 IT IS ESTIMATED THAT 350,000 ACRES WILL BE OFFERED FOR SALE

For information as to the character of the land write for booklet, "INDIAN LANDS FOR SALE," to the Superintendent U. S. Indian School at any one of the following places:

CALIFORNIA:
Hoopa.
COLORADO:
Ignacio.
IDAHO:
Lapwai.
KANSAS:
Horton.
Nadeau.

MINNESOTA:
Onigum.
MONTANA:
Crow Agency.
NEBRASKA:
Macy.
Santee.
Winnebago.

NORTH DAKOTA:
Fort Totten.
Fort Yates.
OKLAHOMA:
Anadarko.
Cantonment.
Colony.
Darlington.
Muskogee, SUPT. OF UNION AGENCY. •
Pawnee.

OKLAHOMA—Con.
Sac and Fox Agency.
Shawnee.
Wyandotte.
OREGON:
Klamath Agency.
Pendleton.
Roseburg.
Siletz.

SOUTH DAKOTA:
Cheyenne Agency.
Crow Creek.
Greenwood.
Lower Brule.
Pine Ridge.
Rosebud.
Sisseton.

WASHINGTON:
Fort Simcoe.
Fort Spokane.
Tekoa.
Tulalip.
WISCONSIN:
Oneida.

WALTER L. FISHER,
Secretary of the Interior.

ROBERT G. VALENTINE,
Commissioner of Indian Affairs.

Figure 16. *Indian Land for Sale.* . . . Broadside, [1911]. U.S. Department of the Interior, signed by Walter L. Fisher, Secretary of the Interior, and Robert G. Valentine, Commissioner of Indian Affairs. Printed Ephemera Collection, Library of Congress, Washington, D.C.

limited." Slavery and the Jim Crow laws that followed formed the basis of a plunder economy in the United States. "In the 1920s," maintains Coates, "Jim Crow Mississippi was, in all facets of society, a kleptocracy. The majority of the people in the state were perpetually robbed of the vote—a hijacking engineered through the trickery of the poll tax and the muscle of the lynch mob." Enslaved Africans, Coates argues, saw their bodies plundered, their families plundered, and their labor plundered. This legacy of plunder created legal conventions such as the one-drop rule and anti-miscegenation laws, and it lived on through Jim Crow. It lives on today in the anti-Black racism of the United States.[4]

Missing from Coates's formulation of the New World and its demand for cheap labor, however, is the recognition of Indigenous dispossession implied by the construct of "boundless" land. One could argue America began with a political economy of plunder that stole Black lives and Indigenous land to launch an experiment in self-government for white men. To imagine the New World as a "boundless" landscape is to see it as an uninhabited or, at least, unsettled land, which it was not. The Western Hemisphere was home to a multitude of Native peoples, Indigenous nations with discrete homelands. The colonization of North America began with the plunder of Native homelands by Europeans who sought land for their New World settlements. Coates is right to identify the settler and the enslaved as two of the crucial elements needed to transform Native North America into the New World. But his formulation misses the third element required for this transformation, the Native. This is the triad of white settlers, Natives, and enslaved Blacks. The theft of Black labor through the theft of Black bodies was necessitated by the theft of Native land and the desire of white settlers to convert this stolen land into private property. As Coates asserts, "African slaves entered the colonies as aliens. Exempted from the protections of the crown, they became early America's indispensable working class—fit for maximum exploitation, capable of only minimal resistance." Settler colonialism provided white settlers with a set of technologies, the most potent and lethal of which is anti-Black racism. It transformed enslaved Black bodies into a technology for transforming land into property while seeking to open land for settlement by eliminating the Native population. Settler colonialism in the United States is an ideology that has attempted to deny Native and

4. Ta-Nehisi Coates, "The Case for Reparations," *Atlantic*, June 2014, https://www .theatlantic.com/magazine/archive/2014/06/the-case-for-reparations/361631.

Black people their rights. It is an ideology that demands constant resistance from Black people, Indigenous people, and other people of color to prevent their erasure.[5]

The consequences of this legacy lasted into the twentieth century, when my grandmother was born, and they remain with us today in the twenty-first century. It is impossible not to see the connection between the history of the political economy of plunder in the Old Northwest and the civil unrest in Ferguson, Missouri, following the shooting death of Michael Brown and the resistance to the expansion of the Dakota Access Pipeline at the Standing Rock Sioux reservation. We are compelled to understand the fugitive slave laws required by all states created via the Northwest Ordinance as a form of anti-Black technology, as are the laws to tax, restrict, and discourage the movement of Black settlers into the states of the Northwest Territory. These laws also represent the Black plunder articulated by Coates.

These anti-Black technologies, along with slavery and land theft, created the economic foundation for the American experiment in self-representative government. These same technologies gave rise to the political climate in Ferguson that led to massive civil unrest after a police officer shot and killed Michael Brown, an unarmed Black teenager, in the summer of 2014. The population of Ferguson is two-thirds Black, yet the city's fifty-person police force had only three Black officers. According to the journalist William Powell, in 2013, the year before Brown's death, "Black people accounted for 86 percent of all traffic stops and 92 percent of searches and arrests." These statistics reflect that the city of Ferguson used policing as a means of generating revenue, and this money was disproportionately raised on the backs of poor and working-class Black people. After investigating Michael Brown's death, the Justice Department cleared the officer who shot him, determining that no prosecutable crime had been committed. A separate Department of Justice investigation, however, concluded that the Ferguson Police Department's focus on generating revenue "has compromised the institutional character of Ferguson's police department, contributing to a pattern of unconstitutional policing, and has also shaped its municipal court, leading to procedures that raise due process concerns and inflict unnecessary harm on members of the Ferguson community." This report also asserted that these

5. Ibid. For "the settler-native-slave triad," see la paperson [K. Wayne Yang], *A Third University Is Possible* (Minneapolis, Minn., 2017), 8.

policing practices exacerbated racial tensions and created racial dispari-
ties that adversely impacted the African American population.[6]

In short, the Justice Department found that the Ferguson Police Department acted with discriminatory intent, practicing racist policing
to generate cash for the city. Thus, even though the Justice Department
found no cause to prosecute the officer who shot Michael Brown, the use
of deadly force against an unarmed man could be considered a form of
Black plunder. At the very least, his death, like the 2014 shooting deaths of
twenty-two-year-old John Crawford in August and twelve-year-old Tamir
Rice in November by police officers who mistook toys for weapons, reflects a system of governance that systematically denies the full humanity
of African American people. Coates has argued that the political climate
and the policing practices that led to Michael Brown's death are the result
of a system of governance tempered by white supremacy. "White supremacy is the technology," he writes, "to ensure that what is yours inevitably
becomes mine." "This technology," he concluded, "has proven highly effective throughout American history." The through line of Black plunder
connecting slavery to present-day moments like Ferguson is clear. But so,
too, is the link between these incidents and the political economy of plunder in the Northwest Territory, which stripped Native peoples of land and
wealth and subjected free Black settlers to fugitive slave and anti-Black
laws. Present-day racist policing in Ferguson and the deaths of multiple
unarmed African Americans at the hands of law enforcement can only
be understood in relation to this history of governance through plunder.[7]

In the short time between my submitting this book manuscript for
peer review and its return to me for revision, more Black citizens had died
as a result of violent acts committed by the police. The murder of George
Floyd by the police in Minneapolis during the summer of 2020, captured
in an excruciating video, set off a wave of national protests in support
of the Black Lives Matter movement, which seeks to end the systematic

6. William Powell, "The Roots of Violence in Ferguson," *Atlantic*, Aug. 16, 2014,
https://www.theatlantic.com/national/archive/2014/08/racial-tension-in-ferguson
-isnt-over/378625; United States Department of Justice, Civil Rights Division, *Investigation of the Ferguson Police Department*, Mar. 4, 2015, 2, 4, https://www.justice
.gov/sites/default/files/opa/press-releases/attachments/2015/03/04/ferguson_police
_department_report.pdf; Ta-Nehisi Coates, "The Gangsters of Ferguson," *Atlantic*, Mar. 5, 2015, https://www.theatlantic.com/politics/archive/2015/03/The-Gangsters
-Of-Ferguson/386893.

7. Coates, "Gangsters of Ferguson," *Atlantic*, Mar. 5, 2015.

anti-Black racism that daily affects the lives of African Americans, too often with lethal consequences.

It is the same connection to a history of governance through plunder that led the U.S. government to sanction the construction of the Dakota Access Pipeline under the Missouri River near the Standing Rock Sioux reservation. The pipeline connects the Bakken oil fields in North Dakota to a refinery in Illinois. The Army Corps of Engineers approved the construction of this pipeline without adequately consulting the tribal council of the Standing Rock Sioux reservation, as they were legally bound to do according to the 1868 Fort Laramie Treaty. Article 2 of the treaty guarantees "undisturbed use and occupation" of reservation lands in the area where the pipeline was being built. Energy Transfer Partners, the company building the pipeline, originally planned to cross the Missouri River near the city of Bismarck but moved the route when city officials expressed concerns that any spills would contaminate the drinking water of the state capital. The altered route instead crosses the Missouri near the Standing Rock Sioux reservation on land taken from the tribe without their consent in 1958, when the Army Corps of Engineers built a series of dams in the region. In April 2016, in response to the advancing pipeline, which was being built on a "fast track" without an environmental impact study, members of the Standing Rock Sioux nation began to resist. Attempting to physically block its construction, they were soon joined by thousands of Native protesters from more than one hundred Indigenous nations as well as a large number of non-Native protestors.[8]

Those who showed up to oppose the construction of the pipeline at Standing Rock insisted that they were not protestors but were water protectors, reframing their act of resistance around the assertion of Native rights and environmental justice. Under the Obama administration, construction of the pipeline was halted to assess the potentially adverse environmental impact of the pipeline's construction. The Trump administration reversed this decision, allowing oil to flow through the Dakota Access Pipeline. In a statement about his decision to allow pipeline construction to move forward, President Donald Trump remarked: "Nobody thought any politician would have the guts to approve that final leg. And

8. Bill McKibben, "A Pipeline Fight and America's Dark Past," *New Yorker*, Sept. 6, 2016, https://www.newyorker.com/news/daily-comment/a-pipeline-fight-and-americas-dark-past. For the Fort Laramie Treaty, see "Treaty with the Sioux . . . , 1868," Apr. 29, 1868, in Charles J. Kappler, comp. and ed., *Indian Affairs: Laws and Treaties*, II, *Treaties* (Washington, D.C., 1904), 998 ("undisturbed").

I just closed my eyes and said 'Do it.'" In contrast, David Archambault, chairman of the Standing Rock Sioux, said, "There's an uneasy feeling that any moment this pipeline could pose a threat to our way of life." President Trump's decision to allow a company to extract wealth and resources at the expense of Native peoples is not an exceptional political act; it is history repeating itself. So, too, is Archambault's anguish. The theft of Native land to build an oil pipeline struck many contemporary U.S. citizens as unconscionable. The resistance at Standing Rock drew widespread support from non-Native people and galvanized Native peoples from tribal communities across the United States. Yet stealing Native land to generate wealth for white citizens of the United States is not an aberration. It is a feature, not a bug, in the system of governance created by the United States in North America.[9]

Most citizens of the United States recognize the need to create laws and a political climate that seeks equality for all members of society, citizens of tribal nations, people of color, people of European descent—everyone. This is the promise of America: that the Republic will function as a system of self-government empowered by all of its citizens. However, this vision of the United States has not always aligned with reality. The United States took shape through a political economy of plunder that pillaged Black lives and Indigenous land to institute a republic for white men. We live with the legacy of this history to this day. We must acknowledge this past, remembering how Anishinaabewaki was turned into Michigan and Wisconsin. But we must seek to end this legacy, which otherwise will continue to resurface, as we have seen in Ferguson, Minneapolis, and Standing Rock.

9. Robinson Meyer, "Oil Is Flowing through the Dakota Access Pipeline," *Atlantic*, June 9, 2017, https://www.theatlantic.com/science/archive/2017/06/oil-is-flowing -through-the-dakota-access-pipeline/529707.

APPENDIX

Summaries of Select Treaties between the United States and Indigenous Nations in the Old Northwest, 1795–1855

For the full text of each treaty listed below, see Charles J. Kappler, comp. and ed., *Indian Affairs: Laws and Treaties*, II, *Treaties* (Washington, D.C., 1904). Page numbers for each of the treaties appear in parentheses following the treaty's formal name.

Treaty of Greenville, 1795
Formal name: "A Treaty of Peace between the United States of America and the Tribes of Indians, Called the Wyandots, Delawares, Shawanoes, Ottawas, Chipewas, Putawatimes, Miamis, Eel-river, Weea's, Kickapoos, Piankashaws, and Kaskaskias" (39–45)
Alternate names: Treaty of Fort Greenville
U.S. signatory: Anthony Wayne, major general of the United States Army
Land ceded: Parts of the Northwest Territory (most of the future state of Ohio and portions of the future states of Indiana, Illinois, and Michigan)
Annuity: $20,000 in goods and an additional $9,500 in goods annually in perpetuity (article 4)
Other notable provisions: Land relinquished by the United States for use by Indigenous nations can be sold only to the United States (article 5); Indigenous nations retain hunting rights on ceded lands as long as they do not injure U.S. citizens (article 7)

Treaty of Detroit, 1807
Formal name: "Articles of a Treaty Made at Detroit, This Seventeenth Day of November in the Year of Our Lord, One Thousand Eight Hundred and Seven, by William Hull, Governor of the Territory of Michigan, and Superintendent of Indian Affairs . . . with the Several Nations of Indians, North West of the River Ohio, on the One Part,

and the Sachems, Chiefs, and Warriors for the Ottoway, Chippeway,
Wyandotte, and Pottawatamie Nations of Indians, on the Other
Part . . ." (92–95)

Land ceded: The southeast quarter of the Lower Peninsula of Michigan
and a section of Ohio north of the Maumee River

Annuity: $10,000 in money, goods, implements of husbandry, or
domestic animals, and $2,400 in perpetuity (article 2)

Other notable provisions: Indigenous nations retain hunting rights on
ceded land (article 5); land reserved for Indigenous nations (article
6); "The said nations of Indians acknowledge themselves to be under
the protection of the United States, and no other power" (article 7)

Treaty at the Foot of the Rapids, 1817

Formal name: "Articles of a Treaty Made and Concluded, at the Foot
of the Rapids of the Miami of Lake Erie, between Lewis Cass and
Duncan McArthur Commissioners of the United States . . . and the
Sachems, Chiefs, and Warriors, of the Wyandot, Seneca, Delaware,
Shawanese, Potowatomees, Ottawas, and Chippeway, Tribes of
Indians" (145–155)

Alternate names: Treaty of Fort Meigs; Treaty of the Rapids of the
Miami of Lake Erie; Treaty of the Maumee Rapids

Lands ceded: Parts of Ohio, Indiana, and the Michigan Territory

Annuity: An annual payment in perpetuity of $4,000 to the Wyandots,
$500 to the Senecas, and $2,000 to the Shawnees; an annual
payment for fifteen years of $1,300 to the Patawatomis, $1,000 to the
Odawaag, $1,000 to the Ojibweg; and a single payment of $500 to the
Delawares (article 4); additional cash payments to allied Indigenous
nations for damages suffered during the War of 1812 (article 12)

Other notable provisions: Land reserved for Indigenous nations
(article 6); land granted to persons "connected with the said Indians,
by blood or adoption" (article 8); Indigenous nations retain hunting
rights and the right to make sugar on ceded lands (article 11); the
United States reserves the "right to make roads through any part of
the land granted or reserved" and "the right of establishing taverns
and ferries for the accommodation of travellers" (article 14)

Treaty of Saint Mary's, 1818 (Delawares)

Formal name: "Articles of a Treaty Made and Concluded at St. Mary's,
in the State of Ohio, between Jonathan Jennings, Lewis Cass, and

Benjamin Parke, Commissioners of the United States, and the Delaware Nation of Indians" (170–171)

Land ceded: The Delawares' claim to land in Indiana

Annuity: The full value of improvements to the land ceded; 120 horses (not to exceed $40 each), "perogues" to transport them to reserved land on the west side of the Mississippi, and provisions for the journey (article 3); $4,000 in perpetuity (article 5); support for a blacksmith (article 6); a sum not exceeding $13,312.25 "to satisfy certain claims against the Delaware nation" (article 8)

Other notable provisions: Land provided to the Delaware nation "upon the west side of the Mississippi" (article 2); sections of land granted to specified individuals and their heirs ("all of whom are Delawares") that cannot be transferred without the approval of the U.S. president (article 7)

Treaty of Saint Mary's, 1818 (Miamis)

Formal name: "Articles of a Treaty Made and Concluded, at St. Mary's, in the State of Ohio, between Jonathan Jennings, Lewis Cass, and Benjamin Parke, Commissioners of the United States, and the Miami Nation of Indians" (171–174)

Land ceded: Parts of Ohio and the Michigan Territory

Annuity: $15,000 in perpetuity; one gristmill, one sawmill, support for a blacksmith and a gunsmith, agricultural implements, and 160 bushels of salt annually (article 5)

Other notable provisions: Land reserved for the use of the Miami nation (article 2); land granted to specified individuals, "Miami Indians by birth, and their heirs" (article 3); the U.S. president must approve transfers of the land reserved to individuals specified in article 3 (article 6)

Treaty of Saginaw, 1819

Formal name: "Articles of a Treaty Made and Concluded at Saginaw, in the Territory of Michigan, between the United States of America, by Their Commissioner Lewis Cass, and the Chippewa Nation of Indians" (185–187)

Land ceded: Part of the Michigan Territory

Annuity: $1,000 annually in perpetuity (article 4); the value of improvements on ceded land (article 6); the support of a blacksmith as well as farming utensils, cattle, and labor to aid with agriculture (article 8)

Other notable provisions: Land reserved for the use of the Ojibwe nation (article 2); land reserved for specified individuals and their heirs, "all Indians by descent" (article 3); the United States reserves the right to build roads on reserved lands (article 7); the Ojibwe nation retains hunting rights and the right to make sugar on ceded lands (article 11)

Treaty of Chicago, 1821

Formal name: "Articles of a Treaty Made and Concluded at Chicago, in the State of Illinois, between Lewis Cass and Solomon Sibley, Commissioners of the United States, and the Ottawa, Chippewa, and Pottawatamie, Nations of Indians" (198–201)

Land ceded: Parts of the Michigan Territory, Indiana, Illinois

Annuity: For the Odawa nation: $1,000 annually in perpetuity and $1,500 for ten years to support a blacksmith, a teacher, and a person to aid with agriculture as well as to purchase cattle and farm utensils. For the Potawatomi nation: $5,000 annually for twenty years and $1,000 annually for fifteen years to support a blacksmith and a teacher; land for the blacksmith and the teacher to reside (article 4)

Other notable provisions: Land reserved for use of the Indigenous nations (article 2); land reserved for specified individuals, "all Indians by descent," that cannot be leased or conveyed without the permission of the U.S. president (article 3); Indigenous nations retain hunting rights on ceded land (article 5); the United States has the right to build and use a road through "Indian country from Detroit and Fort Wayne, respectively to Chicago" (article 6)

First Treaty of Prairie du Chien, 1825

Formal name: "Treaty with the Sioux and Chippewa, Sacs and Fox, Menominie, Ioway, Sioux, Winnebago, and a Portion of the Ottawa, Chippewa, and Potawattomie, Tribes" (250–255)

U.S. signatories: William Clark and Lewis Cass, commissioners

Land ceded: None; established boundaries among Indigenous nations

Annuity: None

Other notable provisions: Parties agree to a perpetual peace among the Indigenous nations in the region, particularly the Sioux and the Ojibweg (article 1); the Indigenous nations "acknowledge the general controlling power" of the United States (article 10); the United States may intervene to maintain peace (article 14)

Treaty of Fond du Lac, 1826

Formal name: "Articles of a Treaty Made and Concluded at the Font du Lac of Lake Superior This Fifth Day of August, in the Year of Our Lord One Thousand Eight Hundred and Twenty-Six, between Lewis Cass and Thomas L. McKenney, Commissioners on the Part of the United States, and the Chippewa Tribe of Indians" (268–273)

Land ceded: None; ensured the full assent of the Ojibwe nation to the Treaty of Prairie du Chien

Annuity: 640 acres of land on the islands and shore of Saint Mary's River for use by "half-breeds" (article 4); $2,000 annually in money or goods (article 5); $1,000 for "Indian youths" for a school on Saint Mary's River (article 6)

Other notable provisions: The United States has the right to obtain "metals or minerals from any part of their country" (article 3); the Ojibweg "acknowledge the authority and jurisdiction of the United States" (article 8)

Treaty of Washington, 1836

Formal name: "Articles of a Treaty Made and Concluded at the City of Washington in the District of Columbia, between Henry R. Schoolcraft, Commissioner on the Part of the United States, and the Ottawa and Chippewa Nations of Indians, by Their Chiefs and Delegates" (450–456)

Land ceded: Part of the Michigan Territory

Annuity: $30,000 annually for twenty years; $5,000 annually for twenty years for education; $3,000 for missions; $10,000 for agricultural implements and cattle; $300 annually for medicine and physicians; $2,000 for provisions; 6,500 pounds of tobacco, 100 barrels of salt, and 500 "fish barrels" annually for twenty years; $150,000 in goods and provisions on ratification of treaty; $200,000 to change the permanent status of reservations to five years (article 4); $300,000 for payment of debts (article 5); $150,000 for "half-breed relatives" (article 6); support for interpreters, a dormitory, two blacksmiths, a gunsmith, two farmers and assistants, and two mechanics (article 7); $48,148 for specified "half-breed claims" (article 9); $30,000 to "the chiefs" (article 10); $100 annually to "one of their aged chiefs," "Ningweegon or the Wing," and $50.00 annually to "Chusco of Michilimackinac" (article 11)

Other notable provisions: Land reserved for the use of Indigenous
nations for five years (articles 2 and 3); United States agrees to send
a deputation to the southwest of the Missouri River "to select a
suitable place for the final settlement of said Indians" that it "will
forever guaranty and secure" (article 8); Indigenous nations retain
hunting rights on ceded land (article 13)

Treaty of Saint Peters, 1837

Formal name: "Articles of a Treaty Made and Concluded at St. Peters
(the Confluence of the St. Peters and Mississippi Rivers) in the
Territory of Wisconsin, between the United States of America, by
their Commissioner, Henry Dodge, Governor of Said Territory, and
the Chippewa Nation of Indians, by Their Chiefs and Headmen"
(491–493)

Alternate names: Treaty with the Chippewa; White Pine Treaty

Land ceded: Parts of the Wisconsin Territory

Annuity: An annual payment for twenty years of $9,500 in money,
$19,000 in goods, $3,000 for establishing three blacksmith shops,
$1,000 for farmers and agricultural implements, $2,000 in provisions, $500 in tobacco (article 2); $100,000 to the "half-breeds of
the Chippewa nation" (article 3); $70,000 for "claims against the
Indians" (article 4)

Other notable provisions: The Ojibwe nation retains hunting, fishing,
and gathering rights on ceded land (article 5)

Treaty of La Pointe, 1842

Formal name: "Articles of a Treaty Made and Concluded at La Pointe of
Lake Superior in the Territory of Wisconsin, between Robert Stuart
Commissioner on the Part of the United States, and the Chippewa
Indians of the Mississippi, and Lake Superior by Their Chiefs and
Headmen" (542–545)

Land ceded: Upper Peninsula of the Michigan Territory and Wisconsin
Territory

Annuity: An annual payment for twenty-five years of $12,500 in specie,
$10,500 in goods, $2,000 in provisions and tobacco, $2,000 to
support two blacksmith shops, $1,000 for two farmers, $1,200 for two
carpenters, and $2,000 for schools; $5,000 as an agricultural fund;
$75,000 for the full satisfaction of debts; and $15,000 to "half breed
relatives" (article 4)

Other notable provisions: The Ojibwe nation retains hunting rights on ceded land until the U.S. president removes the right (article 2); "Unceded lands belonging to the Indians of Fond du Lac, Sandy Lake, and Mississippi bands, shall be the common property and home of all the Indians, party to this treaty" (article 3); "Indians residing in the Mineral district, shall be subject to removal therefrom at the pleasure of the President of the United States" (article 6)

Second Treaty of La Pointe, 1854

Formal name: "Articles of a Treaty Made and Concluded at La Pointe, in the State of Wisconsin, between Henry C. Gilbert and David B. Herriman, Commissioners on the Part of the United States, and the Chippewa Indians of Lake Superior and the Mississippi, by Their Chiefs and Head-Men" (648–652)

Land ceded: Parts of Wisconsin

Annuity: An annual payment for twenty years of $5,000 in coin; $8,000 in goods, household furniture, and cooking utensils; $3,000 in agricultural implements and cattle, carpenters, and building materials; and $3,000 for moral and educational purposes. Additionally, $90,000 to chiefs; $6,000 in agricultural implements, household furniture, and cooking utensils to "mixed bloods"; 200 guns, 100 rifles, 500 beaver traps, $300 of ammunition, and $1,000 of "ready-made clothing, to be distributed among the young men of the nation, at the next annuity payment" (article 4); the support of a blacksmith and assistant "at each of the points herein set apart for the residence of the Indians" (article 5); $10,000 to the "Bois Forte Indians" along with $10,000, "in five equal annual payments," for blankets, cloth, nets, guns, ammunition, "and such other articles of necessity" as well as support for a blacksmith and "two persons to instruct them in farming" (article 12)

Other notable provisions: Land reserved for the use of the Ojibweg (article 2); "No spirituous liquors shall be made, sold, or used on any of the lands herein set apart for the residence of the Indians" nor sold in the ceded territory (article 7)

Treaty of Detroit, 1855

Formal name: "Articles of Agreement and Convention Made and Concluded at the City of Detroit, in the State of Michigan, This the Thirty-First Day of July, One Thousand Eight Hundred and

Fifty-Five, between George W. Manypenny and Henry C. Gilbert, Commissioners on the Part of the United States, and the Ottawa and Chippewa Indians of Michigan, Parties to the Treaty of March 28, 1836" (725–731)

Land ceded: None; reaffirmed the right of the Indigenous nations to remain on reserved land in Michigan

Annuity: $40,000 to liquidate debt (article 1); and a total of $538,400: $80,000 for education purposes, paid in ten equal annual installments; $75,000 in five equal annual installments for agricultural implements and carpenters' tools, household furniture, building materials, cattle, labor, and all such articles necessary in removing; $42,400 to support blacksmiths; $306,000 in coin; and $35,000 in ten annual payments to the Grand River Odawaag (article 2); support for interpreters for five years (article 4)

Other notable provisions: Specific allotments of land reserved for the use of the Odawa and Ojibwe nations (article 1); "The Ottawa and Chippewa Indians hereby release and discharge the United States from all liability on account of former treaty stipulations" (article 3); "The tribal organization of said Ottawa and Chippewa Indians" is dissolved (article 5)

States, 228; on Treaty of Saint Peters and removal, 257; on value of lumber, 314

Boyd, George, 138

Brant, Joseph, 64–66

Brewster, William, 193

Briggs, George, 334

British: and threat of alliance with Natives peoples, 45, 75–76, 124–125, 136–137, 227, 258–259, 303–304

British Canada: and protection of border with United States, 9

Brother, 111–112

Brown, Michael, 343–344

Brunet, François, 179–181, 292–293

Brunet, Jean Baptiste, 243–244

Brunson, Alfred: on unfairness of treaties, 310–315, 319; on role of Native women and mixed-race Native peoples, 317–318; on rights of mixed-race Native peoples, 319–320

Brunson, Ida, 229–231

Buffalo, Amons, 339

Burnet, Jacob, 277, 286

Burnett, Thomas, 228–231

Bushnell, Daniel, 249, 258, 261; on status of mixed-race Native people, 263–266

Cadotte, Charlotte, 295

Cadotte, Esther, 292

Cadotte, Jean-Baptiste, 162, 292

Cadotte, Michel, Jr., 162–163, 260–261, 292–293

Cadotte, Michel, Sr., 292

Calhoun, John C., 128–133, 136–139, 159n. 13

Calloway, Colin G., 43n. 11, 44n. 12, 45n. 14, 53n. 27

Calumet ceremony, 200, 334–335

Campau, Louis, 139–146

Campbell, Elizabeth, 161, 178, 185

Campbell, John, 161

Capitol Rotunda, 81–88

Captive adoptees: and gender, 120n. 47; status of, 149. *See also* Zhaazhaawanibiisens

Carpenter, John, 49

Cass, Charles, 139

Cass, Lewis: as advocate for removal, 8, 147–148, 196–197; on Native peoples' inability to become civilized, 75–78, 80; and Zhaazhaawanibiisens, 119; and renegotiation of Treaty at the Foot of the Rapids, 131–133; on captive adoptees, 134; on cession of lands in Michigan, 136–139; and Treaty of Saginaw, 139–146; on annuities, 140; on Native peoples' reliance on American goods, 158–159; on U.S. strength, 169; on intra-Native warfare, 173; and Native delegates to Washington, D.C., 192, 194, 197–210; on Native peoples as emotional, 221n. 9; and Chi-Amik, 239; and Seminoles, 301

Catlin, George, 28

Charles II (king of England), 86

Chase, Salmon P., 60–62, 253

Cherokee nation, 196n. 69, 198n. 72

Cherokee removal, 334

Chi-Amik, 236–241

Chigawaasking: and murder of Aitkin, 217–221; capture of, 223–225; trial of, 228–231, 246, 262, 268; release of, 255

Chippewas. *See* Anishinaabeg; Ojibwe nation

"Chippeway" Indians, 108–109. *See also* Anishinaabeg; Ojibwe nation

Civilization: as antithesis of Native, 34n. 26; Native peoples' exclusion from, 38–41, 133–134; and presumption of assimilation as inevitable, 62, 69–73, 80, 88, 126–131, 155; and presumption of assimilation as impossible, 76–78, 80, 88, 155–156, 210, 273–274, 282–283, 302;

Hamelin, Augustin, Jr., 191–207
Hamilton, Alexander, 33
Harmar, Josiah, 48–53, 63–64, 66–68, 101–102
Haudenosaunee, 63–66
Haveman, Christopher D., 203n. 78, 252n. 51
Hawkins, Benjamin, 237n. 31
Head, Francis Bond, 5–6, 9
Henry, Alexander, 112
Hidatsa nation, 110
Holiday, John, 200, 207
Holiday, Mary, 200, 207
Houghton, Douglass, 176
Hudson's Bay Company. *See* Fur trade
Hull, William, 233
Huron confederacy: and war with Iroquois confederacy, 105
Hyde, Anne F., 155n. 8, 164n. 21

Indian Citizenship Act (1924), 339
Indian Liberating Army, 1–4, 10–15, 304
Indian princess, trope of, 315–316
Indian raids: purpose of, 101–103
Indian Removal Act (1830), 29, 79, 193, 214–215
Infrastructure: as enticement for westward settlement, 300–301
Inini, 184
Intermill, Jessica, 31
Iroquois confederacy, 37n. 3, 105
Irvine, William, 50–51

Jackson, Andrew, 31, 78–80, 199
Jay Treaty, 56, 67
Jefferson, Thomas: on assimilation and civilization of Native peoples, 34n. 26, 71–73, 80; and meeting with Native leaders, 35–38; on Native peoples and dominion over land, 38–41; and trade and land settlement committee, 46–48; and westward expansion as inevitable, 155

Jefferson-Hartley map, 46–48
Jeffersonian republicanism, 48
Jeffries, Parker, 273–277
Jesuit missionaries, 103–105
Johnson, Walter, 80n. 69
Johnston, Anna Maria, 298
Johnston, George, 166–167, 244
Johnston, John, 122–123, 128, 166
Jones, Martha S., 273n. 1

Kabamappa, 293
Katawbidai, 162
Ketawkah, 233–236
Kewabishkim, 233–236
Kickapoos, 171
King, Tiffany, 325n. 81
Kinship: and identity and belonging, 119–120, 218–220, 287, 292–300, 308–316; and role of women, 180–184, 213–214; and fur trade, 218–220; obligations of, 223–225; and patrilineal ties and mixed-race families, 225
Knaggs, George, 144–145
Knaggs, Peter, 144–145
Knaggs, Whitmore, 128, 141
Knox, Henry, 51, 63–66

Lauzon, Antoine, 232–233, 237
Lea, Luke, 330–332
Legion of the United States, 67
Lewis, Jan Ellen, 278n. 7
Lewis, Meriwether, 35
Lex talionis, 242–243
Little Traverse Bay reservation, 29–34
Locke, John, 39, 285
"Logic of elimination," 72n. 57
Louisiana Purchase, 35, 40
Lumber, 314
Lyon, Lucius, 266, 268; and Treaty of Saint Peters annuity disbursement, 287–300

Maajigaabaw, 176, 188, 213, 249–253, 268

Maangozid, 168, 189–191

Mackadepenessy, 204–205

Mackinac Indians, 108–109, 111, 112

Madison, William, 233

Mandan nation, 92, 110

Manidoogiizhig, 102, 115, 119, 232–233

Marietta (town), 58–63

Marshall, John, 98n. 11

Martin, 310–312

Mason, Steven, 148

McArthur, Duncan, 123

McBean, Charles, 3

McCoy, Isaac, 192, 207–208

McIntosh, William, 25n. 12

McKay, James, 11

McKenzie, John George, 11

McLeod, Alexander, 3, 12

McLeod, Martin, 3–5, 10, 12, 14

McLoughlin, John, 3, 12

Megiss Ininee, 199, 203–204

Meigs, Josiah, 138

Mesquakie, 171

Miami nation, 131–133

Miles, Tiya, 197n. 69

Miller, Thomas, 108–109

Mining, 330

Mishenenanonequet, 141–142

Miskwabunokwa, 114, 116–117

Missionaries: Baptist, 192, 207–208. *See also* American Board of Commissioners for Foreign Missions (ABCFM)

Missouri Compromise, 214

Mixed-race Native peoples: on Indian empire, 2; whites' views on, 3–4; racial categorization of, 23–25, 161, 164–165, 228–231, 244, 246; and land grants, 143–145, 147–149; and citizenship and whiteness, 217, 222–223, 225–226, 266–271, 273–277, 320–322; and patrilineal kinship ties, 225; and French language, 231; exclusion of, from reservations, 250–251, 321; role of, in treaty negotiations, 260–261; and dual nature of citizenship, 260–264, 287, 291–300; vulnerability of, 261–271, 320–322; and right of suffrage, 267–268, 283–284, 287; rights of, to annuities, 287–289, 291–300; as civilized, 291–300, 314–316; and Black ancestry, 296; and social status, 321

Mixenene, 144

Monaco, C. S., 28

Monroe, James, 128

Montezuma II, 1–4

Muckatosha, 192, 199, 203

Murders: and right of revenge, 222–223, 241–247; in American settlements, 236–241. *See also* Aitkin, Alfred

Murphy, Lucy Eldersveld, 120n. 47, 179n. 42, 182n. 48, 231n. 22, 268n. 70, 300

Naadinookwa, 102–103, 109–114

Nabunagiizhig, 199

National mythology, 81–88

National security, 124–125

Native delegations to Washington, D.C., 35–38, 128–131, 191–196, 333–336

Native New World: explanation of, 74–75, 94–96

Native sovereignty: failed elimination of, by U.S. government, 127–128; versus state, 211–212, 237–241, 274; in U.S. territories, 232–236; and impossibility of civilizing mission, 302

Natural law, 6, 31, 38–41, 77–78, 97–98, 284–286, 299

Naugunnee, 143–144

Neome, 143–144

Nindipens, 189–191, 213

Noodin, 258, 292

Norris, Charles, 49
North West Company. *See* Fur trade
Northwest Indian War, 87
Northwest Ordinance, 19–21, 53–62
Northwest Territory: U.S. possession of, 42; slavery in, 55–57, 61–62, 149, 281–282; as Indigenous space, 97, 274; comparison of, to other regions, 210–211, 214–215, 323–325
Norvell, John, 194–196
Nourse, William, 2–3

Oakes, Charles H., 162, 169, 294
Oakes, George Henry, 294
Oakes, Julia, 162, 294
Obama, Barack, 345
Odawa nation: and Michigan land dispute (2015), 29–34; and cession of lands, 121–125
Ogamawkeketo, 141–142
Ogemainini (Joseph Wakazo), 231–232, 238
Ogenaw-gizzhigokwe, 162, 294
Ogimagigido, 202–203
Ohio Company, 58–62
Ojibwe nation: alliances of, with other Native peoples, 91–94; and Treaty of Paris (1783), 97; and cession of lands, 121–125; and conflict with Dakota, 169–177; as decentralized politically and socially, 248–249, 256–259; delegation of, to Washington, D.C., 333–336
Okewa, 242
Onuf, Peter S., 20n. 6, 21, 147n. 93
Ordinance of 1784, 46–50
Osceola, 26–28, 301
Oshkosh, 242
Oshoge, 333–336
Osterhammel, Jürgen, 33n. 25, 60n. 36
Ozhaawshkodewikwe, 166

Pan-Indian Nativism, 101, 115–116
Pateman, Carole, 38n. 5, 261n. 62

Paternalist language: U.S. government's use of, 129–131, 247–253, 305–307; and Native peoples' rejection of subordination, 141–142, 175; and Native peoples as children, 200; Native peoples' use of, 203, 248–253, 307, 310–312, 332
Pelly, John H., 3, 11
Pemmican, 117–118
Penn, William, 86–87
Perfect settler sovereignty, 340
Perkins, James, 61–62
Peshaube, 110–113
Peterson, Jacqueline, 24n. 10
Pilgrims, 83–86
Pocahontas, 83, 315–316
Political economy of plunder: creation of, 17–23, 146–149, 253; continued presence of Native peoples as necessary to, 215–216, 336–337; and traders' use of annuities to collect debt, 252–253, 304; and decline of fur trade, 260; role of mixed-race people in, 264–269; non-Native profit from, 289–290, 330–332; white criticism of, 313–315, 329; and value of land, 322–323; legacy of, in twenty-first century, 339–346
Powell, William, 343
Proclamation Line of 1763, 43, 100, 117–118
Pyant, Josette, 187

Ramsey, Alexander, 327–329
Raps (unauthorized settler), 49
Rautawaubet, 26
Redix, Erik, 328–329
Red River Rebellion, 13
Rese (bishop), 195
Rice, Tamir, 344
Richardville, Jean Baptiste, 132
Riel, Louis, 13
Rivers and waterways, 52, 54, 73, 101, 111, 137

Robbins, Obediah, 52–53
Robinson, Rix, 192, 207
Romanticization of Indigenous peoples, 25–28
Ross, John, 25n. 12
Rothman, Adam, 78n. 67
Roulette, Joseph, 247

Sachs, Honor, 50n. 22, 54n. 31, 98n. 10
Saler, Bethel, 23n. 9, 218n. 3, 300n. 42, 322
Sauk, 171
Saulteaux ("Soetis") Indians, 107
Scalp dance ceremony, 173–174
Schoolcraft, Helena Maria Evelyn, 298
Schoolcraft, Henry Rowe: and Treaty of Detroit, 29; civilizing mission of, 165–177; and Nindipens, 189; and political economy of plunder, 192–196, 290; and Treaty of Washington, 197–210; and Treaty of Saint Peters, 231, 256–257; on murders in Indian country, 231–232
Schoolcraft, James, 298
Second Great Awakening, 174, 177
Selkirk, Thomas Douglas, earl of, 116–119
Seminole nation, 252n. 51, 259, 266; relationship of, with the Spanish in Cuba, 303
Seminole Wars, 26–28, 300–301, 318, 334
Seneca nation, 121–125, 131–133
Settler contract, 18n. 3
"Settler-native-slave triad," 13–14, 321–325, 342–346
Seven Oakes, battle of, 118
Seven Years' War, 6, 42, 87; and Proclamation Line of 1763, 43, 100, 117–118
Shabagajick, 237, 243
Shankman, Andrew, 21n. 7

Shawnee nation, 53, 101; and cession of lands, 121–125, 131–133
Shire, Laurel Clark, 161n. 15, 175n. 36, 266n. 68, 270n. 73
Sibley, Henry, 247, 303–304
Sibley, Solomon, 234–236
Simpson, George, 1–3, 11–12
Sioux nation. *See* Dakota nation
Slater, Leonard, 192, 199, 207–208
Slavery: and fur trade, 55; in Northwest Territory, 55–57, 61–62, 149, 281–282; compromises over, 60–62; in South, 323–325
Sleeper-Smith, Susan, 48n. 19, 60n. 36, 69n. 52, 97n. 9, 110n. 28
Smallpox, 209–210
Smith, Jacob, 143–146
Smith, John, 83
Snyder, Christina, 79n. 68
Spencer, John, 303–305, 312
Sproat, Greenville, 187
Standing Rock Sioux reservation, 343–346
Statehood: process for, 53, 197; attainment of, 73–74
St. Clair, Arthur, 55, 64–66, 281
Stevens, Jedediah, 159
St. Onge, Evelyn, 339
Straumann, Benjamin, 39n. 5
Stuart, Robert, 302–303, 319; and council for Treaty of La Pointe, 305–312; and criticism of process for Treaty of La Pointe, 318
Suffrage: African Americans and lynching for, 13–14; and nonwhite peoples, 267–268, 273–277; and free white males, 280, 285; and debate over "white" versus "free," 283–285

Tagaweninne, 103, 109
Taliaferro, Lawrence, 225–228, 246; on Treaty of Saint Peters, 256–257
Tanner, Edward, 134
Tanner, James, 299

Ulrick, Charles, 233
University of Michigan: land grant for, 124
"Unthinkable history," 33–34
Unwattin, 17, 25–28
U.S. citizenship: and whiteness, 23, 217, 231; Native peoples' exclusion from, 130, 277, 339; Native and Black exclusion from, as linked, 275–277, 286. *See also* Suffrage
U.S. military: and policing of western lands, 48–53; confrontations of, with Native peoples, 68, 211; weakness of, 259

Vanishing Indian, trope of: and myth of annihilation, 10–13, 74–78; and romanticization of Indigenous peoples, 26–28; and known falsehood of land as unoccupied, 29–34, 42, 274; and exercise of dominion, 151–156, 269–271; and proximity of Natives to white settlers, 207; versus cost of settler colonialism, 211–213; Seminole Wars as challenge to, 301
Varnum, James, 58, 62
Veracini, Lorenzo, 38n. 4
Vickers, Daniel, 21n. 7
Vizenor, Gerald, 156n. 9

Waabenemickee, 243–244
Waabojig, 166
Waasese, 110–111
Wabooz, 108, 111–112
Wagetoat, 112
Waishkee, 192, 202
Wakazo, Joseph (Ogemainini), 231–232, 238
Wamegonabiew, 109
Wampanoag nation, 83–86
Wampler, Joseph, 138
Wampums, 5–6, 170
War of 1812, 75–76

Warren, Lyman: ties of, to Native community, 162; and Treaty of Saint Peters, 249, 252–253, 256–257, 261; and annuity claims for mixed-race Native peoples, 295; as translator, 310–312
Warren, Mary Cadotte, 162, 295
Warren, Truman, 295
Washington, George, 43–45, 68
Watrous, John, 332–333
Waub Ojeeg, 298
Wayne, Anthony, 67
Wea nation, 131–133
Wendall, Abraham, 140
Westward settlement: as settler colonialism, 20n. 6, 36–38, 40–41, 323; and Revolutionary War, 43; and statehood, 44–45; and unauthorized settlements, 45–53; and promise of unsettled land, 51; U.S. government facilitation of, 53–60; Native peoples' resistance to, 62–68; deterrents to, 125–126, 137–138, 227
Wheeler, Leonard, 305
White, Bruce M., 19n. 5
White, Richard, 36n. 2, 41n. 8
White Crow, 308–312
White Thunder, Margaret, 298–299
Widder, Keith R., 160n. 14
Williams, Robert A., Jr., 41n. 8
Wisconsin Death March, 328–330
Wolfe, Patrick, 58n. 35, 72n. 57
Women: labor of, 110, 160, 179–181, 185–187, 213–214; role of, in American expansion, 161; as translators, 161, 178, 185–187; and kinship ties, 180–184, 213–214; and civilizing mission, 213–214; and U.S. marriage and property laws, 299–300
Woodbridge, William, 136, 239–241, 243
Woodward, Augustus, 56
Wright, Gavin, 322–323

Wyandot nation, 53, 101, 121–126, 128–133

XY Company, 105

Yang, K. Wayne (la paperson), 324n. 80

Zhaagobe, 255
Zhaazhaawanibiisens (John Tanner): and intra-Native relationships, 91–94, 107; captivity of, 98–103; and hunting and trapping, 109–113; identity of, as Ojibwe, 113–114; and pan-Indian movement, 115–116; and rivalry of trading companies, 117–118; return of, to United States, 118–121, 134–135; European view on, 158; descendants of, 299
Zhingobiins, 189, 307